教育部、国家语委重大文化工程
　　"中华思想文化术语传播工程"成果
国家社会科学基金重大项目
　　"中国核心术语国际影响力研究"（21&ZD158）
"十四五"国家重点出版物出版规划项目
获评第二届向全国推荐中华优秀传统文化普及图书

学习强国
每日中华文化专词双译

XUEXI—
Everyday Wisdom
in Chinese Thought
and Culture

《中华思想文化术语》编委会 ◎ 编

外语教学与研究出版社
FOREIGN LANGUAGE TEACHING AND RESEARCH PRESS
北京

图书在版编目（CIP）数据

学习强国：每日中华文化专词双译：汉英对照 /《中华思想文化术语》编委会编. —— 北京：外语教学与研究出版社，2024.6
ISBN 978-7-5213-5050-0

Ⅰ. ①学… Ⅱ. ①中… Ⅲ. ①中华文化-术语-汉、英 Ⅳ. ①K203-61

中国国家版本馆 CIP 数据核字 (2024) 第 046046 号

出 版 人	王　芳
项目统筹	杨馨园
责任编辑	牛茜茜
责任校对	赵璞玉
封面设计	马庆晓
出版发行	外语教学与研究出版社
社　　址	北京市西三环北路 19 号（100089）
网　　址	https://www.fltrp.com
印　　刷	北京盛通印刷股份有限公司
开　　本	710×1000　1/16
印　　张	30.5
字　　数	644 千字
版　　次	2024 年 6 月第 1 版
印　　次	2024 年 6 月第 1 次印刷
书　　号	ISBN 978-7-5213-5050-0
定　　价	78.00 元

如有图书采购需求，图书内容或印刷装订等问题，侵权、盗版书籍等线索，请拨打以下电话或关注官方服务号：
客服电话：400 898 7008
官方服务号：微信搜索并关注公众号"外研社官方服务号"
外研社购书网址：https://fltrp.tmall.com

物料号：350500001

"中华思想文化术语传播工程"专家团队
（按音序）

Scholars Participating in the Project "Key Concepts in Chinese Thought and Culture: Communication Through Translation"

顾问（Advisors）

李学勤（Li Xueqin）　　　林戊荪（Lin Wusun）
叶嘉莹（Florence Chia-ying Yeh）　张岂之（Zhang Qizhi）
楼宇烈（Lou Yulie）　　　王　宁（Wang Ning）

专家委员会（Committee of Scholars）

主任（Director）
韩　震（Han Zhen）

委员（Members）

晁福林（Chao Fulin）　　　陈德彰（Chen Dezhang）　　　陈明明（Chen Mingming）
冯志伟（Feng Zhiwei）　　韩经太（Han Jingtai）　　　　黄友义（Huang Youyi）
金元浦（Jin Yuanpu）　　　静　炜（Jing Wei）　　　　　李建中（Li Jianzhong）
李雪涛（Li Xuetao）　　　李照国（Li Zhaoguo）　　　　聂长顺（Nie Changshun）
潘公凯（Pan Gongkai）　　王　博（Wang Bo）　　　　　王柯平（Wang Keping）
叶　朗（Ye Lang）　　　　袁济喜（Yuan Jixi）　　　　袁行霈（Yuan Xingpei）
张　晶（Zhang Jing）　　　张立文（Zhang Liwen）　　　张西平（Zhang Xiping）
郑述谱（Zheng Shupu）

特邀汉学家（Scholars of China Studies）

艾　恺（Guy Salvatore Alitto）　　安乐哲（Roger T. Ames）　　白罗米（Luminița Bălan）
包华石（Martin Joseph Powers）　陈瑞河（Madaras Réka）　　狄伯杰（B. R. Deepak）
顾　彬（Wolfgang Kubin）　　　　韩安德（Harry Anders Hansson）　韩　裴（Petko Todorov Hinov）
柯鸿冈（Paul Crook）　　　　　　柯马凯（Michael Crook）　　　斯巴修（Iljaz Spahiu）
王健、李盈（Jan & Yvonne Walls）　魏查理（Charles Willemen）

学术委员会（Academic Committee）

白振奎（Bai Zhenkui）	蔡力坚（Cai Lijian）	曹轩梓（Cao Xuanzi）
陈海燕（Chen Haiyan）	陈少明（Chen Shaoming）	程景牧（Cheng Jingmu）
丁　浩（Ding Hao）	付志斌（Fu Zhibin）	干春松（Gan Chunsong）
郭晓东（Guo Xiaodong）	韩志华（Han Zhihua）	何　淼（He Miao）
何世剑（He Shijian）	胡　海（Hu Hai）	贾德忠（Jia Dezhong）
姜海龙（Jiang Hailong）	柯修文（Daniel Canaris）	黎　臻（Li Zhen）
李存山（Li Cunshan）	李恭忠（Li Gongzhong）	李景林（Li Jinglin）
林敏洁（Lin Minjie）	林少阳（Lin Shaoyang）	刘　佳（Liu Jia）
刘　璐（Liu Lu）	刘　青（Liu Qing）	吕玉华（Lü Yuhua）
梅缵月（Mei Zuanyue）	孟庆楠（Meng Qingnan）	裴德思（Thorsten Pattberg）
彭冬林（Peng Donglin）	乔　希（Joshua Mason）	任大援（Ren Dayuan）
邵亦鹏（Shao Yipeng）	沈卫星（Shen Weixing）	施晓菁（Lynette Shi）
陶黎庆（Tao Liqing）	童孝华（Tong Xiaohua）	王丽丽（Wang Lili）
王　琳（Wang Lin）	王明杰（Wang Mingjie）	王维东（Wang Weidong）
王　鑫（Wang Xin）	温海明（Wen Haiming）	吴根友（Wu Genyou）
吴礼敬（Wu Lijing）	夏　晶（Xia Jing）	谢远笋（Xie Yuansun）
辛红娟（Xin Hongjuan）	徐明强（Xu Mingqiang）	徐亚男（Xu Yanan）
许家星（Xu Jiaxing）	严学军（Yan Xuejun）	张　静（Zhang Jing）
张子尧（Zhang Ziyao）	章思英（Zhang Siying）	章伟文（Zhang Weiwen）
赵　桐（Zhao Tong）	赵　悠（Zhao You）	郑　开（Zheng Kai）
周云帆（Zhou Yunfan）	朱绩崧（Zhu Jisong）	朱良志（Zhu Liangzhi）
朱　渊（Zhu Yuan）	左　励（Zuo Li）	

出版说明

"学习强国"学习平台是为深入贯彻习近平总书记关于建设马克思主义学习型政党、推动建设学习大国的重要指示精神,由中宣部主管主办、中宣部宣传舆情研究中心建设和运营的,以学习宣传习近平新时代中国特色社会主义思想为主要内容的线上学习平台。"学习强国"学习平台自2019年1月1日正式上线以来,依靠"内容融合、技术融合、传播渠道融合、服务功能融合、受众终端融合"的融合发展模式,吸引了不同年龄、不同职业、不同文化程度、不同兴趣爱好的读者上线学习,引领了全媒体时代的网络学习风尚。如今,运用"学习强国"学习平台学思想、览时政、习知识、听慕课、赏文艺,已成为广大党员干部和群众利用碎片化时间随时随地学习的新习惯。

"中华思想文化术语"是由中华民族所创造或构建,凝聚、浓缩了中华哲学思想、人文精神、思维方式、价值观念,以词或短语形式固化的概念和核心词,是中华民族千百年来对宇宙万物、社会伦常、人与自然关系进行独立探索与理性思考的智慧结晶,代表了中华民族的思想基因、精神追求、文明标识。

为做好中华思想文化术语的整理和传播工作,经国务院批准,"中华思想文化术语传播工程"(以下简称"工程")于2014年启动,并建立了由教育部、国家语委作为召集单位,多个部委(单位)为成员的部际联席会议机制，负责统筹协调中华思想文化术语传播工作。"工程"的设立旨在梳理反映中国文化特征和民族思维方式、体现中国核心价值的思想文化术语，用易于口头表达、交流的简练语言客观准确地予以诠释，推荐在政府机构、社会组织、传播媒体等对外交往活动中使用，传播好中国声音，讲好中国故事，让世界更多了解中国国情、历史和文化。

"工程"深入学习贯彻党和国家建设学习大国的重要指示精神，充分发挥资源优势，与中宣部宣传舆情研究中心在"学习强国"学习平台，自2019年7月起合作推出"中华文化专词双译"专题，刊登"工程"已正式发布的术语词条。至2023年12月，"中华文化专词双译"专题已刊登术语词条1100余条。本书编者选取已发布词条中阅读量居前365位的术语，包括大家耳熟能详的天下为公、民惟邦本、为政以德、革故鼎新、任人唯贤、天人合一等，为广大普通读者了解中华思想文化提供一个入门级的中英文对照手册。希望借助本书，读者可以一窥中华思想文化大厦的基石。此外，本书的每个术语词条均配有平台链接二维码，读者可以通过智能手机扫码"听书"，体验线上线下融合的阅读乐趣。

2021年5月31日在主持中央政治局第三十次集体学习时，习近平总书记强调，要更好推动中华文化走出去，以文载道、以文传声、以文化人，向世界阐释推介更多具有中国特色、体现中国精神、蕴藏中国智慧的优秀文化。本书所收的365个术语词条即是对"具有中国特色、体现中国精神、蕴藏中国智慧的优秀文化"的具体阐释。这些历千百年而弥新的思想文化术语至今仍在人类文明的天空熠熠生辉，它们是中华先哲留给今人的伟大精神遗产，也是中华民族贡献给世界的珍贵精神财富。

希望读者们读有所得，开卷有益！

"中华思想文化术语传播工程"秘书处
外语教学与研究出版社
2024年5月

目录
Contents

1. àimín 爱民
   Love the People ············ 1

2. àimínzhěqiáng 爱民者强
   Power Comes from Caring for the People. ············ 3

3. ānjū-lèyè 安居乐业
   Live in Peace and Work in Contentment ············ 4

4. ānpín-lèdào 安贫乐道
   Be Content with a Simple but Virtuous Life ············ 5

5. ānshí-chǔshùn 安时处顺
   Face Reality Calmly ············ 6

6. āntǔ-zhòngqiān 安土重迁
   Attached to the Land and Unwilling to Move ············ 7

7. bǎixì 百戏
   Baixi (All Performing Arts) ············ 8

8. bàofǎ-chǔshì 抱法处势
   Upholding Law by Means of Power ············ 10

9. běnmò 本末
   Ben and *Mo* (The Fundamental and the Incidental) ············ 11

10. běnsè 本色
    Bense (Original Character) ············ 12

11. bǐdé 比德
    Virtue Comparison ············ 14

12 biānsàishī 边塞诗
    Frontier Poetry ············ 15

13 biàntǐ 辨体
    Style Differentiation ············ 16

14 biāojǔ-xìnghuì 标举兴会
    Distinctiveness and Spontaneity ············ 18

15 biécái-biéqù 别材别趣
    Distinct Subject and Artistic Taste ············ 20

16 biéjí 别集
    Individual Collection ············ 21

17 bōrě 般若
    Prajna / Wisdom ············ 23

18 bó'ài 博爱
    Extensive Love to Benefit All People ············ 24

19 bóshī-jìzhòng 博施济众
    Deliver Extensive Benefits to the People and Relieve the Suffering of the Poor ············ 25

20 bù xué《shī》, wú yǐ yán 不学《诗》，无以言
    You Won't Be Able to Talk Properly with Others Without Studying *The Book of Songs*. ············ 26

21 bùyánzhījiào 不言之教
    Influence Others Without Preaching ············ 27

22 bùzhàn'érshèng 不战而胜
    Win Without Resorting to War ············ 28

23 cái 才
    Talent / Capability / Attribute ············ 29

24 cānyàn 参验
    Cross-checking and Verification ············ 30

25 cángfùyúmín 藏富于民
    Keep Wealth with the People ············ 31

26 Chángchéng 长城
    The Great Wall ············ 33

27 chàngshén 畅神
    Free Flow of One's Mind ············ 35

28 chéngrén 成人
Complete Man ·········· 36

29 chéngzhúyúxiōng 成竹于胸
Have a Complete Image of the Bamboo Before Drawing It / Have a Fully Formed Picture in the Mind's Eye ·········· 37

30 chéng 诚
Sincerity ·········· 39

31 chéngyì 诚意
Be Sincere in Thought ·········· 40

32 chéng 城
Fortress / City ·········· 41

33 chóngběn-xīmò 崇本息末
Revere the Fundamental and Dismiss the Specific ·········· 42

34 chǔcí, 《Chǔcí》楚辞
Chuci / Odes of Chu ·········· 43

35 chuánqí 传奇
Chuanqi (Legendary Story / Legendary Play) ·········· 45

36 chuánshén-xiězhào 传神写照
Convey the Spirit and Capture the Person ·········· 47

37 chūnjié 春节
Spring Festival ·········· 49

38 chúnwáng-chǐhán 唇亡齿寒
Once the Lips Are Gone, the Teeth Will Feel Cold. ·········· 50

39 cídá 辞达
Expressiveness ·········· 51

40 císhàngtǐyào 辞尚体要
Succinctness Is Valued in Writing. ·········· 52

41 cuòcǎi-lòujīn 错彩镂金
Gilded and Colored ·········· 53

42 dàjié 大节
Major Principles ·········· 54

43 dàtóng 大同
Universal Harmony ·········· 56

44 dàxué 大学
Daxue (Great Learning) ·········· 57

45 dàzhàngfu 大丈夫
Great Man 59

46 dānqīng 丹青
Painting in Colors 60

47 dànbó-míngzhì, níngjìng-zhìyuǎn 淡泊明志，宁静致远
Indifference to Fame and Fortune Characterizes a High Aim in Life, and Leading a Quiet Life Helps One Accomplish Something Lasting. 62

48 dāngháng 当行
Professionalism 63

49 dāngrén-bùràng 当仁不让
When Facing an Opportunity to Exercise Benevolence, Do Not Yield. 64

50 dào 道
Dao (Way) 65

51 dàofǎzìrán 道法自然
Dao Operates Naturally. 67

52 dédào-duōzhù, shīdào-guǎzhù 得道多助，失道寡助
A Just Cause Enjoys Abundant Support While an Unjust Cause Finds Little. 68

53 dé 德
De (Virtue) 69

54 déxìngzhīzhī 德性之知
Knowledge from One's Moral Nature 70

55 diǎntiě-chéngjīn 点铁成金
Turning a Crude Poem or Essay into a Literary Gem 71

56 dòngjìng 动静
Movement and Stillness 73

57 dū 都
Capital / Metropolis 74

58 dúhuà 独化
Self-driven Development 75

59 duótāi-huàngǔ 夺胎换骨
Express the Ideas in Earlier Literary Works in a New Way 76

60 èrbǐng 二柄
Two Handles 78

61   èr rén tóng xīn, qí lì duàn jīn 二人同心，其利断金
        If Two People Are of the Same Mind, Their Combined Strength Can Break Metal. ············ 79

62   fǎ 法
        Law / Dharma ············ 80

63   fǎbù'ēguì 法不阿贵
        The Law Does Not Favor the Rich and Powerful. ············ 82

64   fàn'ài 泛爱
        Broad Love Extending to All ············ 83

65   fāngbiàn 方便
        Upāya / Expediency ············ 84

66   fēigōng 非攻
        Denouncing Unjust Wars ············ 85

67   fēimìng 非命
        Rejection of Fatalism ············ 86

68   fēngròu-wēigǔ 丰肉微骨
        Fleshy Body and Soft Bone Structure ············ 87

69   fēnggǔ 风骨
        Fenggu ············ 88

70   fēng-yǎ-sòng 风雅颂
        Ballad, Court Hymn, and Eulogy ············ 90

71   fúróng-chūshuǐ 芙蓉出水
        Lotus Rising Out of Water ············ 92

72   fù-bǐ-xìng 赋比兴
        Narrative, Analogy, and Association ············ 93

73   gǎnwù 感物
        Sensed Externalities ············ 94

74   gànchéng 干城
        Shield and Fortress / Dukes and Princes ············ 95

75   gāngróu 刚柔
        Toughness and Softness ············ 96

76   gāngyì 刚毅
        Firm and Resolute ············ 97

77   gégù-dǐngxīn 革故鼎新
        Do Away with the Old and Set Up the New ············ 99

78　géming 革命
　　Changing the Mandate / Revolution ············ 100

79　gé 格
　　Examine / Study ············ 101

80　géwù-zhìzhī 格物致知
　　Study Things to Acquire Knowledge ············ 102

81　géyì 格义
　　Matching Meanings ············ 103

82　gōnggōngsīsī 公公私私
　　Public Property Belonging to the Public, Private Property to Individuals ············ 105

83　gōng shēng míng, lián shēng wēi 公生明，廉生威
　　Fairness Fosters Discernment and Integrity Creates Authority. ············ 106

84　gōngzhèng 公正
　　Fair / Just ············ 107

85　gòngmíng 共名
　　General Name ············ 108

86　guàyáo 卦爻
　　Trigrams / Hexagrams and Component Lines ············ 109

87　guāng'érbùyào 光而不耀
　　Bright but Not Dazzling ············ 111

88　guójiā 国家
　　Family-state / Country ············ 112

89　guótài-mín'ān 国泰民安
　　Stable Country and Peaceful People ············ 113

90　guótǐ 国体
　　Guoti ············ *114*

91　guó yǐ yì wéi lì 国以义为利
　　A State Should Regard Righteousness as a Benefit. ············ 115

92　guòyóubùjí 过犹不及
　　Going Too Far Is as Bad as Falling Short. ············ 116

93　hǎinèi 海内
　　Within the Four Seas / Within the Country ············ 117

94　hǎiwài 海外
　　Outside the Four Seas / Overseas ············ 117

95 hánxù 含蓄
Subtle Suggestion 118

96 hányǒng 涵泳
Be Totally Absorbed (in Reading and Learning) 120

97 hànyuèfǔ 汉乐府
Yuefu Poetry 122

98 háofàngpài 豪放派
The *Haofang* School / The Bold and Unconstrained School 123

99 hé tóngyì 合同异
Unify Commonality and Difference 125

100 hé'érbùtóng 和而不同
Harmony but Not Uniformity 126

101 héwéiguì 和为贵
Harmony Is Most Precious. 127

102 hòudé-zàiwù 厚德载物
Have Ample Virtue and Carry All Things 128

103 hòujī-bófā 厚积薄发
Build Up Fully and Release Sparingly 130

104 huáxià 华夏
Huaxia / The Han People 131

105 huà gāngē wéi yùbó 化干戈为玉帛
Beat Swords into Plowshares / Turn War into Peace 132

106 huàgōng / huàgōng 化工 / 画工
Magically Natural, Overly Crafted 133

107 huàxìng-qǐwěi 化性起伪
Transform Intrinsic Evil Nature to Develop Acquired Nature of Goodness 134

108 huàdào 画道
Dao of Painting 135

109 huàlóng-diǎnjīng 画龙点睛
Add Pupils to the Eyes of a Painted Dragon / Render the Final Touch 137

110 Huáng Hé 黄河
The Yellow River 138

15

111 **huìxīn** 会心
Heart-to-heart Communication ⋯⋯⋯ 139

112 **huì shì hòu sù** 绘事后素
The White Silk First, the Painting Afterwards / Beauty from Natural Simplicity ⋯⋯⋯ 140

113 **hùndùn** 浑沌
Chaos ⋯⋯⋯ 141

114 **huófǎ** 活法
Literary Flexibility ⋯⋯⋯ 143

115 **jī** 几
Ji (Omen) ⋯⋯⋯ 145

116 **jǐsuǒbùyù, wùshīyúrén** 己所不欲，勿施于人
Do Not Do to Others What You Do Not Want Others to Do to You. ⋯⋯⋯ 146

117 **jìtuō** 寄托
Entrust One's Thoughts and Feelings to Imagery ⋯⋯⋯ 147

118 **jiān'ài** 兼爱
Universal Love ⋯⋯⋯ 148

119 **jiànlì-sīyì** 见利思义
Think of Righteousness in the Face of Gain ⋯⋯⋯ 149

120 **jiànwénzhīzhī** 见闻之知
Knowledge from One's Senses ⋯⋯⋯ 150

121 **jiànxián-sīqí** 见贤思齐
When Seeing a Person of High Caliber, Strive to Be His Equal. ⋯⋯⋯ 151

122 **jiàngǔ-zhījīn** 鉴古知今
Review the Past to Understand the Present ⋯⋯⋯ 152

123 **jiāngshān** 江山
Rivers and Mountains / Country or State Power ⋯⋯⋯ 153

124 **jiǎngxìn-xiūmù** 讲信修睦
Keep Good Faith and Pursue Harmony ⋯⋯⋯ 154

125 **jiéqì** 节气
The Twenty-four Solar Terms ⋯⋯⋯ 155

126 **jiěyī-pánbó** 解衣盘礴
Sitting with Clothes Unbuttoned and Legs Stretching Out ⋯⋯⋯ 156

127 jīngjì 经济
Govern and Help the People / Economy ············ 158

128 jīngshì-zhìyòng 经世致用
Study of Ancient Classics Should Meet Present Needs. ············ 160

129 jīngqì 精气
Vital Energy ············ 161

130 jìngyīnzhīdào 静因之道
Governance by Being Aloof ············ 162

131 jìngjiè 境界
Jingjie (Visionary World) ············ 163

132 jìngshēngxiàngwài 境生象外
Aesthetic Conception Transcends Concrete Objects Described. ············ 165

133 jiǔzhōu 九州
Nine *Zhou* (Regions) ············ 167

134 jū'ān-sīwēi 居安思危
Be on Alert Against Potential Danger When Living in Peace ············ 168

135 jǔxián-róngzhòng 举贤容众
Recommend People of Virtue and Be Magnanimous Toward the Masses ············ 169

136 jūn 君
Lord / Nobility / Monarch ············ 170

137 jūnzhě-shànqún 君者善群
A Ruler Should Keep People Together. ············ 171

138 jūnzǐ 君子
Junzi (Man of Virtue) ············ 172

139 jūnzǐzhījiāo 君子之交
Relations Between Men of Virtue ············ 173

140 kāiwù-chéngwù 开物成务
Understand Things and Succeed in One's Endeavors ············ 174

141 kējǔ 科举
The Imperial Civil Examination System ············ 175

142 kèjǐ-fùlǐ 克己复礼
Restrain Yourself and Follow Social Norms ············ 177

143 Kǒng-Yán zhī lè 孔颜之乐
　　The Happiness of Confucius and Yan Hui ············ 178

144 kūdàn 枯淡
　　Dry Plainness ············ 179

145 kuángjuàn 狂狷
　　Proactive Versus Prudent ············ 181

146 lài yǔ Xīshī, dào tōng wéi yī 厉与西施，道通为一
　　A Scabby Person and the Beautiful Lady Xishi Are the Same in the Eyes of Dao. ············ 182

147 líxíng-désì 离形得似
　　Transcend the Outer Form to Capture the Essence ············ 183

148 lǐ 礼
　　Li (Rites / Social Norms / Propriety) ············ 184

149 lǐ 理
　　Li ············ 186

150 lǐqù 理趣
　　Philosophical Substance Through Artistic Appeal ············ 187

151 lǐyī-fēnshū 理一分殊
　　There Is But One *Li* (Universal Principle), Which Exists in Diverse Forms. ············ 188

152 lìcí 丽辞
　　Ornate Parallel Style ············ 190

153 lìyòng-hòushēng 利用厚生
　　Make Full Use of Resources to Enrich the People ············ 191

154 liángzhī 良知
　　Liangzhi (Conscience) ············ 192

155 liǎngyí 两仪
　　Two Modes ············ 193

156 liùyì 六义
　　The Six Basic Elements ············ 194

157 lóng 龙
　　Chinese Dragon ············ 196

158 máodùn 矛盾
　　Paradox of the Spear and the Shield / Contradiction ············ 197

159 méngyǐyǎngzhèng 蒙以养正
　　Enlighten the Ignorant and Make Them Follow the Right Path ………… 198

160 miàowù 妙悟
　　Subtle Insight ………… 199

161 mínbāo-wùyǔ 民胞物与
　　All People Are My Brothers and Sisters, and All Things Are My Companions. ………… 201

162 mínwéibāngběn 民惟邦本
　　People Are the Foundation of the State. ………… 202

163 mín wú xìn bù lì 民无信不立
　　Without People's Trust the State Will Not Survive. ………… 203

164 míngshí 名实
　　Name and Substance ………… 204

165 mìng 命
　　Mandate / Destiny ………… 205

166 nǐróng-qǔxīn 拟容取心
　　Compare Appearances to Grasp the Essence ………… 206

167 nǐwù-lìxiàng 拟物立象
　　Create Images Through Object Imitation ………… 208

168 nián 年
　　Lunar Year / Year ………… 209

169 qíwù 齐物
　　See Things as Equal ………… 210

170 qízhèng 奇正
　　Qi or *Zheng* (Surprise or Normal) ………… 211

171 qì 气
　　Qi (Vital Force) ………… 213

172 qìgǔ 气骨
　　Qigu (Emotional Vitality and Forcefulness) ………… 214

173 qìxiàng 气象
　　Prevailing Features ………… 215

174 qì 器
　　Qi (Vessel) ………… 217

175 qīnqīn 亲亲
　　Affection for One's Kin ………… 218

19

176	qīnrén-shànlín 亲仁善邻
	To Be Benevolent and Friendly Towards Neighboring Countries 219

177	qīngcí-lìjù 清词丽句
	Refreshing Words and Exquisite Expressions 221

178	qīngmíng 清明
	The Qingming Festival 222

179	qíng 情
	Qing 223

180	qíngjǐng 情景
	Sentiment and Scenery 224

181	qǔjìng 取境
	Qujing (Conceptualize an Aesthetic Feeling) 225

182	qù 趣
	Qu 227

183	réndào 人道
	Way of Man 228

184	rénwén-huàchéng 人文化成
	Edify the Populace to Achieve a Harmonious Society 229

185	rén 仁
	Ren (Benevolence) 230

186	rénmín-àiwù 仁民爱物
	Have Love for the People, and Cherish All Things 231

187	rénzhě-àirén 仁者爱人
	A Benevolent Person Loves Others. 233

188	rénzhě-wúdí 仁者无敌
	The Benevolent Person Is Invincible. 234

189	rènrén-wéixián 任人唯贤
	Appoint People Only on Their Merits 235

190	rìxīn 日新
	Constant Renewal 237

191	róngcái 镕裁
	Refining and Deleting 238

192	sāncái 三才
	Three Elements 239

193　sānsī'érxíng 三思而行
　　　Think Carefully Before Taking Action ············ 240

194　sānxǐng-wúshēn 三省吾身
　　　Reflect on Oneself Several Times a Day ············ 242

195　sānxuán 三玄
　　　Three Metaphysical Classics ············ 243

196　shānshuǐshī 山水诗
　　　Landscape Poetry ············ 244

197　shàngbīng-fámóu 上兵伐谋
　　　The Best Strategy in Warfare is to Foil the Enemy's Strategy. ············ 245

198　shàngdì 上帝
　　　Supreme Ruler / Ruler of Heaven ············ 246

199　shàngshàn-ruòshuǐ 上善若水
　　　Great Virtue Is Like Water. ············ 247

200　shěshēng-qǔyì 舍生取义
　　　Give One's Life to Uphold Righteousness ············ 248

201　shèjì 社稷
　　　Gods of the Earth and the Five Grains / State / State Power ············ 249

202　shényǔwùyóu 神与物游
　　　Interaction Between the Mind and the Subject Matter ············ 250

203　shényùn 神韵
　　　Elegant Subtlety ············ 252

204　shèndú 慎独
　　　Shendu (Ethical Self-cultivation) ············ 253

205　shēngshēng 生生
　　　Perpetual Growth and Change ············ 255

206　shēng yī wú tīng, wù yī wú wén 声一无听，物一无文
　　　A Single Note Does Not Compose a Melodious Tune, Nor Does a Single Color Make a Beautiful Pattern. ············ 256

207　shèngtángzhīyīn 盛唐之音
　　　Poetry of the Prime Tang Dynasty ············ 257

208　shīchū-yǒumíng 师出有名
　　　Fighting a War with a Moral Justification ············ 258

209　shīfǎzhīhuà 师法之化
　　　Enlightenment Through Education ………… 260

210　shīshǐ 诗史
　　　Historical Poetry ………… 261

211　shī yán zhì 诗言志
　　　Poetry Expresses Aspirations. ………… 262

212　shī yuán qíng 诗缘情
　　　Poetry Springs from Emotions. ………… 263

213　shī zhōng yǒu huà, huà zhōng yǒu shī
　　　诗中有画，画中有诗
　　　Painting in Poetry, Poetry in Painting ………… 264

214　shízhōng 时中
　　　Follow the Golden Mean ………… 266

215　shíshì-qiúshì 实事求是
　　　Seek Truth from Facts ………… 267

216　shǐ 史
　　　History ………… 268

217　shìwài-táoyuán 世外桃源
　　　Land of Peach Blossoms / Land of Idyllic Beauty ………… 270

218　shūdào 书道
　　　The Way of Calligraphy ………… 271

219　shūqì 书契
　　　Documents on Bamboo or Wooden Slips ………… 273

220　shū zhě, sǎn yě 书者，散也
　　　Calligraphy Expresses Inner Conditions. ………… 274

221　shuàixìng 率性
　　　Acting in Accordance with Human Nature ………… 275

222　shuǐmòhuà 水墨画
　　　Ink Wash Painting ………… 276

223　shùntiān-yìngrén 顺天应人
　　　Follow the Mandate of Heaven and Comply with the Wishes of the People ………… 278

224　sī 思
　　　Reflecting / Thinking ………… 279

225 sīwén 斯文
Be Cultured and Refined ………… 280

226 sìduān 四端
Four Initiators ………… 281

227 sìhǎi 四海
Four Seas ………… 282

228 sìhǎi zhī nèi jiē xiōngdì 四海之内皆兄弟
All the People Within the Four Seas Are Brothers. ………… 283

229 sìshū 四书
Four Books ………… 284

230 sìxiàng 四象
Four Images ………… 285

231 suìhán-sānyǒu 岁寒三友
Three Friends of Winter / Steadfast, Loyal Friends ………… 286

232 tàixū 太虚
Taixu (Great Void) ………… 287

233 tǐ 体
Ti ………… 289

234 tǐyòng 体用
Ti and *Yong* ………… 290

235 tiān 天
Tian (Heaven) ………… 291

236 tiānjīng-dìyì 天经地义
Natural Rules and Orderliness ………… 292

237 tiānmìng 天命
Mandate of Heaven ………… 293

238 tiānmìng-mǐcháng 天命靡常
Heaven-bestowed Supreme Power Is Not Eternal. ………… 295

239 tiānrén-héyī 天人合一
Heaven and Man Are United as One. ………… 296

240 tiānrénzhīfēn 天人之分
Distinction Between Man and Heaven ………… 297

241 tiānshí dìlì rénhé 天时地利人和
Opportune Time, Geographic Advantage, and Unity of the People ………… 298

242   tiānxià 天下
     Tianxia (All Under Heaven) ············ 300

243   tiānxià-wéigōng 天下为公
     The World Belongs to All. ············ 301

244   tiānzǐ 天子
     Son of Heaven ············ 302

245   tiányuánshī 田园诗
     Idyllic Poetry ············ 303

246   tóngguī-shūtú 同归殊途
     Arrive at the Same Destination via Different Routes / Rely on a Common Ontological Entity ············ 304

247   tuījǐ-jírén 推己及人
     Put Oneself in Another's Place ············ 305

248   wǎnyuēpài 婉约派
     The *Wanyue* School / The Graceful and Restrained School ············ *307*

249   wángzhě-fùmín 王者富民
     A Ruler Should Enrich People. ············ 308

250   wéibiān-sānjué 韦编三绝
     Leather Thongs Binding Wooden Strips Break Three Times. ············ 309

251   wéizhèng-yǐdé 为政以德
     Governance Based on Virtue ············ 310

252   wèijǐzhīxué 为己之学
     Learning for Self-improvement ············ 311

253   wēngù-zhīxīn 温故知新
     Review the Old and Learn the New ············ 312

254   wēnróu-dūnhòu 温柔敦厚
     Mild, Gentle, Sincere, and Broad-minded ············ 314

255   wénmíng 文明
     Wenming (Civilization) ············ 315

256   wénqì 文气
     Wenqi ············ *316*

257   wénxué 文学
     Literature / Scholars / Education Officials ············ 317

258   wényǐzàidào 文以载道
     Literature Is the Vehicle of Ideas. ············ 319

259　wénzhāng　文章
　　　Literary Writing ………… 320

260　wénzhī　闻知
　　　Knowledge from Hearsay ………… 321

261　wòyóu　卧游
　　　Enjoy Sceneries Without Physically Travelling ………… 322

262　wúwéi　无为
　　　Non-action ………… 323

263　wúwéi'érzhì　无为而治
　　　Rule Through Non-action ………… 324

264　wúyù-zégāng　无欲则刚
　　　People with No Covetous Desires Stand Upright. ………… 326

265　Wú-Yuè-tóngzhōu　吴越同舟
　　　People of Wu and Yue Are in the Same Boat. ………… 327

266　wǔjīng　五经
　　　Five Classics ………… 328

267　wǔxíng-xiāngshēng　五行相生
　　　The Five Elements, Each in Turn Producing the Next ………… 329

268　wǔyīn　五音
　　　The Five Notes ………… 330

269　wùhuà　物化
　　　Transformation of Things ………… 332

270　xǐmù-lìxìn　徙木立信
　　　Establish One's Credibility by Rewarding People for Moving a Log ………… 333

271　xiāngfǎn-xiāngchéng　相反相成
　　　Being both Opposite and Complementary ………… 334

272　xiāoyáo　逍遥
　　　Carefree ………… 336

273　xiǎorén　小人
　　　Petty Man ………… 337

274　xiǎoshuō　小说
　　　Fiction ………… 338

275　xiào　孝
　　　Filial Piety ………… 340

25

276 xīn 心
Heart / Mind 341

277 xīnzhāi 心斋
Pure State of the Mind 342

278 xīnzhī 心知
Mind Cognition 343

279 xìn yán bù měi, měi yán bù xìn 信言不美，美言不信
Trustworthy Words May Not Be Fine-sounding; Fine-sounding Words May Not Be Trustworthy. 344

280 xīnglì-chúhài 兴利除害
Promote the Beneficial; Eliminate the Harmful 346

281 xíngjǐ-yǒuchǐ 行己有耻
Conduct Oneself with a Sense of Shame 347

282 xíngshū 行书
Running Script 348

283 xíngxiān-zhīhòu 行先知后
First Action, Then Knowledge 350

284 xíng'érshàng 形而上
What Is Above Form / The Metaphysical 351

285 xíng'érxià 形而下
What Is Under Form / The Physical 351

286 xíngjù-shénshēng 形具神生
Physical Form Gives Birth to Spirit. 352

287 xìng 兴
Evocation 353

288 xìng-guān-qún-yuàn 兴观群怨
Stimulation, Contemplation, Communication, and Criticism 355

289 xìngjì 兴寄
Xingji (Association and Inner Sustenance) 357

290 xìngqù 兴趣
Xingqu (Charm) 358

291 xìngfèn 性分
Natural Attribute 360

292   xìnglíng 性灵
         Xingling (Inner Self) ············ 361

293   xìngsānpǐn 性三品
         Human Nature Has Three Levels. ············ 363

294   xiū-qí-zhì-píng 修齐治平
         Self-cultivation, Family Regulation, State Governance, Bringing Peace to All Under Heaven ············ 364

295   xū 虚
         Xu (Void) ············ 365

296   xūjìng 虚静
         Void and Peace ············ 366

297   xūyī'érjìng 虚壹而静
         Open-mindedness, Concentration, and Tranquility ············ 367

298   xuánlǎn 玄览
         Xuanlan (Pure-minded Contemplation) ············ 368

299   xuányánshī 玄言诗
         Metaphysical Poetry ············ 369

300   xuánliáng-cìgǔ 悬梁刺股
         Tie One's Hair on the House Beam and Jab One's Side with an Awl to Keep Oneself from Falling Asleep while Studying ············ 370

301   xué 学
         Learn ············ 372

302   xuèqì 血气
         Vitality / Vital Force ············ 373

303   xúnmíng-zéshí 循名责实
         Hold Actualities According to Its Name ············ 374

304   yǎsú 雅俗
         Highbrow and Lowbrow ············ 375

305   yánbùjìnyì 言不尽意
         Words Cannot Fully Express Thought. ············ 377

306   Yán-Huáng 炎黄
         The Fiery Emperor and the Yellow Emperor / Emperor Yan and Emperor Huang ············ 378

307   yǎngmín 养民
         Nurture the People ············ 380

308 yǎngqì 养气
　　Cultivate *Qi* ············ 381

309 yèluò-guīgēn 叶落归根
　　Leaves Fall Returning to the Roots. ············ 382

310 yī 一
　　The One ············ 383

311 yīwù-liǎngtǐ 一物两体
　　One Thing in Two Fundamental States ············ 384

312 yīyán-xīngbāng 一言兴邦
　　A Single Remark Makes a Country Prosper. ············ 385

313 yīyǐguànzhī 一以贯之
　　Observe a Fundamental Principle Throughout One's Pursuit ············ 386

314 yífēng-yìsú 移风易俗
　　Change Social Practices and Customs ············ 388

315 yǐ wú wéi běn 以无为本
　　Wu Is the Origin. ············ 389

316 yǐxíng-mèidào 以形媚道
　　Natural Shapes Adapting to Dao ············ 390

317 yǐyì-zhìshì 以义制事
　　Handle Matters According to Morality and Justice ············ 391

318 yǐzhí-bàoyuàn 以直报怨
　　Repay a Grudge with Rectitude ············ 392

319 yì 义
　　Righteousness ············ 393

320 yìfǎ 义法
　　Yi Fa (Guidelines for Writing Good Prose) ············ 394

321 yìshù 艺术
　　Art ············ 395

322 yìjìng 意境
　　Aesthetic Conception ············ 397

323 yìxiàng 意象
　　Yixiang (Imagery) ············ 400

324 yìxìng 意兴
　　Inspirational Appreciation ············ 401

325 yīnyáng 阴阳
Yin and Yang ············ 402

326 yīn 音
Musical Sounds ············ 403

327 yǐnxiù 隐秀
Latent Sentiment and Evident Beauty ············ 404

328 Yǒngmíng tǐ 永明体
The Yongming Poetic Style ············ 406

329 yǒngshǐshī 咏史诗
Poetry on History ············ 407

330 yǒng 勇
Courage ············ 408

331 yǒu dé zhě bì yǒu yán 有德者必有言
Virtuous People Are Sure to Produce Fine Writing. ············ 409

332 yǒujiào-wúlèi 有教无类
Education for All Without Discrimination ············ 410

333 yǒuróng-nǎidà 有容乃大
A Broad Mind Achieves Greatness. ············ 412

334 yǒuwú 有无
You and *Wu* ············ 413

335 yúgōng-yíshān 愚公移山
The Foolish Old Man Who Moved the Mountains ············ 414

336 yǔmín-gēngshǐ 与民更始
Make a Fresh Start with the People ············ 416

337 yuánqǐ 缘起
Dependent Origination ············ 417

338 yuànběn 院本
Jin Opera / Scripts Used by Courtesans ············ 418

339 zàizhōu-fùzhōu 载舟覆舟
Carry or Overturn the Boat / Make or Break ············ 419

340 záobì-jièguāng 凿壁借光
Borrow Light from a Next Door Neighbor ············ 420

341 zhèngmíng 正名
Rectification of Names ············ 421

29

342 zhèngxīn 正心
Rectify One's Heart / Mind ············ 422

343 zhèngyì 正义
Correct Meaning / Justice ············ 424

344 zhèngzhě-zhèngyě 政者正也
Governance Means Rectitude. ············ 424

345 zhīcháng-dábiàn 知常达变
Master Both Permanence and Change ············ 426

346 zhī chǐ ér hòu yǒng 知耻而后勇
Having a Feeling of Shame Gives Rise to Courage. ············ 427

347 zhīxíng-héyī 知行合一
Unity of Knowledge and Action ············ 428

348 zhīxiān-xínghòu 知先行后
First Knowledge, Then Action ············ 430

349 zhīyīn 知音
Resonance and Empathy ············ 431

350 zhí 直
Rectitude ············ 432

351 zhíxún 直寻
Direct Quest ············ 433

352 zhǐgēwéiwǔ 止戈为武
Stopping War Is a True Craft of War. ············ 434

353 zhìnèi-cáiwài 治内裁外
Handling Internal Affairs Takes Precedence over External Affairs. ············ 435

354 zhìshìzhīyīn 治世之音
Music of an Age of Good Order ············ 436

355 zhōngdào 中道
The Middle Way ············ 437

356 zhōngguó 中国
Zhongguo (China) ············ 439

357 zhōnghé 中和
Balanced Harmony ············ 440

358 zhōnghuá 中华
Zhonghua ············ 441

359   zhōngyōng 中庸
       Zhongyong (The Golden Mean) ············ 442

360   zhūgōngdiào 诸宫调
       Song-speech Drama ············ 443

361   zhuǎnyì-duōshī 转益多师
       Learn from Many Masters, and Form Your Own Style ············ 445

362   Zhuāng Zhōu mèng dié 庄周梦蝶
       Zhuangzi Dreaming of Becoming a Butterfly ············ 446

363   zìqiáng-bùxī 自强不息
       Strive Continuously to Strengthen Oneself ············ 447

364   zìyóu 自由
       Acting Freely / Freedom ············ 449

365   zōngfǎ 宗法
       Feudal Clan System ············ 450

       中国历史年代简表 A Brief Chronology of Chinese History ······ 451

爱民
/àimín/

Love the People

  仁爱民众；爱护百姓。它不仅是治国者应该具有的对百姓的一种情怀，而且是治国理政必须遵循的重要原则。古人认为，治国者应该通过具体的政策、措施，使民众获利，安居乐业，免受痛苦和无端侵害。这也是治国者获得民众尊崇的前提或基础。"爱民"不仅是重要的政治理念，而且延伸到军事领域，成为兴兵作战的重要原则。依照这个原则，敌我双方的民众都应该受到爱护。它是中华"民本""仁义"思想的展现。

This term means to love and care for the common people. This is not only a sentiment which those who govern should have for the common people, but also an important principle which must be adhered to in governance. The ancient Chinese believed that those who govern should use specific policies and measures to benefit the people and enable them to live and work peacefully, free from sufferings and unwarranted infringements. This is the precondition or basis for those who govern to win the respect of the people. "Loving the people" was not only an important political concept – it also extended to the military sphere and became an important principle when raising armies to make war. According to this principle, the people of both one's own side and that of the enemy should receive caring love. This is a manifestation of the Chinese thinking "people first" and "benevolence and righteousness."

引例 Citations：

◎文王问太公曰："愿闻为国之大务，欲使主尊人安，为之奈何？"太公曰："爱民而已。"文王曰："爱民奈何？"太公曰："利而勿害，成而勿败，生而勿杀，与而勿夺，乐而勿苦，喜而勿怒。"（《六韬·文韬·国务》）

（周文王问姜太公："我想知道治理国家最重要的事情是什么，要使君主得到尊崇、民众得到安宁，应该怎么办呢？"姜太公说："只要爱民就可以了。"周文王问："怎样爱民呢？"姜太公说："使民众获利而不去妨碍他们，帮助民众成事而不去毁坏他们，利于民众生存而不去伤害他们，给予民众实惠而不是从他们手中夺走，使民众快乐而不是使他们痛苦，使民众高兴而不是使他们愤怒。"）

King Wen of Zhou asked Jiang Taigong, "I would like to ask: what are the most important things in governing a country that must be done for the ruler to enjoy respect and the people to have peace?" Jiang Taigong replied, "Just love the people." King Wen asked, "How does one love the people?" Jiang Taigong said, "Allow the people to gain profits and do not obstruct them; help the people achieve successes and do not ruin them; let the people live and do not harm them; give the people benefits and do not take them; bring the people joy and not suffering; make the people happy and not angry." (*The Six Strategies*)

◎ 古者以仁为本、以义治之之谓正。……战道：不违时，不历民病，所以爱吾民也；不加丧，不因凶，所以爱夫其民也；冬夏不兴师，所以兼爱其民也。(《司马法·仁本》)

（古人以仁爱为根本、以治军合乎道义为正道。……战争的原则是：不在农忙时兴兵，不在民众流行疫病时兴兵，为的是爱护自己的民众；不趁敌国有国丧时发动战争，不趁敌国有灾荒时发动战争，为的是爱护敌国的民众；不在冬夏两季兴兵，为的是爱护敌我双方的民众。）

The ancient people considered benevolent love to be the foundation of society, and the use of force in ethical ways as the proper way... The principles of warfare are to not assemble an army during the harvest season or when there is an epidemic among the people, because you love your own people; to not start a war when the enemy state is in mourning or has a natural disaster, because you love its people; to not assemble an army during the winter or summer, because you love both your people and your enemy's people. (*The General Commander's Treatise on War*)

爱民者强

/àimínzhěqiáng/

Power Comes from Caring for the People.

爱护百姓的国家才真正强大。治国者制定、推行政策措施只有顺应民心、代表百姓的根本利益，才会获得百姓的信任和拥护，也才能上下一心，众志成城。它是由"爱民"理念衍生的新命题——爱民是国力强盛的根本动因，也是"民惟邦本""仁者爱人"思想的延展与发扬。

A state which takes good care of its people is one with true power. A ruler will be trusted and supported by the people, and the state under such a ruler will be a solid stronghold only when the policies and measures made and implemented meet the people's requirements and represent the people's fundamental interests. This is a new theme derived from the concept of "loving the people," which is the fundamental driving force of a state's becoming strong and prosperous. It is also an extension and development of the concepts that "people are the foundation of the state," and "a benevolent person loves others."

引例 Citation：

◎爱民者强，不爱民者弱。(《荀子·议兵》)

（爱护百姓的国家强盛，不爱护百姓的国家衰弱。）

A state that takes good care of its people is strong and prosperous; a state that does not care about its people is waning and weak. (*Xunzi*)

安居乐业
/ānjū-lèyè/
Live in Peace and Work in Contentment

安定地生活，愉快地工作。"安居"，安于居所，指平平安安地生活。"乐业"，乐于本业，以自己的职守为乐，指快乐地从事自己的本职工作。形容国家、社会治理得非常好，天下太平无事，人们各得其所，各安生计，幸福快乐。它是普通民众所抱有的基本社会理想，也是有所作为的政治家、管理者所追求的社会治理的目标。作为政治理想，它体现着以民为本、注重民生的基本精神。

Live a stable life and work happily. *Anju* (安居) literally means a secure house and by extension living a happy life. *Leye* (乐业) means enjoying one's work. Together they refer to the general state of good governance, with peace prevailing and everyone in their proper place, satisfied with work and content with life. It is the longing of the common people as well as the goal of good governance. It is a people-oriented political aspiration centering on securing people's livelihood.

引例 Citations：

◎ 至治之极……民各甘其食，美其服，安其俗，乐其业。(《史记·货殖列传》引《老子》)

(治理国家的最高境界……是使民众觉得吃的饭很香甜，穿的衣服很漂亮，习惯于他们的习俗，乐于他们所从事的行业。)

The highest state of good governance is one in which people feel satisfied with their food, clothes, willingly observe social norms, and love their trade. (*Laozi*, as cited in *Records of the Historian*)

◎ 普天之下，赖我而得生育，由我而得富贵，安居乐业，长养子孙，天下晏然，皆归心于我矣。(仲长统《理乱篇》，见《后汉书·仲长统传》)

(普天下的人，依赖我而得以生存生长，因为我而得以享受富贵，安于居所，乐于本职，养育子孙，天下太平，那么人们就都会真心诚意地归附于我了。)

If I can ensure that all the people under heaven survive and develop, are well-off, live in peace and work in contentment, and raise their children in a secure world, then they will willingly pledge allegiance to me. (Zhong Changtong: On Governance and Turmoil)

安贫乐道

/ānpín-lèdào/

Be Content with a Simple but Virtuous Life

安于贫困而乐于守道。在孔子（前551—前479）与儒家看来，对于道义的学习与执守，并不是出于任何功利的目的，而是发自内心的认同，是毕生追求的最高目标。因此，以道义为最高准则的人，不会以违背道义的方式去追求富贵，即便在物质生活上陷于贫困，也能够以执守道义为乐。

When leading a poor life, one should still stick to moral principles. Confucius (551 - 479 BC) and Confucian scholars believe that it is not for fame and wealth that one should observe moral principles. Rather, such observance comes from one's heart and represents his lifetime pursuit. So those who are guided by high moral standards will never seek wealth and fame at the expense of justice, and they can live up to such standards even when they live in poverty.

引例 Citations：

◎子曰："贤哉，回也！一箪食，一瓢饮，在陋巷，人不堪其忧，回也不改其乐。贤哉，回也！"（《论语·雍也》）

（孔子说："颜回真是有贤德啊！一筐饭食，一瓢饮水，居住在简陋的巷子里，别人都忍受不了这种忧苦，颜回却不改变自有的快乐。颜回真是有贤德啊！"）

Confucius said: "Virtuous indeed is Yan Hui! He has simple meals, just drinks cold water, and lives in a humble alley. While others would find such living unbearable, Yan Hui remains cheerful. What a virtuous man!" (*The Analects*)

◎子贡曰:"贫而无谄,富而无骄,何如?"子曰:"可也。未若贫而乐,富而好礼者也。"(《论语·学而》)

(子贡说:"贫穷而不谄媚,富有而不骄纵,怎么样?"孔子说:"可以了。但不如贫穷而乐于道,富有而喜好礼。")

Zigong said: "One does not fawn on others when being poor; one is not arrogant when being rich. How do you find such quality?" Confucius said: "Good! But it is even better to be poor and upright and to be rich and courteous." (*The Analects*)

安时处顺

/ānshí-chǔshùn/

Face Reality Calmly

坦然面对现实,安于时运,顺其自然。这是古代哲学家庄子(前369?—前286)所提出的一种处世态度和人生智慧。庄子认为,一切事物都是不以人的意志为转移的,面对死生等变化所造成的境遇,人们要泰然处之。但它并非要人们消极地逆来顺受,而是强调人本身精神的适应性和超越性;提示人们用一种坦然、超拔的心态对待自己的生命和境遇,获得自我安顿,达到自由境界。它是老子"道法自然"命题的延伸与发挥。

One should face reality calmly and follow its natural course. This is an attitude to life espoused by the ancient philosopher Zhuangzi (369?-286 BC). He believed that all things undergo spontaneous transformations independent of man's will and that humans should face the changes of life and death calmly. However, this does not mean passivity or resignation. It means that people should look upon life with detachment, be at ease with changes and follow life's natural path. This is an extension of Laozi's principle that "Dao operates naturally."

引例 Citations：

◎ 夫得者，时也；失者，顺也。安时而处顺，哀乐不能入也。(《庄子·大宗师》)

（生命的获得是时运所致，生命的失去是顺应自然。安于时命而顺应变化，悲哀和欢乐就不能进入内心。）

What is gained in life is due to changes in nature; loss of life is the natural course of things. When one follows the law of nature, he will not be disturbed by grief or joy. (*Zhuangzi*)

◎ 富贵福泽，将厚吾之生也；贫贱忧戚，庸玉汝于成也。存，吾顺事；没，吾宁也。(张载《正蒙·乾称》)

（富贵福禄，看作天地用来丰厚我的生活；贫贱忧戚，看作天地用来助我成就一番事业。活着，我顺应事情变化；死时，我平静而去。）

Wealth, honor, good fortune, and favors are bestowed on me to enrich my life, while poverty, low status, grief, and distress push me to seek fulfilment. In life, I follow the natural course; when I die, I will face it calmly. (Zhang Zai: *Enlightenment Through Confucian Teachings*)

安土重迁

/āntǔ-zhòngqiān/

Attached to the Land and Unwilling to Move

安于故土生活，不轻易迁往他处。这是传统农业社会一般民众普遍具有的一种思想观念和情感。其实质，首先是离不开土地，因为土地是农业社会人们赖以生产、生活的基本资源；其次是离不开祖宗坟茔和血亲家族，因为传统中国是宗法制社会，祖宗崇拜是基本信仰，聚族而居是社会常态。此外，离开自己生于斯长于斯的环境和社会，人们会感到不便或不安。这种思想观念和情感偏于消极或保守，但也体现了人们热爱家乡、热爱土地、热爱亲人、热爱和平的纯良品格。

This term means feeling attached to the native land and reluctant to move to another place. This was a widespread way of thinking and sentiment among the common people in a traditional agricultural society. In essence, it is because they depended on the land to make a living, since the land served as their basic resource for production and livelihood. Also, they were loath to leave the burial place of their ancestors as well as their family and relations. In the Chinese clan system, ancestor worship was a basic belief and living together with one's clan was the social norm. People felt it upsetting and inconvenient to leave the environment and society in which they grew up. This concept and sentiment may seem passive and conservative, but it reflects the Chinese people's simple love for their homeland, relatives, and a peaceful life.

引例 Citation：

◎安土重迁，黎民之性；骨肉相附，人情所愿也。(《汉书·元帝纪》)

（安于故土生活，不轻易迁往他处，是普通百姓共通的情性；亲人相互依存，不愿分离，是人们共有的心愿。）

Attached to the land and unwilling to move – this is the nature of the common people. Interdependent among relatives and reluctant to leave them – this is a shared feeling. (*The History of the Han Dynasty*)

百 戏

/bǎixì/

***Baixi* (All Performing Arts)**

中国古代歌舞杂技表演的总称。包括武术、魔术、驯兽、歌舞、滑稽戏表演，及空中走绳、吞刀、踏火等各种杂技，内容丰富，形式多样，表演比较自由而随意，追求娱乐效果，具有民间性和通俗性。汉代开始流行，随着各民族的文化交流与融汇，乐舞杂技表演形式也不断融合、丰富，"百"是表示其种类繁多。南北朝以后其义同于"散乐"。唐代进一步盛行。宋代以后，散乐侧重指文人创作、艺人表演的歌舞、戏剧，百戏则相当于民间杂技。有时，统治者会因为百戏耽误正业甚至影响风气而颁布禁令。总的来说，百戏孕育了歌舞、戏剧等高雅艺术，留下了中国杂技这一非物质文化遗产，丰富了人们的精神文化生活。

It's a generic term in history for performing arts, including martial arts, magic, taming animals, song and dance, farce, tightrope walking, knife swallowing, walking on fire, and other acrobatic performances. Such performing arts were diverse in both form and content and the performance could easily take place, the only criterion being to entertain the popular audience. Such performances began in Han times, and as culture and art forms from different ethnic groups were slowly integrated into local practice, performing arts and acrobatics came to be increasingly diversified. The term *baixi* (百戏) literally means "a hundred forms of performances," and suggests, different kinds of performing arts. After the Southern and Northern Dynasties another term, *sanyue* (散乐), became synonymous with *baixi*. During the Tang Dynasty the performing arts became even more popular. In Song times *sanyue* came to refer mainly to song and dance performances or operas created by men of letters; while *baixi* came to mean principally acrobatic shows by folk artists. At times the authorities would impose a ban on *baixi*, believing that such performing arts exerted a bad influence on social customs. Still it is fair to say that *baixi* gave birth to high-brow song and dance as well as operas. It turned acrobatics into a form of intangible cultural heritage, enriching the cultural life of the people.

引例 Citation：

◎秦汉已来，又有杂伎，其变非一，名为百戏，亦总谓之散乐。(郭茂倩《乐府诗集》卷五十六引《唐书·乐志》)

（自秦汉以后，又加入了各种杂技，演变出的种类很多，总称为"百戏"，也总称为"散乐"。）

From the Qin and Han dynasties onward, there appeared different kinds of acrobatic shows and a great variety of performing arts, which were referred to as *baixi*, and were also called *sanyue*. (*The History of the Tang Dynasty*, as cited in Guo Maoqian: *Collection of Yuefu Poems*)

抱法处势

/bàofǎ-chǔshì/

Upholding Law by Means of Power

坚守法度，凭借权势。"抱法处势"是韩非子（前280？—前233）提出的一种法治观念。"法"是所有民众都必须共同遵守的法令，规范着人们的行为与是非善恶的判定。"势"是指统治者占有的地位和掌握的权力。"抱法处势"即要求统治者凭借自己占有和掌握的"势"，以赏罚的手段确保法令的执行，从而维护统一的社会秩序与价值。

This expression means to uphold the law by means of power. This is a way of governance advocated by Hanfeizi (280?-233 BC). Law is what all people have to abide by, regulating people's conduct as well as the judgment of right or wrong, good or evil. "Power" refers to the position and strength of the ruler. "Upholding law by means of power" requires the ruler to use his power to ensure that the law is enforced through reward and punishment so as to maintain social order and social values.

引例 Citation：

◎ 中者，上不及尧、舜而下亦不为桀、纣，抱法处势则治，背法去势则乱。（《韩非子·难势》）

（普通的统治者，上不能企及于尧、舜，下也不至于成为桀、纣，坚守法度、凭借权势则能实现政治安定，背离法度、放弃权势则会导致政治混乱。）

An ordinary ruler, not as good as Yao or Shun, yet not descending to the ways of Jie or Zhou, upholds the law by means of power to realize social stability. If he turns his back on the law and abnegates his power, society will fall into disorder. (*Hanfeizi*)

本末
/běnmò/

Ben and *Mo* (The Fundamental and the Incidental)

本义指草木的根和梢，引申而为中国哲学的重要概念。其含义可以概括为三个方面：其一，指具有不同价值和重要性的事物，根本的、主要的事物为"本"，非根本的、次要的事物为"末"；其二，世界的本体或本原为"本"，具体的事物或现象为"末"；其三，在道家的政治哲学中，无为之治下的自然状态为"本"，各种具体的道德、纲常为"末"。在"本末"对待的关系中，"本"具有根本性、主导性的作用和意义，"末"由"本"而生，依赖"本"而存在，但"本"的作用的发挥仍需以"末"为载体。二者既相互区别，又相互依赖。

The two characters literally mean the different parts of a plant, namely, its root and its foliage. The extended meaning is an important concept in Chinese philosophical discourse. The term can be understood in three different ways. 1) *Ben* (本) refers to what is fundamental or essential, while *mo* (末) means what is minor or incidental, two qualities that differ in value and importance. 2) *Ben* refers to the existence of the world in an ontological sense, while *mo* represents any specific thing or phenomenon. 3) In Daoist political philosophy *ben* is a state in which rule is exercised by not disrupting the natural order of the world, while *mo* refers to moral standards and fundamental principles governing social behavior. In any *ben-mo* relationship, *ben* is most important and plays a dominant role, while *mo* exists thanks to *ben*. On the other hand, it is through the vehicle of *mo* that *ben* exerts its influence. Thus the two, though different, are mutually dependent.

引例 Citations：

◎子夏之门人小子，当洒扫应对进退，则可矣，抑末也。本之则无，如之何？（《论语·子张》）

（子夏的学生，叫他们做打扫、接待、应对的工作，那是可以的，不过这只是末节罢了。而那些最根本性的学问却没有学习，这怎么行呢？）

Zixia's students can clean, receive guests, and engage in social interaction, but these are trivial things. They have not learned the fundamentals. How can this be sufficient? (*The Analects*)

◎崇本以举其末。(王弼《老子注》)

(崇尚自然无为之本以统括道德礼法之末。)

One should respect, not interfere with, the natural order of the world, and apply this principle when establishing moral standards, social norms, and laws and regulations. (Wang Bi: *Annotations on Laozi*)

本色
/běnsè/

Bense (Original Character)

原义指本来的颜色，引申指本来的样子、面貌。作为文学批评术语，主要有三种含义：其一，指符合文体规定的艺术特色和风貌；其二，指符合作家艺术个性的特色和风貌；其三，指作品中真率自然地贴近生活原貌、表达自己真实思想或感情的风格。本色不仅是对作者的要求，也是对作品的要求。宋代文论中，本色多用于评述文体的特性；明清文论中，本色多指诗人作家的个性风格，也用来倡导不加雕饰地贴近生活原貌的创作风格。"本色"常与"当行"连用，相当于"本真"，往往与道家自然之道的思想相联系，用来反对过分雕琢的创作态度与作品风格。

The term originally referred to true colors and has been extended to mean true appearance. As a term of literary critique, *bense* (本色) has three meanings: 1) the artistic style and literary features that are compatible with a given genre; 2) the style and literary features that remain true to the writer's individual character; and 3) the style that makes it possible for the writing to remain true to the author's own experience and that gives truthful expression to his thoughts and feelings. *Bense* is not only a requirement for the writer but also for his works. In the literary criticism of the Song Dynasty, *bense* was often used to describe and evaluate the special qualities of different genres. In the literary criticism of the Ming and Qing dynasties, *bense* usually referred to the individual style of poets and writers and also those styles of writing that remained true to life experience and eschewed literary embellishment. *Bense* is often used together with *danghang* (当行 professionalism) to mean "original and genuine"; it is often associated with the Dao of nature in classical Daoist philosophy, in opposition to the attitude and styles that stress literary embellishment.

引例 Citations：

◎退之以文为诗，子瞻以诗为词，如教坊雷大使之舞，虽极天下之工，要非本色。(陈师道《后山诗话》)

(韩愈以写文章的方法来写诗，苏轼以写诗的方法来写词，就像教坊里的艺人雷大使跳女子舞蹈，虽然技巧高明无比，但并不符合诗词的本色。)

Poems written by Han Yu read like essays and *ci* lyrics by Su Shi read like poems. This is like Master Dancer Lei of the Song Palace Music School performing dances choreographed for women. Although they were good writers, what they wrote was incompatible with the original characters of the genres. (Chen Shidao: *Houshan's Understanding of Poetry*)

◎近来觉得诗文一事只是直写胸臆，如谚语所谓开口见喉咙者。使后人读之，如真见其面目，瑜瑕俱不容掩，所谓本色。此为上乘文字。(唐顺之《与洪方洲书》)

(最近觉得写诗作文只需要直接写出心中所想，就像俗语所说的"开口看见喉咙"。让后人读到这样的作品，就能看到作者的真面目，优点、缺点都不掩饰，这就是本色。能体现本色的作品才是最好的文字。)

Recently I have come to realize that in writing poetry or prose, all that is needed is to write what I have in mind. This is like the Chinese saying, "When you open the mouth, others can see your throat." When readers read such works, they will come to know what the author is actually like. Without hiding either strengths or weaknesses, the author makes his true character fully apparent. The writing that best embodies the author's original character is most desirable. (Tang Shunzhi: *Letter to Hong Fangzhou*)

◎世事莫不有本色，有相色。本色，犹俗言正身也；相色，替身也。(徐渭《〈西厢〉序》)

（世上之事莫不有本色，有相色。本色，好比说是本来之我；而相色，好比替身。）

Everything in the world has its true appearance and its surrogate. True appearance is what I am, while a surrogate is a substitute. (Xu Wei: Foreword to *Romance of the Western Chamber*)

比德
/bǐdé/

Virtue Comparison

　　用自然物包括动植物的某些特性比附人的道德品格。引申到文学审美领域，一般是用美好的事物直接比喻高尚的人格精神，将自然现象看作是人的某些精神品质的表现和象征，体现出儒家将审美与文艺道德化的思维模式。人比德于自然，意味着对自然的欣赏其实就是对人自身特别是人所具有的伦理品格的欣赏。后成为修辞与诗歌创作的一种方式。

The term means likening certain characteristics of things in nature, including plants and animals, to human virtues. When extended to the domain of literary appreciation, it generally involves likening desirable objects to a noble personality. To perceive a natural phenomenon as a reflection or symbol of human characteristics is typical of the Confucian school, which takes aesthetic quality as a moral standard for people as well as literature and arts. Likening humans to nature implies that appreciation of nature is actually appreciation of humanity itself, particularly its moral character. It later became a technique employed in rhetoric and poetry.

引例 Citations：

◎昔者君子比德于玉焉，温润而泽，仁也。(《礼记·聘义》)

（从前，君子的道德人格可以和美玉相比，温润而有光泽，体现出的就是仁。）

In the past, the moral integrity of a man of virtue was likened to fine jade, which is smooth, mellow, and lustrous, an exact embodiment of benevolence. (*The Book of Rites*)

◎ 及三闾《橘颂》，情采芬芳，比类寓意，又覃及细物矣。（刘勰《文心雕龙·颂赞》）

（到了屈原作《橘颂》，情志和文采都极为美好，它用相类的事物比拟并寄寓自己的情志，又将"颂"的内容推及细微之事物了。）

In Qu Yuan's "Ode to the Orange Tree," both his sentiment and literary style were highly refined. The work used similar things to analogize and convey the author's own sentiment, and extended its content into subtle things. (Liu Xie: *The Literary Mind and the Carving of Dragons*)

边塞诗
/biānsàishī/

Frontier Poetry

一种以塞外风光、边境战事及戍边生活为主要创作题材的诗歌流派。其作品或描绘奇异鲜明的塞外风光，或反映惨烈的战争场景与艰苦的戍边生活，有些则重点刻画戍边将士们的离别、思乡、报国之情或其配偶之闺怨及对前方亲人的思念等。边塞诗往往反映作者对战争的深切感受和思考，表现出个体生命价值与时代精神之间的一种张力。边塞诗以唐代为主，之后虽也有边塞之作，但规模与气象远不能与唐代相比。

Poems of this kind depicted frontier scenery as well as fighting along the northern border area and the life of soldiers garrisoned there. These poems described the scenic splendor north of the Great Wall, fierce war scenes, or hardships endured by frontier guards. Some of the works were about soldiers' agony caused by long separation from families and about their homesickness, but many such poems also extolled their patriotism. Some of the works voiced the longing for reunion of women left at home when husbands and sons went to the frontier. Frontier poems showed the poets' attitude towards and reflections on war, highlighting the tension between valuing individual lives and the need to respond to call to duty. The most compelling frontier poems were written in the Tang Dynasty. Frontier poems of later generations could not rival the powerful expression of Tang frontier poems.

引例 Citation：

◎ 盛唐诸公五言之妙，多本阮籍、郭璞、陶潜……边塞之作则出鲍照、吴筠（yún）也。唐人于六朝，率揽其菁华、汰其芜蔓，可为学古者之法。（王士禛《居易录》卷二十一）

（盛唐诗人们的五言诗，其精妙之处多取法于阮籍、郭璞、陶渊明等人的作品……而边塞诗则是学习鲍照、吴筠的作品。唐代诗人于六朝人的作品中，多能采撷它们的精华而去除它们芜杂枝蔓的毛病，这可以作为向古人学习的典范。）

Five-character-a-line poems written during the prime of the Tang Dynasty emulated the poetic style of Ruan Ji, Guo Pu, and Tao Yuanming, whereas frontier poems in this period were more influenced by Bao Zhao and Wu Yun. Tang poets drew inspiration from the poetry of the Six Dynasties while discarding its defects of random extension and disorderliness. Their poems were therefore representative of classical poetry that we should learn from. (Wang Shizhen: *Records of a Secure and Peaceful Life*)

辨体
/biàntǐ/

Style Differentiation

　　辨明文学作品的体式与风格。指创作时根据所要表达的思想感情选择合适的文学体式与风格，从而创作出内容与形式高度和谐一致的优秀作品。古代的文学家在从事文学创作时往往首先考虑文章的体式。魏晋南北朝时的文学批评家们详尽探讨了各种文体的艺术特征和艺术规律，强调创作者应根据思想感情表达的需要选择相应的文体进行写作，并应严格遵守所选文体的创作风格、语言形式与表达技巧，这样才能写出优秀的作品。与之相对的是"破体"，指打破各类文章体式与风格的界限，使之相互融合。"辨体"有时也指辨别与追求高尚的文学品格与境界。

The term refers to the differentiation of the form and style of a literary work. It means that before putting words on paper, one needs to decide on the form and style appropriate to the thoughts and feelings to be expressed so as to produce a fine literary work with a high degree of harmony between form and content. In creating literary works, ancient scholars tended to decide on the style before writing. Literary critics in the Wei, Jin, and Southern and Northern dynasties discussed in detail the artistic features and rules of all literary styles and stressed that authors must choose an appropriate form or style to express their thoughts and sentiments and strictly follow the rules of the style, language form, and writing technique required by the chosen form or style. This, they believed, was the only way to create excellent literary works. Contrary to the term "style differentiation," the term *poti* (破体) or "breaking-down styles" refers to the integration of different styles or forms of literary works by breaking down their boundaries. Style differentiation sometimes refers to differentiating the form or style of a literary work in order to attain a lofty character and realm of literature.

引例 Citations：

◎夫情致异区，文变殊术，莫不因情立体，即体成势也。势者，乘利而为制也。（刘勰《文心雕龙·定势》）

（作品所表达的思想情趣既有所区分，文章的创作手法也要因之变化，但都是依照思想感情确定文章的体式，就着体式形成文章的气势。文章的这种气势，是就着文体自身的特点进行创作而形成的。）

Since literary works express different ideas, temperaments, and tastes, the writing skills and techniques used should also differ in order to suit the content. It is the content of a literary work that determines its style, which in turn gives strength to the work. Such strength comes from writing in accordance with the style of the literary work. (Liu Xie: *The Literary Mind and the Carving of Dragons*)

◎夫诗人之思，初发取境偏高，则一首举体便高；取境偏逸，则一首举体便逸。（释皎然《诗式·辨体有一十九字》）

（诗人刚开始构思的时候，如果取境偏于高迈，那么整首诗的意境就高迈；如果取境偏于飘逸，那么整首诗的意境就飘逸。）

When the poet starts to compose a poem, if his conception of the poem tends towards grandeur, then the aesthetic conception of the poem will be grand; if his conception of the poem is free and easy, so will the aesthetic conception of the poem be. (Shi Jiaoran: *Poetic Styles*)

◎ 先辨体裁，引绳切墨，而后敢放言也。（章太炎《国故论衡·文学总略》）

（先辨明文章体裁，遵循文章体式的要求分出段落，而后才敢放开写作。）

One should first decide on the style or form of an article, decide paragraphs following the rules required by the chosen style or form for the article, and then start writing. (Zhang Taiyan: *Overview of Traditional Chinese Scholarly Learning*)

标举兴会

/biāojǔ-xìnghuì/

Distinctiveness and Spontaneity

亦作"兴会标举"。"标举"有"标明、突出"之义，后来引申出"鲜明、高超、独特"等众多含义。"会"是会聚，"兴会"是创作主体为外物所激发的创作状态及由此产生的丰富的心理感悟，是文学创作时灵感勃发而自然生成的浓厚兴致与意趣。"标举兴会"指文学创作中由"兴"所生发的丰富的心理感悟与情感特征，亦指作品中所呈现的浓厚而强烈的兴致与意趣。"标举兴会"既是一个文学批评术语，也是一种创作理念，它与崇尚自然、反对造作的写作态度相对应，推崇创作者的才华与激情，强调直觉基础上的自由想象和灵感勃发状态下的自由创造。

Also "spontaneity and distinctiveness." *Biaoju* (标举) originally meant "to mark out or stand out." It later extended to mean "superior, unique, distinctive, and outstanding." *Hui* (会) means "to get together." *Xinghui* (兴会) refers to one's passionate creative state and rich perceptions sparked by an object, and keen, naturally-inspired interest and charm in literary creation. The term, as a whole, indicates distinctive, spontaneous perceptions and emotions in literary creation, and intense interest and charm possessed by literary work. It is both a term of literary criticism and a concept of literary creation. Opposing false sentimentality, the term holds in esteem spontaneity, writers' talents and enthusiasm, and emphasizes free imagination based on intuition and free creation in a state of bursting inspirations.

引例 Citations：

◎灵运之兴会标举，延年之体裁明密，并方轨前秀，垂范后昆。(《宋书·谢灵运传论》)

(谢灵运的诗作意旨鲜明、情致高超，颜延之的诗作结构严谨、语言明晰，他们都取法于前代作家的优秀传统，成为后辈写作的典范。)

The spontaneity and distinctiveness of Xie Lingyun's poems as well as the closely-knitted structure and lucidity of Yan Yanzhi's poems, which both draw inspiration from poets before them, have stimulated poets of later time. (*The History of Song of the Southern Dynasties*)

◎一用兴会标举成诗，自然情景俱到。(王夫之《明诗评选》卷六)

(只要将直觉感受到的鲜明物象与灵感激发的独特感悟写成诗，自然有情有景，情景交融。)

A poem with spontaneity and distinctiveness will automatically blend one's sentiments and the natural setting. (Wang Fuzhi: *A Selection of Ming Poetry with Commentary*)

◎原夫创始作者之人，其兴会所至，每无意而出之，即为可法可则。……情偶至而感，有所感而鸣，斯以为风人之旨。(叶燮《原诗·内篇下》)

(推究诗歌的创作者，当兴会来临时，往往在无意间写出了至美的作品，这些作品即成为后世学习的典范。……心中的情偶然与外在的物相感，自然要将心中所感说出来，这就是诗人创作的本旨。)

A careful examination shows that a poet, when inspired, creates excellent works without knowing it. Such poems will thus become a model for future generations to emulate… When the poet's inner feelings interact with the external world, he naturally has the urge to express them. That is what poetry writing is all about. (Ye Xie: *Studies on the Purpose of Poetic Writing*)

别材别趣

/biécái-biéqù/

Distinct Subject and Artistic Taste

诗歌应具有的特殊题材和特殊的人生趣味。北宋以来，在黄庭坚（1045—1105）的倡导下，江西诗派追求学问，以议论入诗，忽略诗歌自身的感兴特点。南宋严羽（？—1264）对此深为不满，在《沧浪诗话》中提出这个概念，旨在划清诗与非诗的界限，说明诗歌的本质是吟咏情性，而不是堆砌书本知识、卖弄学问；诗歌重在表现感受、传达意味，而不是单纯阐发义理，诗的义理应融化在审美意象中。"别材别趣"的提出，说明文论家注意到了诗歌自身的审美特性，倡导回归唐诗的创作方式和风格。

Poetry should have its distinct subject and artistic taste. In the Northern Song Dynasty, inspired by Huang Tingjian (1045-1105), poets of the Jiangxi School used poetry as a means to express views on public issues. In doing so, they tended to overlook the use of inspiring and evocative language unique to poetic expression. In *Canglang's Criticism on Poetry*, literary critic Yan Yu (?-1264) of the Southern Song Dynasty expressed his dismay at this trend. He argued that poetry should have its distinctive subject and purpose and that poetry should express the poet's sentiment and emotion rather than piling book knowledge or showing off learning or presenting theories. The message of a poem should be expressed through its aesthetic imagery. The advocating of distinct subject and artistic taste by Yan Yu shows that by the time of the Southern Song Dynasty, literary critics had recognized the distinctive features of poetic expression and called for return to the creative style of poetry writing of the Tang Dynasty.

引例 Citations：

◎夫诗有别材，非关书也；诗有别趣，非关理也。（严羽《沧浪诗话·诗辨》）

（诗歌有特殊的题材，跟书本知识没有关系；诗歌有特别的旨趣，跟论理没有关系。）

Poetry has its distinct subject matter and is not about book learning. It also has distinct artistic taste and is not about presenting theories. (Yan Yu: *Canglang's Criticism on Poetry*)

◎三百年间虽人各有集，集各有诗，诗各自为体；或尚理致，或负材力，或逞辨博，少者千篇，多者万首，要皆经义策论之有韵者尔，非诗也。（刘克庄《竹溪诗序》）

（宋朝三百年之间，虽然人人有文集，集中都有诗，诗又各有自己擅长的体式，这些诗或者崇尚义理情致，或者自负才学，或者逞辩夸博，少的上千篇，多的上万首，全都是阐发儒家经义或论述时政对策的文章，只不过押上韵罢了，根本不能算诗。）

During the 300 years of the Song Dynasty, a lot of people published collections of literary works, many of which contained poems dealing with different subject matters. In these poems, some authors showcased their arguments, while others paraded their learning or indulged in scholarly debate. Some published 1,000 poems, and others published even 10,000 poems; but most of them were merely rhymed essays that expounded Confucian classics or discussed current policies. They were just not poetry. (Liu Kezhuang: Preface to *A Collection of Lin Xiyi's Poems*)

别集
/biéjí/

Individual Collection

　　汇集某一作家个人诗文作品的集子（与汇集多人诗文作品的"总集"相对）。西汉刘歆（？—23）《七略》有"诗赋略"，录有屈原（前340？—前278？）、唐勒、宋玉等66家的作品，皆以作家为单位，是图书"别集"之始。东汉以后别集渐繁，两汉魏晋南北朝别集见于《隋书·经籍志》的就有886部，历代文人学者几乎人人有集。只收诗作的称为诗集，单收文或诗文并收的称为文集。别集常以作家姓名、字号、谥号、籍贯、居住地等命名。别集保存了某一作家的全部传世作品，是作家心灵世界的真实展示，也是后人认识和研究作家思想与文学成就的主要材料。

The term refers to a collection of works by an individual author, in contrast to an anthology which amalgamates the works of many writers. In the Western Han Dynasty, Liu Xin (?-23) composed *Seven Categories*, one of the categories being "The Catalogue of *Shi* and *Fu*," which collects the literary works of 66 writers including Qu Yuan (340?-278? BC), Tang Le, and Song Yu. Organized by author, "The Catalogue of *Shi* and *Fu*" was regarded as the beginning of individual collections. Many more individual collections were compiled in the Eastern Han Dynasty, as exemplified by the 886 collections of writers from the Han through Wei and Jin to the Southern and Northern Dynasties, recorded in *The History of the Sui Dynasty*. Nearly every author had his own collection. Collections devoted to poetry were usually entitled collection of poems while those concerned with prose or both poetry and prose were entitled collection of writings. An individual collection might be entitled after the author's name, pen name, posthumous title, birth place, or residence. Containing all the major works of an author, an individual collection enables readers to learn about the author's aspirations and therefore provides a valuable source for the study of his ideas and literary achievements for later generations.

引例 Citation：

◎别集之名，盖汉东京之所创也。自灵均已降，属（zhǔ）文之士众矣，然其志尚不同，风流殊别。后之君子，欲观其体势而见其心灵，故别聚焉，名之为集。（《隋书·经籍志》）
（别集的名称，大概是东汉时创立。自屈原以下，写作文章的文士太多了，但他们各自的志向和崇尚不同，风格和遗韵也相差很大。后代的人想通过文章考察作家的风格气势并窥见其内心世界，于是把他们的作品单独汇总在一起，称之为"集"。）

What is known as *bieji* (别集) appeared in the Eastern Han Dynasty. Literary history since Qu Yuan witnessed an increasing number of creative writers with distinctive aspirations, preferences, literary features, and tastes. To examine the style, strength, as well as the spiritual world of a specific author, later generations put together all his works and called it *ji* (集) or collection. (*The History of the Sui Dynasty*)

般若
/bōrě/

Prajna / Wisdom

梵文prajñā的音译（或译为"波若"）。意为"智慧"，指能洞见一切事物本性、认识万物真相的最高的智慧。佛教认为，"般若"是超越一切世俗认识的特殊智慧，是觉悟得道、修成佛或菩萨的所有修行方法的指南或根本。然而，这种智慧本身无形无相，不可言说，仅能依赖各种方便法门而有所领悟。

The term is the transliteration of the Sanskrit word *prajñā*, meaning wisdom. It refers to the supreme wisdom with insight into the nature and reality of all things. Buddhism believes that such wisdom surpasses all secular understandings, and therefore is the guide for or essence of the effort aimed at achieving enlightenment and attaining Buddhahood or bodhisattvahood. This wisdom has no form, no appearance, and cannot be expressed in words. It can only be achieved by undertaking a variety of accessible Buddhist practices.

引例 Citation：

◎般若无所知，无所见。（僧肇《肇论》引《道行般若经》）
（般若这种智慧不是普通的知识，也超越一切具体的见闻。）

Prajñā is the wisdom that surpasses all common or ordinary knowledge and specific understandings. (*The Perfection of Wisdom in Eight Thousand Lines and Its Verse Summary*, as cited in Seng Zhao: *Treatise of Seng Zhao*)

博 爱
/bó'ài/

Extensive Love to Benefit All People

广泛地爱，惠及所有的人。"博"即广泛、广大；"爱"即"惠"，惠及众人。古人认为，"安民则惠"（使民众安定生活就是惠），"爱"是"仁"的体现，而"仁"则是与人亲密。"博爱"犹言爱民、惠民，首先是一种执政理念，意在使国家的制度、法令、政策、措施的受益面尽可能最大化，使更多的人得到好处。它也指与众人亲密相处、友善相待、相互扶助的一种社会伦理、个人品格或情怀。

Bo（博）means extensive, wide; *ai*（爱）is synonymous with *hui*（惠）which means benefit to all. Ancient Chinese believed that ensuring the people a life of peace and security is *hui*. Love in turn is an expression of *ren*（仁）, or benevolence, which is based on close human relationships. The term applies primarily to a concept of governance of "love for and benefit to the people," as demonstrated through its systems, laws, policies, and measures which should be as inclusive as possible. The term also refers to a kind of social morality and personal integrity based on harmonious engagement with others, goodwill, and mutual help.

引例 Citations：

◎先王见教之可以化民也，是故先之以博爱，而民莫遗其亲；陈之以德义，而民兴行……（《孝经·三才》）

（从前的贤明君主发现教育可以感化民众，所以先倡导博爱，民众因此没有遗弃双亲的；向民众讲述道德、礼义，民众于是起而遵行……）

Wise rulers in the past discovered that education could change people for the better so they advocated extensive love, and consequently no people abandoned their parents. They taught people about morality and rules of conduct, and consequently they all acted accordingly... (*Classic of Filial Piety*)

◎人君之道，清净无为，务在博爱，趋在任贤……（刘向《说苑·君道》）

（君主的治国理念或原则，在于顺其自然、不随便干预，努力惠及更多的人，努力任用有才德的人……）

The principles of a ruler should be to govern according to natural laws without unduly interfering, to benefit as many people as possible, and to select the talented and upright for office… (Liu Xiang: *Garden of Stories*)

◎博爱之谓仁，行而宜之之谓义，由是而之焉之谓道，足乎己无待于外之谓德。（韩愈《原道》）

（广爱众人就叫做"仁"，践行"仁"而行为合宜就叫做"义"，遵循"仁义"而前行就叫做"道"，无需借助外力达到自身完满就叫做"德"。）

To have a broad love for humans is benevolence, to implement benevolence and behave in the correct way is to have righteousness, and to act with benevolence and righteousness is to attain the proper way. To achieve a consummate personal state without outside intervention is to attain virtue. (Han Yu: *The Origins of Dao*)

博施济众

/bóshī-jìzhòng/

Deliver Extensive Benefits to the People and Relieve the Suffering of the Poor

广泛地给予百姓好处并救济困苦的民众。"博施济众"是对为政者的一项很高的要求。"博施济众"的实现要求为政者以仁爱之心对待治下的百姓，体察百姓的需求与困苦，并在为政中广泛地施予好处、帮助。做到"博施济众"的为政者即具备了"圣"的德性。

Delivering a wide range of benefits to the people and relieving the suffering of the poor is crucial for good governance. It requires that a ruler must treat his subjects with benevolence, be responsive to people's needs and their difficulties and bring extensive benefits to them. Such a ruler deserves to be called a sage.

引例 Citation：

◎子贡曰："如有博施于民而能济众，何如？可谓仁乎？"子曰：

"何事于仁，必也圣乎！尧舜其犹病诸。"(《论语·雍也》)

（子贡问："如果有为政者做到广泛地给予百姓好处并救济困苦的民众，怎么样呢？可以称得上仁德吗？"孔子说："何止于仁德，那一定是圣德了！尧和舜都难以做到呢。"）

Zigong asked: "If a ruler delivers extensive benefits to his people and relieves the suffering of the poor, how would you rate him? Do you consider him benevolent and virtuous?" Confucius said: "He is far more than benevolent and virtuous. I would call him a sage. Even virtuous rulers such as Yao and Shun could not match him." (*The Analects*)

不学《诗》，无以言
/bù xué《shī》, wú yǐ yán/

You Won't Be Able to Talk Properly with Others Without Studying *The Book of Songs*.

不学习《诗经》，就不能提高与人交流和表达的能力。孔子（前551—前479）时代，《诗经》象征着一个人的社会身份与文化修养。不学习《诗经》，就无法参与君子间的各种交往，就不能提高语言表达能力。孔子对《诗经》与社会交往关系的论述，实际阐明了文学的教育功能或者说文学在教育中的重要地位。

In Confucius' (551 - 479 BC) time, how well one understood *The Book of Songs* was a sign of his social status and cultural attainment. If one did not study it, one would find it difficult to improve one's ability to express oneself and to converse with people of high social status. Confucius' elaboration on the relationship between studying *The Book of Songs* and social interaction actually expounds on the importance of literature in education.

引例 Citation：

◎尝独立，鲤趋而过庭。曰："学《诗》乎？"对曰："未也。""不学

《诗》，无以言。"(《论语·季氏》)

（孔子曾独自站在堂上，儿子伯鱼从堂下庭院经过，孔子问他："学习《诗经》了吗？"伯鱼回答："没有。"孔子说："不学习《诗经》，就不会交流与表达。"）

Confucius was standing alone in the central hall when his son Boyu walked across the front yard. Confucius asked, "Have you studied *The Book of Songs*?" "Not yet," was the reply. Confucius then said, "If you do not study it, you will not be able to express yourself properly." (*The Analects*)

不言之教

/bùyánzhījiào/

Influence Others Without Preaching

　　以不言说的方式施行的教化。这是老子提出的一种符合"无为"原则的教化方式。古代一般意义上的教化，是统治者通过言语表达的各种命令、训导，使百姓的言行乃至心灵符合礼法的要求。老子反对这种"有为"的教化方式，认为统治者不应按照自己的意志命令、训导百姓，而应以"无为""无言"的方式，因循、保全百姓的自然状态。后多用"不言之教"指以自身的品行来影响、引导他人。

Laozi advocated "influencing others without preaching" as part of his philosophy of *wuwei* (无为) or non-action. In ancient times, rulers issued orders and instructions to shape their subjects' speech, thoughts and behavior so as to conform to the proprieties. Laozi was against this kind of direct action, believing that instead of imposing their own will on the people, the sovereign should employ non-action and non-preaching methods to preserve and protect the natural state of their subjects. Later, the term came to mean influencing and guiding others by one's moral conduct.

引例 Citations：

◎是以圣人处无为之事，行不言之教。(《老子·二章》)

（因此圣人以无为的方式处理世事，以不言的方式教导百姓。）

Therefore, sages deal with the world's affairs by way of non-action, and teach people without uttering a word. (*Laozi*)

◎不言之教，无为之益，天下希及之。(《老子·四十三章》)

（"不言"的教化，"无为"的益处，天下很少有人能够做到。）

Few can truly teach others without preaching, and do good through non-action. (*Laozi*)

不战而胜

/bùzhàn'érshèng/

Win Without Resorting to War

不用交战就已战胜敌人。源于古代著名的军事家孙武。孙武提出，最高明的用兵方略是"不战而屈人之兵"，方法有二：其一"伐谋"，挫败敌方的计谋，使敌人无计可施；其二"伐交"，破坏敌方的外交，使敌人孤立无援。由此造成敌必败、我必胜的战略态势，最终迫使敌人屈服。这是一种融政治、军事、外交于一体的大军事观，为历代有作为的军事家所推崇。时至今日，这一思想被广泛运用于国际关系、企业"商战"等众多领域。其核心是：做好自己，搞好联合。

This saying comes from Sunzi, the well-known military strategist, who said that the best military strategy is "to defeat the enemy without going to war." He listed two ways for achieving this: 1) the use of stratagems to foil the enemy's plans; 2) the use of diplomacy to totally isolate the enemy. The opponent is thus forced into a hopeless situation and compelled to submit. This is an over-arching vision of military strategy that combines politics, force, and diplomacy, and has been the ideal of generations of successful commanders. This thinking is prevalent up to the present day in international relations, "business wars," and other areas. At its heart is the dictum "build yourself and form alliances."

引例 Citation：

◎百战百胜，非善之善者也；不战而屈人之兵，善之善者也。故上兵伐谋，其次伐交，其次伐兵，其下攻城。攻城之法，为不得已。(《孙子·谋攻》)

（百战百胜，并不是最高明的用兵谋略；不用交战就使敌人屈服，才是最高明的用兵谋略。所以用兵的上策是挫败敌方的计谋，其次是破坏敌方的外交，再次是攻打敌方的军队，最下策是进攻敌方的城邑。攻城是不得已采取的办法。）

Winning every battle is not the wisest use of force. Making the enemy surrender without fighting is the best military strategy. The preferred way is to foil the enemy's plans, the next best to use diplomacy, failing that to attack the enemy's forces, and the least desirable is to assault the enemy's cities. Assaulting cities is a last resort when all else has failed. (*The Art of War*)

才

/cái/

Talent / Capability / Attribute

人的才能、材质。具体而言，"才"有两种不同的含义：其一，指人应对、处理事务的才能、才干。在这个意义上，"才"是因人而异的。人有才与不才之分，也有兼才与偏才的不同。其二，指人天生所具有的材质，通"材"，接近或等同于"性"的概念。与对"性"的理解相似，人们对"才"之善恶也有着不同的看法。

This refers to a person's ability and attributes. To be specific, it has two meanings. First, it refers to a person's ability to respond to and handle things. In this regard, such ability differs from person to person. A person may or may not have talent.

There are people who have many talents, and there are also those who have one special talent. Second, it refers to one's attributes one is born with. Attributes of a well-rounded person are close or even equal to that of a person with perfect human nature. People differ in views on whether talent is good or evil, just like their views on human nature.

引例 Citations：

◎ 仲弓为季氏宰，问政。子曰："先有司，赦小过，举贤才。"(《论语·子路》)

（仲弓担任季氏的总管，向孔子询问政事。孔子说："将政务先分派给下面的官员，宽赦他们轻微的过错，举用有贤能的人才。"）

Zhonggong, manager of the Ji family, asked Confucius about governance. Confucius said: "Assign administrative work to your subordinates first, pardon those who make errors and promote those who are virtuous and capable." (*The Analects*)

◎ 孟子曰："富岁，子弟多赖；凶岁，子弟多暴。非天之降才尔殊也，其所以陷溺其心者然也。"(《孟子·告子上》)

（孟子说："丰年，年轻子弟多善行；灾年，年轻子弟多暴虐。并不是天赋的材质有所不同，而是由于恶劣的环境使他们丧失了善心。"）

Mencius said: "In a year of bumper harvest, young people tend to do good deeds; in a year of natural calamity, young people tend to be violent. Not that they are different in nature, but that harsh circumstances make them lose virtuous intent." (*Mencius*)

参 验

/cānyàn/

Cross-checking and Verification

通过观察、比较获得验证，是检验认识与言论正确与否的一种方法。"参验"之法在先秦时期即屡被提及，韩非子（前280？—前233）

对这一方法做出了较为深入的阐发。韩非子认为，要判断某一认识或言论的正确性，需要从天、地、物、人等多方面进行比较、检验，这就是"参验"。"参验"应注重认识或言论的实际功用。只有通过比较、检验而证明能够发挥实际功用的认识或言论才是正确的。如果不经"参验"就盲目加以肯定，是愚昧的做法。

One way to confirm whether one's assessments and opinions are correct is to verify them through observation and comparison. The method of cross-checking and verification was frequently mentioned in the pre-Qin period. Hanfeizi (280?-233 BC) expounded this method in detail. He believed that to determine whether something was correct or not, it was necessary to compare, check, and verify from various perspectives: from heaven, earth, objects, and human beings. In using this method, one should focus on the practical effects of assessments and opinions. Only such assessments and opinions that can be proven to produce real effects through comparison, cross-checking, and verification are correct. To blindly confirm something without cross-checking and verification is foolish.

引例 Citation：

◎ 循名实而定是非，因参验而审言辞。(《韩非子·奸劫弑臣》)

（依循名号与实体是否一致而确定是非，依据参验的结果而审察言辞是否正确。）

Right or wrong, it should be determined by whether a name conforms to an entity or matter. Whether one's opinions are correct or not should be judged by cross-checking and verification. (*Hanfeizi*)

藏富于民

/cángfùyúmín/

Keep Wealth with the People

　　将财富贮存在民众手中。这是中国古已有之的政治经济思想，先秦时期儒、墨、道、法、兵等各个流派对此均有阐发。它要求为政者薄敛节用，不要与民争利，搜刮民财；另一方面对百姓要实行宽惠政策，允许、鼓励百姓合理谋利致富。其中隐含有关于民富与国富统一性的认识：民富是国富的基础，也是国家赢得民心的根本保障；而国富的根本不仅在于财富，更在于民心。它是"民本"思想的延伸。时至今日，藏富于民已成为现代文明的根本特征之一。

The concept of keeping wealth with the people has long been a part of Chinese political economy. Prior to the Qin Dynasty, the Confucian, Mohist, Daoist, and Legalist scholars as well as military strategists all expounded on this subject. A ruler is expected to be frugal and will not compete with the people for benefits, nor plunder their riches. Policies that are generous towards the people should be adopted, so as to permit and encourage them to become rich through justified means. The underlying assumption here is that a wealthy populace and a wealthy state are one and the same. A wealthy populace is the foundation of a state's wealth as well as the fundamental guarantee for the state to win popular support. A state's wealth is more than just about its riches, but about people's support as well. This is an extension of the concept of "putting the people first," and in the present day, keeping wealth with the people has become a defining feature of modern civilization.

引例 Citations：

◎善为国者，必先富民，然后治之。(《管子·治国》)

(善于治理国家的人，一定会将使百姓富裕放在首位，然后才考虑如何治理百姓。)

A person good at governing a state will always first enrich his people before considering their governance. (*Guanzi*)

◎取于民有度，用之有止，国虽小必安；取于民无度，用之不止，国虽大必危。(《管子·权修》)

(对人民征收赋税有限度，使用上也有节制，国家即使小但一定能安定；若对人民征收赋税没有限度，使用上也不加以节制，国家即使大也一定会有危险。)

If there are limits to taxes levied on the people and the use of such taxes is under control, a state will enjoy stability even if it is small. If there are no limits to the taxes levied on the people and there is no control on how such taxes are spent, a state will face peril even if it is large. (*Guanzi*)

◎ 善为国者，藏之于民。(《三国志·魏书·赵俨传》)
(善于治理国家的人，让民众拥有、存储财富。)

A ruler good at governing a state will let his people keep their wealth. (*The History of the Three Kingdoms*)

长城
/Chángchéng/
The Great Wall

也称"万里长城"。由城墙、敌楼、关城、烽火台等多种建筑工事构成的完整的防御体系。公元前3世纪，秦王朝在统一中国后，为防御匈奴南侵，将战国时期燕、赵、秦等诸侯国修筑的长城连成一体并加固延长，修筑了西起临洮（今甘肃岷县）东至辽东（今辽宁省）、蜿蜒一万余里的长城。此后，两汉、北朝、隋等各代都曾在与北方游牧民族接壤的地带修筑长城。明朝是最后一个大修长城的朝代，自洪武（1368—1398）至万历（1573—1620）年间，先后修筑长城18次，今天人们看到的长城多是明长城。明长城西起嘉峪关，东至山海关，总长度为8851.8千米。长城是中国古代最伟大的军事防御工程，后世常用"长城"或"万里长城"比喻担负国家重任的人，长城还成为中华民族团结一心、众志成城、坚不可摧的一种文化象征。

The Great Wall, also known as the "10,000-*li* (5,000 kilometer) long Great Wall," was a complete defensive system consisting of walls, watchtowers, gated passes, and beacon towers. After unifying China in the 3rd century BC, the Qin Dynasty sought to ward off southward incursions of the northern nomadic tribes known as the Xiongnu by linking up and fortifying sections of the defense walls which had been built by the feudal states of Yan, Zhao, and Qin during the Warring States Period that had just ended. Extending about 10,000 *li*, the Great Wall wound its way from Lintao in the west (present-day Minxian County, Gansu Province) to Liaodong in the east (present-day Liaoning Province). Later dynasties including the Western and Eastern Han, the Northern Dynasties, and the Sui Dynasty all added sections to the Great Wall in places abutting on northern nomadic tribal areas. The Ming Dynasty was the last Chinese dynasty to engage in extensive construction of the Great Wall, which was rebuilt 18 times between the reigns of Hongwu (1368-1398) and Wanli (1573-1620). A great part of the Great Wall that still stands today is from the Ming Dynasty. The Ming Great Wall extends from the Jiayu Pass in the west to the Shanhai Pass in the east, with a total length of 8851.8 km. The Great Wall is the greatest defense work built in ancient China. Later the term a "great wall" or a "10,000-*li* long great wall" often alludes to a person or a group of people who are a bulwark of the country. This term is also a symbol of fortitude and unity of the Chinese nation.

引例 Citations：

◎ 乃使蒙恬北筑长城而守藩篱，却匈奴七百余里，胡人不敢南下而牧马……（贾谊《过秦论》）

（[秦始皇]于是派遣蒙恬到北方修筑长城、镇守边境，使匈奴后退七百余里，使胡人不敢南下中原来牧马……）

The First Emperor of the Qin Dynasty then sent General Meng Tian north to build the Great Wall and guard the border. This forced the Xiongnu people to pull back over 700 *li*, no longer daring to go south to raise their horses… (Jia Yi: *On the Shortcomings of the Qin*)

◎ 吞珪既丧，坏了万里长城，国中精锐已尽，如何是好？（陈忱《水浒后传》第十二回）

（吞珪死了，国家的栋梁毁坏了，国中的精锐没有了，怎么办好呢？）

As Tian Gui is dead, the country's great wall has collapsed, and its elite are lost. What should we do? (Chen Chen: *Sequel to Outlaws of the Marsh*)

畅神

/chàngshén/

Free Flow of One's Mind

  指精神与自然合一时所达到的自由舒畅的一种审美状态。特指欣赏山水画、山水诗时精神融入自然及物象的审美效应。南朝画家宗炳（375—443）在《画山水序》中指出，欣赏山水画可以领悟古代圣贤寄寓在山水中的哲理与乐趣，可以进入一种摒弃了一切外物和杂念的绝对虚无境界，它是一种全身心的极度愉悦和精神的最高自由。他提出这一术语，不仅揭示了山水画、山水诗及自然美的特殊审美功能，也反映了传统文学艺术对天人和谐、心灵和谐的价值追求。

The term describes a state of mind one achieves when appreciating an artwork, in which process one's inner feelings interact freely and joyfully with nature. In particular, it describes one's aesthetic experience of appreciating landscape paintings and landscape poems, when one feels absorbed with the natural scenes and images depicted. In his "On the Creation of Landscape Paintings," Zong Bing (375 - 443), painter of the Southern Dynasties, pointed out that by watching landscape paintings, one can appreciate the philosophy and pleasure which sages of past times drew from landscape. When doing so, one becomes oblivious to the external world and is totally free from worldly considerations, thus achieving full satisfaction of both body and mind. This term not only reveals the unique aesthetic function of landscape paintings, landscape poems, and natural beauty, but also demonstrates traditional literature and arts' pursuit of harmony between nature and man and between mind and heart.

引例 Citation：

◎圣贤映于绝代，万趣融其神思，余复何为哉？畅神而已。（宗炳《画山水序》）

（古代的圣贤已经通过想象与思考领略融汇了自然山水中的万般旨趣，我还需要做什么呢？只需体会畅神所带来的快乐就可以了。）

As sages of remote past already discovered the philosophical wisdom inherent in nature through imagination and contemplation, what more do I need to do now? All I have to do is relishing the joy when my mind interacts freely with the depicted landscape. (Zong Bing: On the Creation of Landscape Paintings)

成人

/chéngrén/

Complete Man

具备了健全德性与全面技能的人。在古人看来,"成人"的标志并不是年龄的增长所带来的身体的成熟,而是通过学习、修养获得了健全的德性和全面的技能。"成人"需要具备智慧、勇气,能够节制自己的欲望,并掌握各种技能,从而恰当地应对、处理生活中的各种事务,使自己的言行始终合于道义。

A complete man refers to a person of sound moral integrity who also has command of various skills that in ancient times were needed to deal with social life. In the view of the ancient Chinese, a complete man did not just mean that a man reached adulthood. It also meant that a person had acquired sound morals and the skills required to adapt to society. A complete man needed to have wisdom, courage, and self-restraint and also to have mastered the skills necessary to appropriately deal with all types of matters in life, so that his words and deeds met the requirements of moral principles and justice.

引例 Citations:

◎子路问成人。子曰:"若臧武仲之知,公绰之不欲,卞庄子之勇,冉求之艺,文之以礼乐,亦可以为成人矣。"曰:"今之成人者何必然?见利思义,见危授命,久要不忘平生之言,亦可以为成人矣。"(《论语·宪问》)

(子路请教何谓"成人"。孔子说:"像臧武仲那样有智慧,像孟公绰那样寡欲,像卞庄子那样勇敢,像冉求那样有才艺,再用礼乐加以修饰,也就可以称为'成人'了。"又说:"现在所说的'成人'何必一定这样?看到利益考虑是否正当,遇到危险肯付出生命,长久处于穷困仍不忘记平日的诺言,也可以说是'成人'了。")

Zilu asked what qualities a complete man needed to have. Confucius said, "If someone has the wisdom of Zang Wuzhong, is free from covetousness as Meng Gongchuo is, has the courage of Bian Zhuangzi and the versatile skills of Ran Qiu, and is versed in rites and music, he can then be considered a complete man."

Confucius then continued, "Now, what is the necessity of a complete man having all of these virtues? When faced with the temptation of self-interest, he thinks of the principle of justice. When at danger, he is ready to put his life at risk if necessary. When long in dire straits, he never forgets his past promises. Such a person can be said to be a complete man!" (*The Analects*)

◎德操然后能定，能定然后能应，能定能应，夫是之谓成人。(《荀子·劝学》)

(有道德操守然后能够志行坚定，志行坚定然后能够应对外物变化。能坚定，能应变，就可以称作"成人"了。)

With moral integrity, one can have strong willpower and are resolute in action; and with strong willpower and being resolute in action, one can respond to all changes with ease. Such a person can be called a complete man. (*Xunzi*)

成竹于胸
/chéngzhúyúxiōng/

Have a Complete Image of the Bamboo Before Drawing It / Have a Fully Formed Picture in the Mind's Eye

在文艺创作开始前，艺术形象已在头脑中生成。这一术语揭示了文艺创作运用形象思维的特点，也是对文艺创作乃至工艺设计提出的要求。对于文艺创作者来说，思想观念、情感、意志与物象结合，在心中形成审美意象，艺术构思已经完成，然后才是运用技巧、借助物质材料外化为具体可感的作品。对于工艺设计者来说，则有更多的理性思考，允许修改，而成竹在胸则是一种理想状态。

This term means to have an image of the art in one's mind prior to artistic creation. It describes the use of mental imagery in the course of artistic creation, and also sets a requirement for both artistic creation and for design in craftsmanship.

For the creator of an artwork, concepts, feelings, intentions and objects should be integrated in the mind to form an aesthetic image. After this artistic conceptualization is completed, technique is used in conjunction with physical materials to form a tangible work. For a craft designer, the emphasis would be more on rational thinking, and revisions would be permissible. Having a fully formed picture in advance is an ideal state.

引例 Citations：

◎ 故画竹必先得成竹于胸中，执笔熟视，乃见其所欲画者，急起从之，振笔直遂，以追其所见，如兔起鹘落，少纵则逝矣。（苏轼《文与可画筼筜谷偃竹记》）

（所以说画竹一定要先在心中生成竹子的整体形象，拿着画笔仔细观察竹子，然后才可能在心中出现所想要画的竹子，这时要急速起身追赶这一形象，挥笔作画，一气呵成，捕捉住心中所想的竹子，就像兔子跃起、鹰隼俯冲一样迅速，稍一放松，竹子的形象就消失了。）

Thus when drawing bamboo, you must first have a complete image of the bamboo in your mind's eye. First hold the pen while carefully observing the bamboo; only then will the bamboo you wish to draw appear in your mind's eye. Then, as quickly as a leaping hare or a swooping raptor, you must wield your pen and capture this image in one go. The slightest letup and the image of the bamboo will be lost. (Su Shi: An Essay on Wen Yuke's Drawing "The Valley of Bamboos")

◎ 文与可画竹，胸有成竹；郑板桥画竹，胸无成竹。浓淡疏密，短长肥瘦，随手写去，自尔成局，其神理具足也。（郑板桥《板桥题画·竹》）

（文与可画竹，心里先有竹子的完整形象；郑板桥画竹，心中没有竹子的完整形象。竹子颜色是浓是淡，枝叶是疏是密，竹身是短是长、是肥是瘦，都是随手而画，自成一种形态，也都充分表现出了竹子的纹理神韵。）

When Wen Yuke draws bamboo, he already has a complete image of the bamboo in his mind. When Zheng Banqiao draws bamboo, he does not have a complete image of the bamboo in his mind. The colors of his bamboo might be dark or pale; the leaves might be dense or sparse, the stems might be short or long, thick or slender – they are all drawn spontaneously, assuming a form of their own and fully displaying their own textures and charms. (Zheng Banqiao: *Banqiao's Calligraphies in Paintings*)

诚

/chéng/

Sincerity

真实无妄。"诚"是儒家思想的核心概念之一，儒家认为，"诚"是"天道"或"天理"的本质，是万物得以存在的根据。同时，"诚"也是道德的本原和基础，一切道德的行为必须建立在内心真实无妄之上，否则便是虚妄，《中庸》称之为"不诚无物"。圣人以"诚"为本性，其言行自然与"天道""天理"相合；君子则以"诚"作为道德修养的目标以及达于"天道""天理"的途径。

Sincerity is among the core concepts of the Confucian school of thought. Basically, it means truthfulness without deceit. Confucians believed that sincerity is the essence of the "way of heaven" or "principles of heaven," a basis on which everything else is built. At the same time, sincerity is also the root and foundation of morality. All moral deeds must be conducted on the basis of sincerity from the bottom of the heart. Otherwise, they are nothing but pretensions. *The Doctrine of the Mean* maintains, "Nothing can be achieved without sincerity." Sages are sincere by nature. Therefore, their words and deeds are naturally consistent with the "way of heaven" and the "principles of heaven." *Junzi* (a man of virtue) upholds sincerity as his goal for moral attainment and an approach to achieving the "way of heaven" and the "principles of heaven."

引例 Citations：

◎诚者，天之道也；诚之者，人之道也。(《礼记·中庸》)

("诚"，是天的法则；达到"诚"，是人的修养路径。)

Being as it is is the way of nature; being true to human nature is the way to achieve self-refinement. (*The Book of Rites*)

◎诚者，真实无妄之谓，天理之本然也。(朱熹《中庸章句》)

("诚"就是真实不伪诈，是天理本来的状态。)

Sincerity means utter truthfulness without any pretensions or deceit. It is the natural state of the principles of heaven. (Zhu Xi: *Annotations on The Doctrine of the Mean*)

诚意
/chéngyì/

Be Sincere in Thought

使追求日用伦常之道的意愿真实无妄。"诚意"出自《大学》，与格物、致知、正心、修身、齐家、治国、平天下并称"八条目"，是儒家所倡导的道德修养的一个重要环节。"诚意"以"致知"为前提。在知晓日用伦常之道的基础上，确立起内心对此道的认同与追求。内心的真实意愿会自然地表现于言行之中。个人的道德行为应出于真实的意愿，而不应在没有真实意愿的情况下仅仅使外在的言行符合道德规范。

The pursuit of moral principles in daily life should be true and sincere. "Being sincere in thought" is one of the "eight essential principles" from the philosophical text *The Great Learning*, the other seven being "studying things," "acquiring knowledge," "rectifying one's mind," "cultivating oneself," "regulating one's family well," "governing the state properly," and "bringing peace to all under heaven." Those constitute important stages in the moral cultivation advocated by Confucian scholars. "Sincerity in thought" has as its preceding stage the "extension of knowledge." One can only identify and follow the principle of "sincerity in thought" on the basis of understanding the moral principles in daily life. One's true desire will then naturally reflect itself in one's daily behavior. An individual's moral conduct must stem from a genuine wish and must not just conform superficially to the moral principles without true intention of practicing them.

引例 Citations：

◎ 所谓诚其意者，毋自欺也。如恶恶臭，如好好色，此之谓自谦（qiè）。(《礼记·大学》)

（所谓诚意，就是不要自己欺骗自己。如同厌恶难闻的味道，如同喜爱美色，这叫做自我满足。）

Being sincere in one's thought is to tolerate no self-deception, as one hates undesirable smells or likes lovely colors. That is what is called satisfied with oneself. (*The Book of Rites*)

◎诚其意者，自修之首也。（朱熹《大学章句》）

（"诚意"是个人自我修养的首要任务。）

Being sincere in thought is of primary importance in self-cultivation. (Zhu Xi: *Annotations on The Great Learning*)

城

/chéng/

Fortress / City

　　四周由城墙环绕的城邑。"城"本指城墙、城郭，是筑土而成的、具有军事防御及防洪功能的设施，城外一般挖有护城河。古代王朝国都、诸侯封地、卿及大夫的封邑，都以筑有城墙的聚落为中心，所以称为"城"。"城"音"盛（chéng）"，意思是"容纳民众"。其根本功能为保护民众，是"民惟邦本"这一政治理念的具体体现。

Cheng (城) is a city with walls surrounding it. The Chinese character for *cheng* originally referred to inner and outer city walls built of earth, with military defense and flood control functions. Usually, it was surrounded by a moat. In ancient times, the state capital of a monarch, the fief of a prince, and a manor estate granted by a monarch to a minister or a senior official all had a walled settlement as the center, hence the name *cheng*. The Chinese character for *cheng* is pronounced the same way as another character meaning accommodating. Here, *cheng* means having the capacity to accommodate people. The primary function of a *cheng* is to protect its residents. This is a concrete manifestation of the political notion that "people are the foundation of the state."

引例 Citations：

◎城者，所以自守也。（《墨子·七患》）

（城是可以用来守卫自己的[设施]。）

A fortress / city is a facility used to defend the people inside. (*Mozi*)

◎ 城，以盛民也。（许慎《说文解字·土部》）

（城是用来容纳百姓的。）

A fortress / city is for accommodating people. (Xu Shen: *Explanation of Script and Elucidation of Characters*)

◎ 城为保民为之也。（《穀梁传·隐公七年》）

（城是为了保护人民而修建的。）

A fortress / city is built to protect people. (*Guliang's Commentary on The Spring and Autumn Annals*)

崇本息末
/chóngběn-xīmò/

Revere the Fundamental and Dismiss the Specific

　　尊崇"本"以止息"末"，是对待"本""末"关系的一种方式。王弼（226—249）在解释老子思想时提出了"崇本息末"的思想，与"崇本举末"相对。这里的"本"指无形、无名者，即"道"；"末"指人为造作的各种形、名。"崇本息末"即是要发挥"道"或"无"的作用以实现万物的自然，同时止息对人为造作的各种形名之物的追逐。在政治领域，"崇本"特指君主以"道"为依据，施行无为之治。君主通过"崇本"，止息有关道德、礼法的教化以及各种浮华、虚伪的言行。

This term deals with the relationship between the fundamental and the specific. In interpreting Laozi, Wang Bi (226-249) put forth the idea of "revering the fundamental and dismissing the specific," as opposed to the idea of "revering the fundamental and keeping the specific unchanged." The fundamental here means Dao which is shapeless and nameless, while the specific refers to man-made things in various forms and names. The term "revere the fundamental and dismiss the specific" is meant to give full rein to Dao and void so as to maintain the inherent nature of all things and at the same time stop the pursuit of all kinds of manmade things in various forms and names. Politically, "revere the fundamental" means that a sovereign should govern on the basis of Dao and do nothing that goes against nature. At the same time, he should dismiss the rigid inculcation of moral values and rules and stop all false and pretentious rhetoric and behaviors.

引例 Citation：

◎ 故见素朴以绝圣智，寡私欲以弃巧利，皆崇本以息末之谓也。(王弼《老子指略》)

(因此呈现素朴的言行以杜绝圣、智的运用，减少对私欲的追求以摒弃巧、利的诱惑，这都是所说的"崇本息末"。)

Saying simple ideas and doing practical deeds rather than following sagacity and dogma, rejecting the pursuit of selfishness and resisting the temptation of trickery and vanity: this is what revering the fundamental and dismissing the specific is about. (Wang Bi: *An Outline of Laozi*)

楚辞

/chǔcí,《Chǔcí》/

Chuci / Odes of Chu

楚辞是由屈原（前340？—前278？）创作的一种诗体，后来又成为代表中国古代南方文化的第一部诗歌总集，楚辞运用楚地（今湖南、湖北一带）的文学体式、方言声韵，叙写楚地的山川人物、历史风情，具有浓厚的地域特色，因而得名。"楚辞"之名，西汉初期已有之，后刘向（前77？—前6）辑录成集，收战国时期楚国人屈原、宋玉以及汉代淮南小山、东方朔（前154—前93）、严忌、王褒、刘向等人作品共16篇，后来王逸作《楚辞章句》时增加了自己的一篇，共17篇。楚辞通过独特的文体与文化内涵，反映出南方楚国文化的特点，抒情色彩浓厚，想象丰富，保存了上古许多神话故事，彰显出不同于《诗经》传统的一种全新的文学精神与文学体式，成为与《诗经》并驾齐驱的文学形态，后世称这种文体为"楚辞体"或"骚体"，称研究《楚辞》的学问为"楚辞学"。

Chuci (楚辞 ode of Chu) was a poetic genre first attributed to Qu Yuan (340?-278? BC). It later became the title for the first anthology of poetry depicting the culture in south China. *Chuci* was so named because it made use of Chu (now Hunan and Hubei provinces) dialect, accent, and local special genres to describe the unique landscape, history, and folklore of the State of Chu. The term *chuci* first appeared in the early Western Han Dynasty, and later Liu Xiang (77?-6 BC) compiled a literary collection including 16 pieces written by Qu Yuan, Song Yu, Huainan Xiaoshan (a group of authors of the Western Han Dynasty), Dongfang Shuo (154-93 BC), Yan Ji, Wang Bao, and Liu Xiang. When Wang Yi later compiled *Annotations on Odes of Chu*, he added a work of his own to the collection, making it an anthology of 17 works. Through its distinctive genre and unique cultural elements, *chuci* reflected the special culture of the Chu region in southern China. As a genre, *chuci* is characterized by profound emotions, wild imagination, and rich allusions to the remote historical mythology from the dawn of Chinese history. It demonstrates an innovative and distinctive literary genre and spirit, standing with *The Book of Songs* as twin literary pinnacles. Later generations called this genre *Chuci* Style or *Sao* Style (Flowery Style), and its research *chuci* studies.

引例 Citations：

◎ 固知《楚辞》者，体宪于三代，而风杂于战国，乃雅颂之博徒，而词赋之英杰也。（刘勰《文心雕龙·辨骚》）

（可以肯定，《楚辞》取法于三代的圣贤之书，但也掺杂有战国的风气，比起《诗经》来，要逊色一些，但却是词赋中的精品。）

It can be ascertained that *Odes of Chu* borrowed literary elements from the classics of the past ages, but also blended some stylistic features from the Warring States Period. Though less outstanding than *The Book of Songs*, they were masterpieces in poetry. (Liu Xie: *The Literary Mind and the Carving of Dragons*)

◎ 盖屈宋诸骚,皆书楚语,作楚声,纪楚地,名楚物,故可谓之"楚辞"。（黄伯思《新校〈楚辞〉序》）

（大体上说，屈原、宋玉的诸多骚体之作，都是用楚地的方言，用楚地的音乐，描写楚国的地理，称说楚地的风物，因此可称作"楚辞"。）

Generally speaking, the literary works of Qu Yuan and Song Yu used Chu dialect and exploited Chu rhythm and tunes to depict the landscape and scenery in Chu, hence called *chuci*, or odes of Chu. (Huang Bosi: Preface to *Odes of Chu [Revised Edition]*)

传奇
/chuánqí/

Chuanqi (Legendary Story / Legendary Play)

作为文艺术语，含义有三：其一，指唐宋时期的一种短篇小说体裁。或认为由六朝时的志怪小说演变而来，内容扩展到对社会生活及各种人情世态的描写。"传"为传说，"奇"为奇异，本义指记述传说或奇异的故事。唐代裴铏的《传奇》一书可能是该术语的最早应用。宋代时以唐代小说《莺莺传》为传奇，元代时称唐人小说为"唐传奇"。与唐传奇相比，宋代传奇更为贴近生活和口语。其二，指宋元时期的诸宫调、戏文、杂剧等戏曲文学类作品。因这一时期的说唱文学、戏曲创作等多取材于唐传奇，故称。其三，指明清时期以唱南曲为主的长编戏曲。由南戏发展而来，也融合了元杂剧的特点，如梁辰鱼（1519—1591）的《浣纱记》、孔尚任（1648—1718）的《桃花扇》、洪昇（1645—1704）的《长生殿》等。各个时期的"传奇"概念，既有题材的沿用与拓展，又有手法的继承与创新，其核心"传奇特之事、演奇特之人"是一以贯之的。

This is a term for a literary form. It refers to three types of artistic works:
1) A type of short story in the Tang and Song dynasties that might be evolved from tales of the supernatural in the Six Dynasties. Later its subjects widened to include social life, and stories about people and events. *Chuan*（传）means "legendary" and *qi*（奇）means "strange and unusual," so the term originally means recounting tales of strange and extraordinary events that have been passed down by word of mouth. The work *Legendary Stories* by Pei Xing in the Tang Dynasty is probably

the earliest work that uses the term. In the Song Dynasty, the Tang novel *The Story of Yingying* is considered a *chuanqi*, while the Yuan people called all Tang stories *chuanqi* of Tang. Song Dynasty *chuanqi* were more realistic and vernacular than those of the Tang.

2) Song-speech drama, Southern opera and Yuan *zaju* in the Song and Yuan dynasties, most of which were based on Tang stories.

3) Full-length operas in the Ming and Qing dynasties, which were based on the Southern opera (*Nanxi*), and also included some Yuan *zaju* features. Typical works include *The Story of Washing Gauze* by Liang Chenyu (1519-1591), *Peach Blossom Fan* by Kong Shangren (1648-1718), *The Palace of Eternal Life* by Hong Sheng (1645-1704). The ancient style of *chuanqi* has evolved and been innovated over the centuries, both in story content and performance techniques. However, its main purpose is still to "tell stories of strange happenings and unusual people."

引例 Citations：

◎金元创名"杂剧"，国初演作"传奇"。杂剧北音，传奇南调。杂剧折惟四，唱止一人；传奇折数多，唱必匀派。杂剧但摭一事颠末，其境促；传奇备述一人始终，其味长。（吕天成《曲品》卷上）
（金元时期的"杂剧"名称，到了明朝初年演变为"传奇"。杂剧是北方音乐，传奇是南方曲调。杂剧只有四折，一人主唱；传奇的折数很多，演唱也按角色均匀分派。杂剧只取一件事的首尾，故事情境未免局促；传奇详细演绎主人公的故事原委，自然意味深长。）

The term *zaju* of the Jin and Yuan dynasties became *chuanqi* in the early Ming Dynasty. *Zaju* is northern music, while *chuanqi* is from the south. *Zaju* are composed of only four acts, each with one main performer, while in *chuanqi* there are many acts with several characters of equal importance. In *zaju* the plot is only about one event, which narrows the story, whereas in *chuanqi* the various accounts of the main characters are followed in great detail, which naturally makes it all the more interesting. (Lü Tiancheng: *Comments on Qu Drama: Composers and Their Works*)

◎古人呼剧本为"传奇"者，因其事甚奇特，未经人见而传之，是以得名。可见非奇不传。新，即奇之别名也。若此等情节业已见之戏场，则千人共见，万人共见，绝无奇矣，焉用传之？是以填词之家，务解"传奇"二字。（李渔《闲情偶寄·词曲部·结构》）
（古代人把剧本称为"传奇"，是因为其中所讲述的故事非常奇特，没有人亲眼见过却能在世间流传，所以用这个名称。可见不是奇事就不会流传。"新"就是奇特的另一说法。如果这个情节已经在戏场里演过，则成千上万的人都一同见过，大家绝不会感到新奇了，还用得着特别去"传"吗？因此填写戏曲剧本的人，务必要明白"传奇"二字的含义。）

The ancients called drama scripts *chuanqi* because the extraordinary events, which no one had actually experienced, were passed down the ages. In other words, without the strangeness, no one would bother to pass them on. "Novel" or *xin* is just another term for "strange and unusual." If this particular plot line has been performed before and is familiar to thousands upon thousands of people, then there is nothing novel about it, then what is the need to pass it on? It is thus important for those who write scripts to understand the meaning of *chuanqi*. (Li Yu: *Occasional Notes with Leisure Motions*)

传神写照

/chuánshén-xiězhào/

Convey the Spirit and Capture the Person

　　指文学艺术作品中所描绘或刻画的人物生动逼真、形神兼备。"传神"是将人物内在的精神世界完全表现出来，使人物栩栩如生；"写照"就是画像，所绘人物形象逼真，如在目前。初为画论术语，后引入文学领域，是画家、文学家在塑造人物形象及一切艺术形象时所追求的艺术境界。

This term refers to literary descriptions of characters which are accurate both in form and in spirit. *Chuanshen* (传神), to "convey the spirit," is to fully express the spiritual world within the character, so that he comes to life; *xiezhao* (写照), to "capture the person," is to create a vivid physical depiction of him. These expressions were originally used in discussions of art but were later introduced into literature. They represent an artistic state which artists and writers try to achieve as they create images of people as well as all artistic images.

引例 Citations：

◎四体妍蚩（chī），本无关于妙处，传神写照，正在阿堵中。（刘义庆《世说新语·巧艺》）

（人物形象的美丑，本来显现不出画作的高妙之处；真正能够让人物形神兼备、生动鲜活起来的地方，就是那个眼睛。）

The heights of artistry do not lie in whether or not someone's physical shape is well portrayed. Rather, it is the eyes which convey the spirit and capture the person. (Liu Yiqing: *A New Account of Tales of the World*)

◎空中荡漾最是词家妙诀。上意本可接入下意，却偏不入。而于其间传神写照，乃愈使下意栩栩欲动。（刘熙载《艺概·词概》）

（在本应接着抒情表意的地方故意转写他事从而留出意义上的空白，是填词高手的妙诀。抒情表意本可前后相接，但作者偏偏没有接写反而转向其他的描写或叙事，通过空白愈发将人物的内心活动鲜活地传达出来，使得接下来的抒情表意更为鲜明灵动、栩栩如生。）

It is a subtle trick of great lyric writers to deliberately change the subject or to leave something unsaid. Where one thought can give rise to another, the author deliberately refrains from doing so, and instead turns to other descriptions or narratives, thus creating a void which conveys the spirit and captures the person. By doing so, lyrical expression becomes even more vivid and lifelike. (Liu Xizai: *Overview of Literary Theories*)

◎描画鲁智深，千古若活，真是传神写照妙手。（李贽《李卓吾先生批评忠义水浒传》）

（作者所刻画的鲁智深，即使千年以后也还活在人们眼前，真是善于传神写照的高手啊！）

The image of Lu Zhishen portrayed by the author remains lifelike even after a thousand years. He is truly a master who can convey the spirit and capture the person! (Li Zhi: *Li Zhi's Annotations on Outlaws of the Marsh*)

春节
/chūnjié/
Spring Festival

中华民族及海外华人最重要的传统节日。狭义的春节指农历新年第一个月的第一天，广义的春节是指从农历最后一个月的23日（祭灶）到新年第一个月的15日（元宵节）这一段时间。现代意义的春节实际上是古代一年之始与立春节气两者的混合。春节期间，人们会祭拜神灵和祖先，张贴春联和年画，置办年货，吃团圆饭，给压岁钱，除夕守岁，燃放爆竹，走亲访友，等等。它凝结着中国人的伦理情感、宗教情怀、生命意识，具有深厚的历史内涵和丰富的节俗内容。在伦理与宗教层面，除了祭祀，祈求祖先和神灵对家人的庇佑，春节更多体现了中国人对家族团圆、和睦及亲情的重视；在时间与生命意识上，在辞旧迎新、驱除邪祟的同时，表达人们对新年的祝福及对未来生活的美好期待。受中华文化影响，中国周边一些国家和民族也有庆祝春节的习俗。

This is the most important traditional festival for the Chinese nation and overseas Chinese. In the narrow sense, it is the first day of the Lunar New Year. In a broader sense, it refers to the festival that occurs between the 23rd day of the last lunar month (the day of Offerings to the Kitchen God) and the 15th day of the first lunar month (the Lantern Festival). In a modern sense, Spring Festival is a mixture of the beginning of the New Year and the Beginning of Spring on the lunar calendar. During the Spring Festival, people pay tribute to deities and their ancestors, post auspicious couplets and New Year paintings, buy new year's goods and put on new clothes, have a family reunion dinner, give children gift money, stay up the whole night on New Year's Eve to say goodbye to the departing year, set off firecrackers and visit relatives and friends. In terms of family relationships and religion, people make sacrifices to ancestors and deities for the protection of their family members. In addition, Spring Festival reflects the importance Chinese people attach to family reunion, harmony within a family and kinship. When it comes to the Chinese people's sense of life and sense of time, they not only bid farewell to the departing year and express their welcome to the new year, they also express their expectation for a better future. Through the influence of Chinese culture, some of China's neighboring countries also celebrate Spring Festival.

引例 Citation：

◎爆竹声中一岁除，春风送暖入屠苏。千门万户曈（tóng）曈日，总把新桃换旧符。（王安石《元日》）

（爆竹声中，旧的一年缓缓离去；春风送来温暖，全家人聚在一起品尝着屠苏美酒。太阳升起，朝霞照亮了千门万户；为了除旧迎新，家家争先恐后地换上新的桃符。）

The year departs amid the sound of fireworks, and a warm breeze helps to ferment the wine. When the light of dawn shines upon thousands of homes, every family puts up New Year couplets. (Wang Anshi: New Year's Day)

唇亡齿寒
/chúnwáng-chǐhán/

Once the Lips Are Gone, the Teeth Will Feel Cold.

嘴唇没有了，牙齿就会感到寒冷。比喻相互间关系密切，相互依存，有共同的利害关系。据《左传·僖公五年》载，晋国向虞国借道，以便攻打虞国的邻国虢国。虞国的大夫宫之奇向国君进谏说：虢是虞的屏障，虢亡，虞必随之而亡，虞和虢是唇亡齿寒的关系。这实际反映华夏民族自古以来重视邻国关系和与邻友善、务实的地缘政治思想。

When two things are interdependent, the fall of one will endanger the other. According to the early chronicle *Zuo's Commentary on The Spring and Autumn Annals*, when the State of Jin wanted to march through the State of Yu in order to attack Yu's neighbor, the State of Guo. Gongzhiqi, a minister of Yu, remonstrated with his ruler, saying, "Guo provides a protective shield for Yu. If Guo falls, Yu will soon follow. The relationship between Yu and Guo is like that between lips and teeth." This shows that since ancient times the Chinese nation has been keen to maintain friendly ties with neighboring countries. It represents pragmatic geopolitical thinking of maintaining amity with close neighbors.

引例 Citation：

◎且赵之于齐楚，扞蔽也，犹齿之有唇也，唇亡则齿寒。今日亡赵，明日患及齐楚。(《史记·田敬仲完世家》)

（而且赵国对于齐、楚两国来说，就是屏障，就像牙齿有嘴唇一样。嘴唇没有了，牙齿就会感觉寒冷。今天[秦国]灭了赵国，明天就会祸及齐国和楚国。）

To the states of Qi and Chu, the State of Zhao serves as a protective shield, just like the lips protecting the teeth. Once the lips are gone, the teeth will feel cold. If Zhao is defeated by the State of Qin today, the same fate will befall Qi and Chu tomorrow. (*Records of the Historian*)

辞达
/cídá/

Expressiveness

说话、写文章要能简明扼要地表达内心的意思。孔子（前551—前479）反对过度追求辞藻华丽，强调文辞只要能确切而简洁地传达出思想感情即可，并倡导"文质彬彬"的审美观念。这一术语后来经过刘勰（465？—520？或532？）、韩愈（768—824）、苏轼（1037—1101）等人不断继承与发展，形成了中国文学追求语言自然凝练、反对过分雕琢的美学旨趣与风格。

The term means to put forth one's thoughts in a clear and concise way when speaking and writing. Confucius (551-479 BC) opposed excessive efforts in pursuit of extravagant writing styles. He stressed that writings need only to express one's ideas and feelings clearly and precisely, and he advocated a concept of aesthetics that valued the combination of elegance and simplicity. This concept was successively inherited and developed by Liu Xie (465?-520? or 532?), Han Yu (768-824), Su Shi (1037-1101), and others, resulting in a Chinese literary style that strives for natural and pithy expression as opposed to extravagant embellishment.

引例 Citations：

◎子曰："辞达而已矣。"(《论语·卫灵公》)

（孔子说："言辞能把意思表达清楚就行了。"）

Confucius said, "It's good enough if you express yourself clearly." (*The Analects*)

◎辞至于能达，则文不可胜用矣。（苏轼《答谢民师书》）

（文辞如果能够做到达意，那么文采的运用也就无穷无尽了。）

If one can write expressively, his potential to achieve literary grace is boundless. (Su Shi: A Letter of Reply to Xie Minshi)

辞尚体要
/císhàngtǐyào/

Succinctness Is Valued in Writing.

　　文辞要切实简要地传达文章想要表达的主要意思或主要内容。"体要"，体现精要。源于《尚书》，原指政令、法规的文辞应体现精要或切实简要，刘勰（465？—520？或532？）将它引入文学批评，强调文辞须切实精当，体现文章的要义。这一术语体现了中国文化推崇的"尚简"传统，即以简练精当的文辞传达出充实、概括性的内容，不能为了追求文辞上的标新立异而忽略文章本来要表达的主要内容。这一要求，后来成为古文写作的基本要求，对文学创作起着重要的指导作用。

Writing should be substantive and succinct in expressing main ideas or key content. "Succinctness" means to capture the essence. The idea comes from *The Book of History*, originally referring to the requirement that government edicts and regulations should be terse and to the point. Liu Xie (465?-520? or 532?) applied this into literary criticism, emphasizing that writing should be both substantive and pithy, striving to capture the essence. This term reflects the traditional pursuit for "succinctness" in Chinese culture, which prefers to convey a rich message in a concise way rather than seek novel expressions that may overshadow the essence of the writing. Later on, this became a fundamental requirement for the classical style of writing and provided important guidance for literary creation.

引例 Citations：

◎ 政贵有恒，辞尚体要，不惟好异。(《尚书·毕命》)
(国家的大政贵在稳定持久，国家的话语贵在切实简要，不能一味追求标新立异。)

What is most valuable for governance lies in its sustained stability, advocating substantial and straightforward wording, not seeking novelty. (*The Book of History*)

◎ 盖《周书》论辞，贵乎体要；尼父陈训，恶乎异端。(刘勰《文心雕龙·序志》)
(《周书》里讲到文辞，认为重在体现要义；孔子陈述教训，憎恨异端邪说。)

When discussing writing, *The Book of Zhou (of The Book of History)* believes that succinctness matters most. When recounting past lessons, Confucius detested unorthodox beliefs. (Liu Xie: *The Literary Mind and the Carving of Dragons*)

错彩镂金

/cuòcǎi-lòujīn/

Gilded and Colored

涂饰彩色，雕镂金银。形容艺术作品雕饰华美。用于文学作品，主要指诗歌辞藻华丽，讲究技巧。在审美境界上，"错彩镂金"不如"芙蓉出水"高妙："错彩镂金"注重外在形态，处于审美表象阶段；而"芙蓉出水"超越表象，直达本体，是审美意趣的自然呈现。

The term is used to describe an excessively exquisite artistic work as if it were an object painted in bright colors and inlaid with gold and silver. In the literary context, it refers to poems written in a highly rhetorical style. Aesthetically, what is "gilded and colored" is considered undesirable, and the style of "lotus rising out of water" is preferred. The former focuses only on external form and appearance, whereas the latter, as a natural presentation of aesthetic ideas, penetrates appearances and brings out the essence.

引例 Citations：

◎ 延之尝问鲍照己与灵运优劣，照曰："谢五言如初发芙蓉，自然可爱；君诗若铺锦列绣，亦雕缋（huì）满眼。"(《南史·颜延之传》)

（颜延之曾经询问鲍照，自己的作品和谢灵运的作品相比哪个更好，鲍照说："谢灵运的五言诗像刚出水的荷花，自然可爱；您的诗像铺开的锦绣，满眼都是雕饰彩绘。"）

Yan Yanzhi asked Bao Zhao, "Whose works are better, mine or Xie Lingyun's?" Bao said, "Xie's five-word-to-a-line poems are as natural and lovely as lotus having just risen out of water in bloom, while yours are like embroidery embellished with colored decorations." (*The History of the Southern Dynasties*)

◎ 丹漆不文，白玉不雕，宝珠不饰，何也？质有余者，不受饰也。（刘向《说苑·反质》）

（红色的漆不需要花纹，纯白的玉不需要雕琢，珍贵的明珠不用装饰，为什么呢？本身已非常完美的东西，无需再装饰。）

Red lacquer needs no decorated patterns, white jade needs no carving, and precious pearls need no adornment. Why? Because they are too good to be worked on. (Liu Xiang: *Garden of Stories*)

大节
/dàjié/

Major Principles

行事的根本原则与节度。"大节"与"小节"相对，规定着不同身份的人所应担负的根本职责以及相应的行事法则，是人必须持守的节度。

在日常的人伦生活中，人们虽有过错，但一般不会违背"大节"。而"大节"的失守，往往是由于禁受不住巨大的压力或诱惑。因此，持守"大节"是对人的严峻考验。

This term means fundamental principles and standards of behavior. In comparison with minor principles, major principles are about the fundamental duties borne by people of different social status and how they should be performed; they are standards of conduct that people must observe. In ethical human relations, people may commit mistakes, but generally they will not defy major principles. If they should lose control of themselves, it may be the result of failing to withstand great pressure or to resist great temptation. Therefore, remaining true to major principles becomes a major challenge.

引例 Citations：

◎国之大节有五，女皆奸（gān）之：畏君之威，听其政，尊其贵，事其长，养其亲。五者所以为国也。(《左传·昭公元年》)
（国家有五条"大节"，你都违犯了：畏惧君主的权威，听从君主的政令，尊敬地位尊贵之人，侍奉长辈，赡养亲人。这五者都是治国的重要法则。）

The state has five major principles and you have disobeyed them all: hold the monarch in awe, obey his policies, respect people of higher status, serve seniors, and support relatives. These are five major principles of governance. (*Zuo's Commentary on The Spring and Autumn Annals*)

◎曾子曰："可以托六尺之孤，可以寄百里之命，临大节而不可夺也。君子人与？君子人也。"(《论语·泰伯》)
（曾子说："可以托付给他幼小的孤儿，可以委托他执掌诸侯国的政令，面对'大节'的考验而不会动摇。这种人是君子吗？是君子啊。"）

Zengzi said: "Suppose there was an individual who could be entrusted with the care of a young orphan, and could be commissioned with authority over a state, and who would not be driven to abandon major principles in the face of difficulties – is such a man a man of virtue? Indeed, he is a man of virtue." (*The Analects*)

大同
/dàtóng/

Universal Harmony

儒家理想中的天下一家、人人平等、友爱互助的太平盛世（与"小康"相对）。儒家认为它是人类社会发展的最高阶段，类似于西方的乌托邦。其主要特征是：权力和财富归社会公有；社会平等，安居乐业；人人能得到社会的关爱；货尽其用，人尽其力。清末民初，"大同"又被用来指称西方传来的社会主义、共产主义、世界主义等概念。

This term refers to the time of peace and prosperity envisioned by Confucian scholars when all the people under heaven are one family, equal, friendly, and helpful to each other (as opposed to *xiaokang* [小康] – moderate prosperity). Confucianism takes universal harmony as the supreme stage of the development of the human society, somewhat similar to the idea of utopia in the West. Its main features are: All power and wealth belong to the whole of society; all people are equal and live and work in peace and contentment; everyone is cared for by society; everything is used to its fullest and everyone works to his maximum potential. In the late Qing Dynasty and the early Republic of China, the term referred to the concepts of socialism, communism, or cosmopolitanism that had been introduced to China from the West.

引例 Citation：

◎ 大道之行也，天下为（wéi）公。选贤与能，讲信修睦。故人不独亲其亲，不独子其子，使老有所终，壮有所用，幼有所长，矜寡孤独废疾者，皆有所养……是谓大同。(《礼记·礼运》)

（大道实行的时代，天下为天下人所共有。品德高尚、才能突出的人被选拔出来管理社会，人与人之间讲求诚实与和睦。所以人们不仅仅爱自己的双亲，不仅仅抚养自己的子女，而是使老年人都能终其天年，壮年人都有用武之地，幼童都能得到抚育，无妻或丧妻的年老男子、无夫或丧夫的年老女子、丧父的儿童、无子女的老人以及残障者都能得到照顾和供养……这就叫做大同社会。）

When the Great Way prevails, the world belongs to all the people. People of virtue and competence are chosen to govern the country; honesty is valued and people live in harmony. People not only love their parents, bring up their children, but also take care of the aged. The middle-aged are able to put their talents and abilities to best use, children are well nurtured, and old widows and widowers, unmarried old people, orphans, childless old people, and the disabled are all provided for… This is universal harmony. (*The Book of Rites*)

大学
/dàxué/

***Daxue* (Great Learning)**

人们在不同意义上使用"大学"的概念。其一，从学校制度而言，"大学"指由国家设立的最高等级的学校，即"太学"，有别于地方设立的"塾""庠（xiáng）""序"等。其二，从教学内容而言，"大学"即所谓成人之学，主要讲授为人处事、治国理政的道理与原则，有别于学习文字或具体礼仪、技艺的"小学"。其三，从教学目标而言，"大学"旨在帮助学生确立健全的人格与德性，培养治国理政的人才。

The concept means different things in different contexts. In terms of institutions of learning, it refers to the institution of highest learning, the imperial academy, established by the state, which is different from local schools. When it comes to content of learning, it refers to what a complete man should learn, namely, general rules and principles on governance and human relationship, which are different from that of *xiaoxue* (小学 little learning), namely, learning of words and specific rites or skills. In terms of objective, great learning aims to help students develop sound personality and moral integrity and thus make them qualified for exercising governance.

引例 Citations：

◎古之教者，家有塾，党有庠（xiáng），术（suì）有序，国有学。比年入学，中年考校。一年视离经辨志，三年视敬业乐群，五年视博习亲师，七年视论学取友，谓之小成。九年知类通达，强立而不反，谓之大成。夫然后足以化民易俗，近者说（yuè）服，而远者怀之，此大学之道也。(《礼记·学记》)

（古代的教育，家族中设有塾，每一党设有庠，每一遂设有序，诸侯国的国都设有学。学生每年入学，隔年考核。第一年考察经文断句、理解经典的能力及学习志向，第三年考察是否专注学业、友爱同学，第五年考察是否博学、亲爱老师，第七年考察学问上是否有独立见解和选取良友的能力，称为小成。第九年考察是否能够触类旁通、通达无碍，坚定独立而不违反所学的道理，称为大成。如此之后足以教化民众、改易风俗，附近的民众都对他心悦诚服，而远方的民众也都来归附他，这就是大学教育的步骤和目标。）

The educational system in ancient times consisted of small schools for each clan in a village, higher level schools for every 500 households, even higher level schools for every 12,500 households and institutions of higher learning at the capital of a ducal state. Students were enrolled every year, and examinations were held every other year. During the first year, students learned how to punctuate classics and studied them, and they developed motivation through learning. By the third year, students should immerse themselves in learning and develop fraternity with fellow students. During the fifth year, students should gain comprehensive knowledge and hold their teachers in reverence. In the seventh year, students should learn enough to form independent judgment and they should make true friends, which was called secondary attainment. In the ninth year, they should gain a keen sense of what connects different things, have self-confidence, and be independent in thinking without going against what they've learned. This was called great attainment. A scholar trained this way could educate others and improve social mores, and thus enjoyed the respect of people both near and afar. This is what great learning should achieve. (*The Book of Rites*)

◎ 大学之道，在明明德，在亲民，在止于至善。(《礼记·大学》)

（大学的宗旨，在于彰显光明的德性，在于亲和民众，在于达到言行的至善。）

Great learning aims to foster moral integrity, forge close ties with the people and attain consummate virtue in both words and deeds. (*The Book of Rites*)

大丈夫

/dàzhàngfu/

Great Man

　　一种对理想人格的称谓。是否能成为"大丈夫",并不是由个人的功业大小所决定的。评判"大丈夫"的根本标准,在于其对"道"的认知与坚守。不过由于各家对"道"的理解不同,因此对"大丈夫"的具体要求也有所差别。孟子(前372？—前289)强调"大丈夫"应有行道于天下的远大志向,并始终坚守道义,立身端正,不受外在事物的影响。老子则认为"大丈夫"应舍弃浮华的礼仪规范,以无为的方式回归朴实的自然状态。

This is a term used to describe someone of ideal moral quality. How much one achieves does not determine whether he can be called a great man. The criterion is whether or not a person can know and hold fast to Dao. Given that there are different interpretations of Dao, the specific requirements for a great man are also different. Mencius (372?-289 BC) stresses that a great man should have high aspirations to carry out Dao, adhere to moral integrity, stay upright, and his observation of Dao should not be influenced by external matters (as opposed to his inner world). Yet, another ancient Chinese philosopher Laozi believes that a great man should abandon ostentatious rites and norms, and return to the natural state through non-action.

引例 Citations：

◎居天下之广居,立天下之正位,行天下之大道;得志,与民由之;不得志,独行其道。富贵不能淫,贫贱不能移,威武不能屈,此之谓大丈夫。(《孟子·滕文公下》)

(居处在天下最广阔的住所,立身于天下最恰当的位置,遵行天下的大道。得志的时候,与民众一起遵行大道;不得志的时候,独自遵行其道。富贵不能使其行止失度,贫贱不能使其改变遵行的原则,权势不能使其屈服。这就是所谓的"大丈夫"。)

Living in the broad residence under heaven, staying in the proper place under heaven, one should observe the essential Dao under heaven. When having achieved one's ambitions, one should practice Dao along with the people; when failing to succeed in one's ambitions, one should observe Dao alone. Neither riches nor honors can corrupt him; neither poverty nor humbleness can make him swerve from his principles; neither threat nor force can subdue him. Such a person can be called a great man. (*Mencius*)

◎ 夫礼者，忠信之薄而乱之首。前识者，道之华而愚之始。是以大丈夫处其厚，不居其薄；处其实，不居其华。故去彼取此。(《老子·三十八章》)

（礼，标志着忠信的不足，是祸乱的端始。预设的种种规范，是道的浮华，是愚昧的端始。因此大丈夫处事敦厚，不为浇薄；处事朴实，不为浮华。所以舍弃浇薄浮华，而采取敦厚朴实的方式。）

Rites indicate a lack of loyalty and sincerity, and portend disorder. Preset norms are ostentatious representations of Dao and usher in stupidity. So a great man should be earnest rather than superficial, be simple rather than ostentatious. Such a person abandons everything superficial or ostentatious, and leads a simple and honest life. (*Laozi*)

丹青
/dānqīng/

Painting in Colors

　　丹和青是中国古代绘画常用的两种颜色，早期中国画常用丹砂、青䨼（huò）一类矿物颜料"勾线填色"，因而用"丹青"代指绘画。代表性的丹青作品有西汉马王堆一号墓帛画，北魏、隋唐时期的敦煌壁画等。后丹青逐渐为水墨所代替。由于丹青颜色鲜艳绚丽，且不易褪色，古代用丹册纪勋、青史纪事。史家多以丹青比喻一个人功勋卓著，永载史册，不会磨灭。

Dan (丹 cinnabar) and *qing* (青 cyan) were two colors frequently applied in traditional Chinese painting. Cinnabar is red and cyan is bluish green. In early times, Chinese paintings often used minerals such as cinnabar and cyan to draw lines or fill in colors. Hence the term *danqing* (丹青) made from the combination of *dan* and *qing* could stand for painting in general. Representative works of this kind included silk paintings unearthed at Tomb No. 1 of Mawangdui of the Han Dynasty as well as the Dunhuang frescoes of the Northern Wei period and the Sui and Tang dynasties. Later, colors made from cinnabar and cyan were gradually replaced by ink and wash. Partly because of their bright, contrastive colors, and partly because mineral colors do not deteriorate appreciably over time, people used red-character books to record merits and bluish-green-character books to record historical events. Historians often use *danqing* to refer to a man's outstanding, indelible work that deserves to be put down in history.

引例 Citations：

◎ [顾恺之]尤善丹青，图写特妙。谢安深重之，以为有苍生以来未之有也。(《晋书·顾恺之传》)

(顾恺之尤其擅长绘画，画出来的人物奇特精妙。谢安非常器重他，认为他是自有人类以来从未有过的杰出画家。)

Gu Kaizhi was particularly skillful in painting. The figures he portrayed are amazingly vivid and lovely. Xie An held him in high esteem, and regarded him as superior to all other artists, past and present. (*The History of the Jin Dynasty*)

◎ 故丹青画其形容，良史载其功勋。(曹丕《与孟达书》)

(是以画家画下他的相貌，史家记载他的功劳。)

Thus a painter portrays a person's physical features, just as a historian records his accomplishments. (Cao Pi: A Letter to Meng Da)

淡泊明志，宁静致远
/dànbó-míngzhì, níngjìng-zhìyuǎn/

Indifference to Fame and Fortune Characterizes a High Aim in Life, and Leading a Quiet Life Helps One Accomplish Something Lasting.

淡泊名利才能明确自己的志向，心神宁静才能达到远大的目标。"淡泊"，恬淡寡欲，不重名利；"宁静"，安宁恬静，不为外物所动；"致远"，到达远处，即实现远大目标。这是古代中国人所追求的自我修养的一种境界，其核心是对待名利的态度。它希望人们不要贪图名利，为名利所累；要始终胸怀远大理想，专心一意地为实现远大理想而努力。

This saying, with the attitude to fame and fortune at its core, refers to a way in which people in ancient China sought to practice self-cultivation. People should not be greedy for fame and fortune and be burdened by such greed. Instead they ought to cherish noble ideals and work heart and soul to achieve them.

引例 Citations：

◎ 是故非澹薄无以明德，非宁静无以致远，非宽大无以兼覆，非慈厚无以怀众，非平正无以制断。(《淮南子·主术训》)

（所以，不淡泊名利就不能彰明道德，不心神宁静就不能达到远大目标，不心胸广阔就不能兼蓄并包，不慈爱宽厚就不能安抚大众，不公平中正就不能掌控决断。）

Hence, unless he is indifferent to fame and fortune, he cannot demonstrate his virtue; unless he stays calm and quiet, he cannot reach afar; unless he is magnanimous, he cannot learn from others and be inclusive; unless he is kind and warm-hearted, he cannot embrace the people; unless he is even-handed and righteous, he cannot take control and make decisions. (*Huainanzi*)

◎ 非淡泊无以明志，非宁静无以致远。（诸葛亮《诫子书》）

（不恬淡宁静就无法拥有崇高的志向，不安宁平静就无法实现远大的目标。）

Unless he is indifferent to fame and fortune, he cannot have aspirations; unless he stays calm and quiet, he cannot reach afar. (Zhuge Liang: Letter of Warning to My Son)

当行
/dāngháng/

Professionalism

　　内行，在行。最初用于诗歌评论，指诗歌创作完全契合诗歌的体制规范。后发展成为中国古典戏曲理论的重要术语。主要含义有二：其一，指戏曲语言质朴自然、浅显通俗，符合人物性格并适合舞台表演；其二，指戏曲中的角色创造及故事情景，真实传神，具有强烈的艺术感染力，能让观众沉浸其中。在明代戏曲理论中，"当行"经常与"本色"连用，能当行、具本色的戏曲作品就是上乘佳作。

The expression was first used in poetry criticism to mean that a poem fully met poetic stylistic standards. It later became an important term in Chinese classical operatic theory. It has two meanings. One is that the language used by a character in a play is simple, natural, easy to understand, and appropriate for the character. The other is that characters and plot of the play are true to life with a strong artistic attraction. In Ming-dynasty operatic theory, "professionalism" and "being true to life" are often used together to describe outstanding opera works.

引例 Citations：

◎曲始于胡元，大略贵当行不贵藻丽。（凌濛初《谭曲杂札》）
（戏曲从元代开始，大体上重视通俗浅显，不重视辞藻华丽。）

Beginning in the Yuan Dynasty, professional simplicity, rather than flowery rhetoric, has gained popularity as an operatic style. (Ling Mengchu: Miscellaneous Notes on Opera)

◎行家者随所妆演，无不摹拟曲尽，宛若身当其处，而几忘其事之乌有，能使人快者掀髯，愤者扼腕，悲者掩泣，羡者色飞。是惟优孟衣冠，然后可与于此。故称曲上乘，首曰当行。（臧懋(mào)循《元曲选·序二》）

（行家根据自己所扮演的角色，无不摹拟相似，曲尽其妙，好像完全置身其中，忘记了所表演的事情并不是真的，能够让人在快乐时胡须张开，在愤怒时握紧手腕，在悲伤时掩面哭泣，在羡慕时神色飞动。只有优孟那样的艺人，才能达到这种效果。因此，说到戏曲上乘，首要的标准就是当行。）

Professional actors can play their roles so vividly as if they were the characters themselves, forgetting that the story is fictional. Their performances can make viewers so happy that their beards will fly up, or make them so angry that they will wring their wrists, or make them so sad that they will sob, or inspire them so much that they will become thrilled. Only artists like Youmeng can create such effect. Therefore, for an opera to be outstanding, it first and foremost must be professional. (Zang Maoxun: *Selected Works of Yuan Opera*)

当仁不让
/dāngrén-bùràng/

When Facing an Opportunity to Exercise Benevolence, Do Not Yield.

面对正义之事，主动担当，不推让。"仁"本指仁德，是孔子（前551—前479）的最高理念，泛指一切应该做的事情，即符合道义、正义的事情。犹言"义不容辞""责无旁贷"。它弘扬的是一种以道义或正义为己任、勇于担当、勇于践行的主体精神。

This phrase means that one should behave ethically and never dodge one's responsibility. *Ren* (仁 benevolence) is the highest virtue upheld by Confucius (551 - 479 BC). In general, it refers to everything that is right to do, namely things compatible with moral principles and social justice. The term is similar in meaning to "committing oneself completely out of a sense of duty," and "feeling morally obliged." It promotes a positive attitude that takes safeguarding morality and justice as one's own responsibility and dares to shoulder and execute that responsibility.

引例 Citations：

◎子曰："当仁不让于师。"（《论语·卫灵公》）

（孔子说："面对着该做的仁义之事，即便是老师，也不和他谦让。"）

Confucius said, "When faced with an opportunity to be benevolent, one should not yield even to one's own teacher." (*The Analects*)

◎勇一也而用不同。有勇于气者，有勇于义者。君子勇于义，小人勇于气。（《二程外书》卷七）

（同样是"勇"，可以用在不同的地方。有的为了逞个人一时之气而表现"勇"，有的为了正义之事而显现"勇"。君子所以"勇"是为了道义，小人所以"勇"是为了逞个人一时之气。）

Courage can serve different purposes. Some people show courage at the spur of momentary emotions, while others do so for the sake of a just cause. A man of virtue becomes courageous when moral principles are at stake, whereas a petty man may be courageous in order to show off momentarily in front of others. (*More Writings of the Cheng Brothers*)

道

/dào/

Dao (Way)

本义指人所行之路，引申而有三重含义：其一，指不同领域的事物所遵循的法则，如日月星辰运行的规律称为天道，人事活动所遵循的规律称为人道；其二，指万事万物所遵循的普遍法则；其三，指事物的本原或本体，超越于有形的具体事物，是万物生成的基始，又是万物存在和人类行为的根据。儒家、道家、佛教等都谈论道，其内涵差异甚大。儒家之道以仁义礼乐为基本内容，佛教和道家之道偏重"空""无"方面的意义。

In its original meaning, *dao* (道) is the way or path taken by people. It has three extended meanings: 1) the general laws followed by things in different spheres, e.g. the natural order by which the sun, moon and stars move is called the way of heaven; the rules that govern human activities are the way of man; 2) the universal patterns followed by all things and beings; and 3) the original source or ontological existence of things, which transcends form and constitutes the basis for the birth and existence of all things, and for the activities of human beings. In their respective discussions of Dao, Confucianism, Daoism, and Buddhism imbue it with very different connotations. While benevolence, righteousness, social norms, and music education form the basic content of the Confucian Dao, the Buddhist and Daoist Dao tends to emphasize *kong* (空 emptiness) and *wu* (无 void).

引例 Citations：

◎ 天道远，人道迩。(《左传·昭公十八年》)

（天之道遥远，人事之道切近。）

The way of heaven is far away; the way of man is near. (*Zuo's Commentary on The Spring and Autumn Annals*)

◎ 形而上者谓之道。(《周易·系辞上》)

（未成形质者称为道。）

What is above form is called Dao. (*The Book of Changes*)

道法自然
/dàofǎzìrán/

Dao Operates Naturally.

　　"道"效法、顺应万物的自然状态。这一命题出自《老子》。"自然"指事物自主、自在的状态。"道"创造、生养万物，但"道"不会对万物发号施令，而是效法、顺应万物之"自然"。"道"与万物的关系，在政治哲学中表现为统治者与百姓的关系。统治者应遵循"道"的要求，节制自己的权力，以无为的方式效法、顺应百姓的自然状态。

Dao operates in accordance with natural conditions of all things. This idea first appeared in the book *Laozi*, according to which "natural" means the natural state of things. Dao creates and nurtures everything, yet it does not command anything. In political philosophy, the relationship between Dao and natural things implies that between the ruler and the people. The rulers should follow the natural requirements of Dao, which places limits on their power, and govern by means of non-interference to allow the people and affairs to take their own natural course.

引例 Citation：

◎人法地，地法天，天法道，道法自然。(《老子·二十五章》)

(人效法地，地效法天，天效法道，道效法万物之自然。)

Man patterns himself on the operation of the earth; the earth patterns itself on the operation of heaven; heaven patterns itself on the operation of Dao; Dao patterns itself on what is natural. (*Laozi*)

得道多助，失道寡助
/dédào-duōzhù, shīdào-guǎzhù/

A Just Cause Enjoys Abundant Support While an Unjust Cause Finds Little.

奉行道义，支持的人就多；违背道义，支持的人就少。"道"即道义、正义。中国人自古推崇道义，认为道义是决定战争或事业成败的根本力量。只有奉行道义，才能赢得内部的团结一致、赢得民心，取得战争或事业的最后胜利；否则就将不得人心，从而陷入孤立无援的境地，归于失败。它是中华"德政"思想与"文明"精神的具体体现。

The Chinese phrase *dedao* (得道) or "obtaining Dao" here refers to having "a just cause." Since ancient times Chinese people have had a high esteem for justice and have thought of justice as a decisive factor determining success or failure in war and other enterprises. Only by upholding justice can one achieve internal unity and popular support, which are essential for the success of a war or a cause; otherwise, popular support is lost and the ruler or leader becomes too isolated and helpless to succeed. This is a specific expression of the Chinese notion of "governance based on virtue" and the spirit of "civilization."

引例 Citations：

◎域民不以封疆之界，固国不以山溪之险，威天下不以兵革之利。得道者多助，失道者寡助。寡助之至，亲戚畔之。多助之至，天下顺之。以天下之所顺，攻亲戚之所畔，故君子有不战，战必胜矣。（《孟子·公孙丑下》）

（使百姓定居下来不能依靠划定疆域的界限，保护国家不能依靠山河的险要，威慑天下不能依靠兵器的锐利。奉行道义，支持的人就多；违背道义，支持的人就少。支持的人少到了极致，连亲戚都背叛他。支持的人多到了极致，天下人都归顺他。凭借天下人都归顺的力量，攻打连亲戚都背叛的人，所以君子不战则已，战就一定取得胜利。）

The people are not confined by boundaries, the state is not secured by dangerous cliffs and streams, and the world is not overawed by sharp weapons. The one who has Dao enjoys abundant support while the one who has lost Dao finds little support. When lack of support reaches its extreme point, even a ruler's own relatives will rebel against him. When abundant support reaches its extreme point, the whole world will follow him. If one whom the whole world follows attacks one whose own relatives rebel against him, the result is clear. Therefore, a man of virtue either does not go to war, or if he does, he is certain to win victory. (*Mencius*)

◎ 桀纣之失天下也，失其民也；失其民者，失其心也。得天下有道，得其民，斯得天下矣。得其民有道，得其心，斯得民矣。得其心有道，所欲与之聚之，所恶勿施尔也。(《孟子·离娄上》)

(桀和纣所以失去天下，是因为失去百姓；所谓失去百姓，就是失去了民心。得到天下有规律，得到百姓，就能得到天下。得到百姓有规律，得到民心，就能得到百姓。得到民心有规律，百姓想得到的，就替他们聚积起来；百姓所厌恶的，就不要施加于他们身上，如此罢了。)

Jie and Zhou lost all under heaven because they lost the people. They lost the people because they lost the people's hearts. There is a way to win all under heaven: if you win the people, you win all under heaven. There is a way to win the people: if you win their hearts, you win the people. There is a way to win their hearts: amass for them what they desire, do not impose on them what they detest, and it is as simple as that. (*Mencius*)

德
/dé/

De (Virtue)

"德"有两种不同含义：其一，指个人的良好品格或人们在社会共同生活中的良好品行。"德"原初的意义与行为有关，主要指外在的道德行为，后兼指与道德行为相应的内在的情感、意识，"德"被认为是外在的道德行为与内在的道德情感、道德意识的结合。其二，指事物从"道"所得的特殊规律或特性，是幽隐无形的"道"的具体显现，也是事物产生和存在的内在依据。

The term has two different meanings. One is an individual's fine moral character, or his proper conduct in society. At first *de* (德) was only related to an individual's behavior, referring to his external moral conduct. Later, it also referred to something that combined external behavior with internal emotions and moral consciousness. The other meaning of *de* refers to the special laws and features obtained from Dao, or the physical manifestation of the hidden and formless Dao, as well as the internal basis for the origination and existence of all things.

引例 Citations:

◎ 天生烝民，有物有则，民之秉彝，好是懿德。(《诗经·大雅·烝民》)

（上天降生众民，有事物就有法则，民众遵守普遍的法则，崇好这样的美德。）

Heaven gives birth to people, provides them with goods and materials, and subjects them to rules. People obey universal rules and value virtues. (*The Book of Songs*)

◎ 道生之，德畜之。(《老子·五十一章》)

（道生成万物，德蓄养万物。）

Dao creates all things under heaven while *de* nurtures them. (*Laozi*)

德性之知

/déxìngzhīzhī/

Knowledge from One's Moral Nature

　　由心的作用而获得的超越于感官经验的认识，与"见闻之知"相对。张载（1020—1077）最先区分了"见闻之知"与"德性之知"。宋儒认为，人对生活世界的认识是通过两种不同方式实现的。通过目见、耳闻所获得的认识，是"见闻之知"；通过内心的道德修养所获得的认识，则是"德性之知"。"德性之知"不依赖于感官见闻，并超越于"见闻之知"，是对于生活世界的根本认识。

The term refers to knowledge derived from the functioning of the mind, which, in contrast to "knowledge from one's senses," transcends knowledge obtained through the sensory organs. Zhang Zai (1020-1077) was the first to differentiate between "knowledge from one's senses" and "knowledge from one's moral nature." Confucian scholars of the Song Dynasty felt that people gained knowledge about the world in which they lived in two ways. Knowledge obtained from seeing and hearing was "knowledge from one's senses," whereas knowledge obtained through moral cultivation of the mind was "knowledge from one's moral nature." "Knowledge from one's moral nature" was not reliant on the sensory organs; it transcended "knowledge from one's senses" and was fundamental knowledge about the world in which one lived.

引例 Citation：

◎见闻之知，乃物交而知，非德性所知；德性所知，不萌于见闻。（张载《正蒙·大心》）

(见闻之知，乃是耳目与外物接触而获得的知识，并不是德性之知；德性之知，不产生于见闻所得的经验知识。)

Knowledge from one's senses comes from contact with external objects and is not knowledge from one's moral nature. Knowledge from one's moral nature does not come from sensory perceptions. (Zhang Zai: *Enlightenment Through Confucian Teachings*)

点铁成金
/diǎntiě-chéngjīn/

Turning a Crude Poem or Essay into a Literary Gem

指高明的作者用平常词句或化用前人的词句创造性地表达出神奇精妙的意蕴。亦指高手修改文章，善于从平凡文字中提炼出闪光点。北宋黄庭坚（1045—1105）沿袭刘勰（465？—520？或532？）的"宗经"思想，强调学习、揣摩经典作品的表达技巧，巧妙化用前人的词句，化平常、腐朽为神奇，使自己的文章主旨鲜明而又富有文采。此说推动了宋代及后世关于诗文创作手法的讨论。

The term "turning a crude poem or essay into a literary gem" means creatively expressing novel and exquisite meaning through the use of simple language or by transforming old phrases from past masters. The expression also can be used to describe the way that an accomplished man of letters edits writings. By minor adjustment, he can bring out the splendor in an otherwise ordinary piece. Huang Tingjian (1045-1105), a poet and scholar of the Northern Song Dynasty, valued and promoted literary critic Liu Xie's (465?-520? or 532?) idea that classics offer excellent examples from which to learn, but he stressed the need to study and employ the expressive techniques found in classic masterpieces by cleverly transforming the words found there, altering common and hackneyed forms of "novelty" so as to impart to one's own writing freshness and literary style. In the Song Dynasty and later, this theory gave rise to many debates about methods of creative writing in poetry.

引例 Citations：

◎古之能为文章者，真能陶冶万物，虽取古人之陈言入于翰墨，如灵丹一粒，点铁成金也。(黄庭坚《答洪驹父(fǔ)书》)

(古代那些擅长写作的大家，确实能够将各种文字和物象融为一体，即使是采用前人的陈旧辞句，也像用一颗灵丹就能点铁成金那样 [表达出神奇精妙的意蕴]。)

In ancient times the most capable writers could render excellent images of virtually anything mentioned in their writing. Even if old expressions or sentences from former masters entered into their writing, they could transform them like an alchemist who, with a single touch, could turn lead into gold. (Huang Tingjian: Letter in Reply to Hong Jufu)

◎"椎床破面枨(chéng)触人，作无义语怒四邻。尊中欢伯见尔笑：我本和气如三春。"前两句本粗恶语，能煅炼成诗，真造化手，所谓点铁成金矣。(吴可《藏海诗话》)

([有人醉酒后]"捶打坐床撕破脸面触犯他人，满嘴说些无情无义的话激怒四周的人。杯中的酒见到你们的丑态觉得可笑：'我'本是性情温和有如三春的饮品。"前两句本是很粗俗的话，能够锤炼成诗句，真是创意点化的高手，可以说是点铁成金了。)

"When drunk, you strike the bed to offend others, and vex your neighbors with vulgar language. The liquor in the cup laughs at you saying: I am a drink as gentle and warm as the spring weather." The first two sentences were crude, yet for you to transmute such material into a fine poem is true mastery. This is what is called a golden touch! (Wu Ke: *Canghai's Remarks on Poetry*)

动静
/dòngjìng/

Movement and Stillness

事物存在的两种基本状态。就具体事物的存在状态而言，事物或运动或静止。两种状态是对立的，但也是相互依赖、相互转换的。但对于事物恒常的或本质的存在状态，古人则有着不同的认识。儒家认为，"动"才是事物更根本的存在状态。天地万物处于永恒的变化与运动之中。道家则认为，运动的具体事物起始于"静"，最终也要归于"静"。佛家则主张，事物本质上都是静止的，人们所看到的运动变化只是虚幻的假象。

The term refers to two fundamental states in the existence of things, namely, movement and stillness. These two kinds of states are antithetic, but they also rely on each other and change into each other. Ancient Chinese had different views about the constant or the intrinsic state of the existence of things. Confucian scholars believed that "movement" was the fundamental state of existence of things, and that all things under heaven and on earth were in perpetual change and motion. Daoist scholars held that concrete things in motion were originally still, and that they would eventually return to stillness. Buddhists maintained that things were inherently all still and that the movements and changes people saw were just illusionary.

引例 Citations：

◎动静有常，刚柔断矣。(《周易·系辞下》)

（事物的动静变化有其规则，由此断定事物的刚柔。）

There is a fundamental rule governing the movement and stillness of things, which determines if a thing is firm or gentle. (*The Book of Changes*)

◎ 凡动息则静，静非对动者也。（王弼《周易注》）

（凡是运动的事物停息则归于静，本体的静不是与具体事物的动相对应的。）

When things stop to move, there is stillness. Fundamental stillness does not correspond to movement in concrete things. (Wang Bi: *Annotations on The Book of Changes*)

◎ 必求静于诸动，故虽动而常静。（僧肇《肇论·物不迁论》）

（必须在各种事物的变动中探究静的本质，那么虽然表面是变动的，但本质上却是恒常静止的。）

One should explore stillness in every movement. By doing so, he can see that beneath movement there lies constant stillness. (Seng Zhao: *Treatise of Seng Zhao*)

都

/dū/

Capital / Metropolis

国都，国君处理政事及所居的城邑。"都"与"邑"的区别是：有宗庙（陈列祖先和前代君主牌位）的城叫做"都"；没有宗庙的叫做"邑"。宗庙是大夫以上贵族统治者祭祀祖先的庙宇，是祖先崇拜的产物、宗法制度的体现，也是"都"的根本标志。周朝时，各诸侯国的政治中心都叫做"都"；秦汉以后，统指国都、帝王的治所。后规模大、人口多的城邑都可称为"都"。

The term refers to the city in which a state ruler resided and conducted government affairs. The difference between a *du* (都) and a *yi* (邑) was that the former had an ancestral temple to enshrine the memorial tablets of ancestors and previous rulers while the latter did not. An ancestral temple used to be a place where rulers, the nobility, and senior officials made offerings to their ancestors. Therefore, an ancestral temple was a product of ancestral worshipping and a symbol of the patriarchal clan system. It is the defining structure of a *du*. During the Zhou Dynasty, the political center of all ducal states was called *du*. From the Qin and Han dynasties onward, *du* referred to the place where the emperor lived. Later, all cities large in scale and population were called *du*.

引例 Citations：

◎凡邑，有宗庙先君之主曰都，无曰邑。(《左传·庄公二十八年》)
(所有城邑中，有宗庙和前代君主牌位的叫做"都"，没有的叫做"邑"。)

All cities with ancestral temples to house the memorial tablets of ancestors and previous rulers are called *du* while those without are called *yi*. (*Zuo's Commentary on The Spring and Autumn Annals*)

◎国，城曰都者，国君所居，人所都会也。(刘熙《释名·释州国》)
(一国的城邑称为"都"，是因为它是国君居住、人口聚集的地方。)

When a city is called *du*, it is where the ruler of the land resides and where there is a large population. (Liu Xi: *Explanation of Terms*)

独化

/dúhuà/

Self-driven Development

　　指天地万物不假外力，自己独立生成、变化。由郭象（？—312）在《庄子注》中提出。具体而言，"独化"包含三重含义：其一，天地万物的生成和变化都是自然而然的。其二，天地万物的生成和变化都是各自独立的。其三，天地万物的生成和变化都是突然发生的，是没有原因和目的的。"独化"观念否定了造物主的存在，同时也否定了一物构成

75

另一物发生与存在的原因。但就世界整体而言，"独化"而成的万物又处于某种和谐的关系之中。

The term indicates that all things in heaven and on earth do not depend on external forces. Rather, they take shape and change by themselves independently. It was put forward by Guo Xiang (?-312) in his *Annotations on Zhuangzi*. Specifically, the term contains three meanings. Firstly, all things in heaven and on earth form and change naturally. Secondly, all things in heaven and on earth form and change independent of one another. Thirdly, all things in heaven and on earth form and change suddenly, without any reason or purpose. The concept of self-driven development denies the existence of a creator. At the same time, it also denies that one thing causes the occurrence and existence of another. However, according to this concept, all things in the universe, naturally formed, co-exist in harmony.

引例 Citation：

◎ 凡得之者，外不资于道，内不由于己，掘然自得而独化也。(郭象《庄子注》卷三)

(事物凡得其自性者，不依赖于外在的道，不依从于内在的诉求，没有原因地自我获得而独立生成变化。)

All that which comes into existence on its own neither depends on external laws nor does it depend internally on itself. Without any reason it came into being by itself and remains independent. (Guo Xiang: *Annotations on Zhuangzi*)

夺胎换骨

/duótāi-huàngǔ/

Express the Ideas in Earlier Literary Works in a New Way

原意为脱去凡胎俗骨而换为圣胎仙骨，后比喻在诗文创作中援用前人作品的意思但能用自己的语言另立新意的一种技法。强调师法前人而不露痕迹并能有所创新。在诗歌创作中主要通过换字、换意凸显主旨、生成新意、造就佳句。"夺胎"是发现前人作品中具有某种意味，而予以阐扬、深化、拓展，乃至生成新意。"换骨"是发现前人作品中具有某种高妙的思想、情意但表现不够充分，而用更为恰切的语言予以重新表现，使之更完善、更鲜明。这一技巧体现文艺创作的传承、流变关系，在作品中可以看到很多具体运用的实例。文化学术的继承和发展也可以借鉴这一策略。

This term, which figuratively means to replace the flesh and bones of an ordinary human being with those of an immortal, is used to describe a literary technique in which a writer uses his own words to express new ideas while quoting those from earlier works. The emphasis is on borrowing from the past without showing any traces, yet forming something new in the process. In poetry, this is achieved primarily by substituting words and ideas to highlight a theme, thus creating a beautiful new phrase. *Duotai* (夺胎) is to identify an idea in an existing work and to imbue it with new meaning by expounding, deepening or broadening it. *Huangu* (换骨) is to identify a brilliant idea or feeling in an earlier work which is insufficiently expressed, and to give it greater refinement and clarity by expressing it with a more appropriate choice of words. This technique exemplifies how literature both perpetuates and yet changes tradition. Cultural scholarship can also borrow from this method to build on the past and to further develop.

引例 Citations：

◎ 然不易其意而造其语，谓之换骨法；窥入其意而形容之，谓之夺胎法。(释惠洪《冷斋夜话》卷一)

(然而不改变前人的意思而换用更恰切的词句，叫做换骨法；从前人作品中领悟到作者的某个意旨而予以深化和充分发挥，叫做夺胎法。)

Huangu is to use more appropriate words without changing the meaning of earlier writers; *Duotai* is to comprehend a certain meaning of an author and then deepen it and express it more fully. (Shi Huihong: *Evening Talks at Lengzhai*)

◎ 文章虽不要蹈袭古人一言一句，然古人自有夺胎换骨等法，所谓灵丹一粒点铁成金也。(陈善《扪虱新话·文章夺胎换骨》)

(文章虽然不应该袭用前人的一字一句，但前人自有一种夺胎换骨的方法，就好像用一粒灵丹来点铁成金 [从而创造出更完美的作品] 一样。)

Though not copying earlier writings word from word, the ancients had a way of "replacing the flesh and bones" which, like a magic pill turning iron into gold, brings forward even better works. (Chen Shan: *Daring Remarks on Literature*)

二柄

/èrbǐng/

Two Handles

　　君主所掌握的两种权柄，即赏罚之权。奖赏与惩罚是政治治理的基本手段，不同学派都有所讨论。韩非子（前280？—前233）特别重视赏罚在政治治理中的作用，认为赏罚应以国家的法令为依据，合乎法令则赏，违背法令则罚。人们畏惧刑罚、喜好奖赏，就会按照法令的规范行事。韩非子同时强调，君主应掌握施加赏罚的权力，以保证赏罚依据法令而行，避免赏罚之权旁落而成为个人谋求私利的工具。

In this context, two handles mean a sovereign ruler has the power to both confer rewards and mete out punishments. Both are basic ways of governance and have been subjects of discussion in different schools of thought. Ancient scholar Hanfeizi (280?-233 BC) attached great importance to the role of rewards and punishments in governance, believing that both should be given according to the law. One who abode by the law should be offered rewards and one who broke the law should be given punishment. This would make people behave in accordance with the law as they love rewards and fear punishment. He also emphasized that a sovereign should exercise his power in such a way so that rewards and punishments were given exactly as the law requires and that such power was not abused as a tool to seek personal gain.

引例 Citation：

◎二柄者，刑、德也。何谓刑、德？曰：杀戮之谓刑，庆赏之谓德。为人臣者畏诛罚而利庆赏，故人主自用其刑德，则群臣畏其威而归其利矣。(《韩非子·二柄》)

（两种权柄，就是指刑和德。什么是刑、德？杀戮称为刑，奖赏称为德。官吏畏惧刑罚而谋求奖赏，因此君主亲自施用赏罚，官吏就会畏惧刑罚的威势而去谋求奖赏之利了。）

The term "two kinds of power" refers to punishments and honors. What is meant by punishments and honors? The answer is: the death penalty is a form of punishment and reward is a form of honor. Officials fear punishments and seek honors. When a sovereign ruler exercises these two powers, his officials will undoubtedly fear punishments and seek honors. (*Hanfeizi*)

二人同心，其利断金

/èr rén tóng xīn, qí lì duàn jīn/

If Two People Are of the Same Mind, Their Combined Strength Can Break Metal.

两人同心，其力量犹如利刃可以斩断金属。"二人"可以指兄弟、夫妻或任何当事的双方；"同心"，有共同的愿景，思想认识一致；"利"，锋利；"断金"，斩断金属。此术语比喻只要当事双方一条心，就能发挥强大力量，克服任何困难，犹言团结起来力量大。它强调的是齐心协力、团结合作的重要意义。

When two people are of the same mind, their combined strength is like a sharp blade which can cut through metal. "Two people" here could mean two brothers, husband and wife, or any two persons working together. "Of the same mind" here means the people sharing the same vision and thinking. This metaphorical term means that people of the same mind will create great strength and can overcome any obstacles. It stresses the importance of concerted efforts and cooperation, which will generate great power.

引例 Citation：

◎二人同心，其利断金。同心之言，其臭如兰。(《周易·系辞上》)

（两人同心，其力量犹如利刃可以斩断金属。心意相同的语言，其气味就像兰草一样芳香。）

If two people are of the same mind, their combined strength can cut through a piece of metal. Words of people with the same mind smell as fragrant as orchids. (*The Book of Changes*)

法
/fǎ/

Law / Dharma

"法"的本义指刑罚，引申而指法律、法令和法律制度。在古代中国，"法"和"礼"都是对人行为的规范："礼"（礼教）旨在扬善，"法"（刑罚）旨在惩恶。古人认为，"法"虽由君王制定和颁布，但是君王和天下的人须共同遵守，它体现了法的正义性与公平性。公元前536年，郑国执政子产（？—前522）将郑国的法律条文铸在象征诸侯权力的鼎上，史称"铸刑书"，这是中国历史上第一次向民众发布成文法。战国时期，产生了以商鞅（前390？—前338）、韩非子（前280？—前233）为代表的法家学说。"法"（dharma）又为佛教术语。在佛教典籍中，"法"主要有三种含义：其一，指真实的存在，即真知的对象。佛教认为日常事物都是依待各种条件合成的，表象所见悉皆不实，通过修行，可以观见其中不可再分的真实要素，包括物质、意识功能等要素上百种。其二，指如实的教导。它既是佛陀言说的教法，也是听法者应当实现的目标。这一观念与阿毗达摩之法相的具体含义虽然有别，却并不相违，因为对于真实的认识基于相应的教导。这些不仅是佛教知识体系的重要组成部分，也是实现解脱的基础。其三，指世间现象。不同于上述指向解脱的法，佛教典籍中亦有"诸法""万法"的说法，在最宽泛的意义上指世间一切现象，它们是不真实的。

The Chinese character *fa* (法), originally meaning "penalty," refers to the legal system consisting of laws, decrees, and regulations. In ancient China, both *fa* and *li* (礼 rite) set standards for individual behavior. In particular, rites rewarded virtue, while laws punished vice. It was generally accepted that while only a sovereign ruler had the right to enact and promulgate laws, everyone, be it a ruler or a subject, had to obey the laws. This point of view reflects the justice and fairness of law. In 536 BC, Zichan (?-522 BC), the chief minister in the State of Zheng, had the legal provisions cast on a bronze *ding*, a tripodal vessel that symbolized the power of the ducal ruler. Zichan's action, known as "casting the penal code," was the very first example of publishing a statute in Chinese history. The Warring States Period witnessed the rise of the Legalists such as Shang Yang (390?-338 BC) and Hanfeizi (280?-233 BC).

Fa (法) is also a Buddhist term. In scriptures, it is the Chinese equivalent of the Sanskrit word *dharma* with three shades of meaning. First, it refers to real being, which is the object of genuine knowledge. Buddhism argues that all things in daily life are produced through the concomitance of causes and conditions. In this sense, what one appears to see or know is unreal in nature. However, one can perceive the dharmas, the indivisible real elements beneath the surface, through mental practices. Indeed, there are more than a hundred types of the elements, such as substance and consciousness. Second, dharma can be defined as the Buddhist teachings. The teachings here not only refer to the words dictated by the Buddha but also what dharma-hearers receive and pursue. This point of view is different from the characteristics of dharma discussed in the *Abhidhamma Piṭaka* (Basket of Advanced Dharma). But they do not contradict each other, because both of them advocate that perception of reality be based on relevant teachings. For Buddhism as a whole, the teachings constitute a significant portion of its knowledge system; for all Buddhists, the teachings pave the way for their personal liberation. Third, dharma denotes the worldly phenomenon, which is clearly distinguishable from the previous meaning. In scriptures, *zhufa* (all dharmas) and *wanfa* (tens of thousands of dharmas) represent all worldly phenomena, unreal in nature, in the broadest sense.

引例 Citations：
◎法者，刑罚也，所以禁强暴也。（桓宽《盐铁论·诏圣》）
（法就是刑罚，是用来禁止强暴的。）

Laws are punishments for the purpose of prohibiting violence and crime. (Huan Kuan: *Discourses on Salt and Iron*)

◎ 夫礼禁未然之前，法施已然之后。(《史记·太史公自序》)
（礼的作用是阻止作恶之事发生，法则是在作恶之事发生之后进行惩罚。）

Rites are practiced before crimes can be committed, while laws as punishments are enforced afterwards. (*Records of the Historian*)

◎ 心、心所法亦非实我，不恒相续，待众缘故。(《成唯识论》卷一)
（意识和由意识产生的各种心智功能也都不是真实的自我，因为这些法都依待各种条件产生，并不能恒久持续。）

Neither mind nor its resulting mental factors belong to the real self. They cannot last permanently, because they are produced through the concomitance of various causes and conditions. (*Collected Commentaries to the Perfection of Consciousness-only*)

法不阿贵

/fǎbù'ēguì/

The Law Does Not Favor the Rich and Powerful.

法律对一切人平等，对权贵也绝不徇情偏袒。古代法家主张，治理国家应该不分贵贱亲疏，一切依据法律规定而予以奖惩。其主旨强调公正执法，法律面前，人人平等。这一主张为历代推崇，是"依法治国"思想的重要来源之一。

The law treats everybody equally, not favoring the rich and powerful. The Legalists in ancient China argued that there should be no distinction between noble and poor or close and distant people; punishment or reward should be meted out strictly in accordance with the law. They believed in fairness in enforcing the law and treating everyone as equal before the law. This belief has been championed through the ages and is a major source of the notion of rule of law.

引例 Citation：

◎ 法不阿贵，绳不挠曲。法之所加，智者弗能辞，勇者弗敢争。刑过不避大臣，赏善不遗匹夫。(《韩非子·有度》)

（法律不偏袒权贵，墨线不随弯就曲。法律所制裁的，即便是智者也不能推脱、勇者也不敢争辩。惩罚罪过不回避大臣，奖励善行不遗漏百姓。）

The law does not favor the rich and powerful, as the marking-line does not bend. What the law imposes, the wise cannot evade, nor can the brave defy. Punishment for wrongdoing does not spare senior officials, as rewards for good conduct do not bypass the common man. (*Hanfeizi*)

泛爱
/fàn'ài/

Broad Love Extending to All

广泛地爱。在语义学层面，它与"博爱"相同；但在思想史层面，"博爱"通常指爱所有人，而"泛爱"则既指爱所有的人，也指爱一切事物，与孟子（前372？—前289）的"仁民爱物"、张载（1020—1077）的"民胞物与"异曲同工。

On the semantic level, *fan'ai* (泛爱), like the term *bo'ai* (博爱), means a broad love that extends to all. However, in the history of Chinese thought, it has been used with a different connotation: while *bo'ai* generally suggests "love of all human beings," *fan'ai* infers "love of all humans as well as all things." It means the same as what Mencius (372?-289 BC) advocated that men of virtue should love others and treasure everything on earth, and what Zhang Zai (1020-1077) proposed that all people are brothers and sisters, and all things are companions.

引例 Citations：

◎子曰："弟子入则孝，出则悌，谨而信，泛爱众，而亲仁。"（《论语·学而》）

（孔子说："弟子们在家要孝顺父母，出门要尊重师长，言行要谨慎诚信，广爱众人，亲近有仁德的人。"）

Confucius said, "At home treat parents with reverence, outside treat elders with respect, be circumspect and honest, love all people, and frequent those who are magnanimous and virtuous." (*The Analects*)

◎泛爱万物，天地一体也。(《庄子·天下》)
（广泛地爱一切事物，天地万物是一个有机整体。）
Love all things and creatures, for they form an organic whole. (*Zhuangzi*)

方便

/fāngbiàn/

***Upāya* / Expediency**

　　方式、方法。"方便"常与"善巧"（kauśalya）连用，指佛陀或菩萨为了教化众生应机说教，使用巧妙的语汇和叙事手法，令不同背景的听众都能理解并领会言外之奥义。"方便"概念是大乘佛教的一个关键，强调包括佛陀言教在内的所有言语表述都依赖于名相概念、不得究竟，在一定意义上都是方便施设，如指月之指，故不应做字面理解，更不可执著。

This concept refers to appropriate skillful means or methods. "Expediency" is often used together with "ingenuity" (*kauśalya*). It refers to the Buddha's or to a bodhisattva's preaching adapting to the circumstances, in order to convert beings. He used adroit words and terms and narrative techniques, so as to allow listeners of different backgrounds all understand and comprehend it and grasp the implied abstruse meaning. The concept of "expediency" is a key to the Great Vehicle (Mahayana) sect of Buddhism. It emphasizes that all verbal expressions, including the Buddha's teaching, depend on the concept of the term and appearance. They cannot obtain the highest level. In a certain sense they are all expedient means, like a finger pointing at the moon. That is why they should not be literally interpreted. One should not cling to them.

引例 Citation：

◎吾从成佛已来，种种因缘、种种譬喻广演言教，无数方便引导众生，令离诸著（zhuó）。(《妙法莲华经》卷一)

（自从我成佛以来，就以各种各样的言行事迹或譬喻故事，详细地演说教义，利用无数巧妙的方法引导众生远离各种执著。）

Since I have become Buddha, I have widely developed and verbally taught several kinds of causality stories and several kinds of similes. With countless skillful means I have guided the beings, so that they would abandon any attachment. (*Scriptural Text: The Lotus Sutra of the Wonderful Dharma*)

非攻
/fēigōng/

Denouncing Unjust Wars

反对、禁止不义的战争。"非攻"是墨家的基本主张之一。墨家认为，违反道义的攻伐战争有着严重危害。不仅被攻伐的国家遭到极大破坏，发动战争的国家也会因战争造成大量的人民伤亡及财产损失，因此应该禁止不义的战争。墨家也通过实际的行动反对并阻止国家间的相互攻伐，并研究了用以防御攻伐的战术、器具。

Opposition to unjust warfare is one of the basic concepts in the Mohist School of thought. It regards immoral and aggressive wars as acutely harmful to society. Not only does the country being attacked suffer great damage, the people of the country that starts the war also suffer serious casualties and property losses. Therefore, Mohists held that unjust wars should be prohibited. They took specific measures to prevent aggressive wars between nations, and conducted research into defensive tactics and armaments.

引例 Citation：

◎今欲为仁义，求为上士，尚欲中圣王之道，下欲中国家百姓之利，故当若非攻之为说，而将不可不察者此也。(《墨子·非攻下》)
（现在想要施行仁义，力求成为上等士人，上要符合圣王之道，下要有利于国家百姓的利益，那么对于非攻之说，就不可不审察了。）

If one wishes to be humane and just and become a gentleman with high moral standards, he must both observe the way of the sage kings, and advance the interests of the state and the people. In order to achieve these goals, the principle of prohibiting unjust wars cannot be disregarded. (*Mozi*)

非命
/fēimìng/

Rejection of Fatalism

反对人事由命运所决定的观念。"非命"是墨家的基本主张之一。墨子（前468？—前376）提出，人民的贫富、国家的治乱都取决于人自身的作为，而不是由命运所决定的。将人事托付于命运，是在推卸行为主体的责任，只会导致国乱民贫。只有依据"兼爱"等道德原则，通过自身的努力作为，才能获得实际的利益。

A belief that events are not predetermined and a denial of fate is a basic component of Mohist thought. Mozi (468?-376 BC) proposed that poverty and turmoil are brought about by our own acts rather than predetermined by fate. Blaming human affairs on fate is nothing other than relieving actors of responsibility for their actions and will only bring chaos to the state and poverty to the people. Only by embracing ethical principles such as impartial love and by our own efforts, can we gain practical benefits.

引例 Citation：

◎ 执有命者，此天下之厚害也，是故子墨子非也。(《墨子·非命中》)

（主张命运决定人事的人，是天下的大害，因此墨子反对他们的主张。）

Those who hold that there is fate are harmful to the world. For that reason Mozi is opposed to their stand. (*Mozi*)

丰肉微骨

/fēnròu-wēigǔ/

Fleshy Body and Soft Bone Structure

原指女性身材娇小、肌肉丰腴而身段柔软，后用于书画品评，指运笔丰肥、媚浮而骨力纤弱。"骨"即骨法，指笔势或结构上的清劲雄健；"肉"指线条的丰肥、妍媚无力或浓墨重彩。古人强调书画创作应有骨有肉、骨肉匀称，既不失妍美而又雄健有力。因此，"丰肉微骨"是差评，而"丰骨微肉"或"骨丰肉润"则各有千秋。这一术语从人物的鉴赏延伸到艺术作品鉴赏，体现了中国美学概念"近取诸身"的特点。

Originally this term indicated that a woman had a delicate figure, that she was fleshy and limber. Later it was used to judge calligraphy and painting, indicating that the circulation of the writing brush was lavish and vigorous, but that the strength of the bone (structure) was weak. Bone (structure) means skeletal structure, indicating weakness or vigor in the strength of the writing brush and in the structure of the work. "Fleshy" indicates that the lines are sumptuous and charming, but without strength, or that the ink is thick and the colors heavy. In the old days, it was stressed that a work of calligraphy or a painting should have a bone (structure) and be fleshy and that there should be a proper balance between the bone and flesh. There should neither be a lack of elegance nor of vigor and strength. Therefore, "fleshy body and soft bone structure" is regarded as a demerit. But when there is a stout bone structure and soft muscles, or when the bone structure is stout and the muscles are smooth, both are considered desirable. This term shifted from depicting human figures to appreciating art works, giving expression to the Chinese aesthetic concept of "using body parts to describe what is near."

引例 Citations：

◎丰肉微骨，调以娱只。(《楚辞·大招》)

（身材娇小而丰腴柔美的女人哪，舞姿和谐令人欢快轻松。）

With delicate, fleshy and soft figures, the lady dancers delighted the audience with their performance. (*Odes of Chu*)

◎善笔力者多骨，不善笔力者多肉；多骨微肉者谓之筋书，多肉微骨者谓之墨猪；多力丰筋者圣，无力无筋者病。（卫夫人《笔阵图》）（笔力强的人，其作品的筋骨多清劲雄健；而笔力弱的人，其作品则是多浓墨。骨法鲜明雄健而着墨少的字叫做"筋书"，用墨浓重而不见骨法的字叫做"墨猪"。筋骨饱满有力的作品最高妙，筋骨少而无力属于很差的作品。）

Those who are good at using the writing brush can create fresh and vigorous calligraphic pieces like a body with strong bone structure, whereas those who are not can only produce inky calligraphic pieces. A vigorous calligraphic work done without much ink is called "a sinewy work," while a less vigorous piece done with much ink is called "an inky piglet." A vigorous work is to be highly appreciated, while a less vigorous one is undesirable. (Lady Wei: On Maneuvers of Calligraphy)

风骨
/fēnggǔ/

Fenggu

指作品中由纯正的思想感情和严密的条理结构所形成的刚健劲拔、具强大艺术表现力与感染力的神韵风貌。其准确含义学界争议较大，但大致可描述为风神清朗，骨力劲拔。"风"侧重指思想情感的表达，要求作品思想纯正，气韵生动，富有情感；"骨"侧重指作品的骨架、结构及词句安排，要求作品刚健遒劲、蕴含丰富但文辞精炼。如果堆砌辞藻，过于雕章琢句，虽然词句丰富繁多但内容很少，则是没有"骨"；如果表达艰涩，缺乏情感和生机，则是没有"风"。风骨并不排斥文采，而是要和文采配合，才能成为好作品。风骨的高下主要取决于创作者的精神风貌、品格气质。南朝刘勰（465？—520？或532？）《文心雕龙》专门列有《风骨》一篇，它是我国古代文学批评史上首篇论述文学风格的文章。

This term refers to powerful expressiveness and artistic impact that come from a literary work's purity of thoughts and emotions, as well as from its meticulously crafted structure. Despite some difference in interpreting the term, people tend to agree that *fenggu* (风骨) can be understood as being lucid and fresh in language while sturdy in structure. *Feng* (风) means "style," which emphasizes that a literary work should be based on pure thoughts, vivid impressions, and rich emotions so as to produce an effect of powerful expressiveness. *Gu* (骨) means "bones" or proper structure, figuratively. It stresses the impact of structure and sentence order, requiring a piece of writing to be robust, vigorous, profound, and yet succinct. If a piece of work is wordy and overly rhetorical but weak in content, then it lacks the impact of a "proper structure," no matter how flowery its expressions are. If such writing is awkward in delivery and has no emotions and vitality, then it lacks expressiveness in "style." *Fenggu* does not preclude, but rather combines with linguistic elegance in order to create a piece of good work. Good command of *fenggu* depends on the personality and dispositions of the author. In *The Literary Mind and the Carving of Dragons*, Liu Xie (465?- 520? or 532?) of the Southern Dynasties devoted a chapter to the discussion of *fenggu*, which is the first essay on writing style in the history of classical Chinese literary criticism.

引例 Citations：

◎ 文章须自出机杼，成一家风骨，何能共人同生活也！(《魏书·祖莹传》)

(文章必须有自己的构思布局，有自己作品的风骨，如何能与他人同一个层次！)

A piece of writing must have its own structure, and its own *fenggu*, that is, expressiveness in style and sturdiness in structure. How can it ever be the same as the writings of other writers! (*The History of Northern Wei*)

◎ 捶字坚而难移，结响凝而不滞，此风骨之力也。(刘勰《文心雕龙·风骨》)

(字句锤炼确切而难以改动，读起来声音凝重有力而不滞涩，这就是风骨的魅力。)

The charm of *fenggu* in a literary work derives from deliberate and precise diction that is hard to alter, and from powerful and controlled sounds that do not sound awkward when read out. (Liu Xie: *The Literary Mind and the Carving of Dragons*)

◎若能确乎正式，使文明以健，则风清骨峻，篇体光华。(刘勰《文心雕龙·风骨》)

(倘若能够定好正确合适的文体，使文采鲜明而又气势刚健，那么自可达到风神清新明朗，骨力高峻劲拔，通篇文章都会生发光彩。)

Once a good and appropriate style is set to make the writing lucid and vigorous, it will produce the effect of being pure, clear and powerfully impressive, making the writing both remarkable and appealing. (Liu Xie: *The Literary Mind and the Carving of Dragons*)

风雅颂

/fēng-yǎ-sòng/

Ballad, Court Hymn, and Eulogy

《诗经》中依体裁与音乐对诗歌所分出的类型。"风（国风）"是不同地区的音乐，大部分是民歌；"雅"是宫廷宴享或朝会时的乐歌，分为"大雅"与"小雅"，大部分是贵族文人的作品；"颂"是宗庙祭祀用的舞曲歌辞，内容多是歌颂祖先的功业。"雅""颂"指雅正之音，而"国风"系民间乐歌，因此"风雅颂"既是《诗经》的体裁，同时也有高雅纯正的含义。"风雅"后来一般指典雅与高雅的事物。

In *The Book of Songs,* the content is divided into three categories according to style and tune: *feng* (ballad), *ya* (court hymn), and *song* (eulogy). Ballads are music from different regions, mostly folk songs. Court hymns, divided into *daya* (major hymn) and *xiaoya* (minor hymn), are songs sung at court banquets or grand ceremonies. They are mostly the works by lettered noblemen. Eulogies are ritual or sacrificial dance music and songs, most of which praise the achievements of ancestors. Court hymns and eulogies are highbrow songs while ballads are lowbrow ones. Therefore, ballads, court hymns, and eulogies not only refer to the styles of *The Book of Songs* but also indicate highbrow songs. Later on *fengya* (风雅) generally referred to anything elegant.

引例 Citations：

◎ 故《诗》有六义焉：一曰风，二曰赋，三曰比，四曰兴，五曰雅，六曰颂。(《毛诗序》)

（所以《诗经》有六项基本内容：即风、赋、比、兴、雅、颂。）

Therefore *The Book of Songs* has six basic elements: ballads, narratives, analogies, associations, court hymns, and eulogies. (Introductions to *Mao's Version of The Book of Songs*)

◎ "三经"是赋、比、兴，是做诗底骨子，无诗不有，才无则不成诗。盖不是赋便是比，不是比便是兴。如风、雅、颂却是里面横弗（chǎn）底，都有赋、比、兴，故谓之"三纬"。(《朱子语类》卷八十)

（《诗经》中的"三经"指赋、比、兴，是作诗的骨架，所有的诗都有，如果没有就不成诗。大概是没有赋就得有比，没比就得有兴。像风、雅、颂在诗歌里面却起横向的贯穿作用，诗歌中都得有赋、比、兴，所以将风、雅、颂称为"三纬"。）

The three "longitudes" of *The Book of Songs* refer to narrative, analogy, and association, which serve as the frame of a poem. Without these, they could not be called poems. If narrative is not used in a poem, analogy must be used; if analogy is not used, association must be employed. Ballads from the states, court hymns, and eulogies play a connecting role in the poems. Since the poems have narrative, analogy, and association serving as the "longitudes," ballads from the states, court hymns, and eulogies are therefore called the three "latitudes." (*Categorized Conversations of Master Zhu Xi*)

芙蓉出水

/fúróng-chūshuǐ/

Lotus Rising Out of Water

　　美丽的荷花从水中生长出来。形容清新、淡雅、自然之美，与"错彩镂金"的修饰之美构成对比。魏晋六朝时崇尚自然，与这种审美理想一致，在艺术创作方面，人们欣赏像"芙蓉出水"一般的天然清新的风格，注重主观意趣的自然呈现，反对过分雕琢修饰。

The term of lotus rising out of water describes a scene of freshness, quiet refinement and natural beauty, in contrast to "gilded and colored" embellishments. During the Wei and Jin dynasties, people valued nature and favored this aesthetic view. In their artistic creations, they pursued the natural and fresh style like lotus rising out of water. They sought natural presentation of their ideas and were opposed to excessive ornamentation.

引例 Citations:

◎谢诗如芙蓉出水，颜如错彩镂金。（钟嵘《诗品》卷中）

（谢灵运的诗清新自然，像荷花出水；颜延之的诗歌修饰雕琢，像涂绘彩色、雕镂金银。）

Xie Lingyun's poems are natural and refreshing like lotus rising out of water, whereas Yan Yanzhi's poems are elegantly embellished, like gilding an object and adding colors to it. (Zhong Rong: *The Critique of Poetry*)

◎清水出芙蓉，天然去雕饰。（李白《经乱离后天恩流夜郎忆旧游书怀赠江夏韦太守良宰》）

（从清水中生长出的荷花，自然天成没有雕饰。）

It is like a lotus rising out of clear water: natural and without embellishment. (Li Bai: *To Wei Liangzai, the Governor of Jiangxia, Written While Thinking of My Friends on My Way into Exile at Yelang Following the War*)

赋比兴

/fù-bǐ-xìng/

Narrative, Analogy, and Association

　　《诗经》创作的三种表现手法。"赋"是铺陈事物直接叙述；"比"是类比；"兴"是先言他物以引出所咏之词，有两层含义，一是即兴感发，二是在感发时借客观景物婉转地表达出某种思想感情。"赋比兴"为汉代儒家所总结和提出，后来演变为中国古代文学创作的基本原则和方法。

These are the three ways of expression employed in *The Book of Songs*: a narrative is a direct reference to an object or an event, an analogy metaphorically likens one thing to another, and an association is an impromptu expression of a feeling, a mood or a thought, or using an objective thing as metaphor for sensibilities. Confucian scholars of the Han Dynasty summarized and formulated this concept of narrative, analogy, and association, which later became the basic principle and method in classical Chinese literary creation.

引例 Citation：

◎ 赋、比、兴是《诗》之所用，风、雅、颂是《诗》之成形。(《毛诗序》孔颖达正义)

(赋、比、兴是《诗经》创作的三种手法，风、雅、颂是《诗经》体制上的定型。)

In *The Book of Songs*, narrative, analogy, and association are three techniques in its creation, whereas ballad, court hymn, and eulogy represent three established styles of the poems. (Kong Yingda: Correct Meaning of "Introductions to *Mao's Version of The Book of Songs*")

感物

/gǎnwù/

Sensed Externalities

  指人为外物所触动产生了创作冲动，经过构思与艺术加工，形成为文艺作品。"物"指直观可感的自然景物、生活场景。古人认为创作缘起于外界事物的感召而激起了创作欲望，文艺作品是外物与主观相结合的产物。这一术语强调了文艺创作源于生活的基本理念。

A person's creative impulse is triggered by one or more externalities, and after conceptualization and artistic treatment, this results in a work of art. Such externalities include both natural sights and scenes from life which can be directly sensed. Ancient Chinese believed that creation resulted from externalities which evoked a desire to create, and that works of art and literature were the result of combining externalities with subjective thinking. This term emphasizes the fundamental idea that artistic creation is rooted in life.

引例 Citations：

◎ 凡音之起，由人心生也。人心之动，物使之然也。感于物而动，故形于声。(《礼记·乐记》)

(一切音乐都起源于人的内心。人的内心之所以产生活动，是受到外物感发的结果。人受外物的感发而产生内心活动，所以会通过音乐表达出来。)

All music originates in people's hearts. Feelings arise in people's hearts because externalities cause them to do so. Hearts are moved by externalities, hence they express themselves through music. (*The Book of Rites*)

◎ 人禀七情，应物斯感，感物吟志，莫非自然。(刘勰《文心雕龙·明诗》)

(人具有喜、怒、哀、惧、爱、恶、欲等七种情感，受到外物的刺激而心有所感，心有所感而吟咏情志，所有的诗歌都出于自然情感。)

People have the seven emotions of joy, anger, sadness, fear, love, loathing and desire. He expresses his feelings and aspirations in a poetical way when he is stimulated by the external world and his heart is touched. All poems come from natural emotions. (Liu Xie: *The Literary Mind and the Carving of Dragons*)

干城

/gànchéng/

Shield and Fortress / Dukes and Princes

　　本指盾与城，后用来比喻诸侯，以及国家政权、理论主张等的捍卫者。"干"本义指盾，是古代的一种防御性武器，引申为捍御；"城"即城墙或城郭，是具有防御功能的建筑设施。用"干城"比喻诸侯，与"崇城"（比喻天子）相对。称天子为"崇城"，表明天子地位之崇高、优越；称诸侯为"干城"，表示诸侯的职责是拱卫天子，必须服从天子号令。后泛指忠实得力的保卫者——不仅指地位低的人保卫地位高的人，有时也指地位高的人保卫地位低的人。

The term originally referred to shield and fortress, but was later used to mean dukes and princes, and then defenders of a regime, theory or proposition. *Gan* (干 shield), a defensive weapon in old days, is used to mean to defend, while *cheng* (城) means inner and outer city walls or a fortress, a structure for defensive purposes. Dukes and princes were likened to *gancheng* (干城), in contrast with *chongcheng* (崇城), which means supreme city, referring to the Son of Heaven and indicating his supreme position. It is meant that dukes and princes, likened to shield and fortress, had the responsibilities to defend the Son of Heaven. Hence, dukes and princes must obey orders from the Son of Heaven. As it has evolved over time, the term generally referred to loyal and efficient defenders. Interestingly, it came to mean that not only people of lower ranks defend their superiors, but also people of high positions defend their subordinates.

引例 Citations：

◎ 天子曰"崇城"，言崇高也；诸侯曰"干城"，言不敢自专，御于天子也。（《初学记》卷二十四引《白虎通义》）

（天子称"崇城"，意思是说天子居于崇高、尊贵的地位；诸侯称"干城"，意思是说诸侯不敢擅自行动，必须听命于天子。）

The Son of Heaven is referred to as *chongcheng*, indicating his supreme and noble status, while dukes and princes are referred to as *gancheng*, meaning that they must not act on their own but pledge their obedience to the Son of Heaven. (*Debates of the White Tiger Hall*)

◎赳赳武夫，公侯干城。(《诗经·周南·兔罝(jū)》)

（雄赳赳的武士，是诸侯的保卫者。）

The valiant warriors are defenders of dukes and princes. (*The Book of Songs*)

◎天下有道，则公侯能为民干城。(《左传·成公十二年》)

（如果国家政治清明，那么诸侯们就能成为百姓的保卫者。）

With good governance, dukes and princes become defenders and protectors of their people. (*Zuo's Commentary on The Spring and Autumn Annals*)

刚柔
/gāngróu/

Toughness and Softness

人和事物所具有的两种相反的属性或德性。主要有三种含义：其一，就自然物或器物而言，"刚"指坚硬，"柔"指柔软。其二，就个人的品格而言，"刚"指为人刚毅、坚强，"柔"指温柔、谦逊。其三，就为政、执法的风格而言，"刚"指严厉，"柔"指宽宥。"刚柔"被认为是"阴阳"的某种具体表现。"刚"与"柔"之间的对立与调和是促成事物运动变化的根本原因。在具体事物或行事中，二者应达到某种平衡，"刚"与"柔"过度都是不好的、危险的。

Two opposing properties or qualities that objects and human beings possess. The term has three different meanings. First, when describing natural or manmade objects, *gang* (刚) means hard and *rou* (柔) means soft. Second, when describing human qualities, *gang* means strong and determined, while *rou* means gentle and modest. Third, when describing a style of governance or law enforcement, *gang* means stern and *rou* means lenient. *Gang* and *rou* are one of the manifestations of yin and yang. Their mutual opposition and accommodation are the basic causes of change, and they must achieve a certain balance within any object or action. Too much of either is inappropriate and dangerous.

引例 Citations：

◎是以立天之道曰阴与阳，立地之道曰柔与刚，立人之道曰仁与义。(《周易·说卦》)

(所以确立天的法则为阴与阳，确立地的法则为柔与刚，确立人世的法则为仁与义。)

The laws governing the ways of heaven are yin and yang, those governing the ways of the earth are *rou* and *gang*, and those governing the ways of human society are benevolence and righteousness. (*The Book of Changes*)

◎刚柔相推，变在其中矣。(《周易·系辞下》)

(刚与柔相互推移转换，变化就在其中了。)

Change occurs when *gang* and *rou* interact. (*The Book of Changes*)

刚毅

/gāngyì/

Firm and Resolute

坚强而果决。"刚"指坚强而不屈，"毅"指果断而不犹豫。人们对于道义的遵守会受到各种干扰。"刚毅"即强调要破除这些干扰，既不为个人的私欲所影响，也不受暴力或强权的胁迫，让自己的言行始终符合道义的要求。儒家认为，"刚毅"作为一种重要的美德，接近于"仁"德。

The first of these two Chinese characters means firm and unyielding; the second one means resolute and decisive. As people often come under undue influences that affect their observance of moral standards, this term emphasizes the need to resist such influences by adhering to ethical rules in their conduct. People should neither succumb to self-driven motives, nor yield to violence and coercion. Confucian scholars regard firmness and resolution as an important virtue which is close to benevolence.

引例 Citations：

◎子曰："刚、毅、木、讷，近仁。"(《论语·子路》)

(孔子说："刚强、果毅、质朴、少言的品德，接近于仁德的要求。")

Confucius said, "Being firm, resolute, simple and sparing with words—this is a virtue that comes close to benevolence." (*The Analects*)

◎儒有可亲而不可劫也，可近而不可迫也，可杀而不可辱也。其居处不淫，其饮食不溽，其过失可微辨而不可面数也。其刚毅有如此者。(《礼记·儒行》)

(儒者可以亲密而不能加以威逼利用，可接近而不能加以胁迫，可杀掉而不能加以侮辱。儒者居住的地方不奢侈，饮食滋味不丰厚，其过错可委婉地指出而不可当面数落。儒者的刚毅有这样一些表现。)

Confucian scholars can be befriended but not be made to act under duress, can be on close terms with others but not coerced, and can be killed but not disgraced. They live simple lives and eat simple food. Their faults may be pointed out in a subtle manner, but not accusingly to their face. Such are their firmness and resolution. (*The Book of Rites*)

革故鼎新
/gégù-dǐngxīn/

Do Away with the Old and Set Up the New

革除旧事物，创建新事物。"革"与"鼎"是《周易》中的两卦。在《易传》的解释中，革卦下卦象征火，上卦象征泽。火与泽因对立冲突不能维持原有的平衡状态，必然发生变化。因此革卦意指变革某种不合的旧状态。鼎卦下卦象征木，上卦象征火。以木柴投入火中，是以鼎烹饪制作新的食物。因此鼎卦象征创造新事物。后人承《易传》之说，将二者合在一起，代表一种主张变化的世界观。

Do away with the old and set up the new. *Ge* (革) and *ding* (鼎) are two trigrams in *The Book of Changes*. In *Commentary on The Book of Changes*, it is explained that the lower *ge* trigram symbolizes fire and the upper *ge* trigram symbolizes water. Since fire and water are opposed and in conflict, and they cannot keep an original state of equilibrium, changes are bound to occur. Consequently, the *ge* trigram implies change of an unsuitable old state of affairs. The lower *ding* trigram symbolizes wood and the upper *ding* trigram symbolizes fire. When people throw the wood into the fire, they can cook their food in a *ding*. Thus, the *ding* trigram signifies the creation of new things. Following the doctrine in *Commentary on The Book of Changes*, later people combined the two together to represent an outlook advocating changes.

引例 Citation：

◎革，去故也；鼎，取新也。(《周易·杂卦》)

(革卦，意味着革除旧事物；鼎卦，意味着创建新事物。)

Ge trigram signifies doing away with the old; *ding* trigram symbolizes setting up the new. (*The Book of Changes*)

革命

/gémìng/

Changing the Mandate / Revolution

变革王命。"革",变革;"命",初指天命,后来指王命,即帝王的政令或帝王的统治权。犹言江山易主、改朝换代,即推翻旧政权,建立新政权。古人认为,"王命"源于"天命"(上天的意志),故"革命"本质上是实施变革以应"天命"。而"革"是宇宙的基本规律,"革命"是这一规律的具体体现;判断"革命"合法性与成功的依据,则在于"革命"的领导者是否顺应了上天的意志和民众的意愿。近代以降,"革命"转指社会、政治、经济制度的重大变革。

The term means taking power from a ruler. *Ge* (革) means to change or remove. *Ming* (命) first referred to the mandate of heaven and later came to mean a ruler's decrees and his mandate to rule. Changing the mandate usually involves replacing a ruler and a change of dynasty, in other words, overthrowing an old regime and establishing a new one. People in ancient China believed that a ruler's mandate to rule was ordained by heaven and therefore any change of the mandate should in essence be carried out in response to the will of heaven. However, change is a basic law of the universe, and the removal of a ruler's mandate is a specific expression of this law. The legitimacy and success of such change depend on whether those who lead the change do so in response to the will of heaven and the popular desire of the people. In modern times, the term is used as an expression meaning revolution, denoting major social, political or economic changes.

引例 Citation:

◎ 天地革而四时成,汤武革命,顺乎天而应乎人。(《周易·彖下》)

(天地有阴阳的变化而形成一年四季。商汤、周武王变革天命[推翻旧政权,建立新政权],是顺应了上天的旨意和人民的意愿。)

Changes of yin and yang in heaven and earth give rise to the four seasons. Following the mandate of heaven and complying with the wishes of the people, King Tang and King Wu overthrew old regimes and established the Shang and Zhou dynasties respectively. (*The Book of Changes*)

格
/gé/

Examine / Study

对人、事、物的考量与推究。是儒家提出的获得正确认识、培养道德良知的途径，具有方法论的意义。"格"亦有规范、准则的意思。用于人物品评，则指人的道德水平和思想境界，即人格。用于文艺批评，主要有三重含义：其一，指诗文写作的基本要求和方法；其二，指作品的品位、品格与境界；其三，指作品的体制、组织结构，是内容特色和形式特征相统一而呈现出的整体格局，仍不离衡量作品水准这一核心意义。

This term means to study or examine things, people or any phenomenon. It is an approach developed by Confucian scholars to help people obtain accurate assessments of things around them and to cultivate morals and ethics, as a kind of methodology. Sometimes the term is used as a noun to refer to a standard or criterion. When the term is used to assess a person's qualifications, it refers to his moral quality which is to say, a person's personality or moral integrity, as well as attainments in learning. In literary criticism, it has three connotations: first of all, it refers to the basic requirements and methods for poem or prose writing; second, it refers to the taste, style, and literary attainment; third, it is about the overall structure of a literary work or how the form and content are integrated. All in all, the term refers to the criteria applied in judging a literary work.

引例 Citations：

◎致知在格物，物格而后知至。(《礼记·大学》)
(获得真知的途径在于推究事实与现象，穷尽事物方方面面的道理，而后才得到真知。)

To study and analyze facts and phenomena is the right approach to obtain knowledge; the truth can only be obtained after facts and phenomena are thoroughly examined and analyzed. (*The Book of Rites*)

◎唐之晚年，诗人无复李、杜豪放之格，然亦务以精意相高。(欧阳修《六一诗话》)

（到了晚唐，诗人们难以再现李杜诗歌那样奔放宏大的境界，但也一定要以构思精巧而一争高下。）

In the late Tang Dynasty, poets no longer possessed the bold, heroic qualities of their predecessors Li Bai and Du Fu. Nonetheless they still competed with each other with regard to the depth of thought and literary refinement. (Ouyang Xiu: *Ouyang Xiu's Criticism of Poetry*)

◎诗之要，有曰格，曰意、曰趣而已。格以辨其体，意以达其情，趣以臻其妙也。（高启《〈独庵集〉序》）

（作诗的关键在于"格"（格局）、"意"（意蕴）和"趣"（趣味）。"格"可以判断其风格体式是否雅正，"意"则是察看其是否表达了真情实感，而"趣"则是衡量其是否达到精妙的境界。）

Structure, content, and appeal are the essentials of poetry. Its structure will reflect the poetic form; its content will convey emotion; and its appeal will determine whether it has achieved a high level of artistry. (Gao Qi: Preface to *Collected Works of Du'an*)

格物致知

/géwù-zhìzhī/

Study Things to Acquire Knowledge

在与事物的接触中体认人伦日用之道。"格物""致知"出自《礼记·大学》，与诚意、正心、修身、齐家、治国、平天下并称"八条目"。"致知"在于"格物"，二者密切相关，故有时并称"格致"。历代学者对"格物致知"的含义有多种不同的理解：或强调在对事物的接触中穷究其"理"；或强调亲自实践以掌握各种德行、技艺；或以心意所在为"物"，进而以内心的修正为"格物"。

The term means to understand how we should conduct ourselves through our contact with things. "Studying things to acquire knowledge" comes from *The*

Great Learning, a section of *The Book of Rites*. Together with "being sincere in thought," "rectifying one's mind," "cultivating oneself," "regulating one's family well," "governing the state properly," and "bringing peace to all under heaven," they are collectively known as the "eight essential principles." Knowledge is acquired through the study of things. Since the two are closely related, they are sometimes together called "study and acquire." Throughout history scholars have had varied understandings of the meaning of the term. Some emphasize a thorough inquiry of principles in contact with things. Others stress personal practice in order to master all kinds of moral conduct and skills. Still others consider their intentions as things, thus reforming their innermost thoughts as studying things.

引例 Citations：

◎事皆有理，至其理，乃格物也。(《二程外书》卷二)
(事物皆有其理，穷究其理，就是"格物"。)

All things have their own principles. An exhaustive inquiry into the principles means the study of things. (*More Writings of the Cheng Brothers*)

◎格物如《孟子》"大人格君心"之"格"。(《传习录》卷上)
("格物"就如同《孟子》中所言"大人格正君主之心"之格正之义。)

Gewu (格物) means setting things right, just like what is said in *Mencius*: A great man may rectify a ruler's mind. (*Records of Great Learning*)

格义
/géyì/
Matching Meanings

　　使用中国本土思想对佛教教义进行转译和阐释的方法。在译介大量佛教经典的魏晋南北朝时期，佛教思想对于汉语世界而言完全陌生，热衷于佛法的时人揣摩佛典的意思，但借用老庄等经典的语汇、概念乃至观念来比附、转译其义理，而被称为"格义"。"格"取量度义。这一时期也因而被称为格义佛教时期。格义作为一种阐释方法，是站在中国本土思想的立场上来解读佛教，建构佛教在汉语世界的思想体系，故而对佛教的中国化产生了奠基性的作用。

This term refers to a method to carry out translation and interpretation using Chinese thought for the Buddhist doctrines. During the Wei, Jin, and the Southern and Northern Dynasties period, when a large quantity of Buddhist scriptures was translated and introduced, Buddhist thought was completely unfamiliar for the Chinese world. The Chinese people, who were keen on the law of Buddha, tried to fathom the meaning of the Buddhist scriptures. They borrowed the vocabulary of the scriptures of Laozi, Zhuangzi, etc. The concepts and even ideas of these scriptures were appended. They developed their argumentation and that was called "matching meanings." "Matching" takes the meaning of measuring. So this period was also called the Buddhist period of matching meanings. "Matching meanings" is a kind of method of interpretation. It is an interpretation of Buddhism from the standpoint of Chinese thought, constructing a system of thought of Buddhism in the world of the Chinese. Therefore, it has produced a fundamental influence in the sinification of Buddhism.

引例 Citation：

◎雅乃与康法朗等，以经中事数拟配外书，为生解之例，谓之"格义"。及毗（pí）浮、相昙等，亦辩格义以训门徒。（释慧皎《高僧传·竺法雅》）

（竺法雅于是与康法朗等人，使用传统经籍中的概念，尝试与外来之书中的教义匹配，作为事例引导人理解教义，这就叫做"格义"。及至毗浮、相昙等人，也使用格义的方法善加辞巧，以教育门徒。）

Then, Zhu Faya, Kang Falang and others matched the doctrines in foreign texts with the original concepts in Chinese classics, and gave instances to bring about the meaning for people to understand them. It was called "matching meanings." Later, monks like Pifu and Xiangtan also used the method of "matching meanings" to instruct their disciples. (Shi Huijiao: *Biographies of Eminent Monks*)

公公私私
/gōnggōngsīsī/

Public Property Belonging to the Public, Private Property to Individuals

以公为公，以私为私；将公共之物视为公共所有，将私人之物视为私人所有。列子认为，公共之物犹如自然生成的天地万物一样，是有机的整体，不能随意分割成为私物；公是公，私是私，公私分明，才是符合天地自然属性的正道。它是道家"无为"理念的发挥，既是国家治理的原则，也是个人修养的境界。

This term means that public property belongs to the public and private property belongs to individuals. Liezi held that public property, like anything naturally formed between heaven and earth, is an organic whole that cannot be divided and given to individuals at random. A clear separation of the public and private interests is in conformity with the law of nature. This concept grew out of the Daoist philosophy of "non-action governance," which is a principle that the government should follow in its rule of a country, and also a state of one's moral cultivation.

引例 Citation:

◎ 天地万物不相离也。刎而有之，皆惑也。……公公私私，天地之德。(《列子·天瑞》)

(天地万物都是不能相互分离的。把它们认作、占为己有，都是糊涂的。……将公共之物视为公共所有，将私人之物视为私人所有，这符合天地的自然德性。)

All things between heaven and earth cannot be separated from each other. It is wrong for a person to regard things that do not belong to him as his own, or possess them for his own use… It is in conformity with nature and social ethics that public property belongs to the public and private property belongs to individuals. (*Liezi*)

公生明，廉生威

/gōng shēng míng, lián shēng wēi/

Fairness Fosters Discernment and Integrity Creates Authority.

　　处事公正才能明察是非，做人廉洁才能树立威望。这是明清两代一些正直廉洁的官吏用以自戒的座右铭。"公"即公正无私；"明"即明察是非，有很强的分辨力和判断力；"廉"即廉洁；"威"即威望，有令人信服的公信力。时至今日，它仍是执政者应当遵循的最重要的为官准则：执政当公平公正，在国家法律和规定程序的框架内进行；官员当以身作则，廉洁自律，克己奉公，不可以权谋私。

Only by being fair can one distinguish between right and wrong; only with moral conduct can one establish authority. These mottoes were used as reminders by upright officials of the Ming and Qing dynasties. *Gong* (公) means fairness and opposing pursuit of selfish interest. *Ming* (明) means discernment, namely, the ability to distinguish right from wrong. *Lian* (廉) means free from corruption. *Wei* (威) means authority or credibility. Today, these teachings have remained important principles which office holders should abide by. They mean that governance should be exercised in a fair and just way and within the framework of laws and regulatory procedures of the state. Officials should lead by example, have moral integrity and be self-disciplined; they should put public interests above their own and not use their power to pursue personal gain.

引例 Citation：

◎吏不畏吾严而畏吾廉，民不服吾能而服吾公。公则民不敢慢，廉则吏不敢欺。公生明，廉生威。（年富《官箴》刻石）

（官吏不害怕我的严厉但害怕我廉洁，百姓不信服我的才能但信服我的公正。我公正，百姓就不敢轻慢；我廉洁，官吏就不敢欺瞒。处事公正才能明察是非，做人廉洁才能树立威望。）

Officials have a sense of awe towards me not because of my being strict with them, but because of my upright conduct. People accept my authority not because of my ability, but because of my fairness. If I am fair, people will not dare to disobey my order; if I am morally upright, officials will not dare to deceive me. Only by being fair can one distinguish between right and wrong; only with moral integrity can one establish authority. (Nian Fu: Mottoes for Officials, from a stone carving)

公正

/gōngzhèng/

Fair / Just

公平正义或公平正直。"公"与"厶（私）"相反，无偏私，不以个人为中心考虑问题；"正"与"曲"相反，有两层含义：其一，有以正义为基础的共同的准则。其二，能以此端正自己与他人的一切行为，不偏斜，不枉曲。"公正"主要体现为国家、社会有共同的道义和规范，所有人都能以此约束自己并对他人行为正确与否作出判断。在现代社会，公正主要体现在制度公正、法律公正、社会财富与公共资源分配公正及人心公正等方面，被认为是培育美好品德、构建美好社会的核心价值之一。

The expression means fair and just. *Gong* (公), the opposite of *si* (私 private), means impartial and not self-centered. *Zheng* (正), the opposite of *qu* (曲 crooked), has two meanings. One is shared norms based on justice, and the other is making oneself comply with these norms in one's behavior and stay unbiased and impartial in one's relationship with others. Fairness is expressed mainly in a state or society having a common morality and norms with which all people are bound and which people use to judge whether others are doing right. In modern society, fairness finds its expression mainly in the way that institutions, laws, and people are just and social wealth and public resources are fairly distributed. It is seen as one of the core values conducive to good morality and society.

引例 Citations：

◎毋以私好恶害公正，察民所恶，以自为戒。（《管子·桓公问》）

（不要以自己的喜欢或不喜欢损害公平正义，要知道百姓所厌恶的做法并以之为戒。）

Do not harm the fairness because of personal likes and dislikes. Find out what the people detest and take that as a warning to oneself. (*Guanzi*)

◎ 太宗曰："古称至公者，盖谓平恕无私。"（吴兢《贞观政要·公平》）

（唐太宗说："古代讲的最公正，大概是说持心公平宽恕、绝无偏私。"）

Emperor Taizong of the Tang Dynasty said, "What the ancient people described as the greatest fairness probably means impartiality and forbearance without any self-interest." (Wu Jing: *Important Political Affairs of the Zhenguan Reign*)

◎ 天下所以平者，政平也；政所以平者，人平也；人所以平者，心平也。（《艺文类聚》卷二十二引）

（天下所以能做到公平，只因有国家政事的公平；国家政事所以做到公平，只因掌管政事的人公平；掌管政事的人所以做到公平，只因他们的内心有公平。）

All under heaven enjoys fairness when its governance is fair. Governance is fair when the men who govern are fair. The men are fair when their minds are fair. (*An Anthology of Pre-Tang Dynasty Literature*)

共名
/gòngmíng/

General Name

　　用以概括同类事物的名称。"共名"是荀子（前313？—前238）所使用的一种名称类别，与"别名"相对。名用以指称实。具有相同属性的同一类事物，可以用一个"共名"来加以概括。具有不同"共名"的事物类别之间若具有相同属性，可以用更高层级的"共名"来加以概括。如此类推，最高层级的"共名"称为"大共名"。

A general name is used to refer to everything in the same category. It is a term used by Xunzi (313?-238 BC) and its opposite is "distinct name." A name should denote the nature of a thing. Things with similar properties can be grouped together under a "general name." These, together with other things with different general names but still sharing some common properties, can have a higher-level "general name." The highest-level "general name" is called "broad general name."

引例 Citation：

◎ 故万物虽众，有时而欲遍举之，故谓之物。物也者，大共名也。推而共之，共则有共，至于无共然后止。(《荀子·正名》)

（因此万物虽然繁多，有时想要全面地概括它们，就称之为"物"。"物"就是最大的"共名"。推演而寻求"共名"，"共名"之上还有更高层级的"共名"，一直到无法再推出更高层级的"共名"为止。）

There are so many things around us, and sometimes we wish to speak of them all in the same breath, so we call them "things." "Thing" is a broad general term. We extend this generalization even more and subsume the general under something more general, until there is nothing more general. (*Xunzi*)

卦爻

/guàyáo/

Trigrams / Hexagrams and Component Lines

"卦"是由"—"和"--"排列组合而成的一套符号系统，其中的"—"为"阳爻"，"--"为"阴爻"。每三"爻"合成一卦，可得"八卦"。每六"爻"合成一卦，可得"六十四卦"。"卦爻"的产生与占筮有关。古人通过分取蓍草，演算其变化之数，从而确定卦爻，以预测吉凶。后人为卦爻赋予各种象征意义，并用以理解和阐发包括人事在内的天地万物的运行变化及其法则。

A *gua* (trigram / hexagram) is a system of symbols consisting of undivided lines (——) and divided lines (— —). The undivided line (——) is a yang line while the divided one (— —) a yin line. Three lines make a trigram, and there are eight such trigrams. When six lines are put together, they together make 64 hexagram combinations. Trigrams / hexagrams and component lines were created partly for the purpose of divination. Ancient Chinese people used yarrow stalks to make hexagrams, calculated the variations they suggested, and consulted them for the purpose of divination. Later on, people used trigrams / hexagrams and component lines symbolically to explain the changes and the laws regulating the changes that occurred in people and everything else, and why and how these changes took place.

引例 Citations：

◎八卦成列，象在其中矣；因而重之，爻在其中矣。(《周易·系辞下》)

（八卦创立分列，万物的象征就在其中了；根据八卦重成六十四卦，所有的爻就都在其中了。）

When the eight trigrams were invented, they embodied the images of all things. When the eight trigrams were multiplied by eight trigrams and permuted into the 64 hexagrams, all the component lines were included. (*The Book of Changes*)

◎圣人有以见天下之动，而观其会通，以行其典礼，系辞焉以断其吉凶，是故谓之爻。(《周易·系辞上》)

（圣人看到天下万物的运动变化，观察其中的会合贯通之处，从而施行制度礼仪，在"爻"下附系文辞以判断吉凶，所以称之为"爻"。）

When sages saw the changes or events happening under heaven, they observed the similarities of the events and responded with appropriate rites and rituals. They judged their implications of the changes by obtaining explanations from the *yao*. (*The Book of Changes*)

光而不耀
/guāng'érbùyào/
Bright but Not Dazzling

　　光明而不刺眼。老子用"光而不耀"来形容执政者对百姓的影响。在老子看来，执政者具有显赫的地位，并且掌握着足以影响百姓生活的权力与资源。从这个意义上来说，执政者对百姓的影响如同光照一样，是显明而不容回避的。但老子同时强调，执政者不应将自己的意志强加给百姓，而应因循、保全百姓的自然状态。百姓受到影响却不被伤害，如同在光明之中而不感到刺眼。"光而不耀"也可用于形容强者对待他人的方式。

This term means to be bright without being dazzling. Laozi used the term to describe the influence of those in power on ordinary people. High status, authority and resources enable them to have a great impact on people's lives, just like a bright light that cannot be avoided. However, Laozi also believed that no person in power should impose his will on the people, whose natural state should be maintained and protected. To be influenced but not harmed is like being surrounded by light but not dazzled by it. The term can be used to describe the way any powerful person should treat others.

引例 Citation：

◎ 是以圣人方而不割，廉而不害，直而不肆，光而不耀。(《老子·五十八章》)

（因此圣人方正而不割伤他人，清廉而不伤害他人，正直而不刺激他人，光明而不刺人眼目。）

The sage is ethical but not hurtful, incorruptible but not disdainful, candid but not offensive, bright but not dazzling. (*Laozi*)

国家

/guójiā/

Family-state / Country

古代指诸侯和大夫的领地。古代诸侯的封地称"国",大夫的封地称"家"。"国家"是"国"与"家"的合称。在古代中国,家庭、家族、国家都是依据血缘、宗法关系构建起来的,在组织结构上具有共通性。这就是所谓的"家国同构"。后演变指一国的全部疆域。近代以来,"国家"又指由一定疆域、人民和政权机构共同构成的政治实体。

Family-state referred to the land owned by feudal lords and officials in ancient China. The land of a feudal lord was called "state" and the land of an official was called "family." In ancient China, family, clan and country shared common structural features, all founded on the basis of blood relationships. This is the so-called "commensurability of family and state." Family-state later referred to the entire territory of a country. In modern times, the term is also used to denote a polity encompassing a territory, a people, and a government.

引例 Citations:

◎君子安而不忘危,存而不忘亡,治而不忘乱,是以身安而国家可保也。(《周易·系辞下》)

(君子安居时不忘危险,生存时不忘灭亡,天下太平时不忘记祸乱,如此自身就能安全、国家就能保全。)

A man of virtue and talent should be aware of potential danger in time of peace, keep in mind possible peril in time of security, and be vigilant of turmoil in time of order. Then he can keep himself safe and his country preserved. (*The Book of Changes*)

◎人有恒言,皆曰"天下国家"。天下之本在国,国之本在家。(《孟子·离娄上》)

(人们常说"天下国家"。"天下"的根本在于"国","国"的根本在于"家"。)

People often mention the following three together: all under heaven, the state, and the family. The root of all under heaven is in the state. The root of a state is in the family. (*Mencius*)

国泰民安

/guótài-mín'ān/

Stable Country and Peaceful People

  国家太平无事，人民安居乐业。与"天下太平"等义近。这是自古以来每一个正常的统治者所努力追求的治理目标和治理状态，也是每一个普通百姓所抱持的生活愿景。其关键在于"泰"与"安"，即安定、平和。它被认为是国家和人民的共同福祉，体现了中国人崇尚和平安定的"文"的精神。

When a country is at peace, its people enjoy a happy life. This term is similar to another ancient concept – "peaceful land." Since ancient times, this has been the goal of governance pursued by all decent rulers. It has also been a vision cherished by commoners. The key to reaching such a state lies with stability and peace. This has been regarded as the common source of well-being for both the country and the people. It also reflects the humanistic spirit of the Chinese people who cherish stability and peace.

引例 Citation：

◎ 每岁海潮大溢，冲激州城。春秋醮祭，诏命学士院撰青词，以祈国泰民安。（吴自牧《梦粱录》卷十四"山川神"）

（每年海水涨溢，冲向州城。每年春秋都举办祭祀仪式，皇上下旨命学士院撰写祷词，祈祷国泰民安。）

Seawater rises and rushes into towns year after year. At sacrificial ceremonies held in both spring and autumn, the emperor orders the imperial academy to write up a prayer, expressing his wish that his country would be stable and the people live in peace. (Wu Zimu: *Notes of Past Dreams*)

国体

/guótǐ/

Guoti

  主要有三种不同的含义：其一，指辅佐国君的重要大臣。这是一种比喻的说法，即国家犹如人的身体，而辅佐国君的大臣犹如这个身体的重要组成部分。其二，指国家的法令制度。其三，指国家的体统或尊严。

The term, literally meaning the state and the body, has three meanings. First, it refers to the important ministers who help the sovereign ruler govern the state. Figuratively, the term suggests that the state is a human body and the ministers are the major components of the body. Second, it refers to the constitution and laws of a state. Third, it means national polity or dignity.

引例 Citations：

◎君之卿佐，是谓股肱，故曰国体。(《榖梁传·昭公十五年》范宁集解)

(辅佐国君的执政大臣，就像人的大腿和胳膊，所以称作"国体"。)

Ministers are like the arms and legs of the sovereign ruler. They constitute the major components of the country. (Fan Ning: *Annotations on Guliang's Commentary on The Spring and Autumn Annals*)

◎国体具存，纪纲不紊。(姚莹《与陆制军书》)

(国家的典章制度完备，政策法令的运行不紊乱。)

The national legal system is well enacted, and the laws and regulations are orderly implemented. (Yao Ying: *A Letter to General Lu*)

国以义为利

/guó yǐ yì wéi lì/

A State Should Regard Righteousness as a Benefit.

　　国家以道义为根本利益。"义利之辨"是中国思想史上历久弥新的议题,"以义为利"则是先哲确立的基本理念。小到一身,大到一国,无利不存,但古人注重利与义的统一,认为利的本质乃是与义相合,实现利与义的和谐统一,不能因利害义,妨害大局。依照这一理念,国对民,不与民争利;国对国,不片面利己;努力达成兼顾、兼得、平衡与共赢。

A state should regard righteousness as a fundamental benefit. The debate over righteousness and benefits has been a constant theme of discussion in the Chinese history of philosophy, because benefits were often seen as personal profits that might be wrongfully gained. Taking righteousness as the most important kind of benefit was a basic concept upheld by ancient philosophers. Neither a person nor a state can survive without benefits. However, ancients emphasized the integration of righteousness and benefits. They believed that benefits could be materialized only when combined with righteousness, and the two should stay in harmony. One must not seek personal gain at the expense of righteousness. According to this concept, a government must not vie with commoners for benefits, nor should a state vie with another state for benefits for itself only. One must always strive for mutual assistance, shared interests, balance, and win-win outcomes.

引例 Citations：

◎利者,义之和也。(《周易·文言》)

(利是义与利的和谐统一。)

Benefit is a combination of righteousness and interests. (*The Book of Changes*)

◎国不以利为利,以义为利也。(《礼记·大学》)

(国家不应以财利为利,而应以道义为利。)

A state should not take pecuniary gain as benefit, but righteousness as its benefit. (*The Book of Rites*)

过犹不及

/guòyóubùjí/

Going Too Far Is as Bad as Falling Short.

　　事物超过一定的标准和没有达到标准同样是不好的。儒家以礼作为个人言语行事及其与天地万物关系的标准，并根据礼的要求判断言行的"过"或"不及"。孔子（前551—前479）分别用"过"与"不及"评价自己的两位学生，认为二者在未能达到礼的要求这一点上是一样的。如果能够按照礼的要求达到无过、无不及的中道，即具备了"中庸"的美德。

It is just as bad to go beyond a given standard as to fall short of it. Confucian scholars use rites as the standards both for individuals' words and actions, and for their relationship with everything in the world. They also judge people's words or actions against the requirements of the rites to see whether they have gone too far or fallen short. Confucius (551 - 479 BC) evaluated one of his students as "going too far" and another as "falling short," considering them to be the same in both failing the requirements set by the rites. If a person can follow the middle way by not going too far or falling short, then he has achieved the virtue of "the golden mean."

引例 Citation：

◎子贡问："师与商也孰贤？"子曰："师也过，商也不及。"曰："然则师愈与？"子曰："过犹不及。"（《论语·先进》）

（子贡问孔子："子张和子夏谁更好一些？"孔子说："子张行事过度，而子夏常有不及。"子贡问："那么子张这样更好一些吗？"孔子说："过与不及一样，都是不好的。"）

Zigong asked Confucius, "Which one is more virtuous, Zizhang or Zixia?" Confucius replied, "Zizhang tends to go too far, while Zixia often falls short." Zigong further asked, "In that case, is Zizhang better?" Confucius said, "Going too far is just as bad as falling short." (*The Analects*)

海内
/hǎinèi/

Within the Four Seas / Within the Country

"四海之内",即古代中国疆域以内。古人认为中国的疆域四周环海,各依方位称"东海""南海""西海"和"北海",合称"四海"。"海内"即指"四海"所环绕的疆土。它隐含着古人以海为界的国土意识,是农耕文明的反映。

Within the Four Seas means within the territory of China. The ancient Chinese thought China's territory was surrounded by the Four Seas (the East, West, North, and South seas). Within the Four Seas refers to the landmass surrounded by the Four Seas. It reflected the ancient Chinese belief that the seas were the natural boundary of a country, demonstrating the influence of an agricultural civilization.

引例 Citation:

◎ 海内存知己,天涯若比邻。(王勃《杜少府之任蜀州》)

(四海之内都会有知己,纵使远隔天涯海角也如近邻一样。)

If you have a bosom friend within the Four Seas, even at world's end he remains close to you. (Wang Bo: Seeing Off a Friend Who Has Been Appointed to a County Post in Shuzhou)

海外
/hǎiwài/

Outside the Four Seas / Overseas

"四海之外",指古代中国疆域之外、国外,也指边远地区。古人认为中国疆域四周环海,各依方位称"东海""南海""西海"和"北海"，合称"四海"，所以称中国以外的地方为海外。其中隐含着古人以海为界的国土意识。它体现出古人以自我为中心而又具开放性的空间感，及其对于境外遥远地方的向往。

Outside the Four Seas refers to the territory outside China, foreign lands, or remote areas. The ancient Chinese thought that China's territory was surrounded by the Four Seas (the East, West, North, and South seas). Therefore, places outside China were outside the Four Seas. It reflected the ancient Chinese belief that the seas were the natural boundary of a country. It also suggested that the ancient Chinese were on the one hand self-focused and on the other open-minded, longing to explore the unknown world outside the Four Seas.

引例 Citation：

◎相（xiàng）土烈烈，海外有截。(《诗经·商颂·长发》)
（相土威武勇猛，边远地区的人都对他一齐顺服。）

Xiangtu was so brave that he was recognized and extolled even by those outside the Four Seas. (*The Book of Songs*)

含蓄
/hánxù/

Subtle Suggestion

文艺作品的一种创作技巧与风格，用简约的语言和浅近的艺术形象委婉表达出丰富深远的情感意蕴，使欣赏者能从中获得回味无穷的美感。中国古代的文学艺术作品中既有直率真实的表现方式，亦有含蓄蕴藉的表达手法。含蓄这一术语源于诗歌的讽谏传统及道家思想，主张作品的情感、意蕴应当内敛，外在形象的描写要借助充实的内在意蕴而感染读者，形成言近旨远、意在言外的审美效果。唐代司空图（837—908）将其列为二十四种诗歌风格之一。含蓄是作家修养、创作技巧与文学作品的风格和境界的高度统一。

A technique or style in creating literary works, it refers to the use of concise language in portraying a simple artistic image, whose rich feelings and implications are elicited in a subtle manner, so that readers can intuit multiple hidden meanings. One finds a straightforward and factual manner of expression in early literary and artistic works in China, as well as the subtle mode of expression. Because this technique originally evolved from Daoist thought and, in the early period, was employed as a means of criticizing powerful individuals in poetry, it stresses the expression of emotion in a subtly suggestive manner, such that the depiction of images should be supported by a rich undertone or hidden meaning that can appeal to readers. The language should be simple and plain but still leave sufficient room for readers to seize upon hidden meanings. Sikong Tu (837-908), a literary critic in the Tang Dynasty, listed it as one of the twenty-four styles of poetry writing. Subtle suggestion imparts a high degree of unity to a writer's cultural attainments, creative technique, as well as his literary style and imagery.

引例 Citations：

◎不著一字，尽得风流。语不涉己，若不堪忧。是有真宰，与之沉浮。(司空图《二十四诗品·含蓄》)

(虽然没有写上一字，却尽得其意蕴之美妙。文辞虽没有直接抒写自己的忧伤，读时却使人好像忧伤不已。这是因为事物有着真实自然的情理，在与作品一起或沉或浮。)

Without penning down a word about it, yet it is overfilled with what it intends to express. Without mentioning the writer's own sorrow, yet one can feel it there. It is because the genuine and natural feelings reside there, that one's mood rises and falls with the work that conveys them. (Sikong Tu: *Twenty-four Styles of Poetry*)

◎语贵含蓄。东坡云："言有尽而意无穷者，天下之至言也。"(姜夔《白石道人诗说》)

(语言表达以含蓄为贵。苏东坡说："用有限的文辞表达无穷的意义，这是天下公认的至理名言啊。")

The merit of expressing oneself lies in presenting one's opinions with subtlety. Su Dongpo once said, "There is a limit to the words one can use in writing a poem, but there is no limit to the meaning a poem may deliver. This is universally acknowledged." (Jiang Kui: *The Poetry Theory of Baishi Daoren*)

◎含蓄无穷，词之要诀。含蓄者，意不浅露，语不穷尽，句中有余

味,篇中有余意,其妙不外寄言而已。(沈祥龙《论词随笔》)
(有着无限的蕴含是作词的要诀。含蓄就是意蕴不要简单肤浅,用词不要将意蕴全都说完,句子要给人留有回味的余地,整部作品有让人进一步思考的空间,其精妙之处不外就是在有限的词句上寄寓无限的意蕴而已。)

The key to writing great *ci* lyrics is the subtle suggestion of limitless meaning. Subtle suggestion means that the meaning is never simply obvious, yet the words will forever echo in one's mind. A line should leave enough room for further thought, and a poem enough meaning for readers to ponder. The beauty of this method lies in expressing unlimited subtle meaning in simple language. (Shen Xianglong: *Essays on Ci Poetry*)

涵泳

/hányǒng/

Be Totally Absorbed (in Reading and Learning)

原指阅读经典作品时,要像潜泳一样沉浸其中、反复玩味,方能有所收获,激发自己的情志和感悟。作为一种读书做学问的方法,它强调调动自己的经验和学养,努力思考书中的问题、观点、材料及事实,使自己的学问如源头活水而常新。作为一种理解与诠释文艺作品的方法,它强调努力进入作品特定的情境,通过反复体会与咀嚼,最终领略作品的深层意蕴及审美意境。它也表明文艺作品具有兴发志意和感化人心的效力。

This term originally refers to an attitude in reading classics, requiring one to become deeply absorbed in the work as if one were submerged in water, repeatedly ruminating on its meaning until one is able to fully digest its significance so that it informs one's own feelings and insights. In time this becomes a way of learning, impelling one to mobilize one's own experience and accumulated knowledge to think deeply about what he is reading so that knowledge is endlessly renewed and refreshed. As a method of understanding and interpreting literary works, it requires one to place one's own thought in the particular world of the work so that one becomes deeply aware of why the work was so written and can master its subtle meanings and aesthetic conception. This method is premised on the understanding that literary works can be deeply inspiring and enlightening.

引例 Citations：

◎学者读书，须要敛身正坐，缓视微吟，虚心涵泳，切己省察。（《朱子语类》卷十一）

（学者读书，必须收腹端坐，慢慢看，轻声念，放空心灵，沉浸其中，并结合自身经验进行思考和体察。）

When a scholar reads a book, he must sit straight, read attentively, read out softly, focus all his thought on the book, be entirely absorbed in it, and meditate on its significance from his own experience. (*Categorized Conversations of Master Zhu Xi*)

◎此等语言自有个血脉流通处，但涵泳久之，自然见得条畅浃洽，不必多引外来道理、言语，却壅滞却诗人活底意思也。（朱熹《答何叔京》）

（这些语言都有内在的血脉连通之处，只要沉潜其中反复玩味，自然能够理清头绪，融会贯通，不必引用很多外来的道理和言论，这样反而遮蔽诗人真正想要表达的意思。）

Such language has an inner coherence and logical line of thought. When a person has been deeply absorbed in it for long, he naturally understands how to articulate its complexities and unite its core ideas. There is no need to rely on theories and discussions extraneous to the work. To do so would only be to stifle what the poet intended to express. (Zhu Xi: In Response to He Shujing)

◎熟绎上下文，涵泳以求其立言之指，则差别毕见（xiàn）矣。（王夫之《姜斋诗话》卷二）

（细致推究上下文的联系，沉浸其中以求把握文章的主旨，那么不同文章的差别就会完全显现出来了。）

By carefully studying the literary context of a text, and by becoming so absorbed in the text as to master its essence, one will be able to discern the essential differences between different literary works. (Wang Fuzhi: *Desultory Remarks on Poetry from Ginger Studio*)

汉乐府

/hànyuèfǔ/

Yuefu **Poetry**

  指汉代的乐府诗。"乐府"本是秦以后由朝廷设立的用来训练乐工、采集民歌并配器作曲的专门官署，后转指由乐府机关所采集、配乐并由乐工演唱的民歌。乐府诗是继《诗经》之后古代民歌的一次创造，是与"诗经""楚辞"并列的诗歌形态。至今保存的汉乐府民歌有五六十首，大都真实反映了当时社会生活的各个方面，表现出纯真质朴的思想感情，并由此形成反映普通民众声音与情感的文学创作传统。其中最有特色与成就的是描写女性生活的作品。汉代以后将可以入乐的诗歌及仿乐府古题而写的诗歌统称为乐府。

Yuefu（乐府）poems were written in the Han Dynasty. Originally, *yuefu* was a government office set up by the imperial court to train musicians, collect folk songs and ballads, compose music, and match musical instruments to it. It later came to refer to folk songs and ballads collected, matched with music, and played by court musicians. Poems of this style represented a new creation of ancient folk songs and ballads in the years after *The Book of Songs* was compiled, and equaled *The Book of Songs* and *Odes of Chu* in importance. About 50 to 60 *yuefu* poems have been handed down to this day. They truthfully depicted various aspects of society at the time and revealed genuine emotions, thus creating a literary tradition reflecting ordinary people's sentiments. In particular, *yuefu* poems were noted for their vivid depiction of women's life. All poems that could be chanted or were written with *yuefu* themes were collectively called *yuefu* poems in later times.

引例 Citations：

◎ 自孝武立乐府而采歌谣，于是有代、赵之讴，秦、楚之风。皆感于哀乐，缘事而发……（《汉书·艺文志》）

（自从汉武帝设立乐府并采集歌谣，这之后就有了代、赵之地的吟唱及秦、楚等地的民歌。它们都是受内心悲喜情绪的影响或者受到某件事情的触发而产生的……）

After Emperor Wu of the Han Dynasty set up an office to collect folk songs and ballads, folk songs from the Dai and Zhao regions, and ballads from the Qin and Chu regions could be heard. They were all created to express people's joy and sorrow or were inspired by certain events… (*The History of the Han Dynasty*)

◎乐府者,"声依永,律和声"也。(刘勰《文心雕龙·乐府》)
(乐府诗,就是"随诗的吟唱而有抑扬疾徐的声音变化,再用音律调和声音"。)

Yuefu poems vary in rhythm and tone and are accompanied by music when chanted. (Liu Xie: *The Literary Mind and the Carving of Dragons*)

豪放派
/háofàngpài/

The *Haofang* School / The Bold and Unconstrained School

宋词两大流派之一。内容多写家国大事、人生情怀,其特点是境界壮阔宏大,气象豪迈雄放,常常运用诗文创作手法及典故,而且不拘音律。最先用"豪放"评词的是苏轼(1037—1101),南宋人已明确将苏轼、辛弃疾(1140—1207)作为豪放词的代表。北宋范仲淹(989—1052)《渔家傲》词开豪放之先,经苏轼大力创作"壮词"而成一派词风。中原沦陷后,南宋政权偏安江南,不以收复失地为意,许多词人报国无望,因而逐渐形成慷慨悲壮的词风,产生了豪放派领袖辛弃疾及陈与义(1090—1139)、叶梦得(1077—1148)、朱敦儒(1081—1159)、张元干(1091—1170?)、张孝祥(1132—1170)、陆游(1125—1210)、陈亮(1143—1194)、刘过(1154—1206)等一大批杰出词人。他们抒发报国情怀,将个体的命运与家国命运紧密联系在一起,进一步拓宽了词的表现领域,丰富了词的表现手法,大大提升了词在文学史上的地位。豪放派词人虽以豪放为主体风格,却也不乏清秀婉约之作,故不可一概而论。有些词作出现议论和用典过多、音律不精或过于散文化，也是毋庸讳言的。

This is one of the two *ci* (词) lyric schools of the Song Dynasty, which mainly dealt with major affairs of the nation and expresses noble aspirations. It featured broad vision and bold expression, often employing the methods of prose poetry and uninhibited by metric stereotypes. The first poet who used the term "bold and unconstrained" was Su Shi (1037-1101) who, together with Xin Qiji (1140-1207), was widely acclaimed by Southern Song critics as the leading poets of this school. The Northern Song writer Fan Zhongyan (989-1052) created this school with his *ci* lyric, A Fisherman's Song, which grew into a major poetic style thanks mainly to Su Shi's contribution. After the Central Plains fell to the Jin forces, the Song court fled south of the Yangtze River and was too weak to recover the lost territory. Many *ci* poets, led by Xin Qiji and supported by other prominent poets such as Chen Yuyi (1090-1139), Ye Mengde (1077-1148), Zhu Dunru (1081-1159), Zhang Yuangan (1091-1170?), Zhang Xiaoxiang (1132-1170), Lu You (1125-1210), Chen Liang (1143-1194), and Liu Guo (1154-1206), expressed their longing to return to the north in verses of a stirring style. They voiced their patriotic sentiments and identified their own fate with that of the whole nation. They thus enriched *ci* lyrics' ways of expression and greatly lifted its status in the history of literature. Although poets of this school wrote in the bold and unconstrained style, they occasionally wrote graceful and subtle *ci* poems. And some of their works contained too many commentaries and allusions, were careless about the use of metric schemes, and read more like prose than poetry.

引例 Citations：

◎词体大略有二：一体婉约，一体豪放。婉约者欲其辞情蕴藉，豪放者欲其气象恢弘。盖亦存乎其人，如秦少游之作多是婉约，苏子瞻之作多是豪放。大约词体以婉约为正。（张綖（yán）《诗余图谱·凡例》）

（词的风格大约有两种，一种是婉约，一种是豪放。婉约风格的词，其词句和情感追求含蓄之美，豪放词则追求气魄宏大。大概是由于作者的气质所致，如秦观的作品多是婉约之作，而苏轼的作品多是豪放之作。大致说来，词的风格以婉约为正宗。）

Ci lyrics can be divided into two types: the graceful and restrained vs. the bold and unconstrained. The first type of poems features subtle expression of one's feelings, whereas the second type is far more explicit and has a broader vision.

This distinction is due to different dispositions of poets. Qin Guan's *ci* lyrics are mostly graceful and subtle, whereas Su Shi's tend to be bold and exuberant. Generally, the graceful and restrained style follows more closely the original spirit of *ci* lyrics than the bold and unconstrained style. (Zhang Yan: *The Metric Schemes of Ci Lyrics*)

◎张南湖论词派有二：一曰婉约，一曰豪放。仆谓婉约以易安为宗，豪放惟幼安称首，皆吾济南人，难乎为继矣！（王士禛《花草蒙拾》）

（张綖论词派有二：一是婉约派，一是豪放派。我认为婉约派以李清照为第一，豪放派以辛弃疾为第一，他们都是我们济南人，之后就后继无人了。）

According to Zhang Yan, *ci* lyrics can either be graceful and restrained or bold and unconstrained. I believe that Li Qingzhao is the best of the former and Xin Qiji the best of the latter. They were both natives of Ji'nan. After them, no great *ci* poet has emerged in our province. (Wang Shizhen: *Random Notes on Ci Poetry*)

合同异

/hé tóngyì/

Unify Commonality and Difference

把事物的同和异合而为一。"合同异"是惠施（前370？—前310？）提出的看待事物同异的一种方式。惠施认为，事物的同异是相对而言的。两个具体事物之间会有或大或小的相同或相异之处。从"同"的角度来看，万物有共同之处，因此可以说万物是相同的；而从"异"的角度来看，则没有完全相同的两个事物，万物是不同的。事物的同异取决于看待事物的角度，因此惠施主张打破同异的界限，也即是"合同异"。

The philosopher Hui Shi's (370?-310? BC) approach to commonality and difference among things was to unite them, regarding similarities and differences as relative.

There are bound to be small or great similarities and differences between any two concrete things. If we look at them from the point of view of commonality, all things have something in common, so they can be said to be similar. If we look at them from the point of view of difference, no two things are completely the same, so they are all different. Whether things are similar or different depends on the perspective from which we look at them. This led Hui Shi to determine that similarities and differences are not separate; that is, they are unified.

引例 Citation：

◎ 大同而与小同异，此之谓"小同异"。万物毕同毕异，此之谓"大同异"。(《庄子·天下》)

（大同小异与小同大异是有区别的，这种区别称为"小同异"。万物完全相同、完全不同，这称为"大同异"。）

There are big commonalities and small differences, or small commonalities and big differences between things, and these are known as the "minor commonality and difference." When things are totally identical or totally different, this is known as the "major commonality and difference." (*Zhuangzi*)

和而不同
/hé'érbùtóng/

Harmony but Not Uniformity

在尊重事物差异性和多样性的基础上实现整体的和谐共存。"同"与"和"是对待、安顿社会群体的两种态度。"同"指对事物差异性的抹杀，"和"则意味着对事物差异性的保存与尊重。不同的事物彼此间相互辅助、补充，才能组成一个充满生机、富于创造性的和谐整体。

The term means achieving overall harmonious co-existence on the basis of respecting differences and diversity. Uniformity and harmony are two different attitudes to treating and accommodating social groups. Uniformity means obliterating differences in everything while harmony is to keep and respect the differences. Allowing different things to complement and supplement each other will create a harmonious whole full of vitality and creativity.

引例 Citations：

◎ 夫和实生物，同则不继。(《国语·郑语》)
（不同的事物相互调和而生成新的事物，只有相同的事物则难以有延续。）
Harmony begets new things; while uniformity does not lead to continuation. (*Discourses on Governance of the States*)

◎ 君子和而不同，小人同而不和。(《论语·子路》)
（君子与人和谐相处却不会盲目附和，小人盲目附和而不能真正和谐相处。）
A man of virtue pursues harmony but does not seek uniformity; a petty man seeks uniformity but does not pursue harmony. (*The Analects*)

和为贵
/héwéiguì/

Harmony Is Most Precious.

　　以和谐为贵。"和"，和谐、恰当，是在尊重事物差异性、多样性基础上的和谐共存。本指"礼"的作用就是使不同等级的人既保持一定差别又彼此和谐共存，各得其所，各安其位，相得益彰，从而实现全社会的"和而不同"，为儒家处理人际关系的重要伦理原则。后泛指人与人之间、团体与团体之间、国家与国家之间和谐、和睦、和平、融洽的关系状态。它体现了中华民族反对暴力冲突、崇尚和平与和谐的"文"的精神。

Make harmony a top priority. *He* (和) indicates congruity and appropriateness. It is a state of congenial co-existence on the basis of due respect for differences and diversity. At first, this phrase referred to the role of *li* (礼 rites / social norms) which is to keep citizens of distinct social status co-existing in a harmonious way, with everybody having his or her own place and staying there contentedly for mutual benefits, resulting in a "harmonious yet diverse" society. It is an important moral concept of the Confucian school in managing inter-personal relations. The term later evolved to refer in general to harmonious, congenial, peaceful, and agreeable relationships among people, groups, and states. It epitomizes the "civil" nature of the Chinese people, who oppose violent conflicts and aspire for peace and harmony.

引例 Citation：

◎有子曰："礼之用，和为贵。先王之道，斯为美，小大由之。有所不行，知和而和，不以礼节之，亦不可行也。"(《论语·学而》)
（有子说："礼的应用，以和谐为贵。古代君主的治国方法，可宝贵的地方就在这里，不论大事小事都依照"和"的原则去做。也有行不通的时候，如果仍一味为了和谐而和谐，而不用礼来加以节制，也是不可行的。"）

Youzi said, "Make harmony a top priority in the application of rites. That is a key feature that characterizes governance by sovereign rulers in ancient past. Always act upon the rule of harmony, no matter whether the issue at hand is minor or major. Sometimes, however, this rule may fail to work. If one insists on seeking harmony just for the sake of harmony instead of qualifying it with rites, then there will be no hope to succeed." (*The Analects*)

厚德载物

/hòudé-zàiwù/

Have Ample Virtue and Carry All Things

以宽厚的德性承载天下万物。多指以宽厚之德包容万物或他人。古人认为，大地的形势和特质是宽厚和顺的，它承载万物，使万物各遂其生。君子取法于"地"，要像大地一样，以博大宽厚的道德容纳万物和他人，包含了对自身道德修养及人与自然、社会和谐一体的追求。这是中国人参照大地山川状貌和特质树立的治国理政和为人处事的理念和理想。它和"自强不息"一起构成了中华民族精神的基本品格。

This term means that one should be broad-minded and care for all things and people. Ancient Chinese believed that with its topography and other natural features being generous and peaceful, the earth sustained all things in the world, allowing them to grow and develop in keeping with their own nature. Men of virtue model themselves on the earth, and just like the earth, care for all things and fellow human beings with open heart and virtue. This embodies the pursuit of moral cultivation and harmony among people and between people and nature. It represents the Chinese views and ideals on governance and human relationship, which were inspired by the formation and features of mountains and rivers in China. Together with the notion of constantly exerting oneself for self-improvement, it forms the fundamental character of the Chinese nation.

引例 Citations：

◎地势坤,君子以厚德载物。(《周易·象上》)

(大地的气势厚实和顺,君子应以宽厚美德容载天下万物。)

Just like the earth, which is generous and peaceful, a man of virtue should have ample virtue and accommodate all things. (*The Book of Changes*)

◎地势之顺，以地德之厚也。厚，故万物皆载焉。君子以之法地德之厚，而民物皆在所载矣。(陈梦雷《周易浅述》卷一)

(大地的形势是和顺的，因为大地具有宽厚的品德。因其宽厚，所以能承载万物。君子效法大地的宽厚品德，百姓、万物就都能被包容了。)

The peaceful nature of the earth is due to its virtue of generosity. Thus, it can accommodate and provide for all things. By modeling himself on the earth, a man of virtue should care for all people and all things. (Chen Menglei: *A Simple Account of The Book of Changes*)

厚积薄发

/hòujī-bófā/

Build Up Fully and Release Sparingly

充分地积累，少量地释放。多指学术研究或文艺创作等先要广泛汲取前人已有的知识和成果，待有了深厚的积累和坚实的基础，再一点儿一点儿地从事学术研究或文艺创作，尝试提出独到见解或在前人的基础上有所创造。也指一个国家、一个企业在某一领域或某一方面经过长期的积累，开始逐步展现其实力、创新力及开拓新的局面等。其核心内涵是，凡事不可急于求成，应注重积累，充分准备，才能把事情做好。

The term means to accumulate as much as possible but to release a little at a time. This often refers to the process of scholarly research or artistic creation, in which one should first extensively absorb the knowledge and results of others to acquire a wealth of knowledge and lay a solid foundation. On this basis, one is engaged in further scholarly studies or artistic creation, attempting to make new accomplishments. It can also refer to a country or a business which, after a long period of building up its strength, begins to gradually unleash its potential and ability to innovate and proceed to break new ground. The message of this expression is that one should never seek quick results; rather, one should pay attention to accumulating knowledge and making full preparations before making advances.

引例 Citation:

◎博观而约取，厚积而薄发，吾告子止于此矣。（苏轼《稼说——送张琥》）

（读书要广博，吸取其精要；学问积累要深厚，慢慢释放出来。我能告诉你的就是这些了。）

Read widely and absorb the best from the books you read; acquire deep learning and share it gradually – that is all I can tell you. (Su Shi: An Allegory for Zhang Hu on Growing Crops)

华夏
/huáxià/

Huaxia / The Han People

古代居住于中原地区的汉民族先民的自称。最早称"华""诸华"或"夏""诸夏"。"华夏"实际表达的是以汉民族为主体的中原先民对其共同的生活、语言、文化特征的一种认同和传承。秦建立以华夏为主体的统一的多民族国家以后,华夏才成为比较稳定的族群。自汉代以后,华夏又有了"汉"这一名称与之并用。后来华夏进一步引申为指中国或汉族。

The forefathers of the Han people living in the Central Plains referred to themselves by this term. Earlier on they called themselves Hua (华), Zhuhua (诸华), Xia (夏) or Zhuxia (诸夏). The term Huaxia (华夏) embodies the common identity of the way of life, language, and culture of the people living in the Central Plains, mainly the Han people, and the inheritance of such identity. The Huaxia people evolved into a fairly stable ethnic group in the Qin Dynasty, which established a unified country of many ethnic groups with Huaxia being the principal group. In the Han Dynasty, the term Han became an alternative name of Huaxia. Later, the term Huaxia was extended to refer to China or the Han people.

引例 Citation:

◎夏,大也。中国有礼义之大,故称夏;有服章之美,谓之华。华夏一也。(《左传·定公十年》孔颖达正义)

(夏的含义是"大"。华夏族的礼仪宏富伟大,所以称为"夏";华夏族的衣服华美出众,所以称为"华"。"华"与"夏"是同一个意思。)

The Chinese character 夏 (xia) means big and great. Since the ancient Huaxia people practiced grand and elaborate rituals, they called themselves *Xia* (great). Their dresses were resplendent, so they were referred to as *Hua* (splendid). Therefore, both *Hua* and *Xia* refer to the Han people. (Kong Yingda: *Correct Meaning of Zuo's Commentary on The Spring and Autumn Annals*)

化干戈为玉帛
/huà gāngē wéi yùbó/

Beat Swords into Plowshares /
Turn War into Peace

消除仇怨，变战争为和平，变冲突为友好。"干""戈"是中国古代用于防御和进攻的两种武器，借指战争、武力冲突；"玉""帛"指圭、璋等玉器和束帛，是古代诸侯会盟、诸侯与天子朝聘时互赠的礼物，后来用于表示和平共处之意。它反映了华夏民族自古崇尚和平、愿意化解暴力冲突的美好期待。

The term means to eliminate animosity in order to turn war into peace and turn conflicts into amity. *Gan* (干) and *ge* (戈) are two weapons of war which were used for defense and attack respectively in ancient China. *Yu* (玉) and *bo* (帛) mean jades (such as jade tablets and jade ornaments) which were gifts exchanged between feudal lords and tribute paid to monarchs. In time, *yu* and *bo* acquired the meaning of peace and co-existence. This term reflects the Chinese people's long-standing aspiration for peace and goodwill to dissolve conflict and violence.

引例 Citation：

◎ 上天降灾，使我两君匪以玉帛相见，而以兴戎。(《左传·僖公十五年》)

(上天降下灾祸，使我[秦、晋]两国国君没有带着玉帛会面，却发动了战争。)

Heaven has struck disaster, bringing our two sovereign lords (of the states of Qin and Jin) to face each other, not with jades and silks, but with the instruments of war. (*Zuo's Commentary on The Spring and Autumn Annals*)

化工 / 画工
/huàgōng / huàgōng/

Magically Natural, Overly Crafted

　　品评文学艺术作品风格自然与否的术语。"化工"指作品的工巧自然天成，毫无雕琢痕迹，达到了出神入化的地步；"画工"则是指作品的工巧由刻意雕琢而成，技巧虽高明，但缺乏自然韵味。"化工"是艺术家的作品，"画工"可以说是匠人的作品。这个评价标准，由明代李贽（1527—1602）《杂说》提出，与他所提倡的写文章要有真情、真心是一致的。从文化渊源上来说，"画工"与"化工"的区分，其实来自道家的纯任自然、弃绝机巧的思想。明代文士大都倡导文艺放任天然，否定雕琢模仿的创作立场。

The expressions are about the naturalness of literary and artistic works. The first one, "magically natural," means that a literary or artistic work is completed naturally and achieves the acme of perfection without any sign of craft. The second, "overly crafted," means that a work is meticulously crafted, but it is overly elaborate in style while lacking naturalness and spontaneity. "Magically natural" is used to refer to works accomplished by artists while "overly crafted" is used to describe works done by craftsmen. These two standards were proposed by Ming writer Li Zhi (1527 - 1602) in his "Random Thoughts," which echoed his idea that writings must reflect the author's true sentiments. Culturally, the distinction between "magically natural" and "overly crafted" is rooted in the Daoist thought of being harmonious with nature while forsaking excessive skills. Most Ming scholars favored literary naturalism and rejected elaboration and imitation.

引例 Citations：

◎ 吴生虽妙绝，犹以画工论。摩诘得之于象外，有如仙翮谢笼樊。吾观二子皆神俊，又于维也敛衽无间（jiàn）言。（苏轼《王维、吴道子画》）

（吴道子的技巧虽然绝妙，只能说是画工之作。王维的高妙之处则是超越了所描绘的物象，就像仙鸟离飞笼子。我看这两位技法都很高超，对于王维则更钦敬，没有任何可挑剔之处。）

Wu Daozi had superb technical skills, but his paintings were over crafted. What is remarkable about Wang Wei is that he gave free rein to his imagination in his paintings, like a bird that had broken free from its cage. Both of them were highly skilled, but I like Wang Wei better; I can find no fault in his works. (Su Shi: The Paintings of Wang Wei and Wu Daozi)

◎《拜月》《西厢》，化工也；《琵琶》，画工也。夫所谓画工者，以其能夺天地之化工，而其孰知天地之无工乎？（李贽《杂说》）
(《拜月亭》《西厢记》属于"化工"之作，《琵琶记》则是"画工"之作。之所以称"画工"，是人们认为它能够取代天地的造化之功，可是，谁知道天地本就没有这样的造化之工呢？)

The Moonlight Pavilion and *Romance of the Western Chamber* were works of magical naturalness, whereas *A Tale of the Pipa* was an overly crafted work. The latter shows that an attempt made to outdo the magic of nature has proved impossible to achieve. (Li Zhi: Random Thoughts)

化性起伪
/huàxìng-qǐwěi/

Transform Intrinsic Evil Nature to Develop Acquired Nature of Goodness

改变人的本性的恶而兴起人为的善。伪：人为。"化性起伪"是荀子（前313？—前238）在"性恶"论基础上提出的一种道德教化的主张。荀子认为，人天生的本性中包含着对外物的欲求。如果放纵本性中的欲望，就会导致人与人之间的纷争，社会将陷入混乱。因此，需要通过后天的教化，在恰当安顿人的欲望的同时，确立起对道德、礼法的认同与遵守。

This term means changing element of evil in one's intrinsic nature and developing acquired nature of goodness. This ethical principle is put forward by Xunzi (313?-

238 BC) based on his belief that human nature is evil. Xunzi believes that the desire for external things is an intrinsic part of human nature. Unrestrained pursuit of such desire leads to rivalry between people and throws society into chaos. Therefore, it is imperative to rein in human desire and make people accept and observe rites and laws.

引例 Citations：

◎不可学、不可事而在人者谓之性，可学而能、可事而成之在人者谓之伪，是性、伪之分也。(《荀子·性恶》)

(不可以通过学习、从事而为人所具备的，称之为"性"；可以通过学习、从事而为人所具备的，称之为"伪"，这是"性"和"伪"的分别。)

Attributes that people have and that cannot be gained by learning and practice are called intrinsic nature. Abilities learned or mastered through practice are called acquired nature. Such is the difference between intrinsic nature and acquired nature. (*Xunzi*)

◎故圣人化性而起伪，伪起而生礼义，礼义生而制法度。(《荀子·性恶》)

(因此圣人改变人的本性的恶而兴起人为的善，人为的善兴起而产生了礼义，礼义产生而后制定法度。)

Thus, what the sage does is to transform the evil element in people's intrinsic nature and develop acquired nature of goodness. The acquired nature of goodness gives rise to rites and ethical standards, which in turn give birth to laws. (*Xunzi*)

画道
/huàdào/

Dao of Painting

绘画之道。有广狭二义：狭义指绘画的各种技法；广义则指画作中蕴含的文化理念、人格精神、艺术风格和审美追求，是"道"与"技"

的完美融合。"道"决定画所要表现的思想主题、艺术法则和美学风格；画是"道"的具体表象，寄托了画家的文化理念、人格精神、艺术风格和审美追求。故道以画显，画因道而获得提升。杰出的画家追求技进乎道、艺与道合。画道，不仅包含了宇宙自然之道，而且折射了社会人生之道，彰显出中国固有的人文精神。

The term has both broad and narrow meanings. Interpreted narrowly, it means various painting techniques. Interpreted broadly, it means the cultural values, personality, artistic style, and aesthetic aspiration embodied in a painting, suggesting a perfect fusion of Dao and skills. Dao determines the theme a painting conveys as well as the painting's artistic principles and aesthetic style. A painting is a concrete image that illustrates Dao. It reflects the cultural principles followed by the painter as well as his personality, artistic style, and aesthetic aspiration. Therefore, paintings illuminate Dao, which in turn enhances the paintings. Prominent painters seek to access Dao through refining their skills and epitomizing Dao in artwork. The Dao of painting not only encompasses the Dao of nature, but also the Dao of social life, demonstrating the commitment to humanism inherent in the Chinese culture.

引例 Citations：

◎ 夫圣人以神法道，而贤者通；山水以形媚道，而仁者乐。不亦几乎？（宗炳《画山水序》）

（圣人精神上效法道，而德才杰出的人可以通达于道；山水以其自然形质婉转契合道，使仁者对之喜爱。这难道不是很微妙吗？）

Sages follow Dao with their spirit. Men of virtue and talent may comprehend and practice Dao. Mountains and rivers conform to Dao through their natural shapes. That is why they are loved by benevolent people. Isn't this subtle and profound? (Zong Bing: On the Creation of Landscape Paintings)

◎ 画之道，所谓宇宙在乎手者，眼前无非生机。（董其昌《画禅室随笔·画源》）

（绘画之道，就是宇宙自然的神奇都能够通过手表现出来，呈现于眼前的全是有生命的景象。）

The Dao of painting enables one to use his hand to depict the wonder of nature and present to viewers a scene full of life. (Dong Qichang: *Essays from Huachan Studio*)

画龙点睛

/huàlóng-diǎnjīng/

Add Pupils to the Eyes of a Painted Dragon /
Render the Final Touch

  比喻文学艺术创作中在紧要处着墨或写出关键性的词句，以创造出最奇妙的神韵和意境来。孟子（前372？—前289）认为，观察一个人，最好观察他的眼睛，因为眼睛最容易表露一个人内心的善良和丑恶。东晋顾恺之（345？—409）画人物，曾数年不肯轻易下笔点睛。他强调人物传神之关键在于画出眼神。南朝画家张僧繇（yáo）绘画技术高超，传说他曾为画好的龙点上眼珠，龙即刻腾空而去。故后世用"画龙点睛"强调文学艺术创作中应抓住要诀，使形象更加生动传神。

The term is a metaphor about giving the finishing touch, which means providing critical details or key words in an artistic or literary work in order to lend it charm and aesthetic conception. Mencius (372?-289 BC) believed that when observing a person, one should look directly into his eyes because the eyes reveal his nature, be it good or evil. When painting portraits, Gu Kaizhi (345?-409) in the Eastern Jin Dynasty did not add pupils to the eyes in haste. He stressed that the key to painting a vivid portrait lied in painting the eyes. Zhang Sengyao, a painter of the Southern Dynasties, was well known for his excellent painting skills. Legend has it that his painted Chinese dragons flew into the sky as soon as he finished their pupils. The term is thus used by later generations to underline the importance of applying critical touches to add life and charm to a literary or artistic work.

引例 Citation：

◎又金陵安乐寺四白龙，不点眼睛，每云："点睛即飞去。"人以为妄诞，固请点之，须臾雷电破壁，两龙乘云腾去上天，二龙未点眼者见在。（张彦远《历代名画记》卷七）

（[张僧繇]在金陵安乐寺墙壁上画了四条白龙，他没有给龙点上眼睛，常说："点上眼睛，龙立刻就会腾空飞走。"人们都认为他的话荒唐虚妄，一再请他点上眼睛，[张僧繇只好提笔点睛，]即刻天空雷电交加，两条龙乘云腾空而去，而另两条没点眼睛的龙还留在墙壁上。）

Zhang Sengyao painted four white Chinese dragons on the wall of the Anle Temple in Jinling. But he did not paint pupils to their eyes, saying that once he did, the dragons would fly into the sky. People considered his words absurd and repeatedly urged him to add pupils to the dragons' eyes. He eventually did it on two of the four dragons. Suddenly, lightning and thunders struck, and the two dragons with pupils added to their eyes flew into the clouds. The other two remained on the wall. (Zhang Yanyuan: *Famous Paintings Through History*)

黄河

/Huáng Hé/

The Yellow River

中国第二大河，发源于青藏高原，自西向东流经青海、四川、甘肃、宁夏、内蒙古、陕西、山西、河南、山东9个省（自治区），注入渤海，全长约5464公里，为世界著名大河。因多泥沙色黄而得名，是中华民族的摇篮和中国古代文化的重要发源地，被称为中国人的"母亲河"。她不仅是一条自然河流，而且已经成为中国人重要的文化意象和文化符号，象征中华民族自强不息、百折不挠、勇往直前的精神品格。

Originating in the Qinghai-Tibet Plateau, the Yellow River is the second longest waterway in China, flowing eastward through the provinces of Qinghai, Sichuan, Gansu, the Ningxia Hui Autonomous Region, and the Inner Mongolia Autonomous Region, as well as the provinces of Shaanxi, Shanxi, Henan, and Shandong before emptying into the Bohai Sea. With a total length of 5,464 kilometers, the Yellow River is one of the major waterways in the world. The river is so named because of its yellowish color caused by the large amount of silts washed into it. Considered the cradle of the Chinese nation and Chinese culture, the river is therefore known as the Mother River among the Chinese, and has become an important cultural image and sign for the Chinese nation. It symbolizes the heroism and perseverance with which the Chinese nation forges ahead against all odds.

引例 Citation：

◎ 白日依山尽，黄河入海流。欲穷千里目，更上一层楼。（王之涣《登鹳雀楼》）

（太阳依傍着西边的大山落下，黄河向着东方的大海奔流。要想眺望千里远，必须再上一层楼。）

The setting sun beyond the mountains glows, the Yellow River seaward flows. Going to the top of the pavilion, and you will have a panoramic river view reaching the horizon. (Wang Zhihuan: Climbing the Guanque Tower)

会心
/huìxīn/

Heart-to-heart Communication

不需言说而彼此心领神会。一般是指志趣、性情投合的朋友心意相通，能够互相理解和欣赏。特指自然美欣赏和文艺作品审美中主客体交融的境界。作者创作出美的意境，而欣赏者心领神会，感受到心与物高度融合及心心相印带来的快乐与慰藉。

The term refers to a situation in which people understand each other without the need to utter a single word. It generally means the spontaneous understanding reached by close friends who share common interests, aspirations, and dispositions. In particular, it refers to an aesthetic state in which the subject and the object interact with each other smoothly with no barrier between them, or in which an artist creates a marvelous image and a viewer appreciates it with emotion and understanding. The culmination of such an experience is joy and satisfaction derived from the perfect harmony between the human heart and its surroundings.

引例 Citations：

◎ 简文入华林园，顾谓左右曰："会心处不必在远，翳然林水，便自有濠濮间想也，觉鸟兽禽鱼自来亲人。"（刘义庆《世说新语·言语》）

（梁简文帝到华林园游玩，转过头对左右随从说："合人心意的地方不一定遥远，这里林木蔽空，其间一湾流水，便自然会产生庄子游于濠水桥上、垂钓于濮水的遐想，觉得鸟兽和鱼儿都主动和人亲近。"）

When Emperor Jianwen of Liang in the Southern Dynasties was touring the Hualin Garden, he turned to his followers and said, "A place which prompts heart-to-heart communication need not be far. This garden is shadowed by trees and has a stream meandering through. Such a place makes one think of Zhuangzi strolling on the bridge of the Haoshui River and angling in the Pushui River, where birds and fish seemed eager to get close to him." (Liu Yiqing: *A New Account of Tales of the World*)

◎《三百篇》美刺箴怨皆无迹，当以心会心。（姜夔《白石道人诗说》）

(《诗经》中的颂美、怨刺与劝谏都没有明显的痕迹，欣赏时应当以心会心。)

The Book of Songs contains odes, satires, and admonitions, but all are veiled. One must engage in a heart-to-heart communication to appreciate them. (Jiang Kui: *The Poetry Theory of Baishi Daoren*)

绘事后素
/huì shì hòu sù/

The White Silk First, the Painting Afterwards / Beauty from Natural Simplicity

原指绘画须先有白绢作底，引申为美感源于自然质朴。孔子（前551—前479）由此阐发仁义为本、礼教为辅的理念，强调礼的教育起源于人的自然本性。后来这一术语引入文艺创作与批评，它倡导雕饰起源于质素，文质相符，彰显天然之美。

The original meaning of this phrase is that a piece of white silk must be prepared before one can paint. The concept was then extended to mean that beauty comes from natural simplicity. From this, Confucius (551-479 BC) put forward the notion that benevolence and righteousness are fundamental and the code of ethics secondary, emphasizing that the teaching of the rites originates in human nature. This concept was later introduced into literary and artistic creation and criticism, which advocates that elaboration should be based on substance, and that style and substance should be compatible and complement each other to bring out the natural beauty.

引例 Citations：

◎子夏问曰："'巧笑倩兮，美目盼兮，素以为绚兮。'何谓也？"子曰："绘事后素。"（《论语·八佾》）

（子夏问道："'美妙的笑靥那样迷人啊，漂亮的眼睛含羞顾盼啊，就像是白绢上画出了绚丽的画啊！'这几句诗是什么意思？"孔子道："先有白绢才能作画。"）

Zixia asked: "A seductive smile with pretty dimples, her lovely eyes sparkling, like a beautiful painting on white silk. What do these lines mean?" Confucius replied: "To paint, one must have a piece of white silk first." (*The Analects*)

◎礼必以忠信为质，犹绘事必以粉素为先。（朱熹《论语集注》卷二）

（礼教必须以忠信为根本，如同绘画必须先要有白绢。）

The ethical code must be based on loyalty and faithfulness, like a painting that must be done on a piece of white silk prepared. (Zhu Xi: *The Analects Variorum*)

浑沌

/hùndùn/

Chaos

"浑沌"又作"混沌"，有两种不同含义：其一，指天地分化形成以前宇宙浑然一体的状态。常以未分化之"气"言之。天地万物皆由"浑沌"分化演变而成。其二，特指《庄子》一则寓言中的中央之帝。中央之帝浑沌无七窍，被南海之帝儵（shū）和北海之帝忽凿开七窍而亡。庄子（前369？—前286）以此形象寓指人无知无识、无善恶彼我之分，与整个世界浑然一体的状态。

The term has two meanings. First, it refers to the state of one whole mass that existed before the universe took shape, often said to exist before *qi* (vital force) emerged. The multitude of organisms on earth all emanated from this state. Second, it refers to Chaos, king of the Central Region in a fable in *Zhuangzi*. According to the fable, Chaos had no eyes, nose, mouth or ears. Shu, king of the South Sea, and Hu, king of the North Sea, drilled seven apertures into Chaos and killed him. Zhuangzi (369?-286 BC) used this story to show the state of chaos of the world in which there is neither knowledge or wisdom, nor distinction between good and evil.

引例 Citations：

◎说《易》者曰："元气未分，浑沌为一。"（王充《论衡·谈天》）
（论说《周易》的人言道："元气没有分化之时，浑然一体。"）

Those who commented on *The Book of Changes* said, "Before *qi* (vital force) appeared, the world was in a state of formless chaos." (Wang Chong: *A Comparative Study of Different Schools of Learning*)

◎南海之帝为儵，北海之帝为忽，中央之帝为浑沌。儵与忽时相与遇于浑沌之地，浑沌待之甚善。儵与忽谋报浑沌之德，曰：人皆有七窍以视听食息，此独无有，尝试凿之。日凿一窍，七日而浑沌死。（《庄子·应帝王》）
（南海之帝是儵，北海之帝是忽，中央之帝是浑沌。儵与忽时常相会于浑沌之地，浑沌待他们很好。儵与忽商量报答浑沌，说：人都有七窍用以视听、饮食、呼吸，唯独浑沌没有，尝试为它开凿出来。于是每天为浑沌开凿一窍，七天之后浑沌死了。）

The king of the South Sea was called Shu, the king of the North Sea was called Hu, and the king of the Central Region was called Chaos. Shu and Hu often met in the territory of Chaos, who treated them very well. They wanted to repay his kindness, and said, "Every man has seven apertures with which to hear, to see, to eat and drink, and to breathe, but Chaos alone has none of them. Let's try and bore some for him." They bored one aperture on Chaos each day, and on the seventh day Chaos died. (*Zhuangzi*)

活法
/huófǎ/
Literary Flexibility

指诗文创作在遵守规矩法度的同时，又不可死守规矩法度，要有所变化和创新。与拘泥于前人格套、不知变通的"死法"相对立。使作品具备活法的途径，是善于学习前人，在广泛涉猎、融会贯通的基础上，不拘泥、不胶着，从自己的情感和作品的美感出发，使作品的文法、语言呈现崭新的意义。宋代文论家们受到了圆转灵活的禅风影响，在诗文领域倡导活法，使之成为诗文创作的重要原则。

Literary flexibility means that one should respect the rules for writing poetry or prose but not be bound by them; one should encourage change and innovation. The opposite of literary flexibility is literary rigidity under whose influence the writer mechanically imitates the forms of established writers without innovation. One way to attain literary flexibility in one's works is to draw inspiration from others extensively and absorb their talent while refraining from sticking mechanically to the model. One should base oneself on his own feelings and the aesthetic principles so as to create new styles and new ways of expression. Influenced by the Chan spirit of liberal flexibility, literary critics of the Song Dynasty championed flexibility in literary pursuit and established it as an important principle guiding poetry and prose writing.

引例 Citations：

◎学诗当识活法。所谓活法者，规矩备具而能出于规矩之外，变化不测而亦不背于规矩也。是道也，盖有定法而无定法，无定法而有定法。知是者则可以与语活法矣。（刘克庄《后村集》卷二十四引吕本中《〈夏均父集〉序》）

（学作诗要懂得活法。所谓活法，就是作诗的各种规矩法度全都具备而又能跳出法度的限制，使诗文产生各种不可预测的变化而且还不违背规矩。这个道理就是，说有恒定的规矩法度又没有恒定的规矩法度，说没有恒定的规矩法度却又有恒定的规矩法度。懂得这个道理的人，就可以与他谈论活法了。）

Those who wish to learn to write poetry should master literary flexibility. By this I mean that, while knowing all the rules for poetry, the poet goes beyond them to reflect unpredictable changes in his poetry yet without compromising the rules. The principle underlying this way of writing is that there should be set rules, yet they are not fixed; where there seem to be no rules, rules do exist. You can discuss literary flexibility with others only if they understand this principle. (Lü Benzhong: Foreword to *The Collected Poetry of Xia Junfu*)

◎文章一技，要自有活法。若胶古人之陈迹，而不能点化其句语，此乃谓之死法。死法专祖蹈袭，则不能生于吾言之外；活法夺胎换骨，则不能毙于吾言之内。毙吾言者，[故为死法；]生吾言也，故为活法。(俞成《萤雪丛说·文章活法》)

(写文章这种技艺，必须有自己的活法。如果只是拘泥于古人的陈法，而不能将他们的词句化陈出新，这就叫死法。死法只会因袭模仿，不能让我的文章在语言之外获得新生。活法则能超凡脱俗，不会让我的文章被语言困死。文章被语言困死，[所以称死法；]使文章在语言之外获得新生，所以称活法。)

In writing essays, it is necessary to maintain literary flexibility. If one is bound by the clichés of the classical masters and fails to produce novel ideas, this is what we call literary rigidity. Literary rigidity refers to mechanically copying others without permitting one's own work to acquire new ideas. Literary flexibility, however, allows one's work to free itself from clichés so that the work will not be stifled by stereotyped style of writing. Literary rigidity leads to a literary dead end, while literary flexibility encourages the birth of new ideas by going beyond the limitations of conventional way of writing. (Yu Cheng: *Reflections from Devoted Reading*)

几

/jī/

Ji (Omen)

事物产生或变化的征兆。古人认为,新事物产生或旧事物发生变化,以及人心善恶的分化之前,都会出现微小的征兆,也即是"几"。"几"或显现于外,或隐藏于旧事物的内部。人应培养发现、把握几兆的能力。只有善于发现事物出现或变化的几兆,并适时加以利用,才能够预见、把握事物发展变化的方向,以实现趋利避害。

Ji (几) refers to an omen indicating the emerging or changing of things. Ancient Chinese believed that a subtle omen would appear before something new emerged or when something old was about to change, or before the differentiation of good and evil in human nature occurred. An omen is either visible or hidden inside something old. One should develop the ability to identify and use an omen. When one is adept at identifying an omen that something is emerging or changing and makes use of it at the appropriate moment, one can foresee and grasp the way things emerge and change, thus pursuing the desired course and avoiding harm.

引例 Citations：

◎几者,动之微,吉凶之先见者也。君子见几而作,不俟终日。(《周易·系辞下》)

("几"是事物变化的微小征兆,预示着吉凶的结果。君子发现几兆就适时行动,不需要长时间等待。)

Ji means a subtle omen of change predicting good or evil. A man of virtue acts at the right moment without hesitation when he sees an omen. (The Book of Changes)

◎几者,动之微,善恶之所由分也。(朱熹《通书注》)

("几"是事物变化的微小征兆,人心的善恶也由此分化。)

Ji means a subtle omen of change in things, and it indicates the differentiation of good and evil in human nature. (Zhu Xi: Annotations on The Gist of Confucian Thought)

己所不欲，勿施于人

/jǐsuǒbùyù, wùshīyúrén/

Do Not Do to Others What You Do Not Want Others to Do to You.

  自己不愿意的，不要强加给别人。这是孔子（前551—前479）所提倡的"恕道"（推己及人的原则），以自己的心意推测、理解别人的心意，亦即今之所谓设身处地，换位思考。其哲学基础是"性相近"（人的本性是相近的）。它是儒家处理人与人关系的重要原则，如今也被引申为反对强权政治的国际关系原则，其基本精神是仁爱、平等与宽容。

Do not impose on others what you do not want yourself. That is the "way of being considerate" advocated by Confucius (551-479 BC). It calls for using one's own mind to infer and understand other people's minds. In today's words, it means to put oneself into others' shoes or to think from their positions. Its philosophical basis lies in the commonality of people's basic natures. It is an important principle put forth by Confucians to govern inter-personal relationships, and is now extended to international relationship management to counter power politics. Its essential elements are benevolence, equality, and tolerance.

引例 Citations：

◎子曰："性相近也，习相远也。"（《论语·阳货》）

（孔子说："人的本性是相近的，由于环境的习染才有了差别。"）

Confucius said, "Human nature is similar at birth, only made different by the environment." (*The Analects*)

◎子贡问曰："有一言而可以终身行之者乎？"子曰："其恕乎！己所不欲，勿施于人。"（《论语·卫灵公》）

（子贡问道："有没有一句教导可以让我终身奉行呢？"孔子说："那就是恕吧！自己不想要的，不要施加于他人。"）

Zigong asked, "Is there any teaching that can serve as a lasting principle for conduct in one's whole life?" Confucius replied, "Surely that is to be considerate! Do not do to others what you do not want others to do to you." (*The Analects*)

寄托
/jìtuō/

Entrust One's Thoughts and Feelings to Imagery

指诗歌作品通过形象化而寄寓作者的主观认识或感受，并能激发读者的联想。"寄"是寄寓一定的思想内容和个人情志，"托"是托物兴咏。是清代常州词派提出的一个文学术语。张惠言（1761—1802）主张词要继承《诗经》的比兴、讽喻传统。周济（1781—1839）进而认为，初学写词应力求有寄托，以提升作品意蕴、激发读者的思考和艺术想象；待入门后，则不能拘于寄托，而要言意浑融，无迹可寻。这一主张实质是反对观念先行，强调文学自身的特性，对于当时的文学创作有积极的导向作用。

The term refers to the entrusting of the poet's subjective understanding or sentiments to imagery in poetic works. It can also stir responsive appreciation of the reader. *Ji* (寄) means having a specific thought or individual feelings, and *tuo* (托) means giving expression to such thought or feelings through the channel of an object. It is a literary term first used by a group of *ci* (词 lyric) poets from Changzhou during the Qing Dynasty. Zhang Huiyan (1761-1802) stressed that lyric writing should follow the tradition of analogies, associations and allegories in *The Book of Songs*. Zhou Ji (1781-1839) further suggested that an aspiring poet should entrust his thought to imagery in order to raise the artistic appeal of his work and stimulate the imagination of the reader. After having established himself, however, the poet should not be bound by the technique of entrusting to imagery; rather, his words and sentiments should blend seamlessly. This view emphasized the primacy of nature of literature as opposed to the primacy of concept and provided a new guidance for literary creation at the time.

引例 Citation：

◎夫词，非寄托不入，专寄托不出。(周济《宋四家词选目录序论》)
(作词，如果没有寄托，就很难深入；如果只专力于寄托，就不能意出词外。)

When writing *ci* poetry, one cannot effectively express one's thoughts and sentiments without entrusting them to imagery. On the other hand, overreliance on imagery will make it hard for one to clearly express his idea. (Zhou Ji: Preface to *Contents of Selected Poems of Four Poets of the Song Dynasty*)

兼爱
/jiān'ài/

Universal Love

　　无差等地相互关爱。"兼爱"一说是墨家的基本主张，它所针对的是儒家所提出的爱有差等原则。"兼爱"强调每个人都应像爱自己一样爱他人，像爱自己的家人、国人一样爱别人的家人、爱别国的人，那么人与人之间就会彼此相爱。这种相爱是不分亲疏远近、尊卑上下的，是平等的、没有差别的爱。如果做到兼相爱，就能够避免人与人、家与家、国与国之间的相互攻伐、侵害，进而实现互利。

Universal love, equal affection for all individuals, is a basic concept of the Mohist school of thought, as opposed to the principle of differentiated love advocated by the Confucian school. Universal love emphasizes that you should love others as you love yourself, and love others' relatives and people of other states as you love your own so that all people would love one another equally. This principle of affection has no regard for blood ties or social status. It is an affection that is exercised equally without differentiating between individuals, families, or nations. If such a principle could be realized, we could avoid conflicts between persons, clans, or nations and bring equal benefit to all.

引例 Citation：

◎天下兼相爱则治，交相恶则乱。(《墨子·兼爱上》)

(天下之人彼此相爱则社会安定有序，相互厌恶则社会纷乱不安。)

Universal love will bring peace and order to the world while mutual animosity can only throw the world into disorder. (*Mozi*)

见利思义

/jiànlì-sīyì/

Think of Righteousness in the Face of Gain

在面对利益之时，首先思考、分辨利益的获取是否符合道义。是儒家用以处理义利关系的准则。对利益的追求与对道义的坚守之间常存在冲突。人们往往会因为贪图私利而忽视道义，行背德违法之事。针对这种情况，孔子（前551—前479）提出了"见利思义"的主张，倡导人们应该在道义的原则之下谋求利益。知晓道义的是君子，一味追求利益的是小人。

When faced with gain one should first consider and distinguish whether the obtainment of gain is in accord with morality. This is a Confucian criterion for dealing with the relation between righteousness and gain. Between the pursuit of gain and the upholding of morality a conflict has long existed. Because people more often than not may covet personal gain and overlook morality, their actions may go against virtue and violate the law. Against this kind of situation Confucius (551 - 479 BC) advanced the stand of "thinking of righteousness in the face of gain," proposing that people should strive for gain on the basis of the principle of morality. He who knows morality is a man of virtue, and he who blindly pursues gain is a petty man.

引例 Citation：

◎见利思义，见危授命，久要（yāo）不忘平生之言，亦可以为成人矣。（《论语·宪问》）

（看见利益时思考该不该得，遇到危险时肯付出生命，经过长久的穷困而不忘记平日的诺言，也可以说是成人了。）

He who when faced with gain thinks of righteousness, who when confronted with danger is ready to lay down his life, and who does not forget a past promise despite enduring poverty, may be considered a true man! (*The Analects*)

见闻之知

/jiànwénzhīzhī/

Knowledge from One's Senses

由耳、目等感官与外物接触而获得的认识，与"德性之知"相对。张载（1020—1077）最先区分了"见闻之知"与"德性之知"。宋儒认为，人对生活世界的认识是通过两种不同方式实现的。通过目见耳闻所获得的认识，即是"见闻之知"。"见闻之知"是人的认识所不可缺少的。但"见闻之知"不足以穷尽对事物的认识，也无法获得对世界本体或本原的认识。

The term refers to knowledge derived from contact between externalities and one's sensory organs such as the ears and eyes, in contrast to "knowledge from one's moral nature." Zhang Zai (1020-1077) was the first to differentiate between "knowledge from one's senses" and "knowledge from one's moral nature." Confucian scholars of the Song Dynasty felt that people acquired knowledge about the world in which they lived in two ways. Knowledge obtained from seeing and hearing was "knowledge from the senses," which was an essential part of human knowledge. However, it was not a complete picture, nor could it provide an understanding of the original source or ontological existence of the world.

引例 Citation：

◎ 闻见之知，非德性之知，物交物则知之，非内也。（《二程遗书》卷二十五）

（闻见之知，不是德性之知，感官与外物相接触则获得了对外界的认知，并非由内心而生。）

Knowledge from one's senses is not knowledge from one's moral nature. It comes from contact with external objects and not from the inner workings of the heart. (*Writings of the Cheng Brothers*)

见贤思齐
/jiànxián-sīqí/

When Seeing a Person of High Caliber, Strive to Be His Equal.

遇见有德才的人，就要想着努力向他看齐。"贤"指德才兼备的人；"齐"是看齐，达到同样的水平。"见贤思齐"是孔子（前551—前479）对自己学生的教导，后成为世人修身养德、增进才智的座右铭。其主旨在于鼓励人们善于发现他人长处，激发内心的自觉，主动向道德、学问、技能等比自己强的人学习看齐，从而不断进步。它体现了中华民族一心向善、积极进取、自强不息的精神。

This term means that when you see a person of high caliber, you should try to emulate and equal the person. *Xian* (贤) refers to a person of virtue and capability; *qi* (齐) means to emulate and reach the same level. This was what Confucius (551-479 BC) taught his students to do. The term has become a motto for cultivating one's moral character and increasing one's knowledge. The main point of this term is to encourage people to discover the strengths of others and take initiative to learn from those who are stronger than themselves in terms of moral qualities, knowledge, and skills so as to make constant progress. The term embodies the Chinese nation's spirit for good, enterprise, and tenacious self-renewal.

引例 Citations：

◎子曰："见贤思齐焉，见不贤而内自省也。"（《论语·里仁》）

（孔子说："遇见有德才的人，就要想着努力向他看齐；遇见德才不好的人，就要在内心反省自己[是否有同样的缺点]。"）

Confucius said, "When you see a person of virtue and capability, you should think of emulating and equaling the person; when you see a person of low caliber, you should reflect on your own weak points." (*The Analects*)

◎君子博学而日参（cān）省乎己，则知明而行无过矣。（《荀子·劝学》）

（君子广泛学习并且每天坚持自我参验、反省，就可以做到智慧明达而行为不会有错了。）

Men of virtue, who study extensively and reflect on themselves every day, become wise and intelligent and are free from making mistakes. (*Xunzi*)

鉴古知今

/jiàngǔ-zhījīn/

Review the Past to Understand the Present

以过去、历史为镜鉴，可以了解现在并预知未来。也说"鉴往知来""知古鉴今"。"鉴"本指镜子，引申为借鉴、参照，审察、考察。所谓"鉴古""鉴往""知古"主要指总结历史上朝代、国家兴衰成败的经验教训，考察历史人物的言行事迹以及是非善恶，来为现实的国家治理和个人的道德修养服务。"知今""鉴今""知来"则是了解现在，以现在为鉴，预知未来。古代执政者为了使自己的决策符合国情、民情，具一定合理性，非常注重从历史中吸取经验教训，以避免重蹈覆辙。它包含着对于历史的现实意义和现实的历史景深的双重关注。与"前事不忘，后事之师"意思接近。

Reviewing the past helps us understand the present and predict the future. It is also said that "reviewing the past we understand the future" and "knowing the past we understand the present." The Chinese word *jian* (鉴) can mean "mirror" and hence to "review the past" as if in a mirror, "understand the past," or "gain knowledge of the past." The lessons of the rise and fall of dynasties and states, the words and deeds of historical figures, as well as right and wrong, and good and evil, help govern the country and improve personal morality. "Understanding the present," "reviewing the present," or "understanding the future" means predicting the future based on the present. The rulers of antiquity saw it as extremely important to draw lessons from history in order to avoid past mistakes and justify their policies by making them conform to the needs of the country and people. The concept of "reviewing the past to understand the present" stresses both the practical significance of history and the historical depth of things present. It is similar to the concept that "past experience, if not forgotten, is a guide for the future."

引例 Citations：

◎监前世之兴衰，考当今之得失，嘉善矜恶，取是舍非。（司马光《进〈资治通鉴〉表》）

（察看前代政权的兴衰，考察当今的得失，赞美善德，戒惧恶行，采纳正确做法，放弃错误做法。）

It is advisable to review the rise and fall of previous dynasties and the achievements and failures of the present dynasty, to commend the good, condemn the evil, and adopt what is right and discard what is wrong. (Sima Guang: Memorial on *History as a Mirror*)

◎知往见今，驱曹荡吴，非同小可也。（无名氏《太平宴》第一折）

（了解过去，作为现在的镜鉴，驱除和消灭曹魏、孙吴，这是了不起的事业。）

It is of great importance to review knowledge of the past to help understand the present, expel the invasion of the State of Wei and wipe out the State of Wu. (*A Peace Banquet*)

江山
/jiāngshān/

Rivers and Mountains / Country or State Power

本义指河流和山岭，代指一个国家的政权及其所覆盖的全部疆域（义同"河山"）。这种用法隐含着这样的观念：河流、山岭地形险要，是卫护国家安全、政权稳固的天然屏障；疆域是国家的构成要素。

The term, similar in meaning to *heshan* (河山), literally means rivers and mountains. It is used to refer to the sovereignty of a state and all its territory. The term has these implications: rivers and mountains provide natural barriers that protect the country and its sovereignty; territory is the key feature of a state.

引例 Citation:

◎ 割据江山，拓土万里。(《三国志·吴书·贺邵传》)

（以武力占据一方，建立政权，开拓大片疆土。）

To seize a region by force, establish a regime there, and extend its territory far and wide. (*The History of the Three Kingdoms*)

讲信修睦
/jiǎngxìn-xiūmù/

Keep Good Faith and Pursue Harmony

崇尚诚信，谋求和睦。语出《礼记·礼运》。它是战国至秦汉之际儒家学者所描述的"大同"社会的重要特征之一。儒家认为最理想的社会应当是，天下是天下人的天下，人与人之间、国与国之间应彼此信任合作，和睦相处。后"讲信修睦"不仅成为儒家所提倡的一种伦理规范，而且成为中国文化中处理人际关系和国家关系的一个重要准则。

This term, from *The Book of Rites*, means attaching great value to good faith and seeking harmonious relations, which was a key feature of the society of "universal harmony" envisioned by Confucian scholars from the Warring States Period through the Qin and Han dynasties. They believed that in an ideal society, the land should belong to all its people, and there should be mutual trust, cooperation and harmonious relations between people and between states. "Keeping good faith and pursuing harmony" subsequently became an ethical norm advocated by Confucian scholars; it later also became an important Chinese cultural norm governing relations between people and between states.

引例 Citation:

◎ 大道之行也，天下为(wéi)公。选贤与能，讲信修睦。(《礼记·礼运》)

（大道实行的时代，天下为天下人所共有。品德高尚、才能突出的人被选拔出来管理社会，人与人之间讲求诚实与和睦。）

When the Great Way prevails, the world belongs to all the people. People of virtue and competence are chosen to govern the country; honesty is valued and people live in harmony. (*The Book of Rites*)

节气
/jiéqì/

The Twenty-four Solar Terms

　　二十四节气的简称，是中国传统农历中特有的现象。古人为了能更好地进行农事活动，从长期的农业实践中总结出了一套用于指导农耕的补充历法。根据太阳一年内在黄道的位置变化以及地面相应发生的气候、物候变化情况，把一年分成二十四段，每一段起始于一个节气，分列于十二个月，这就是二十四节气。二十四节气通常均匀分布于每月，月首的叫"节"，月中的叫"气"（每三年会出现有"节"无"气"或有"气"无"节"的情况，这时需设闰月进行调节）。节气的命名反映了季节、物候、气候三方面的变化。反映季节变化的是立春、春分、立夏、夏至、立秋、秋分、立冬、冬至八个节气；反映物候变化的是惊蛰、清明、小满、芒种四个节气；反映气候变化的有雨水、谷雨、小暑、大暑、处暑、白露、寒露、霜降、小雪、大雪、小寒、大寒十二个节气。二十四节气在秦汉时期就已形成，两千多年来，既有辅助农业生产的实际功效，也成为中国人所特有的时间观念。

"The twenty-four solar terms" is a unique phenomenon on the traditional lunar calendar. To facilitate agricultural production, ancient Chinese people summarized a supplementary calendar that divides a year into 24 segments according to the sun's movement on the ecliptic and seasonal changes in weather and other natural phenomena, with the 24 solar terms proportionally distributed through the 12 months. A solar term that starts in the early part of a month is called *jie* (节), and

155

one that starts in the middle part of a month is called *qi* (气). (Every three years there would be a month which has only a *jie* without a *qi*, or a month which has only a *qi* without a *jie*, in which case a leap month would be added to regulate it.) The solar terms are so named that they represent the changes in season, phenology and climate. The eight solar terms that reflect seasonal changes are Beginning of Spring, Vernal Equinox, Beginning of Summer, Summer Solstice, Beginning of Autumn, Autumnal Equinox, Beginning of Winter, and Winter Solstice; the four solar terms that represent phenological changes are Waking of Insects, Fresh Green, Lesser Fullness, and Grain in Ear; and the 12 solar terms that indicate the changes in climate are Rain Water, Grain Rain, Lesser Heat, Greater Heat, End of Heat, White Dew, Cold Dew, First Frost, Light Snow, Heavy Snow, Lesser Cold, and Greater Cold. First established in the Qin and Han dynasties, the 24 solar periods have not only facilitated agricultural production but also reflected Chinese people's perception of time in the past more than two thousand years.

引例 Citation：

◎ 微雨众卉新，一雷惊蛰始。田家几日闲，耕种从此起。（韦应物《观田家》）

（绵绵细雨伴随百花清新，一声惊雷带来万物复苏。种田的人家哪有几日空闲，自此开始一年的耕种忙碌。）

Drizzles refresh all forms of greenery, / and thunder startles hibernators awake. / Farmers hardly have time to relax, / and tilling the soil starts now. (Wei Yingwu: Watching Farmers Working in Fields in Spring)

解衣盘礴

/jiěyī-pánbó/

Sitting with Clothes Unbuttoned and Legs Stretching Out

原指绘画时全神贯注的样子，引申指艺术家进行艺术创作时排除一切外在干扰而进入一种自由任放的精神状态。《庄子·田子方》讲述了一位画师纯任本性、解衣叉腿恣意作画的情形。"解衣"，敞开胸襟，露出胳膊；"盘（一作'般'）礴"，分开双腿，随意坐着，意谓全神贯注于作画。这一术语揭示了率性不拘、自由无待的精神状态是创作优秀艺术作品的重要条件，对于后世书画理论影响很大。

The term originally referred to the appearance of an artist who is concentrating on painting. It has been extended to mean an unrestrained state of mind free from external interruption when an artist is doing creative work. The book *Zhuangzi* describes a painter drawing freely with his clothes thrown open and legs stretching out. "To unbutton one's clothes" is to expose one's chest and arms; and "to sit with legs stretching out" indicates a casual posture while one is concentrating on painting. This term stresses the importance of a relaxed state and complete freedom of mind to the successful creation of quality artwork. This concept had significant influence on subsequent development of theories on calligraphy and painting in later generations.

引例 Citations：

◎宋元君将画图，众史皆至，受揖而立，舐笔和墨，在外者半，有一史后至，儃（tǎn）儃然不趋，受揖不立，因之舍，公使人视之，则解衣般礴，臝。君曰："可矣，是真画者也。"（《庄子·田子方》）
（昔时宋元君准备作画，所有的画师都赶来了，行礼后毕恭毕敬地站着，舔笔调墨，还有一半的人在外面等着。有一个画师来晚了，他悠闲自得，接受了旨意也不恭候站立，随即回到馆舍里去。宋元君派人去看，只见他袒胸露背，叉开腿而坐［正全神贯注作画］。宋元君说："对呀，这才是真正的画家。"）

Once when King Yuan of the State of Song was to do painting, all the painters came. Half of them, after paying him their respects, stood submissively to prepare brush-pen and ink for him. The other half were waiting outside. One painter, however, arrived late and was casual in manner. After receiving the king's instructions, he returned to his hostel instead of standing there respectfully. The king sent somebody to check on him, and he was seen sitting there painting attentively with his chest and shoulders exposed and both legs stretching out. The king exclaimed, "Yes, that is a real painter!" (*Zhuangzi*)

◎作画须有解衣盘礴、旁若无人意，然后化机在手，元气狼藉，不为先匠所拘，而游于法度之外矣。（恽格《南田画跋·题石谷为王

奉常烟客先生画册》)

(绘画必须解开衣襟、叉腿而坐[排除一切外在干扰],旁若无人,然后手上仿佛握有造化之精微,天地自然之气纵横散布,不再受先前的画匠束缚,而心神驰骋于各种技法之外。)

When doing painting, one should unbutton one's clothes, sit with legs stretching out, keep himself free from all external interruptions, and ignore spectators. That way, one is able to obtain miraculous creative power, draw inspirations from heaven, earth, and nature, go beyond the rules of previous painting masters, and freely use various painting techniques. (Yun Ge: *Nantian's Comments on Paintings*)

经济
/jīngjì/

Govern and Help the People / Economy

治理世事,救助百姓。"经世济民"的略语。"经世"即治理国家和社会事务,使之有条理;"济民"即帮助百姓,使之远离困境。"经济"是中国传统知识分子治学立世的目标和准则之所在,体现了他们学以致用、贡献国家、造福百姓的务实、民本精神。近代以降,"经济"转指创造、转化、实现价值,满足人们物质文化生活需要的社会活动等。

The term is an abbreviation of an expression meaning public governance and support for the people. *Jing* (经) means managing state and social affairs in an orderly manner; *ji* (济) means helping people who are in difficulty. This dual-pronged approach to governance is aimed at making the nation and society prosperous and ensuring that the people live in peace and contentment. The concept of *jingji* (经济) embodies the goals and principles followed by traditional Chinese intellectuals in the pursuit of scholarship and learning, and reflects their commitment to apply learning to the service of the country and for the benefit of the people. In modern times, the term is used to mean "economy," namely, social activities that create, transfer or realize value, and satisfy people's material and cultural needs.

引例 Citations：

◎而国家乃专以辞赋取进士，以墨义取诸科士，皆舍大方而趋小道，虽济济盈庭，求有才有识者十无一二，况天下危困，乏人如此，将何以救之乎？教以经济之业，取以经济之才，庶可救其不逮。（范仲淹《上仁宗答诏条陈十事》）

（朝廷专以诗赋选拔进士，以经义选拔其他科目的士子，都是舍弃了最重要的东西而追逐小技，这样选拔出的人即使济济一堂，但想寻求真有才识的人十个人中找不出一两个。况且天下形势危急，人才如此缺乏，用什么来拯救呢？将经世济民的内容教给士子，用经世济民的才能作为选拔人才的标准，只有这样或可解决人才匮乏的问题。）

The state selects talent through imperial civil service examinations solely on the basis of their literary ability and qualifies scholars only on the basis of their knowledge of the classics. This is ignoring the truly important and choosing the trivial. Even if we have an abundance of candidates, it will be hard to pick one or two competent ones out of every ten. In the current dire situation facing the empire and with paucity of talent, how can we save the country? Only by teaching scholars how to govern and help the people and by selecting talent in those areas can we hope to meet the demand for competent professionals. (Fan Zhongyan: Presentation of Ten Proposals in Response to Emperor Renzong's Proclamation)

◎古来经济才，何事独罕有？（杜甫《上水遣怀》）

（为什么治国安民的人才自古少有？）

Why is it that there have been so few people adept at governance and helping the people since ancient times? (Du Fu: Reflections While Going Upstream)

经世致用

/jīngshì-zhìyòng/

Study of Ancient Classics Should Meet Present Needs.

学术要对国家和社会的治理发挥实际效用。"经世"即治理国家和社会事务，"致用"即发挥实际效用。17世纪思想家顾炎武（1613—1682）、王夫之（1619—1692）、黄宗羲（1610—1695）、李颙（yóng，1627—1705）等人倡导学术研究要关注现实，通过解释古代典籍，阐发自己的社会政治见解，解决社会实际问题，以增进国家治理、民生安定、社会改良。这一思想强调知识的政治价值和知识分子的现实担当，体现了中国传统知识分子讲求功效、务实的思想特点和"以天下为己任"的情怀。

Learning should contribute to good governance. *Jingshi* (经世) means governance of the country and society, and *zhiyong* (致用) refers to meeting practical needs. In the 17th century, thinkers such as Gu Yanwu (1613-1682), Wang Fuzhi (1619-1692), Huang Zongxi (1610-1695), and Li Yong (1627-1705) argued that scholarly studies should be geared to meet current needs. They held that while interpreting ancient classics, scholars should expound their views on the social and political issues of their day, solve practical problems, enhance governance of the country, improve people's livelihood, and promote social reform. This view stressed the practical value of knowledge and the practical responsibilities of intellectuals. It reflects the pragmatic character of traditional Chinese intellectuals as well as their concern for the well-being of the people and eagerness to shoulder responsibility for the whole nation.

引例 Citations：

◎ 凡文之不关于"六经"之指、当世之务者，一切不为。（顾炎武《与人书·三》）

（凡是与"六经"本旨、当世要务无关的文章，一概不作。）

No articles should be written except those that are concerned with what the Six Classics teach us about the current state affairs. (Gu Yanwu: *Letters to a Friend*)

◎学人贵识时务，《奏议》皆识一时之务者也。……道不虚谈，学贵实效。学而不足以开物成务，康济时艰，真拥衾之妇女耳，亦可羞已！（李颙《二曲集》卷七）

（学者贵在通晓时务，《历代名臣奏议》中的文章都是通晓当时事务的。……道是不可以空谈的，学问贵在讲求实效。学问如果不足以揭示事物真相，确定处理事务的方法，有助于解救时局艰难，那不过是如同拥被自覆不能见人的妇女罢了，实在是可羞愧的呀！）

Scholars should value knowledge of current affairs. Essays in *Memorials to the Throne by Famous Officials Through History* should be about such affairs... There should be no empty talk on abstract theories. The value of knowledge lies in dealing with practical matters. Scholars whose studies do not reveal the essence of things or put forward ways of coping with difficult situations should feel ashamed as an uneducated woman! (Li Yong: *Collected Works of Li Yong*)

◎［先君］益自奋励，自理学及经世致用书，靡不究览。（崔述《先府君行述》）

（先父更加发奋努力，从理学到经世致用的书籍，全都详细研读。）

My late father was very diligent. He read a wide range of works, from Neo-Confucian theories to books on dealing with practical matters. There was nothing he did not study in depth. (Cui Shu: An Account of My Late Father)

精气
/jīngqì/

Vital Energy

最精致细微的"气"。对"精气"较为详细的解释，最早见于《管子》。在《管子·内业》等篇的讨论中，"精气"指"气"中最精致细微的部分，是"道"的具体呈现。一切有形之物及人类都是由"精气"构成的。此外，人的生命、精神、智慧也被看作是"精气"作用的结果。

Vital energy refers to the finest and most subtle energy. The earliest detailed explanation of vital energy is found in *Guanzi*. According to the book, the finest and most subtle energy is a concrete manifestation of Dao. All things with shapes and all human beings are made up of vital energy; one's life, sense, and intelligence are also believed to derive from vital energy.

引例 Citations:

◎ 凡物之精，此则为生。下生五谷，上为列星。流于天地之间，谓之鬼神；藏于胸中，谓之圣人。(《管子·内业》)

（大凡事物所包含的"精气"，是事物得以生成的依据。在地生成五谷，在天生成众星。"精气"流转在天地之间，便称作鬼神；藏纳于胸中，便成为圣人的智慧。）

Everything is generated by its vital energy. Vital energy produces crops on the earth and forms stars in the sky. When vital energy comes between heaven and earth, it creates ghosts and spirits; when it goes into the heart of a human being, a sage is created. (*Guanzi*)

◎ 人之所以生者，精气也，死而精气灭。(王充《论衡·论死》)

（人之所以能够生存，依赖于精气，人死而精气消亡。）

People depend on vital energy for survival. When they die, their vital energy vanishes. (Wang Chong: *A Comparative Study of Different Schools of Learning*)

静因之道

/jìngyīnzhīdào/

Governance by Being Aloof

虚静因循的为政方式。"静因之道"出自《管子》，一般被认为代表了黄老学的思想。黄老学继承了老子的"无为"思想，认为君主应避免依凭政治权力去干预百姓的生活，要以虚静的姿态因循百姓自身所固有的法则，使百姓能够按照自然的方式生存、发展。君主对待百姓的这种虚静、因循的方式，就是"静因之道"。

This term, first mentioned in *Guanzi*, refers to being aloof in exercising governance. It is regarded as representing the doctrines of the Yellow Emperor and Laozi. This school of thought built on Laozi's concept of non-action and held that a ruler should avoid using political power to interfere with the people's daily life. Rather, he should be aloof so that the people would follow their own ways and practices and live and work in a natural way.

引例 Citation：

◎ 是故有道之君，其处也若无知，其应物也若偶之，静因之道也。（《管子·心术上》）

（因此有道的君主，他自处的时候好像毫无智慧，他应对事物好像自然契合事物的固有法则，这就是"静因之道"。）

Therefore, a ruler who practices the Way (Dao), when being by himself, seems without knowledge. And he adapts to things which follow their natural course of development. This is called being aloof in governance. (*Guanzi*)

境界
/jìngjiè/

***Jingjie* (Visionary World)**

"境界"本指疆域边界、土地边界，后来在佛经翻译中，"境界"一词被用于精神领域，指人破除对于物质世界的沉迷后所达到的精神层次或修为境域。作为文艺术语，主要指文艺作品中所表现出的审美层次和境域，是作者的创造力、理解力和审美能力在精神层面的综合呈现。有境界的作品是作者真实人格的显现，具备超越凡俗的意味，更能引发读者的共鸣，激发读者的想象，甚至提升读者的感受。"意境"形成较早，而"境界"主要受中唐以后佛教思想的影响而形成。近代学者王国维（1877—1927）《人间词话》对境界的阐释最多。王国维往往将"意境"与"境界"概念通用。他构建了融合西方美学与中国古典美学为一体的"境界论"。但一般说来,意境侧重作者主观寓意与作品形象的完满融会,通过鉴赏使想象得到发挥,而境界则突出心灵感悟使艺术形象得到升华,强调心灵世界对于作品层次的提升。

Jingjie (境界) originally meant border or boundary. Later, it was used to translate the idea of a mental realm in Buddhist sutras, a state of spiritual cultivation achieved after having overcome bewilderment in the material world. As a literary and artistic term, *jingjie* is mainly used to indicate the aesthetic depth in a literary work so as to give full expression to the author's creativity, comprehension, and aesthetic faculties. A work reaching a high level of *jingjie* manifests the author's true personality, transcends the ordinary, strikes a responsive chord in the heart of the reader, stimulates the reader's imagination, and thus enhances the reader's appreciation of his work. The term *yijing* (意境 aesthetic conception) came into being earlier than *jingjie* which was formed under the influence of Buddhism in the mid-Tang period. In his *Poetic Remarks in the Human World,* modern scholar Wang Guowei (1877-1927) wrote extensively about *jingjie*. He often used *yijing* in the same sense as he used *jingjie* or the other way round. He created the theory of *jingjie*, in which he blended classical Western and classical Chinese aesthetics. Generally speaking, *yijing* refers to a perfect combination of the message the author conveys with the images he uses in his works, and it gives full rein to reader's imagination. The concept of *jingjie*, however, foregrounds the sublimation of artistic images through mental insight, and emphasizes the role of the mental world in elevating the work of art to a higher level.

引例 Citations:

◎ 山水不出笔墨情景,情景者境界也。(布颜图《画学心法问答》)
(画山水的要素无非就是用笔和墨描绘情与景,情与景融为一体就是境界。)

Painting landscapes is about depicting with brush and ink the artist's affective response to a natural scene. When the artist's sentiments interact intensely with the natural scene, a realm of what we call the visionary world is reached. (Buyantu: *How to Paint*)

◎ 言气质,言神韵,不如言境界。有境界,本也;气质、神韵,末也。有境界而二者随之矣。(王国维《〈人间词话〉删稿》)
(与其用气质、神韵做评价标准,不如用境界来评价。境界是根本,气质、神韵是末节。有了境界，气质、神韵必然也就随之出现了。）

The visionary world achieved in literary works serves as a better criterion for making critical evaluation than one's personal character or charm. The visionary world is primary, whereas one's personal character and charm are secondary. Once the visionary world is reached, personal character and charm will naturally follow. (Wang Guowei: *Poetic Remarks in the Human World* [*The Deleted Part*])

境生象外
/jìngshēngxiàngwài/

Aesthetic Conception Transcends Concrete Objects Described.

诗文中的审美意境往往在物象之外，需要鉴赏者领悟其中的精神之美。"境"指作品所创造的审美意境，"象"是作品中所呈现出的具体物象。诗歌由语言文字写成，所描写的都是一个个物象，在这些具体的物象之外，能够形成整体的审美情境。唐代诗人刘禹锡（772—842）首次提出这个命题，表达对诗歌意趣的思考，强调文字与物象是确切的，而审美情境却是微妙而难以言传的。在古典诗论意境说的形成过程中，"境生象外"是一个重要的发展阶段。

The aesthetic conception evoked by a poem or prose transcends what a physical object denotes, and a reader needs to perceive and appreciate the beauty of such aesthetic conception. *Jing* (境) here refers to an aesthetic conception created by a poem or prose, while *xiang* (象) refers to the image of a concrete object portrayed in such writing. Composed of words, a poem describes individual objects through which it evokes a coherent poetic conception beyond the physical appearance of such objects. This proposition was first put forward by poet Liu Yuxi (772-842) of the Tang Dynasty to express his understanding of poetry. He pointed out that words and images were concrete while aesthetic conceptions were abstract and subtle and therefore hard to describe. Liu's proposition, namely, aesthetic conception transcending concrete objects described, marked an important stage in the development of the theory of aesthetic conception in classical Chinese poetry.

引例 Citations:

◎ 夫境象非一，虚实难明，有可睹而不可取，景也；可闻而不可见，风也；虽系乎我形，而妙用无体，心也；义贯众象，而无定质，色也。凡此等，可以偶虚，亦可以偶实。（释皎然《诗议》）

（"境"和"象"不是同一个东西，"虚"和"实"也是难以分清。有的可以看到却不能取用，比如景致；有的可以听到却不能看到，比如风；有的虽然与我的形体有关联，而它神奇的应用却不受形体的局限，比如思想；有的其义理贯穿于万物，本身却无固定的形质，比如色彩。所有这些，可以蕴含于"虚写"，也可以蕴含于"实写"。）

Aesthetic conception and imagery are not the same thing, and it is not always easy to distinguish between what is actual and what is implied. Some things like scenery can be seen but not taken, while others such as wind can be heard but not seen. Still others are like thought: it exists in our body but is not restricted by the body. Some pervades everything but possesses no particular shape, like color. All these can be expressed concretely or indirectly by implication. (Shi Jiaoran: *Comments on Poetry*)

◎ 诗者其文章之蕴耶？义得而言丧，故微而难能。境生于象外，故精而寡和。（刘禹锡《董氏武陵集纪》）

（诗歌难道是高度凝练的文章吗？有文章的意蕴却无需那么多语言，所以非常隐微，很难写得非常好。诗的意境往往产生于所描写的物象之外，所以非常精妙，很少有人能臻于完美。）

Is poetry highly condensed prose? A poem can convey the same meaning of a prose without using many words. Therefore, poetry is implicit and subtle, an art that is hard to master. Poetic conception often transcends what is denoted by the objects described, therefore it is subtle and difficult to achieve. (Liu Yuxi: *A Preface to Dong's Notes from Wuling*)

九州
/jiǔzhōu/

Nine *Zhou* (Regions)

中国的别称。《尚书·禹贡》中将中国划分为九州，分别是冀州、兖州、青州、徐州、扬州、荆州、豫州、梁州、雍州。同时代或稍后的典籍《周礼》《尔雅》《吕氏春秋》等有关"九州"的说法大同小异。"九州"作为行政区划在历史上并未真正实行过，但它反映了春秋末期以来中华先民栖息生活的大致上的地理范围。

This term is an alternative designation for China. According to *The Book of History*, the country consisted of nine *zhou* (州), namely Jizhou, Yanzhou, Qingzhou, Xuzhou, Yangzhou, Jingzhou, Yuzhou, Liangzhou, and Yongzhou. There are similar references to the nine *zhou* in classic works of the same or later period, such as *The Rites of Zhou*, *Er Ya*, and *Master Lü's Spring and Autumn Annals*. The nine *zhou* were never adopted as actual administrative divisions of the country, but they did show the general geographical area inhabited by the Chinese people since the late Spring and Autumn Period.

引例 Citations：

◎九州生气恃风雷，万马齐喑究可哀。我劝天公重抖擞，不拘一格降人才。（龚自珍《己亥杂诗》其一百二十五）

（九州生机勃勃靠的是风雷激荡，万马齐喑的局面实在令人悲哀。我奉劝上苍定要重振精神，打破一切清规戒律降生更多人才。）

The vitality of China depends on wind and thunder, unfortunately not a single horse's neighing is heard. I urge the Lord of Heaven to once again lift his spirits and, breaking all bonds and fetters, send talent of all kinds to the human world. (Gong Zizhen: *Miscellaneous Poems Written in the Year of 1839*)

◎吾恐中国之祸，不在四海之外，而在九州之内矣。（张之洞《劝学篇·序》）

（我恐怕中国的祸患，不在中国之外，而在中国之内。）

As I see it, the cause of China's disasters lies not overseas but within the country. (Zhang Zhidong: *Exhortation to Study*)

居安思危
/jū'ān-sīwēi/

Be on Alert Against Potential Danger When Living in Peace

处在安宁的环境中，要想到可能出现的危难。历代有抱负的统治者都希望国家长治久安，常常提醒自己不要沉湎于安逸享乐，而要勤于政事，励精图治，及时化解社会矛盾，防患于未然。这是一种长远、积极的忧患意识。它不仅成为历代有为的统治阶级时时警醒自己的治政理念，而且也成为现代企业经营的重要指导原则和一般民众积极进取的一种精神。

One should always be on alert against potential danger in time of peace. All ambitious rulers in history hoped to maintain enduring stability. They often reminded themselves not to indulge in pleasure and comfort, but to conduct diligent governance, work hard to make their country prosperous, and resolve social conflicts in a timely manner so as to prevent them from developing into crises. This keen awareness of potential danger was a quality of accomplished rulers in Chinese history. This notion has also become a principle for modern enterprise management, and been adopted by common people in their pursuit of progress.

引例 Citation：

◎若能思其所以危则安矣，思其所以乱则治矣，思其所以亡则存矣。（吴兢《贞观政要·刑法》）

（如果能思考为什么会有危险，国家就安全了；想到为什么会有战乱，国家就太平了；想到为什么会有覆亡，国家就能保存了。）

If one keeps thinking about danger that could emerge, then there can be safety; if one keeps reminding oneself of the possible outbreak of war, then there can be peace; if one keeps thinking about the possible fall of the nation, then the nation can be preserved. (Wu Jing: *Important Political Affairs of the Zhenguan Reign*)

举贤容众
/jǔxián-róngzhòng/

Recommend People of Virtue and Be Magnanimous Toward the Masses

　　推举有才德的人，包容一般人。治国理政要达到良好状态，必须选拔、任用有品德、才能出众的人，但对于德行、资质都很一般的人也能放开襟怀，予以包容。这是中国传统政治思想中"尚贤"与"仁爱"精神的有机结合。

To govern a state well, the ruler must select and employ those with outstanding virtue and talent. However, he must also be tolerant and inclusive toward people of ordinary virtue and aptitude. This is a successful combination of the traditional Chinese political concepts of "exalting the worthy" and "being compassionate."

引例 Citation：

◎博学而不穷，笃行而不倦；幽居而不淫，上通而不困；礼之以和为贵，忠信之美，优游之法，举贤而容众，毁方而瓦合。（《礼记·儒行》）

（广泛学习而无止境，专心行道而不倦息；隐居独处行为不会放荡，仕途通达也能力行正道；依礼去做以和为贵，以忠信为美德，以宽和为法则。推举有才德的人而能包容德行、资质一般的人，必要时也可毁弃原则而迁就众人。）

One must learn extensively and endlessly, never be weary of the pursuit. One must never give way to licentiousness even when living in isolation and acting alone, and always follow the right paths even though smoothly promoted in officialdom. One must act in accordance with etiquette, value generosity and harmony, regard loyalty and honesty as virtue, tolerance and benevolence as benchmarks. One should recommend people with virtue and talent, and yet tolerate and be magnanimous toward those of ordinary virtue and aptitude. If necessary, one may even bend principles in order to accommodate the wishes of the general public. (*The Book of Rites*)

君

/jūn/

Lord / Nobility / Monarch

最早指包括天子、诸侯、卿、大夫等在内地位尊崇并拥有一定土地、百姓的统治者，后专指诸侯国国君和帝王。"君"的字形由"尹""口"构成，"尹"即治理，指管理国家，治理百姓；"口"即发令。古人认为，为"君"者须具备四个条件：一有"德"，即具备非凡的德行与才能；二有"命"，即秉承"天命"（上天的旨意）；三有"地"，即拥有自己的土地或领地；四有"群"，即管理"群下"（群臣、民众）并为群下所诚心归附。

Originally, the term referred to the Son of Heaven, dukes or princes, ministers, and senior officials who owned land and ruled the common people. It later referred to ducal monarchs and the emperor only. The Chinese character 君 is composed of two parts, namely, 尹 and 口. The top part 尹 means to run a country and govern its people, and the lower part 口 means to give orders. Ancient Chinese believed that a monarch or nobility must possess four qualities: first, having extraordinary virtues and be competent; second, having the mandate of heaven; third, in possession of land or manor; and fourth, having the ability to govern officials and common people, and enjoying their unfailing loyalty.

引例 Citations：

◎天子、诸侯及卿大夫有地者皆曰"君"。(《仪礼·丧服》郑玄注)

（天子、诸侯、卿、大夫，凡拥有自己领地的人，都称作"君"。）

The Son of Heaven, dukes or princes, ministers, and senior officials who own land are all regarded as the nobility or lord. (Zheng Xuan: *Annotations on The Book of Rites and Rituals*)

◎君，群也，下之所归心。(《白虎通义·三纲六纪》)

（君即群，指为群臣、民众所诚心归附。）

The lord, monarch or nobility rules over common people who pledge loyalty to their authority. (*Debates of the White Tiger Hall*)

君者善群
/jūnzhě-shànqún/

A Ruler Should Keep People Together.

　　"君"的含义就是指善于使人们凝聚成群。"君"本指君主，泛指领导者；"群"指的是由人聚合而成的社会群体。荀子（前313？—前238）认为，群居而生是人的本性，违背了这个本性，人就不能生存；而组织群众使之成为集体或社会，则是领导者的根本职能和本质规定性之所在。此术语不仅揭示了"君"与"群"的关系，而且隐含着社会与国家的构造原理。

A ruler has the duty to keep people together. According to ancient Chinese philosopher Xunzi (313?-238 BC), people by nature want to live in community. People cannot survive if they go against this nature. Keeping people together so that they form a community or a society is the fundamental duty of a ruler. This term defines the relationship between a ruler and the people, and implies the way in which a society or a state should be structured.

引例 Citation：

◎君者，善群也。群道当，则万物皆得其宜。(《荀子·王制》)
（"君"的含义就是善于使人们凝聚成群。组织社会群体的原则恰当，那么万事万物就都能得到适当的安置。）

A ruler is someone whose duty is to bring people together. If he follows this principle in organizing the people into a community, all things will fall into the right place. (*Xunzi*)

君子
/jūnzǐ/

Junzi (Man of Virtue)

　　"君子"最初用以指称人的社会身份与地位，一般指统治者和贵族男子。但自孔子（前551—前479）始，"君子"更多地被赋予了道德的意义，德行出众者被称为"君子"，反之为"小人"。在儒家传统中，"君子"成为一种介乎士和圣贤之间的人格理想，它标志着道德人格的确立。"君子"有志于追寻和实践作为价值理想的"道"，并把"道"而不是权力或利益等视为生命意义的根本。

Junzi (君子) was originally used to indicate a person's social status, generally referring to a ruler or a member of the aristocracy. Beginning with Confucius (551 - 479 BC), the term acquired an additional moral dimension and came to mean someone of true virtue. The opposite of *junzi* is *xiaoren* (小人), which roughly means the "petty man." In the Confucian tradition, *junzi* is someone who is above a scholar and below a sage in terms of moral influence. A man of virtue pursues and practices the ideal known as Dao and regards Dao as the fundamental meaning of life above power or gains.

引例 Citations：

◎君子喻于义，小人喻于利。(《论语·里仁》)
（君子知晓并遵循义，小人知晓并追逐利。）

A man of virtue understands and observes what is morally right; while a petty man only has his eyes on and goes after what brings personal gains. (*The Analects*)

◎君子，成德之名。(朱熹《论语集注》卷一)
（君子是对道德成就者的称谓。）

A man of virtue is someone who has achieved moral integrity. (Zhu Xi: *The Analects Variorum*)

君子之交
/jūnzǐzhījiāo/

Relations Between Men of Virtue

君子之间的交往。与"小人之交"相对。"君子"是品德高尚的人，他们之间的交往是因为志同道合，看似平淡，实则情深义重；"小人"是品德低下的人，他们之间的交往是为了谋取私利，表面亲密，实则利尽义绝。"君子之交"自古即为中国人所崇尚。它是"义利之辨"和"君子小人之辨"在人际交往中的体现，蕴涵着重道义、轻私利，褒君子、贬小人的健康的价值观念。

Relations between men of virtue are the opposite of those between petty men. The former are people with moral integrity and their relations are based on shared values. These relations may not seem close, but they are in fact strong and deep. The latter have low moral character and their relations are based on the pursuit of personal gains. These relations may seem intimate, but they will come to an end when nothing more is to be gained from them. Relations between men of virtue has been extolled by the Chinese since ancient times. This term distinguishes between moral integrity and pursuit of personal gains and between men of virtue and the petty men in the context of social interactions. It represents values of moral integrity possessed by men of virtue while censuring selfish pursuit of the petty man.

引例 Citations：

◎君子之交淡若水，小人之交甘若醴。君子淡以亲，小人甘以绝。（《庄子·山木》）

（君子之间的交往像水一样淡然，小人之间的交往像甜酒一样甘美。君子之间淡然却内心亲近，小人之间甜蜜却利断义绝。）

The relations between men of virtue are plain like water, while those between petty men are delicious like sweet wine. For the men of virtue the bland flavor leads to closeness; for the petty men the sweet flavor easily leads to rupture. (*Zhuangzi*)

◎君子之接如水，小人之接如醴。君子淡以成，小人甘以坏。（《礼记·表记》）

（君子之交淡如清水，小人之交甘如甜酒。君子因其淡泊 [不图私利] 而相互成就，小人因其甜美 [贪图私利] 而彼此败坏。）

The relations between men of virtue are plain like water, while those between the petty men are like sweet wine. The former helps achieve success, while the latter can only lead to discord. (*The Book of Rites*)

◎君子之交也，以道义合，以志契亲，故淡而成焉。小人之接也，以势利结，以狎慢密，故甘而败焉。（葛洪《抱朴子·疾谬》）

（君子交往，因为道义相合走到一起，因为志趣相投而亲近，所以相处淡然却能彼此成就。小人交往，因为权势、财利而结交，因亲昵不敬而密切，所以虽然亲热却彼此败坏。）

The relations between men of virtue are based on shared values and aspirations. Because of this, these men become friends. Their ties are not that close but they provide support for each other. The relations between petty men are based on connections of power and pursuit of selfish gains. These people may have intimate ties but do not really respect each other. And their relations easily go sour. (Ge Hong: *Baopuzi*)

开物成务

/kāiwù-chéngwù/

Understand Things and Succeed in One's Endeavors

揭示事物的真相并据以做成事情。"开物"即揭开事物真相，弄清事物的内在联系和规律；"成务"即根据事物的内在联系和规律，确定适当方法，把事情做好做成。这是古人从《周易》的变化规律及社会功用中所悟出的认识世界、改造世界、服务自身的思想方法和行动纲领，蕴含着朴素的科学精神。

This term means to find out the truth of things, and act accordingly to succeed in what one does. *Kaiwu* (开物) means to reveal the truth of things and understand their intrinsic relations and rules. *Chengwu* (成务) means to use proper methods to do things successfully according to their intrinsic relations and rules. This was a perception and guide to action that the ancient Chinese learned from *The Book of Changes* and everyday life, which they used to understand the world, change the world, and serve themselves. This concept represents a fundamental principle of social science.

引例 Citation:

◎夫《易》，开物成务，冒天下之道，如斯而已者也。(《周易·系辞上》)

(《易》这本书，旨在揭示万物真相，确定行事原则并做好事情，总括天下万物的基本法则，如此而已。)

The Book of Changes aims to reveal the truth of all things on earth, point out how to handle affairs, and do them right. It covers the basic rules governing all things on earth. (*The Book of Changes*)

科举

/kējǔ/

The Imperial Civil Examination System

通过分科考试选用官吏的制度。隋文帝（541—604）统一中国后，废除以门第、品级为主的选人制度。隋炀帝（569—618）大业元年（公元605年）正式开科取士。历代科举，在考试科目、内容、录取规则上均有变化。各科之中，以进士科最难，也最为士人所重。元明以后，考试内容以《四书》《五经》文句命题，答题是写一篇文章，格式为八股文，观点需以《四书章句集注》等为依据。1905年光绪皇帝（1871—1908）下诏废科举。科举制促进了贵族政治向官僚政治的转换，同时兼具教育、选官、考试、社会分层、文化传承等多种功能。它是隋朝以后1300年间中国最主要的"选举"方式，对中国社会发生的影响是极其深广的。

This is the system in which officials were selected through different levels of examinations. After Emperor Wen of the Sui Dynasty (541-604) reunified China in 581, he abolished the system of selecting officials on the basis of family background or moral character. In 605, the first year of the reign of Emperor Yang of the Sui Dynasty (569-618), the system to select officials through imperial civil examinations was officially established. From then on, examination subjects, content, and recruitment standards varied from dynasty to dynasty. The *jinshi* exam was the most difficult of imperial civil examinations, and was always the most revered by scholars. Since the Yuan and Ming dynasties, examination content had been based on the Four Books and the Five Classics and had to be answered in the form of the stereotyped "eight-part" essay and refer to *Commentaries on the Four Books* and other classics. In 1905 Emperor Guangxu of the Qing Dynasty (1871-1908) issued an edict abolishing the imperial civil examination system.

For 1,300 years since the Sui Dynasty, the imperial civil examination system was the main method for selecting officials, which had a broad and profound influence on Chinese society. It hastened the transformation of aristocracy-based politics to bureaucracy-based politics and had multiple functions such as educating people, selecting officials, choosing talent through examinations, social stratification, and carrying forward the traditional culture.

引例 Citations:

◎［宋］太宗即位，思振淹滞，谓侍臣曰："朕欲博求俊彦于科场中，非敢望拔十得五，止得一二，亦可为致治之具矣。"(《宋史·选举志一》)

（宋太宗即位后，打算给那些有德有才却久遭埋没的人提供机会，对身边的大臣说："我想通过科举考试广求德才出众的人，并不指望选上十个人就有五个人出众，只要其中有一两个出众的，就可以把科举考试作为实现政治清平的手段了。"）

Soon after Emperor Taizong of the Song Dynasty ascended the throne, he wanted to help people with both moral integrity and professional competence come to prominence, so he said to his ministers, "By recruiting remarkable people through the imperial civil examination system, I do not expect five out of ten of those recruited to excel. If one or two out of ten do, the imperial civil examination system can be used as an effective means to maintain political stability." (*The History of the Song Dynasty*)

◎科举必由学校，而学校起家，可不由科举。(《明史·选举志一》)
(科举必须经由学校，但从学校推举上来的人才，可以不经过科举考试。)

The imperial civil examination system had to be implemented through schools, but those recommended by schools to official positions do not necessarily need to take the imperial civil examinations. (*The History of the Ming Dynasty*)

克己复礼
/kèjǐ-fùlǐ/

Restrain Yourself and Follow Social Norms

克制自己的言行以符合礼的要求。出自《论语》，是孔子（前551—前479）提出的实现仁德的基本方法。孔子认为，仁德的养成应以礼为标准。个人的言行应受到外在的礼的规范，但更重要的是通过约束自身的私欲，使自己的所见、所闻、言语、行为都符合礼的要求。能够做到"克己复礼"，就达成了仁德。

Restrain your words and deeds to comply with social norms. This term comes from *The Analects*. It is the fundamental method Confucius (551 - 479 BC) recommended for achieving benevolence. According to Confucius, social norms should be the standard for cultivating benevolence. Externally, your words and deeds should be subject to social norms, but more importantly, you should restrain your own selfish desires in order to see, listen, speak, and act within such norms. Once you can "restrain yourself and practice propriety," you will have achieved benevolence.

引例 Citation：

◎颜渊问仁。子曰："克己复礼为仁。一日克己复礼，天下归仁焉。为仁由己，而由人乎哉？"(《论语·颜渊》)
(颜渊请教何谓仁。孔子说："克制自己的言行以符合礼的要求就是仁。一旦能够克制自己的言行以符合礼的要求，天下都称许你的仁德。践行仁德依赖于自己，还要依赖别人吗？")

Yan Yuan asked about benevolence. Confucius said, "To restrain yourself and practice propriety is benevolence. Once you can restrain yourself and practice propriety, everyone else will praise you for your benevolence. You must practice benevolence yourself; how can others practice it for you?" (*The Analects*)

孔颜之乐

/Kǒng-Yán zhī lè/

The Happiness of Confucius and Yan Hui

孔子（前551—前479）、颜回（前521—前481）的自得之乐。"孔颜之乐"是儒家尤其是宋明理学家所推崇的一种精神境界。常人往往不堪忍受贫困的生活，但孔子、颜回却能不受简陋的物质条件的困扰，而保持一种快乐的精神境界。"孔颜之乐"体现着对物质欲求的超越，是在对天理、人伦的深刻体认与追求中所获得的一种内在的快乐与幸福。

This term means the happiness and contentment of Confucius (551 - 479 BC) and Yan Hui (a disciple of Confucius, 521 - 481 BC). The happiness of Confucius and Yan Hui is a mental outlook admired and advocated by Confucian scholars, especially by Song and Ming Neo-Confucianists. Most people do not want to put up with poverty, but poor material conditions could not keep Confucius and Yan Hui from maintaining a happy state of mind. The expression "Happiness of Confucius and Yan Hui" embodies an inner joy and happiness obtained from the transcending of material desires and from the profound understanding and quest for principles of heaven and ethical principles.

引例 Citations：

◎子曰："饭疏食，饮水，曲肱而枕之，乐亦在其中矣。不义而富且贵，于我如浮云。"（《论语·述而》）

（孔子说："吃粗粮，喝生水，弯着手臂做枕头，也能感受到其中的快乐。靠不正当的做法获得富贵，在我看来就像浮云一样。"）

Confucius said: "If I have coarse grain to eat, cold water to drink, and my bended arm for a pillow, there is joy to be found in these things. Riches and honors acquired by unrighteous means are like floating clouds to me." (*The Analects*)

◎子曰："贤哉，回也！一箪食，一瓢饮，在陋巷，人不堪其忧，回也不改其乐。贤哉回也！"（《论语·雍也》）
（孔子说："颜回真是有贤德啊！一筐饭食，一瓢饮水，居住在简陋的巷子里，别人都忍受不了这种忧苦，颜回却不改变自己的快乐。颜回真是有贤德啊！"）

Confucius said: "Virtuous indeed is Yan Hui! He has simple meals, just drinks cold water, and lives in a humble lane. While others would find such living unbearable, Yan Hui remains cheerful. What a virtuous man!" (*The Analects*)

枯淡

/kūdàn/

Dry Plainness

指诗文作品所呈现的质朴干枯、平和清淡的艺术风格。枯淡不是枯涩寡味、平庸浅薄，而是指外表看似干枯平淡、内里丰腴醇厚的一种表现手法，旨在用质朴平淡的语言和描写来表现丰富深刻的思想内容，创造出含蓄深邃、醇厚高远的意境。北宋初期，雕琢华艳的文风盛行，梅尧臣（1002—1060）、欧阳修（1007—1072）等人倡导诗文革新，标举平淡深邃的风格，认为诗歌的根本在于性情，无需刻意而为。苏轼（1037—1101）以陶渊明（365或372或376—427）、柳宗元（773—819）的诗歌为典范，进一步提出了"枯淡"的概念。"枯淡"与"平淡""淡泊""冲淡"等概念内涵接近，是道家冲和之美与儒家典雅之美的合流。

This refers to a literary style that appears plain and dry, mild and moderate. Here, dry and plain does not mean insipid, dull, common or shallow; rather, it suggests a means of expression that, while appearing prosaic, is rich in substance within. Its aim is to convey, in plain and simple language, a message that is not lacking in breadth or profundity and to create a deep and subtle, rich and far-reaching effect. In the early years of the Northern Song Dynasty, an ornate and sumptuous style prevailed in literature. Men of letters such as Mei Yaochen (1002-1060) and Ouyang Xiu (1007-1072) argued for literary renewal and endorsed a plain and penetrating style. They held that the essence of poetry lies in authenticity and true feeling and that there was no need to be too rhetorical. With the classical examples of Tao Yuanming's (365 or 372 or 376-427) and Liu Zongyuan's (773-819) poetry in mind, Su Shi (1037-1101) went on to put forth the notion of "dry plainness." It comes close in meaning to "calm," "unassuming," or "unpretentious" – a convergence of the peaceful and profound beauty of Daoism and the elegant beauty of Confucianism.

引例 Citations:

◎所贵乎枯淡者，谓其外枯而中膏，似淡而实美，渊明、子厚之流是也。若中边皆枯淡，亦何足道。（苏轼《评韩柳诗》）

（我之所以看重枯淡，是因为它形似干枯而内里丰腴，看似平淡而实际很美，像陶渊明、柳子厚等人的诗歌就是这样。如果中间、边侧都枯淡，那还有什么可称道的呢！）

I value the style of dry plainness because it looks withered and dry outside but is rich inside; it appears plain but is in fact beautiful. Poetry by such writers as Tao Yuanming and Liu Zongyuan is like this. If inner and outer were equally dry, why praise it? (Su Shi: A Critique of Poems by Han Yu and Liu Zongyuan)

◎故观之虽若天下之至质，而实天下之至华；虽若天下之至枯，而实天下之至腴。如彭泽一派，来自天稷者，尚庶几焉，而亦岂能全合哉！（包恢《答傅当可论诗》）

（所以，看起来虽像天下最质朴的，实际上却是天下最华美的；看起来虽像天下最枯槁的，实际上却是天下最丰腴的。像陶渊明等人的诗歌，自然天成，大致达到了这种境界，然而也不能完全符合啊！）

Therefore, what seems most plain in the world is in fact the most resplendent, and what seems most dry and withered is in fact the most fruitful. Poems by people like Tao Yuanming and his followers read naturally; they more or less achieved this artistic effect, though not completely! (Bao Hui: Reply to Fu Dangke's Discussion of Poetry)

狂狷

/kuángjuàn/

Proactive Versus Prudent

激昂进取与拘谨持守。孔子以"狂"和"狷"来指称两种为人处世的态度和作风。孔子（前551—前479）认为，理想的处事方式是不偏不倚，无过或不及。而"狂"和"狷"各有所偏："狂"则激昂进取，弘扬道义而不做任何妥协；"狷"则拘谨持守，谨慎退让但不失节操。二者虽有所偏颇，但都合乎道义，皆有可取之处。

Proactive and prudent were used by Confucius (551-479 BC) to refer to two opposing attitudes and styles of behavior. Proactive persons tend to be radical and won't make any compromise in upholding moral principles and justice. Prudent persons, on the other hand, tend to be cautious and ready to make compromise but without sacrificing moral integrity. Confucius believed that the ideal conduct in life is keeping to the mean, neither going too far nor falling short. While proactive and prudent may be extreme to some extent, both have their own advantages as both adhere to moral principles and justice.

引例 Citation:

◎子曰："不得中行而与之，必也狂狷乎？狂者进取，狷者有所不为也。"（《论语·子路》）

（孔子说："不能与遵循中道的人相交，也一定要结交狂者或狷者。狂者激昂进取，狷者不做有违道义的事。"）

Confucius said, "If one cannot make friends with those who adhere to the middle way, at least be close to aspiring or uninhibited minds. The former aims high whereas the latter never violates moral laws." (*The Analects*)

厉与西施，道通为一
/lài yǔ Xīshī, dào tōng wéi yī/

A Scabby Person and the Beautiful Lady Xishi Are the Same in the Eyes of Dao.

身长癞疮的人与美丽的西施，从道的角度看都可相通为一。厉，通"癞"，指长有癞疮的人。这是庄子（前369？—前286）关于审美相对性的著名论述。原意指身长癞疮的人与著名的美女没有区别，因为她们都是"道"的产物及体现。美丑的判断只是人们主观上的感觉而已，而且美丑之间还可相互转化。庄子的这一思想，强调从造物的本原看，美丑都符合道，都具有内在的同一性。这个思想启发后世的文艺评论家从相反相成的维度去看待自然万物与文学创作。

This is a famous statement made by Zhuangzi (369?-286 BC) on how beauty is relative. Originally it meant there was no difference between a beauty and an ugly person, because they both came from and reflected Dao. The character 厉 (*lai*) meant 癞 (*lai*, covered in scabs) in ancient Chinese. Whether a person is beautiful or ugly is but a subjective perspective in the mind of the beholder. Besides, beauty can turn into ugliness, and vice versa. Zhuangzi, from the perspective of the origin of all things, stressed that beauty and ugliness are both in accord with Dao and are inherently the same. This idea has encouraged later literary critics to look at all things, including literary works, from the perspective that opposite things complement each other.

引例 Citations：

◎举莛与楹，厉与西施，恢恑（guǐ）憰（jué）怪，道通为一。（《庄子·齐物论》）

（细小的草茎与高大的庭柱，身长癞疮的人与美丽的西施，还有各种诡变怪异的事物，从道的角度来说都可相通为一。）

In the light of Dao, a small blade of grass or a tall pillar, someone as ugly as a favus patient or someone as beautiful as Lady Xishi, as well as crafty and strange things, are all the same. (*Zhuangzi*)

◎大用外腓（féi），真体内充。返虚入魂，积健为雄。（司空图

《二十四诗品·雄浑》）

（大道呈现于外显得雄浑阔大，真实的本体则充满于内。唯有返回虚静，内心才能到达浑然之境；积蓄精神力量，笔力才能雄放豪健。）

The grand appearance is an external manifestation of Dao, while the true vitality permeates itself internally. Reverting to a tranquil void, one may gain fullness and amass inner strength, and he will produce powerful works. (Sikong Tu: Twenty-four Styles of Poetry)

离形得似
/líxíng-désì/

Transcend the Outer Form to Capture the Essence

文艺创作描绘对象时要善于超越外形而捕捉其精神特征，达到高度真实。庄子（前369？—前286）认为生命的根本在于精神而非形体，应该忘记形体存在而让精神自由驰骋。晚唐诗人司空图（837—908）借鉴这一观点，认为诗歌描绘对象也要追求神似而超越形似。这一诗歌创作理念和批评术语后来也在书法、绘画领域得到贯彻。

When describing something, literary writing should be able to go beyond external appearance to capture the essence so as to reflect a high degree of reality. Zhuangzi (369?-286 BC) considered that the essence of life lies in the inner spirit rather than the physical form. One should forget one's physical existence and give full free rein to the spirit. The late Tang poet Sikong Tu (837-908) adopted this view and believed that poetic description should likewise focus on essence rather than form. This concept of poetic creation and critique was later applied in calligraphy and painting as well.

引例 Citations：

◎有生必先无离形，形不离而生亡者有之矣。（《庄子·达生》）

（生命的存在必定要以形体健全为前提，但是形体没有离开生命而生命已经死亡的人也是有的啊。）

Life exists in a physical body. However, there are people who are dead due to lack of spirit although they are alive physically. (*Zhuangzi*)

◎ 离形得似，庶几斯人。(司空图《二十四诗品·形容》)

(做到离形得似，那才是真正善于描写对象的诗人。)

He who can transcend the outer form aside and capture the essence is truly a great poet. (Sikong Tu: Twenty-four Styles of Poetry)

◎ 离形得似，书家上乘，然此中消息甚微，不可死在句下。(姚孟起《字学臆参》)

(做到离形得似，即是书法作品中的上乘之作，不过这其中的道理很微妙，不能死抠字面意思。)

The work that transcends the outer form and captures the essence is a masterpiece. However, the theory underpinning this ability is very subtle and is not to be understood mechanically. (Yao Mengqi: *Personal Reflections on the Art of Calligraphy*)

礼

/lǐ/

Li (Rites / Social Norms / Propriety)

　　社会秩序的总称，用以规范个人与他人、与天地万物乃至鬼神之间的关系。"礼"通过各种有关器物、仪式、制度的规定，明确了个人特定的身份及相应的责任、权力，从而区别了个人在社会群体中长幼、亲疏、尊卑的差等。"礼"以这样的区别来实现对个体的安顿，并由此达成人与人、人与天地万物之间的和谐。

Li (礼) is a general term for social norms which regulate an individual's relationship with other people, everything else in nature, and even ghosts and spirits. By setting various regulations about ceremonial vessels, rituals, and systems, rites define an individual's specific status and corresponding duty and power, thereby differentiating between people in a community in terms of age, kinship, and social status. With such differentiations, the rites determine the proper position of each individual, thus achieving harmony among human beings, and between humanity and everything else in nature.

引例 Citations:

◎ 夫礼，天之经也，地之义也，民之行也。(《左传·昭公二十五年》)

（礼是天地运行的法则，民众行为的规范。）

Rites are the rules governing the movement of heaven and earth as well as code of conduct for the people. (*Zuo's Commentary on The Spring and Autumn Annals*)

◎ 夫礼者，所以定亲疏、决嫌疑、别同异、明是非也。(《礼记·曲礼上》)

（礼是确定亲疏关系、决断疑惑之事、区别同异、辨明是非的依据。）

Rites are the basis for determining proper human relations, clarifying ambiguities, differentiating between things, and telling right from wrong. (*The Book of Rites*)

◎ 礼之用，和为贵。先王之道斯为美，小大由之。有所不行，知和而和，不以礼节之，亦不可行也。(《论语·学而》)

（礼的应用，以和谐为贵。古代君主的治国方法，可宝贵的地方就在这里，不论大事小事都依照"和"的原则去做。也有行不通的时候，如果仍一味为了和谐而和谐，而不用礼来加以节制，也是不可行的。）

Make harmony a top priority in the application of rites. That is a key feature that characterizes governance by sovereign rulers in ancient past. Always act upon the rule of harmony, no matter whether the issue at hand is minor or major. Sometimes, however, this rule may fail to work. If one insists on seeking harmony just for the sake of harmony instead of qualifying it with rites, then there will be no hope to succeed. (*The Analects*)

理

/lǐ/

Li

本义指玉石的纹理，引申而有三重含义：其一，指具体事物的样式或性质，如短长、大小、方圆、坚脆、轻重、白黑等物理属性；其二，指万事万物所遵循的普遍法则；其三，指事物的本原或本体。后两种含义与"道"相近。宋明时期的学者特别注重对"理"的阐发，以"理"为最高范畴，因此宋明时期占主导地位的学术体系被称为"理学"。

The original meaning of *li* (理) was the texture of jade; later it was extended to contain three meanings: 1) the physical forms or proprieties of things, such as length, size, shape, tensile strength, weight, and color; 2) the universal laws followed by all things and beings; and 3) the original source or ontological existence of things. The last two meanings are similar to those of Dao. Scholars of the Song and Ming dynasties were particularly interested in describing and explaining the philosophy known as *li* (理), and considered it as the highest realm, giving rise to the School of Principle which dominated academic thought in the period from the Song to the Ming dynasties.

引例 Citations：

◎物无妄然，必由其理。（王弼《周易略例·明象》）

（事物没有随意而为的，必然会因循其理。）

Nothing happens at random; each follows its own *li* (laws). (Wang Bi: *A Brief Exposition of The Book of Changes*)

◎有物必有则，一物须有一理。（《二程遗书》卷十八）

（每一事物的存在必有其法则，但所有事物都须有万物皆同的理。）

Everything exists according to its objective law but all things must follow the common *li* (law). (*Writings of the Cheng Brothers*)

理 趣

/lǐqù/

Philosophical Substance Through Artistic Appeal

指文学作品通过艺术形象而展示给人们的某种哲理和审美趣味，亦指读者通过对作品的阅读欣赏而领略到的其中所蕴含的哲理启示与审美趣味。魏晋南北朝出现的玄言诗崇尚玄理，宋人好以议论入诗，皆为后人诟病。因而有些诗歌评论家反对脱离艺术形象而单纯说"理"的创作理念，主张将"理"寄寓在艺术形象中，化为鲜活生动的审美趣味，所以称作理趣。这里的"理"是人生体悟，而非知识和学问，不能用逻辑概念去表达。这里的"趣"是一种审美情趣，是体悟人生哲理后的内心喜悦。"理趣说"将诗歌能否说理的争议转化为哲理与情趣相结合的理论主张，有助于辩证看待一切寄寓思考与体悟的文学作品。

This term refers to the philosophical substance of a work as well as its literary appeal conveyed to readers through its artistic image. In other words, it means the philosophical insights and aesthetic engagement that readers acquire through the process of appreciatively reading classic literary works. For example, poets of the Wei, Jin, or Southern and Northern dynasties were fond of entertaining abstruse schools of philosophy in their poems, while Song-dynasty poets often used poetry to comment on the society of their time. Both practices were treated as faults by some critics of later times. Some later critics even maintained that philosophical content should never figure into a poem apart from artistic images. Instead they insisted that the substantial content of the poem should be conveyed only by means of artistic images so that it could be grasped by readers through their appreciation of the work's artistic features, thus the term "substance through artistic appeal." *Li* (理) in this phrase refers to insights derived from the experience of life rather than bookish knowledge and learning. It is not something that can be acquired or expressed through logical argument. *Qu* (趣) refers to the aesthetic delight readers obtain when they acquire insight into life through reading classic literary works. This concept turns the dispute over whether poems could present logical arguments into a theory of the integration of reason and taste in poetic writing. It helps critics appreciate dialectically those literary works that contain both logic and insight.

引例 Citations：

◎ 盖古人于诗不苟作、不多作，而或一诗之出，必极天下之至精。状理则理趣浑然，状事则事情昭然，状物则物态宛然。（包恢《答曾子华论诗》）

（大约古人作诗，不轻易作，也不多作，只要创作一首诗，就一定追求天底下最好。说理则哲理与趣味浑然一体，叙事则事情的来龙去脉很明晰，写物则事物的形态让人感觉真切自然。）

Most likely, when writing poems, the classic poets neither wrote carelessly nor wrote many of them. Once they had decided to write a poem, they would strive to create the best work possible. As for philosophical substance, the argument and its aesthetic appeal should be well integrated; when it came to narration, the logic of the story was made perfectly clear, and descriptions were such that the thing described would appear natural and lifelike. (Bao Hui: *Letter to Zeng Zihua on Poetry*)

◎ 诗不能离理，然贵有理趣，不贵下理语。（沈德潜《清诗别裁集·凡例》）

（写诗不能背离哲理，但贵在将哲理与审美趣味融为一体，不推崇直接写出哲理。）

A poem cannot avoid philosophical content, yet it is best to integrate the argument with aesthetic appeal. Direct argument is inappropriate for poetry. (Shen Deqian: *Collection of Poems in the Qing Dynasty*)

理一分殊

/lǐyī-fēnshū/

There Is But One *Li* (Universal Principle), Which Exists in Diverse Forms.

作为最高范畴的"理"存在于不同事物之中或呈现为不同形态。"理一分殊"是宋明理学家对"理"的存在形式的一个重要理解。由于"理"

的含义不同,"理一分殊"的意义也有所差别:其一,就万物本体或本原之"理"而言,每一事物都禀受了这个"理"。每一事物之"理"并不是分有"理"的一部分,而是禀受了"理"的全部意义。其二,就万物所遵循的普遍法则而言,普遍之"理"在具体事物之中表现为不同的原理。每一事物之"理"是普遍之"理"的具体表现。"理一"保证了世界的统一性,而"分殊"则为事物的多样性与等级秩序提供了依据。

Being a supreme domain in terms of principle, *li* (理) exists in different things and manifests itself in different forms. "There is but one *li*, which exists in diverse forms" – this is an important way in which the Song- and Ming-dynasty thinkers viewed the forms in which *li* exists. As *li* has different meanings, its one-and-diverse composition is also interpreted in different ways. First, as the origin of universe in an ontological sense, *li* runs through all things. The *li* of each thing is not a part of *li*, rather, it is endowed with the full meaning of *li*. Second, representing the universal law governing all things, the universal *li* expresses itself in the form of different guiding principles in specific things. The *li* of each thing or being is a concrete expression of the universal *li*. The concept of *li* being one and same ensures unity of the world, whereas its diversity provides the basis for multifarious things and hierarchical order.

引例 Citations:

◎万物皆有此理,理皆同出一原,但所居之位不同,则其理之用不一。(《朱子语类》卷十八)

(万物都具有这个理,万物所具之理都源自一处,但其所处的情境不同,因此理的具体运用和呈现样式就有不同。)

Li (universal principle) runs through all things, which is derived from one source. But as *li* is present in different things, its functions and forms vary. (*Categorized Conversations of Master Zhu Xi*)

◎盖人物之生,受气之初,其理惟一;成形之后,其分则殊。(罗钦顺《困知记》卷上)

(人和事物在禀气初生之际,他们所具有的理是唯一的;而具有了各自的形体之后,理的具体表现又各不相同。)

When a person or thing comes into being and is endowed with *qi*, or vital force, he or it is governed by only one *li* (universal principle). However, once a person or thing gains a specific physical form, the *li* embodied expresses itself in different ways. (Luo Qinshun: *Knowledge Painfully Acquired*)

丽 辞
/lìcí/

Ornate Parallel Style

　　骈文中运用两两相对的方式遣词造句。"丽"即骈俪、对偶。单音独体汉字比较容易形成前后两句对偶的结构，对偶句具有音节配合、意义呼应的整齐美、和谐美。古人借此术语肯定了语言的形式美但又坚持形式与内容相和谐，以最终创作出文质相符、尽善尽美的作品。

The term refers to a classical Chinese literary style generally known as "parallel prose," largely composed of couplets of phrases with similar structure. Monosyllabic Chinese words, each represented with a single written character, are fairly easy to arrange in pairs of expressions with semantic symmetry and prosodic harmony. The ornate parallel style highlights the beauty of the form of the language without neglecting the harmony between form and content; and it is employed to produce fine works of utmost beauty, with form and content reinforcing each other.

引例 Citations:

◎故丽辞之体，凡有四对：言对为易，事对为难，反对为优，正对为劣。（刘勰《文心雕龙·丽辞》）

（丽辞的格式，大凡有四种：文辞的对偶容易，事典的对偶困难，事理不同而旨趣相合的对偶最佳，物类不同而意义相同的对偶最差。）

Thus, the ornate parallel style has four types of couplets: matching words, which is easy; matching facts, which is difficult; matching contrast, which is excellent; and matching sameness, which is poor. (Liu Xie: *The Literary Mind and the Carving of Dragons*)

◎若气无奇类，文乏异采，碌碌丽辞，则昏睡耳目。(刘勰《文心雕龙·丽辞》)

(如果文章在气势上并无奇异的地方，文辞上也缺乏特别精彩之处，有的只是很平常的对偶句，那就让人昏昏欲睡了。)

If a piece of writing has no original appeal, lacks imaginative polish and is full of crude and common parallel phrases, it will bore people to sleep. (Liu Xie: *The Literary Mind and the Carving of Dragons*)

利用厚生
/lìyòng-hòushēng/

Make Full Use of Resources to Enrich the People

　　充分发挥物力的效用，使民众生活富裕。古人认为，良好的政治在于"养民"，让民众生活富足。"利用"讲的是统治者应当节俭而不奢靡浪费，使物尽其用；"厚生"讲的是减轻徭役赋税，使民众生活安宁、富裕、幸福。它是中国近代民生主义、社会主义的思想渊源之一。

The ancient Chinese believed that good governance allowed people to lead a life of plenty. The ruler should be frugal, not extravagant or wasteful. He should make good use of the country's material resources, reduce the corvée and tax burdens on the people so that they could live peaceful, prosperous, and happy lives. This belief was one of the sources of advocation for the people's livelihood and socialist thinking in modern China.

引例 Citation：

◎德惟善政，政在养民……正德、利用、厚生，惟和。(《尚书·大禹谟》)

(帝王的德行要体现为良好的施政，施政要以养育民众为目的……端正德行、物尽其用、使民众富裕，这三项工作要兼顾协调，配合得当。)

A ruler should manifest his virtue in good governance, and the goal of governance is to bring a good life to the people... The ruler should act in an upright and virtuous manner, and ensure that the country's resources are put to good use and that the people live a prosperous life. These three goals complement one another. (*The Book of History*)

良知

/liángzhī/

Liangzhi (Conscience)

人天生所具有的道德本性与道德上的认识和实践能力。"良知"一词最初由孟子（前372？—前289）提出，认为人不加思虑便能知道的便是"良知"。"良知"的具体内容包括亲爱其父母、尊敬其兄长。而亲爱父母是仁，尊敬兄长是义。"良知"说是孟子性善论的重要内容。明代的王阳明（1472—1529）提出"致良知"，进一步发展了孟子的"良知"说。他认为，"良知"就是天理，一切事物及其规律都包含在"良知"之中。将"良知"扩充到底，即能达到对一切道德真理的认识和实践。

Humans are born with innate conscience and the ability to know and act upon it. The term *liangzhi* (良知) was first used by Mencius (372?- 289 BC), who believed that what man knew by instinct was *liangzhi* (knowledge of goodness). The term includes *ren* (仁), i.e. love for one's parents and *yi* (义), i.e. respect for one's elder brothers. The concept is an important component of Mencius' belief in the innate goodness of human nature. The Ming-dynasty philosopher Wang Yangming (1472-1529) raised the idea of "attaining *liangzhi*." He extended the concepts of Mencius' *liangzhi* to mean the principles of heaven, maintaining that all things under heaven and their laws were covered by *liangzhi*. With *liangzhi* being extended to its fullest (through self-cultivation and moral practice), it is possible to know and put in practice all moral truths.

引例 Citations:

◎所不虑而知者，其良知也。(《孟子·尽心上》)
(人所不加思虑便能知晓的，就是良知。)
What is known without thinking is the innate knowledge of goodness. (*Mencius*)

◎天理即是良知。(《传习录》卷下)
(天理就是良知。)
Principles of heaven and conscience are the same in essence. (*Records of Great Learning*)

两仪

/liǎngyí/

Two Modes

　　事物生成与存在的两种仪则，是用以表现"八卦"生成过程的一个易学概念。《周易·系辞上》言："《易》有太极，是生两仪，两仪生四象，四象生八卦。""太极"分化而形成相互匹配、对立的两面，即是"两仪"。就"两仪"的具体内容而言，古人有不同的理解：其一，从宇宙生成的角度来看，"两仪"或指天、地，或指阴、阳。其二，从占筮的角度来理解，"两仪"指由四十九根蓍草任意划分出的两组，或指画卦中分出的奇偶两画。

Things come into being and exist in two modes, which are used to describe how the eight trigrams are formed. As explained in *The Book of Changes*: "*The Book of Changes* involve *taiji* (太极 the supreme ultimate), which produces two modes. The two modes generate the four images, and the four images give birth to the eight trigrams." *Taiji* divides itself into two mutually complementary but opposite parts, or modes. Ancient Chinese had different views as to what the modes represented. Some believed that from the point of view of the formation of the universe, the two modes could be understood as heaven and earth or as yin and yang. Others thought that as a term in divination, the two modes could refer to two groups formed by randomly dividing up 49 yarrow stalks used in divination, or the two lines, solid or broken, in the hexagrams of *The Book of Changes*.

引例 Citations：

◎ 混元既分，即有天地，故曰"太极生两仪"。(《周易·系辞上》孔颖达正义)

(混一的元气既已分化，即形成了天与地，所以《周易》称"太极生两仪"。)

Once the primordial chaos divided itself, there came into being heaven and earth. Therefore it is said in *The Book of Changes* that taiji (the supreme ultimate) gives birth to the two modes. (Kong Yingda: *Correct Meaning of The Book of Changes*)

◎ 分阴分阳，两仪立焉。(周敦颐《太极图说》)

(分化出了阴与阳，两仪就确立了。)

When yin and yang appeared, the two modes emerged. (Zhou Dunyi: The *Taiji Diagram Explained*)

六义

/liùyì/

The Six Basic Elements

汉代学者从治理国家与社会教化角度总结《诗经》所具有的六方面意义："风"是用来阐发圣贤思想对民风的教化作用，"赋"是直陈时政善恶，"比"是以类比方式委婉批评时政的不足，"兴"是借助其他美好事物来鼓励善行，"雅"是宣扬正道并作为后世的准则，"颂"是歌颂和推广美德。"六义"原本是儒家用来阐述《诗经》创作手法的术语，后来也用它来说明一切诗歌的创作方式以及文学批评的基本原则。

The six basic elements were drawn from *The Book of Songs* by scholars of the

Han Dynasty to promote the state's governance, social enlightenment, and education. The six are: *feng* (ballad), which offers an insight into the influence of a sage's thinking on ordinary folk customs; *fu* (narrative), which directly states the goodness or evilness of court politics; *bi* (analogy), which criticizes mildly the inadequacies of court politics by comparing one thing with another; *xing* (association), which extols a virtue by making an indirect reference to some other laudable thing; *ya* (court hymn), which shows the proper way of doing things as a norm for posterity to follow; and *song* (eulogy), which praises and promotes virtue. All the six elements were originally used by Confucian scholars to expound on the creative techniques in *The Book of Songs*. Later, they were used to emphasize creative styles of all works of poetry. They also served as essential principles of literary criticism.

引例 Citation:
◎风言贤圣治道之遗化也。赋之言铺，直铺陈今之政教善恶。比，见今之失，不敢斥言，取比类以言之。兴，见今之美，嫌于媚谀，取善事以喻劝之。雅，正也，言今之正者，以为后世法。颂之言诵也、容也，诵今之德，广以美之。(《周礼·春官·大师》郑玄注)
(风是从留存的民风习俗了解圣贤的治国之道。赋是铺陈的意思，即直接陈述那些反映时政得失的事情。比是看到时政弊端，但不敢直接指斥，而以类比的方式委婉指出。兴是看到当时政治清明，担心直接赞美好似阿谀谄媚，因此借其他美好事物加以晓谕和勉励。雅是"正"的意思，讲述当今正确的做法，作为后世遵循的准则。颂是"诵"(赞颂)和"容"(仪容)的意思，即通过赞颂仪容来赞美当今君主的品德，并且推广这种美德。)

A ballad tells how to run the country via the customs and folkways that have survived through the ages. A narrative flatly states the positive and negative things in state affairs. An analogy is made when one sees a vice in court politics but dares not directly point it out; it hints at the vice by describing something similar to it. An association, in view of the clean and honest governance of the time, voices its appreciation and support through borrowing from some other commendable thing, in order to avoid arousing suspicions of unscrupulous flattery. A court hymn is related to propriety, describing something rightly done and setting norms for people of later generations to observe. A eulogy praises and promotes a reigning monarch's virtues by admiring his elegant, upright manner. (Zheng Xuan: *Annotations on The Rites of Zhou*)

龙

/lóng/

Chinese Dragon

　　传说中一种神异、祥瑞的动物，其形象综合了多种动物的特征：牛头、鹿角、虾眼、驴嘴、人须、蛇身、鹰爪等；能走、能飞、能游泳，能兴云布雨、善于变化，法力无边。它是中华民族最古老的图腾之一，秦汉以后成为帝王或皇室的象征，后又演化为汉民族及所有中国人共同的精神标记和文化符号。中国"龙"象征统合、强大、尊贵、威严、杰出、吉祥等，与西方神话传说中邪恶、贪婪的dragon有所区别。

The Chinese dragon is a mystique and auspicious animal in Chinese mythology, with its image having the features of a number of animals: bull's head, deer antlers, shrimp's eyes, donkey's mouth, human beard, snake's body, and eagle's claws. It can walk, fly, swim, and even raise clouds and make rain. It holds boundless supernatural powers and can transform itself into different creatures at will. As one of the oldest totems of the Chinese nation, the Chinese dragon became a symbol of the emperor or the imperial house after the Qin and Han dynasties. Later, it further evolved into a common spiritual and cultural symbol of the Han ethnic group and all Chinese people. In China, the dragon represents unity, power, reverence, dignity, excellence and good luck, which is quite opposite to the evil and greedy dragon in Western mythology and tradition.

引例 Citations：

◎龙，鳞虫之长。能幽能明，能细能巨，能短能长；春分而登天，秋分而潜渊。（许慎《说文解字·龙部》）

（龙，有鳞动物之首。能隐能显，能小能大，能短能长；春分时飞到天上去，秋分时潜隐在深水里。）

The most powerful among scaly animals, the Chinese dragon can hide itself or be visible, be small or huge, be short or long. At the Spring equinox it mounts into the sky, and at the Autumn equinox it hides deep in the water. (Xu Shen: *Explanation of Script and Elucidation of Characters*)

◎龙能大能小，能升能隐。大则兴云吐雾，小则隐介藏形；升则飞

腾于宇宙之间，隐则潜伏于波涛之内。……龙之为物，可比世之英雄。（罗贯中《三国演义》第二十一回）

（龙能大能小，能飞能隐。若变大，就能兴起云雾；若变小，就能隐藏形体；若高飞，则能在宇宙间飞腾；若隐藏，则能在波涛内潜伏。……龙作为一种物，可以用来类比人世间的英雄。）

A Chinese dragon can be big or small, and it can soar or hide. When big, it raises clouds and spews mist. When small, it conceals its body and becomes invisible. When soaring, it flies up in space, and when hiding, it lies low in the waves… A true hero should act just like a Chinese dragon. (Luo Guanzhong: *Romance of the Three Kingdoms*)

矛盾
/máodùn/

Paradox of the Spear and the Shield / Contradiction

可以刺穿任何东西的矛和没有任何东西能够刺穿的盾。"矛盾"之说出自《韩非子》。可以刺穿任何东西的矛和没有任何东西能够刺穿的盾，这两个命题是不相容的。一个人不能同时肯定这样两个不相容的命题。后世即以"矛盾"指称事物之间的对立关系，也意指言行自相抵触。

The term comes from a story in *Hanfeizi*. In the story, *mao* (矛) is a spear that is said to be able to pierce anything; *dun* (盾) is a shield that is said to be able to be pierced by nothing. *Mao* and *dun* are a paradox to each other, so a person cannot affirm both propositions at the same time. Later, the term came to mean "contradiction," or "inconsistency between speech and action."

引例 Citation：

◎ 楚人有鬻楯（dùn）与矛者，誉之曰："吾楯之坚，物莫能陷也。"又誉其矛曰："吾矛之利，于物无不陷也。"或曰："以子之矛，陷子

之楯，何如？"其人弗能应也。夫不可陷之楯与无不陷之矛，不可同世而立。(《韩非子·难（nàn）一》)

（有一位楚国人，既卖矛又卖盾，他夸赞自己的盾说："我的盾坚硬无比，没有任何东西能刺穿它。"又夸赞自己的矛说："我的矛非常锋利，任何东西都可以刺穿。"有人问他："那如果用你的矛刺你的盾，结果会怎么样呢？"楚国人无法回答。任何东西都无法刺穿的盾和能够刺穿一切的矛，不可能同时存在于这个世界中。）

A man from the State of Chu was selling spears and shields. He boasted about his shield, saying "It is so tough that nothing can pierce it." He then boasted about his spear, saying, "It is so sharp that it can pierce anything." Someone asked him, "What will happen if you pierce your shield using your spear?" The man was speechless. A spear that can pierce anything and a shield that can be pierced by nothing cannot exist at the same time. (*Hanfeizi*)

蒙以养正

/méngyǐyǎngzhèng/

Enlighten the Ignorant and Make Them Follow the Right Path

通过教育，使人摆脱蒙昧，归于正道（一说从童年开始就要施以正确的教育）。"蒙"即蒙昧、幼稚、无知；"养"即培养、教育；"正"即正道或端正的品性。作为中华教育智慧，"蒙以养正"揭示了教育的功能和价值。

The ignorant should be enlightened through education so that they will follow the right path. (One opinion is that this must begin from early childhood.) *Meng* (蒙 ignorance) here refers to the naivety of the young and their lack of knowledge. *Yang* (养) means education. *Zheng* (正) suggests the right path, the proper way, and upright conduct. This term, which underlies Chinese pedagogy, stresses the importance of function and value of education.

引例 Citation：

◎蒙以养正，圣功也。(《周易·彖上》)

(通过教育，使人摆脱蒙昧，归于正道，这是圣人的功业。)

Enlightening the ignorant through education so that they follow the right path – this is the achievement of sages. (*The Book of Changes*)

妙悟
/miàowù/

Subtle Insight

一种特定情境下形成的心理体验状态，在精神自由放松的状态下，直接领会、感知美，然后呈现于诗歌作品中，从而使诗歌整体的美感超越具体的语言文字，达到极高的审美层次。它能够在瞬间的心理体验中，达到物我两忘的境界，领悟诗歌的本质和永恒的精神之美。在佛、道、玄三家的义理中，"妙"指思维方面的精微玄奥，而"悟"则是一种体验式的、不依赖逻辑推理的认识方式。禅宗提倡通过禅修来达到本心清净、空灵清澈的精神境界，这种境界与文艺审美的精神境界有着密切的联系。南宋严羽（？—1264）《沧浪诗话》借用禅宗的思想，对"妙悟"在诗歌创作中的特征与功用作了充分的阐发，开创以禅喻诗的先河，影响较大。"妙悟"也影响了中国古代的绘画与书法。

This term refers to an inner experience one gains under special circumstances. When the mind is so relaxed and peaceful, it allows one to develop an intimate appreciation and understanding of beauty and then express it in a poem. The beauty of the poem thus inspired transcends words and creates an intense aesthetic experience. Subtle insight enables the reader to appreciate the essence and lasting beauty of a poem by creating a spontaneous experience so engrossing that one becomes oblivious to both himself and the outside world. According to Buddhist, Daoist, and Metaphysical principles, "subtle" refers to the minute and profound nature of thinking, whereas "insight" is an intensely personal experience derived not from logical reasoning. Chan Buddhism promotes meditation as a way to return to the mind's original tranquility and thus achieve a clear and simple state of mind. Such a state of mind comes from literary and artistic experience. In *Canglang's Criticism on Poetry*, literary critic Yan Yu (?- 1264) of the Southern Song Dynasty dealt extensively with the function and features of subtle insight in poetry writing by drawing on Chan philosophy. This book is the first one to apply Chan terms to critical writing on poetry and has thus gained great influence. The concept of subtle insight has also influenced traditional painting and calligraphy in China.

引例 Citations：

◎凝神遐想，妙悟自然，物我两忘，离形去智。(张彦远《历代名画记》卷二)

(凝聚心神，自由畅想，对自然之美的体悟达到绝妙境地，忘记了外在世界，也忘记了自身，脱离形体的束缚，抛弃知识的局限。)

By concentrating one's mind and freeing one's thoughts, one can reach such a fascinating state in appreciating the beauty of nature as to become oblivious to the outside world and one's own self, totally free from the constraints of physical forms and limitations of knowledge. (Zhang Yanyuan: *Famous Paintings Through History*)

◎大抵禅道惟在妙悟，诗道亦在妙悟。且孟襄阳学力下韩退之远甚，而其诗独出退之之上者，一味妙悟而已。(严羽《沧浪诗话·诗辨》)

(一般说来禅修最重要的原则是妙悟，作诗最重要的原则也是妙悟。比如孟浩然的学问才力远远比不上韩愈，但是孟浩然的诗却比韩愈水平高，就是因为他一心妙悟。)

Generally speaking, the most important principle of meditation is to achieve subtle insight, and this is the most important principle underlying poetry writing as well. For example, while Meng Haoran is no equal to Han Yu in terms of knowledge and talent, his poems surpass those of Han Yu because he is able to create subtle insight. (Yan Yu: *Canglang's Criticism on Poetry*)

民胞物与

/mínbāo-wùyǔ/

All People Are My Brothers and Sisters, and All Things Are My Companions.

　　世人都是我的同胞，万物都是我的同伴。北宋张载（1020—1077）认为人和万物都是天地自然之气化生的，本性相同，因此提出"民胞物与"，主张爱世上一切人和物。这一思想超越了以人类为中心的窠臼，达到了人我、物我的统一与和谐，与"厚德载物"的内在精神是一致的，是宋明理学思想的重要组成部分。

This idea was first put forward by Zhang Zai (1020 - 1077) of the Northern Song Dynasty, who held that people and things are all created by the vital force of heaven and earth, and thus are similar in nature. He advocated love for all people and things in the world, and his view transcended the old anthropocentric viewpoint and aimed to reach harmony between oneself and other human beings as well as between oneself and other creatures and things. It is the same as the idea that a true gentleman has ample virtue and cares for all things. This notion is an important part of the School of Principle of the Song and Ming dynasties.

引例 Citation：

◎ 故天地之塞，吾其体；天地之帅，吾其性。民，吾同胞；物，吾与也。（张载《西铭》）

（所以，充塞天地的[气]构成了我的形体；支配天地的[道]构成了我的本性。世人都是我的同胞，万物都是我的同伴。）

Therefore, what fills heaven and earth constitutes my body; what governs heaven and earth forms my nature. All people are my brothers and sisters, and all things are my companions. (Zhang Zai: The Western Inscription)

民惟邦本

/mínwéibāngběn/

People Are the Foundation of the State.

指民众是国家的根本或基础。只有百姓安居乐业、生活稳定，国家才能安定。最早见于古文《尚书》所载大禹的训示。这与战国时代孟子（前372？—前289）提出的"民为贵，社稷次之，君为轻"，荀子（前313？—前238）提出的"水能载舟，亦能覆舟"的思想一脉相承，并由此形成儒家所推崇的"民本"思想。

This term means that the people are the essence of the state or the foundation upon which it stands. Only when people live and work in peace and contentment can the state be peaceful and stable. This saying, which first appeared in the "Old Text" version of *The Book of History* as an instruction by Yu the Great, can be traced to Mencius' (372?-289 BC) statement: "The essence of a state is the people, next come the god of land and the god of grain (which stand for state power), and the last the ruler," and Xunzi's (313?-238 BC) statement, "Just as water can float a boat, so can water overturn it." This idea gave rise to the "people first" thought advocated by Confucianism.

引例 Citation：

◎皇祖有训：民可近，不可下。民惟邦本，本固邦宁。(《尚书·五子之歌》)

（我们的祖先大禹曾经告诫说：民众可以亲近，不能认为他们卑微。民众是国家的根本，根本稳固了国家才能安宁。）

Our ancestor Yu the Great warned: (A ruler) must maintain a close relationship with the people; he must not regard them as insignificant. They are the foundation of a state, and a state can enjoy peace only when its foundation is firm. (*The Book of History*)

民无信不立

/mín wú xìn bù lì/

Without People's Trust the State Will Not Survive.

若是得不到百姓的信任，国家政权就不会稳固。中国人自古重"信"（诚信、信任）；孔子（前551—前479）把它放在了官民关系上，并提到了事关政权稳固与否的高度。其意为：国家或国家的治理者要对百姓讲诚信，不倚仗权势而妄为，以使百姓信任自己，而百姓对自己也因此讲诚信。这是政权建立、坚固的基础和保障。它也是"民惟邦本"思想的引申表达。

Without the trust of the people, the government will not be stable. Chinese people have since antiquity put high value on "trust" (good faith). Confucius (551 - 479 BC) applied it to the relationship between officials and the people and saw it as a crucial factor in the stability of the state. What this means is that the government or the ruler should be honest in dealing with the people, not acting recklessly with force or power, so that the people will trust the authorities and act in good faith in regard to them. This is the solid basis and guarantee of state power. It is also an extension of the notion that "people are the foundation of the state."

引例 Citation：

◎子贡问政，子曰："足食，足兵，民信之矣。"子贡曰："必不得已而去，于斯三者何先？"曰："去兵。"子贡曰："必不得已而去，于斯二者何先？"曰："去食。自古皆有死，民无信不立。"（《论语·颜渊》）

（子贡问怎样治理国家。孔子说，"粮食充足，军备充足，老百姓信任统治者。"子贡说："如果不得不去掉一项，那么在三项中先去掉哪一项呢？"孔子说："去掉军备。"子贡说："如果不得不再去掉一项，那么这两项中去掉哪一项呢？"孔子说："去掉粮食。自古以来人总是要死的，如果老百姓对统治者不信任，那么国家就不能存在了。"）

Zigong asked about what was needed in governance. Confucius said, "Enough food, enough weapons and people's trust of the ruler." Zigong said, "If you had no choice but to forgo one thing, which of those three should be first?" Confucius said, "Forgo weapons." Zigong said, "If you had no choice but to forgo one thing, which of those two should be first?" Confucius said, "Forgo food. Since ancient times there has always been death, but if the people have no trust, the state does not survive." (*The Analects*)

名实
/míngshí/

Name and Substance

"实"指实存的事物，"名"指赋予事物的名号、称谓。"名"建立在"实"的基础之上，不能脱离对"实"的认识。"名"体现着人们对事物的本质及其相互关系的理解和设计。人们通过命名的方式，将万事万物纳入到一定的秩序之中。事物依据其被赋予的名号、称谓，在有秩序的整体中确立自己的地位和意义。

Shi (实) refers to an existing object, while *ming* (名) refers to a name, a title or an appellation given to an object. A name is given on the basis of substance, and it cannot be separated from the knowledge of the substance. Names give expression to people's understanding about the essence of objects and their interrelations, and the way in which they handle such interrelations. By giving names, people integrate all things and all objects into a certain order. The position and significance of an object in the whole system are determined on the basis of the name, title or the appellation given to it.

引例 Citations：

◎所以谓，名也。所谓，实也。(《墨子·经说上》)

(对实物的称谓就是"名"，所指称的对象就是"实"。)

That by which an object is called is the name. That which a name refers to is a substance. (*Mozi*)

◎物固有形，形固有名，此言不得过实，实不得延名。(《管子·心术上》)

(事物固有其形态，形态固有其名称，因此称说的名不能超过实，实不能延伸于名称所指之外。)

An object has a shape, and a shape has a name. The name must not go beyond the substance, and the substance must not extend beyond its name. (*Guanzi*)

命
/mìng/
Mandate / Destiny

最初指"天命"，即上天对人事的命令。上天根据人的德行状况对人施与奖赏或惩罚。"天命"决定着王朝的更替、国家的兴衰乃至个人的吉凶祸福，被认为是一种不可抗拒的力量。后人逐渐淡化了"命"与"天"的关联，侧重于强调"命"的不可抗拒之义，也即是命运。对人而言，"命"意味着来自外部的某种限制，标志着人力的极限，并在某种意义上体现为人的无可奈何的处境。

The earliest meaning of the term was mandate of heaven, that is, the intentions and instructions that heaven expressed to humans. The implication was that Heaven meted out rewards and punishments on human beings as their moral conduct deserved. The mandate of heaven was considered an irresistible force that determined dynastic changes, the rise and fall of nations, and even the fate of ordinary people. Later, the link with Heaven became weaker; instead, the unavoidable destiny or fate prevailed. For human beings, the term implies the external limits that determine what is possible and what is not. In one sense, it expresses the helplessness of human beings.

引例 Citations：

◎天命靡常。(《诗经·大雅·文王》)
(上天的命令没有恒常不变的。)

Heaven-bestowed supreme power is not eternal. (*The Book of Songs*)

◎知其不可奈何而安之若命。(《庄子·人间世》)

(知道没有办法可以改变，故安然处之顺应其命。)

Knowing that one cannot change his destiny, one should face things calmly and submit himself to fate. (*Zhuangzi*)

拟容取心

/nǐróng-qǔxīn/

Compare Appearances to Grasp the Essence

指诗人在采取比兴手法的时候，通过类比、描摹事物的形象外貌，摄取事物内在的意蕴和义理，从而将原本不同的事物联系、结合在一起。"拟容"说的是重视"比兴"的具体形象；"取心"说的是摄取事物的精神实质，即重视事物形象所包含的内在意蕴和理趣。合起来的意思是，借助能表达一定意义的事物形象，来寄寓、抒写作者的思想感情。见于《文心雕龙·比兴》，由《周易·系辞上》中的"拟物立象"发展而来。刘勰（465？—520？或532？）提出这一术语，主要用以阐释比、兴都是由彼及此，二者又有不同：比为"拟容"，重在贴合事理，忌不伦不类；兴为"取心"，重在感发幽微，以意相联。

This term means a poet uses the techniques of analogy and stimulation to depict the form and the external appearance of things. He takes in internal connotations and the principles of things, thus linking originally different things and combining them. *Nirong* (拟容 comparing appearances) attaches importance to specific forms for *bixing* (比兴 analogy and stimulation). While *quxin* (取心 grasping the essence) aims to get at the spirit and the essence of things, it therefore attaches importance to internal connotations and to the principles contained in the form of things. The combined meaning is that by giving expression to the form of things with a certain meaning, one may imply and express his thoughts and feelings. This notion appeared in *The Literary Mind and the Carving of Dragons*. It developed from *niwu lixiang* (拟物立象 create images through object imitation) in *The Book of*

Changes. Liu Xie (465?-520? or 532?) first used this term, mainly to explain that analogy and stimulation are inter-connected but are different: Analogy here means "comparing appearances." Staying true to the principle of things is most important, and anything far-fetched should be avoided. Stimulation means "grasping the essence," sensing the abstruse and being connected with the meaning.

引例 Citations:

◎诗人比兴，触物圆览。物虽胡越，合则肝胆。拟容取心，断辞必敢。攒杂咏歌，如川之涣。（刘勰《文心雕龙·比兴》）

（诗人在运用比兴手法的时候，能够具体周密地接触、观察事物。即使事物的差异很大，像胡、越一样遥不相及，用比兴合在一起却如同肝胆那样密切。比拟、描摹事物的外在形象，摄取事物的内在意蕴和理趣，判断和措辞一定要果断明白。把繁杂纷纭的事物用比兴纳入诗歌，文思就如同河水一样畅快流淌。）

When a poet uses analogy and stimulation, he comes into close contact with things and observes them thoroughly. Things may be quite disorganized, but when combined they tend to show themselves to be intimately linked. When comparing appearances to grasp the essence of things, one should be concise and resolute in forming judgment. When one incorporates various things in recitations and songs, they will swell and flow like a river. (Liu Xie: *The Literary Mind and the Carving of Dragons*)

◎取象曰比，取义曰兴，义即象下之意。（释皎然《诗式·用事》）

（从事物的外部形象方面着眼是"比"，从事物的内在意蕴方面着眼是"兴"，而意蕴就含在形象之中。）

Analogy means comparing the appearances of things, while association means grasping the essence of things. Meaning is what underlies the appearance. (Shi Jiaoran: *Poetic Styles*)

拟物立象
/nǐwù-lìxiàng/

Create Images Through Object Imitation

通过捕捉自然界和社会生活中具体事物的感性形象，加以模拟与提炼概括，创造出艺术家心目中独有的艺术形象。这一创作理念来源于《周易》。《周易》用设立卦象象征天下的万事万物及其变化规律，启发了文学艺术通过具体的艺术形象对自然界与人类自身进行认识与表达。这种思维方式对中国古代文学、艺术理论产生了深远的影响，孕育了意象理论的产生。

This refers to the process in which an artist creates his unique artistic representations of concrete objects, found in the natural world and social life, by mimicking, refining, and synthesizing their perceptual images. This concept for artistic creation comes from *The Book of Changes*, which uses images of hexagrams to symbolize everything in nature and their rules of change. *The Book of Changes* has inspired literature and art to make use of concrete artistic images to interpret and describe nature and human beings themselves. This mode of thinking has exerted a far-reaching influence on literary and artistic theories in ancient China, nurturing the birth of the theory of imagery.

引例 Citations：

◎ 圣人有以见天下之赜（zé），而拟诸其形容，象其物宜，是故谓之象。(《周易·系辞上》)

（圣人用《周易》卦爻来察见天下万物的奥妙，从而模拟万物的形态，象征事物之所宜，所以称之为象。）

Sages use the hexagrams and trigrams described in *The Book of Changes* to observe the subtleties of all things under heaven and determine what is fitting through the simulation of shapes in different things. Therefore it is called *xiang* (images). (*The Book of Changes*)

◎ 子曰："书不尽言，言不尽意。"然则圣人之意其不可见乎？子曰："圣人立象以尽意……"（《周易·系辞上》）

（孔子说："文字不能完全表达言语的意思，言语不能完全表达人的思想。"那么，圣人的思想难道就不可知道了吗？孔子说："圣人设立卦象就是为了全面表达他的思想……"）

Confucius says: "Writing cannot fully express what is spoken, and what is spoken cannot fully express a speaker's thoughts." Then is it ever possible to know the thoughts of a sage? Confucius says: "Sages expressed their thoughts fully through establishing images…" (*The Book of Changes*)

年

/nián/

Lunar Year / Year

在文字学意义上，"年"的本义指庄稼成熟，即年成。因庄稼大都一岁一熟，"年"渐等同于"岁"，成为历法上的时间单位（一年），后又引申指年节（春节）。在历法意义上，它是指中国传统农历（阴阳合历）的一个时间周期，平年12个月，大月30天，小月29天，全年354或355天；闰年13个月，全年383、384或385天。作为一个时间周期，它与中国古代的农业生产密切相关，反映农耕社会的时间意识和思想观念。近代以来，西方的历法（公历）传入中国，1912年为中华民国正式采用，形成了公历与农历并行的双历法系统，所以"年"现在既指农历的时间周期，也指公历的时间周期，视具体的语境而定。

In the literal sense, the Chinese character *nian* (年) means the ripening of crops. As crops are mostly harvested annually, the Chinese character *nian* has gradually come to refer to the period of one year, and later it is used to refer to the annual Spring Festival. When it comes to the calendar, it refers to the period of one year on the lunar calendar (lunisolar calendar), which has 12 months: 7 months each of 30 days and 5 months of 29 days, altogether 354 or 355 days. A leap year has 13 months, altogether 383 or 384 or 385 days a year. As a lunar calendar, it is closely related to agricultural production cycles in ancient China, and it epitomizes ancient Chinese people's awareness of time and concept in an agrarian society. The Gregorian calendar from the West was adopted by the Republic of China in 1912, ushering in a dual system of lunar and solar calendars. As a result, *nian* (year) refers to a year on the solar or lunar calendar, depending on the context.

引例 Citation:

◎年年岁岁花相似，岁岁年年人不同。(刘希夷《代悲白头翁》)
(每年繁花盛开十分相似，但是前来赏花的人却不同。)

Blossoms look the same season after season; but people enjoying the flowers look different from year to year. (Liu Xiyi: Feeling Sorry for a White-haired Old Man)

齐物
/qíwù/
See Things as Equal

破除事物之间差异与对立的一种认识态度或生活方式。庄子（前369？—前286）在《齐物论》中通过对世界的变化无常的揭示，说明差异与对立的事物之间内在相通。因此在认识层面，应该从世界的相通的本质出发，视万物齐等如一，放弃自我的立场所带来的对事物的分别与好恶。心游离于事物之外，摆脱事物的限制与影响。事物之间差异与对立的表象不再构成内心乃至生命的负担。

This refers to a worldview or lifestyle that seeks to reconcile differences and contradictions among things. In "On Seeing Things as Equal," Zhuangzi (369?-286 BC) analyzes the unpredictable nature of the world to reveal that different or opposing things are inherently interconnected. In striving to understand the world, one should therefore first of all identify the interconnectedness among all things in the world, see all as equal, and abandon personal preferences, likes and dislikes. In this way, one's heart can be above all material things and free from their constraints and influences, and the differences and contradictions among things will no longer burden one's mind or one's life.

引例 Citation：

◎故齐物而偏尚之累去矣。（郭象《庄子注》卷一）

（因此能够做到齐物，则由个人偏好所带来的各种弊端都不存在了。）

Hence if we can see all things as equal, there will be no flaws brought about by our personal preferences. (Guo Xiang: *Annotations on Zhuangzi*)

奇正
/qízhèng/

Qi or *Zheng* (Surprise or Normal)

"奇"是反常的、出其不意的，"正"是正面的、正常的。最早由《老子》提出。主要含义有二：其一，作为军事用语，指两种不同的用兵应敌的方式："正"指在了解敌方作战意图基础上的正面应敌，"奇"指隐蔽自己的作战意图，灵活地运用偷袭、设伏等手段，以达到出其不意的效果。"奇"与"正"的运用需要相互配合。"奇正"有时也被用来处理、应对日常事务。其二，作为文艺批评术语，用来称说文章思想内容上的纯正与奇诡以及文辞上的典雅与巧丽。南朝刘勰（465？—520？或532？）为了矫正齐梁时期的文坛过于重形式、片面追求新奇的弊病，将"奇正"引入文学批评。他认为，文学创作应当在思想内容上以儒家经典为依归，以文辞上的巧丽奇异为配合，只有执"正"（思想纯正）以驭"奇"（文辞巧丽），才能使文章的主旨新颖而不邪乱，词采美丽而不浮夸。后世诗歌评论及戏曲批评也用到这一术语。

Qi（奇）means surprise while *zheng*（正）means direct and normal. First advanced by Laozi, the concept has two main meanings. First, it is a military term about two opposing ways of fighting. *Zheng* means meeting the enemy head-on based on an understanding of its intention, while *Qi* means keeping one's intention to oneself and launching surprise attack and laying ambush on the enemy in order to secure surprise victory. *Zheng* and *qi* need to be applied in a coordinated way.

While a military term, *qizheng* is also used to deal with daily affairs. Second, as a term of literary and art criticism, it means an article is pure and original in terms of theme and elegant and stylish in terms of diction. Liu Xie (465?–520? or 532?) of the Southern Dynasty first introduced *qizheng* in literary criticism to oppose attaching excessive importance to form and novelty, a trend which was popular in the literary circles in the Qi and Liang dynasties. Liu Xie maintained that literary creation should be based on Confucian classics in terms of theme, to be embellished by stylish rhetoric. He believed that pure thought (*zheng*) must come before rhetoric (*qi*) so that an essay would be original in terms of theme and beautiful but unexaggerated in terms of diction. The term *qizheng* was later also used in literary criticism of poetry and opera.

引例 Citations：

◎ 以正治国，以奇用兵，以无事取天下。(《老子·五十七章》)

（以正规的方式（清静之道）治国，以奇诡的方法用兵，以不搅扰人民来治理天下。）

A state should be ruled by the normal way, fighting should be conducted in a surprised way, while ideal governance should let people handle their own affairs. (*Laozi*)

◎ 凡战者，以正合，以奇胜。故善出奇者，无穷如天地，不竭如江海。(《孙子·兵势》)

（大凡用兵作战，都是以正面应敌，以奇兵取胜。所以善于出奇的人，出奇用兵的手段像天地那样无穷无尽，像江海那样长流不竭。）

In all warfare, the direct way is to meet enemy attack head-on, but surprise attack should be launched in order to secure victory. One who is good at using surprise attack will have at his disposal a rich reservoir of such tactics as inexhaustible as Heaven and Earth and as unending as the flow of rivers and streams. (*The Art of War*)

◎ 是以将阅文情，先标六观：一观位体，二观置辞，三观通变，四观奇正，五观事义，六观宫商。(刘勰《文心雕龙·知音》)

（因此阅读和评论文章，先要标明需要考察的六个方面：一是谋篇布局，二是遣词造句，三是对前人作品风格的继承与创新，四是表现手法上的守正与新变，五是援引事例以证立论，六是音律节奏。）

Therefore, we should study and comment a literary work according to the following six criteria: structural layout of writing, choice of words to construct sentences, acceptance and innovation in the style of earlier writers, inheriting and transforming traditional ways of expression, citing examples to support an argument, and musical rhythm. (Liu Xie: *The Literary Mind and the Carving of Dragons*)

气
/qì/

Qi (Vital Force)

　　独立于主观意识之外的物质实体，是构成一切有形之物的原始物质材料，同时也是生命和精神得以发生和存在的基础。此外，某些思想家还为"气"赋予了道德属性。"气"没有具体的形状，永远处于运动变化之中。"气"的凝聚意味着事物的生成，"气"的消散意味着事物的消亡。"气"贯通于所有有形之物的内外。哲学意义上的"气"与常识性的"气体"概念不同，"气体"指各种非液体、非固体的存在；而从哲学层面来看，液体、固体既是有形之物，其生成、存在也是"气"凝聚的结果。

Qi (vital force) has a material existence independent of subjective consciousness and is the basic element of all physical beings. It is also the basis for the birth and existence of life and spirit. In addition, some thinkers have given a moral attribute to *qi*. *Qi* is in constant motion and change, and has no specific shape. Its concentration gives birth to a thing and its evaporation signals the end of that thing. *Qi* permeates all physical beings and their surroundings. *Qi*, as a philosophical concept, is different from what is commonly understood by the word *qi* (气), namely, air. Although things in liquid or solid form are different from things in air form, from the perspective of the ancient Chinese philosophy, their formation and existence are the results of the concentration of *qi*.

引例 Citations：

◎通天下一气耳。(《庄子·知北游》)
（贯通天下万物的就是一个"气"罢了。）

It is *qi* that permeates everything under heaven. (*Zhuangzi*)

◎天地合气，万物自生。(王充《论衡·自然》)
（天地之气相互交合，万物自然而生。）

The convergence of *qi* of heaven and that of earth gives life to all things. (Wang Chong: *A Comparative Study of Different Schools of Learning*)

气骨
/qìgǔ/

Qigu (Emotional Vitality and Forcefulness)

指作品的气势与骨力。多形容文学艺术作品所呈现出的刚健劲拔的精神气度和力度美。"气骨"这一术语出现于南朝，与当时的人物品评风气相呼应，用来形容诗文、书法、绘画等文学艺术作品中劲健的精神气度和内在骨力，与"风骨"含义接近，而与"风姿"（作品外在的风貌姿态）相对。

This term refers to the emotional strength and the vitality of a literary work. It was first used during the Southern Dynasties, resonating with the social practice of making comment on people. The term was used to describe the emotional vigor and forcefulness of artistic works such as poetry, essays, calligraphy, and paintings. It is similar in meaning to *fenggu* (风骨), but contrary to *fengzi* (风姿), a term meaning external elegance of an artistic work.

引例 Citations：

◎言气骨则建安为俦，论宫商则太康不逮。(殷璠（fán）《河岳英灵集·集论》)

（论气势与骨力，能与建安时期的作品相媲美；论音节与韵律，能超过太康时期的作品。）

In terms of its emotional vitality and forcefulness, the poem stands equal to works of the Jian'an Reign period; in terms of its musicality and rhythms, it surpasses the works of the Taikang Reign period. (Yin Fan: *A Collection of Poems by Distinguished Poets*)

◎ 观鲁公此帖，奇伟秀拔，奋有魏晋隋唐以来风流气骨。（黄庭坚《题颜鲁公帖》）

（观颜真卿这个法帖，奇特雄伟，秀美挺拔，全然具备魏晋隋唐以来的神韵气骨。）

This piece of calligraphy by Lord Lu (Yan Zhenqing) is amazing, vigorous, mellow, and forceful, fully illustrating the admirable emotional vitality and strength that characterized the style since the Wei, Jin, Sui and Tang dynasties. (Huang Tingjian: *Inscription on Yan Zhenqing's Calligraphy*)

气象
/qìxiàng/

Prevailing Features

原是自然界中景色物候的总称，也指某个时期社会的总体精神风貌。"气象"兼指气概、气势和景色、景物两方面而言。具体到艺术领域，指艺术作品所呈现出的风格与气概，内涵偏重于宏伟壮大，多用"雄浑""浑厚""峥嵘"等来修饰。唐代文论家们开始用"气象"一词来论述诗歌、文章的神采和风貌。从宋代起，"气象"成为文论的重要概念，用以品评诗歌、文章以及书画作品的风格与气概。"气象"往往反映特定文艺时期的精神风貌，例如盛唐气象实即盛唐时代的诗歌风貌，也与创作者个人的襟抱气度相关。

Qixiang (气象), originally a term about the general state of scenery and physical objects in nature, also refers to the prevailing features of a society in a given period of time. This description carries the meaning of great appeal and impact as well as scenery and objects. When applied to art, it refers to the overall style and appeal in a piece of artistic work. It connotes grandeur and magnificence, and is often used in conjunction with such words as "heroic," "immense," and "sublime." Literary critics of the Tang Dynasty began using the term to comment on the style and features of a poem or an essay. Since the Song Dynasty, the term has become an important concept in literary criticism, used to critique the style and artistic flair of poems, essays, calligraphy, and paintings. It is often thought to reflect the prevailing features in literature and art of a particular period. For instance, during the prime of the Tang Dynasty, the term referred to the appeal of both poems and the poets who wrote them.

引例 Citations:

◎ 盛唐诸公之诗，如颜鲁公书，既笔力雄壮，又气象浑厚。（严羽《答出继叔临安吴景仙书》）

（盛唐诸多诗人的诗作，好比颜真卿的书法作品一样，笔力既雄壮感人，气象又质朴厚重。）

Works of many poets during the prime of the Tang Dynasty struck readers with their powerful expression, just like the calligraphy of Yan Zhenqing. (Yan Yu: Letter in Reply to Uncle Wu Jingxian in Lin'an)

◎ 大凡为文当使气象峥嵘，五色绚烂，渐老渐熟，乃造平淡。（周紫芝《竹坡诗话》引苏轼语）

（一般说来，写文章应该做到气象高峻壮美，语言文采绚丽。随着作者年龄增长、阅历丰富及风格逐渐成熟，最终归于平淡自然。）

Generally speaking, one should strive to achieve an elegant style and powerful expression in writing. However, as a writer becomes more experienced with age, his writing will grow simple and natural in style. (Su Shi, as quoted in Zhou Zizhi: *Zhupo's Remarks on Poetry*)

◎ 五言律体……唯工部诸作气象嵬（wéi）峨，规模宏远。（胡应麟《诗薮·内编四》）

（就五言律诗而言……只有杜甫的作品气象高峻不凡，格局广阔深远。）

Regarding five-character-a-line verses… only Du Fu's poems possess a style that is imposing and original and a quality that is both profound and forceful. (Hu Yinglin: *An In-depth Exploration of Poetry*)

器
/qì/
Qi (Vessel)

　　实在的器物或具体的职官、身份等。"器"是有形的或可以具体描述的。每一种"器"都具有特定的形态、功用或能力。因此，"器"与"器"之间有着明确的界限和差别。但不同的"器"之中又包含着相通的"道"。"器"的存在来自于"道"且依赖于"道"。具体就人事而言，个人在自己的职分中担负着特定的责任，但又应超越具体而有限的器用，致力于对"道"的体认与遵循。

Qi (器) is a real object or a specific official, position, etc. A *qi* is something visible, or something one may describe in concrete terms. Every kind of *qi* has a specific form, function, or capability. Therefore there are clear distinctions between one *qi* and another. However, a common Dao exists in different kinds of *qi*. The existence of a *qi* is based on Dao. In terms of human affairs, an individual assumes a particular responsibility suited to his position; but he should go beyond his specific capabilities and strive to adhere to and obtain Dao.

引例 Citations：

◎形而上者谓之道，形而下者谓之器。(《周易·系辞上》)
（未成形质者称为"道"，已成形质者称为"器"。）

What is above form is called Dao, and what is under form is called "an object." (*The Book of Changes*)

◎子曰："君子不器。"(《论语·为政》)
（孔子说："君子不局限于一才一艺之用。"）

Confucius said, "A virtuous man should not possess one skill only." (*The Analects*)

217

◎朴散则为器，圣人用之则为官长。(《老子·二十八章》)

(真朴的道分散则成为各种器物，圣人善于任使不同功用的"器"，就成为百官的首长。)

Dao disperses and gives birth to tangible objects, and sages who are good at making use of objects of different functions become natural leaders of all officials. (*Laozi*)

亲亲
/qīnqīn/

Affection for One's Kin

爱亲人，尤其是爱父母。"亲亲"既指一种自然的情感，同时也指这种情感在言行上的表现。儒家主张，应将对父母、对亲人的亲爱之情，推及他人，使之成为仁德的基础。但是，过度的"亲亲"，会导致行事上的偏私。因此，儒家提出了以"义"克服"亲亲"可能存在的局限。

This term refers to love for one's kin and particularly for one's parents. It is a natural affection, and it also refers to the way in which such feeling is expressed. Confucianism holds that such a love should also be extended to others so that it will foster public virtue. Excessive affection for one's kin, however, can lead to favoritism in one's conduct. So righteousness is proposed by Confucianism as a means to curb excessive love for one's kin.

引例 Citations：

◎亲亲，仁也；敬长，义也。无他，达之天下也。(《孟子·尽心上》)

(亲爱父母，是仁；尊敬兄长，是义。行善没有其他要求，就是将亲亲、敬长推之于天下之人。)

To love one's parents is benevolent; to hold one's elder brothers in reverence is righteous. Fostering virtue requires nothing but extending one's love for his kin to all the people in the world. (*Mencius*)

◎仁者人也，亲亲为大；义者宜也，尊贤为大。亲亲之杀（shài），尊贤之等，礼所生也。(《礼记·中庸》)

（仁是人天生的本性，以亲亲为最重要的表现；义是行事合宜，以尊贤为最重要的表现。亲亲要有亲疏远近的不同，尊贤也要有差等，因此就产生了礼。）

Benevolence is the nature of man, which finds expression in one's love for his kin. Righteousness means doing the right thing on right occasions, which finds expression in one's respect for virtuous and visionary people. Love for one's kin and others should be extended in order of closeness of different relations, and the same should apply to respect to the virtuous and visionary people. This gives rise to rites. (*The Book of Rites*)

亲仁善邻
/qīnrén-shànlín/

To Be Benevolent and Friendly Towards Neighboring Countries

亲近仁德而与邻国友善。"仁"，狭义的理解指仁者即有仁德之人，广义的理解指仁德、仁义实即道德；"亲仁"表示的是对道德、正义的主动亲近与遵循；"邻"原指相邻的国家，亦可泛指近邻。这一思想最早见于《左传》，中国古人用它作为处理与相邻国家关系的重要指导原则，即邻国之间应当相互尊重、相互友好，共同构筑祥和安定的周边环境，它符合国家和民众的根本利益。从地缘政治角度看，"亲仁善邻"重视国与国之间的友好与和平，和"唇亡齿寒"有相通之处；但它又强调"亲仁"是建立"善邻"关系的基础和前提，即双方都应当共同遵循仁德。它体现了原则性和务实性相统一的国际关系理念以及中华民族崇尚"仁"与"协和万邦"的基本精神。

To be benevolent and friendly towards neighboring countries was first mentioned in *Zuo's Commentary on the Spring and Autumn Annals*. The ancient Chinese used this notion as an important guiding principle in handling relations with neighboring countries: Countries should respect and be friendly to each other, and jointly foster a benign and stable environment. This is in the fundamental interests of all countries and their people. In terms of relations among countries, the pursuit of benevolence and good-neighborliness emphasizes friendship and peace between countries and is similar to the idea that if the lips are gone, the teeth will be cold. This concept also emphasizes moral values as a basis of good-neighborly relations, that is to say, both sides should be guided by moral values in handling their relations. The concept, as applied to international relations, is one of both principle and pragmatism. It embodies the Chinese nation's pursuit of harmonious relations with other nations based on moral values.

引例 Citations:

◎亲仁善邻，国之宝也。(《左传·隐公六年》)

(亲近仁德而与邻国友善，这是国家的法宝。)

To be benevolent and friendly towards neighboring countries is fundamental policy a country should pursue. (*Zuo's Commentary on The Spring and Autumn Annals*)

◎夫亲仁善邻，古之令轨。(《魏书·许谦传》)

(亲近仁德而与邻国友善，这自古就是国家的良法。)

To be benevolent and friendly towards neighboring countries – this has been a good principle observed by our country since its early days. (*The History of Northern Wei*)

◎亲仁善邻，国之美事。其或犹豫以至用兵，夫谁所乐为也？(《元史·外夷传一·日本》)

(亲近仁德而与邻国友善，这对国家来说是好事。或许有时会有迟疑偏离，甚至于发生战争，可又有谁乐意这样做呢？)

To be benevolent and friendly towards its neighbors is obviously in the interest of a country. It is true that sometimes a country may deviate from this policy, and this may even lead to war. But surely no one wants this to happen. (*The History of the Yuan Dynasty*)

清词丽句

/qīngcí-lìjù/

Refreshing Words and Exquisite Expressions

  指立意新颖、情感真挚、物象鲜明而语言清新美妙的诗句。"清"主要针对堆砌辞藻和典故而言，不仅指词句清新自然，还指格调高雅而意境淡远；"丽"指的也不是词语本身的华丽，而是指尽脱俗气，物象鲜明而有真情。作为一个诗学术语，它实际是指包括语言风格在内的诗歌整体风格。

This term refers to verses original in theme, sincere in feeling, distinctive in image, and refreshing in diction. "Refreshing" stands opposed to ornate phrases and excessive literary quotations, and indicates both fresh and natural expressions as well as elegant style and subtle aesthetic conception. What "exquisite" indicates is not that the wording itself is resplendent, but that there is complete freedom from vulgarity, and that the imagery is sharp with real sentiments. As a poetic term, it refers to the general feature of a poem, including its linguistic style.

引例 Citation:

◎不薄今人爱古人，清词丽句必为邻。（杜甫《戏为六绝句》其五）
（学诗既要效法古代名家，也不能轻视当世才俊；一切清新自然、鲜明动人的作品，定要加以亲近揣摩。）

In writing poems, one should emulate past eminent poets. At the same time, he should not ignore contemporary talents either. Every refreshing, natural, distinct, and impressive work should be studied closely. (Du Fu: Six Playful Quatrains)

清明
/qīngmíng/
The Qingming Festival

　　中华民族四大传统节日（春节、清明节、端午节、中秋节）之一，是中国传统岁时体系中唯一与节气合一的节日，通常在4月4或5或6日。唐以前，清明主要作为二十四节气之一，反映自然时节的变化，与农事息息相关。唐宋以后，清明节取代寒食节而成为节日，寒食节原有的祭祖扫墓、吃冷食等成为清明节俗的内容。此时万物生气旺盛，人们顺应季节的变化，又有郊游踏青、插柳、放风筝、荡秋千等活动。时至今日，清明仍是中国人生活中具有特殊意义的节日。2006年5月20日，经国务院批准，清明节被列入中国第一批国家级非物质文化遗产名录。

It is one of the four major traditional festivals, namely, the Spring Festival, the Qingming Festival, the Dragon Boat Festival and the Mid-autumn Festival, that are celebrated by the Chinese. It is the only Chinese festival which occurs on one of the solar terms of the traditional calendar, usually on April 4, 5 or 6. Prior to the Tang Dynasty, Qingming functioned primarily as one of the 24 solar terms that reflected natural changes of seasons and were closely associated with timing of agricultural activities. After the Tang and Song dynasties, Qingming took the place of the Hanshi ("Cold Food") Festival, and the practices of sweeping ancestral graves and eating cold food became prominent features of the Qingming Festival. At this time of year, with the coming of spring, all living things are bursting with vitality, and people go on country outings, plant willows, fly kites and play on swings. Today, Qingming has remained a festival of special significance to the Chinese. On May 20, 2006, it was included in the first batch of the National List of Intangible Cultural Heritage by the Chinese government.

引例 Citations：

◎清明时节雨纷纷，路上行人欲断魂。借问酒家何处有？牧童遥指杏花村。（旧题杜牧《清明》）

（清明时节下着纷纷小雨，路上的行人十分惆怅。向别人询问什么地方有酒家？牧童遥遥地指向杏花村。）

In the drizzling rain of Qingming, / A traveler walks with a heavy heart. / He asks,

"Where can I find an inn?" / In response, a cowherd points to a village where apricot trees are in bloom. (Du Mu: Qingming)

◎燕子来时新社，梨花落后清明。(晏殊《破阵子》)

(燕子飞来的时候是春社，梨花飘落后就到了清明节。)

When the swallows return, it is the Spring Observance; / And after the pear blossoms fall, it is Qingming. (Yan Shu: Pozhenzi)

情
/qíng/

Qing

"情"有三种不同含义：其一，泛指人的情感、欲望。"情"受外物感动而发，是人的自然本能，不是后天习得的。其二，特指人的某些情感、欲望，通常被规定为好、恶、喜、怒、哀、乐等六者，或喜、怒、哀、惧、爱、恶、欲等七者。前者也被称作"六志"或"六情"，后者被称作"七情"。其三，指情实或实情。对于前两个意义上的"情"，历代学者持有不同态度，或主张抑制"情"，或承认"情"的合理性而加以引导和安处。

The term has three different meanings. First, it means human emotions and desires, referring to the natural and instinctive reaction to external circumstances, not a learned response. Second, it refers to specific human emotions and desires, commonly known as the six human emotions: love, hate, delight, anger, sadness, and joy, or as the seven human emotions: happiness, anger, sadness, fear, love, hatred, and desire. Third, it means the true state of affairs, or actual situation. For centuries, scholars have had different interpretations on the first two meanings. Some advocated that emotions should be restrained or controlled, while others believed that emotions and desires were natural and should be properly guided.

引例 Citations：

◎何谓人情？喜、怒、哀、惧、爱、恶、欲，七者弗学而能。(《礼记·礼运》)

(什么叫做人之情？就是喜爱、恼怒、悲哀、恐惧、爱慕、憎恶、欲求，这七者不用学习就能产生。)

What are human emotions? They are happiness, anger, sadness, fear, love, hatred, and desire which are naturally born with people. (*The Book of Rites*)

◎上好信，则民莫敢不用情。(《论语·子路》)

(地位高的人讲求诚信，则民众没有人敢不以实情相待。)

If those in high positions act in good faith, the people will not dare to conceal the truths. (*The Analects*)

情景
/qíngjǐng/

Sentiment and Scenery

指文学作品中摹写景物与抒发情感的相互依存和有机融合。"情"指作者内心的情感，"景"为外界景物。情景理论强调二者的交融，情无景不立，景无情不美。是宋代以后出现的文学术语，相对于早期的情物观念，情景理论更加重视景物摹写与情感抒发、创作与鉴赏过程的互相依赖与融为一体。

This term refers to the mutual dependence and integration of an author's description of scenery and objects, and his expression of feelings in his literary creation. *Qing* (情) is an author's inner feelings, and *jing* (景) refers to external scenery or an object. The theory of sentiment and scenery stresses integration of the two, maintaining that sentiment can hardly be aroused without scenery and that scenery or an object cannot be appreciated without sentiment. This term appeared in the Song Dynasty. Compared with earlier notions about sentiment and scenery, this one is more emphatic about fusing the depiction of scenery with the expression of feelings, and the process of creation with that of appreciation.

引例 Citations：

◎景无情不发，情无景不生。（范晞文《对床夜语》卷二）
（景物若没有情感的注入就不会出现在诗歌中，情感若没有景物的衬托就无从生发。）

Scenery has no place in poetry unless there are feelings for it; feelings cannot be stirred without the inspiration of scenery. (Fan Xiwen: *Midnight Dialogues Across Two Beds*)

◎情景名为二，而实不可离。神于诗者，妙合无垠。巧者则有情中景、景中情。（王夫之《姜斋诗话》卷二）
（情与景虽然名称上为二，但实际上不可分离。善于作诗的人，二者融合巧妙，看不出界限。构思精巧的则会有情中景、景中情。）

Sentiment and scenery seem to be two distinct things, but in fact they cannot be separated. A good poet knows how to integrate them seamlessly. An ingenious combination of sentiment and scenery means scenery embedded in sentiment and vice versa. (Wang Fuzhi: *Desultory Remarks on Poetry from Ginger Studio*)

取境

/qǔjìng/

Qujing (Conceptualize an Aesthetic Feeling)

　　指诗人在诗歌创作中，选取最能表达内心情感的物象并构思符合诗人自己的审美感受的意境。由唐代诗僧皎然（720—796？）在《诗式》中提出。皎然在总结六朝至中唐诗人的创作经验与方式时提出，作诗的时候，要精于构思，立意尽量奇特，不落俗套，在一番苦思冥想之后，灵感迸发、神完气足，才能写出境界上好的诗歌作品。虽然构思险奇，但是最终形成的作品风格要平易自然，不要显露精心思索的痕迹。取境与意境、境界等术语关系密切，属于中国古典诗论中关于"境"的术语系列。

The term means to conceptualize an aesthetic feeling by selecting images that best express a poet's sentiments and appreciation. The term *qujing* (取境) was coined by the Tang monk poet Jiaoran (720-796?) in his *Poetic Styles*. After conducting a review of how poets from the Six Dynasties to the mid-Tang Dynasty wrote poems, he concluded that to write poems, one must structure one's thoughts ingeniously so as to generate a uniquely original conception with no trace of clichés. Then, after some deep thinking, an inspiration will arise and his imagination will run free. In this way, the poet can create a poem with a fine visionary world. Although the conception may be highly original, ultimately the style of the work should be simple and natural without any traces of having been laboriously crafted. This term is closely related to the terms *jingjie* (境界) and *yijing* (意境); together, they are part of a series of terms dealing with *jing* (境) in classical Chinese poetics.

引例 Citations：

◎ 夫诗人之思，初发取境偏高，则一首举体便高；取境偏逸，则一首举体便逸。（释皎然《诗式·辩体有一十九字》）

（诗人刚开始构思的时候，如果取境偏于高迈，那么整首诗的意境就高迈；如果取境偏于飘逸，那么整首诗的意境就飘逸。）

When the poet starts to compose a poem, if his conception of the poem tends towards grandeur, then the artistic conception of the poem will be grand; if his conception of the poem is free and easy, so will the aesthetic conception of the poem be. (Shi Jiaoran: *Poetic Styles*)

◎ 夫不入虎穴，焉得虎子。取境之时，须至难至险，始见奇句。成篇之后，观其气貌，有似等闲不思而得，此高手也。（释皎然《诗式·取境》）

（不进入老虎的洞穴，就抓不住老虎的幼崽。作诗取境的时候，必须从最难最险的地方开始构思，才能创作出奇妙的诗句。全篇完成之后，再看整首诗的气势和面貌，似乎很平常像没经过思索就写成了，这才是作诗的高手。）

Without entering the tiger's den, one cannot catch a cub. When developing one's poetic conception, it is necessary to begin to contemplate what is most difficult and daring before great lines can spring to mind. After one completes a poem, one should review its overall structure and appeal. If it looks so smooth and natural as if written effortlessly, then it will be a great poem. (Shi Jiaoran: *Poetic Styles*)

趣

/qù/

Qu

  指文学艺术作品中所表现的作者的志趣、情趣、意趣等。作者的"趣"决定他们对自然、人生的独特体验和理解，以及对作品主题的选择和作品的表现风格。"趣"是作品中无形的精神韵味，通过审美活动而体现出它的价值与品位高下。

Qu is the aspirations, emotions, and interests expressed in the work of a writer or artist. His pursuit of *qu* determines his unique perception and comprehension of nature and life. It also determines what theme he chooses for his work and how he gives expression to it. *Qu* is invisible but manifests its value and appeal through aesthetic appreciation.

引例 Citations：

◎［嵇］康善谈理，又能属文，其高情远趣，率然玄远。(《晋书·嵇康传》)

（嵇康善谈玄理，又擅长写作，他情趣高雅，率真而旷远。）

Ji Kang was good at explaining profundities and writing. He had a high style and fine taste. A forthright and broad-minded man, indeed! (*The History of the Jin Dynasty*)

◎世人所难得者唯趣。趣如山上之色，水中之味，花中之光，女中之态，虽善说者不能下一语，唯会心者知之。……夫趣得之自然者深，得之学问者浅。(袁宏道《叙陈正甫〈会心集〉》)

（世人难以领悟的只有"趣"。"趣"好比山的颜色、水的味道、花的光彩、女人的姿容，即使擅长言辞的人也不能一句话说清楚，只有领会于心的人知道它。……趣，如果从自然之性中得来，那是深层次的"趣"；如果从学问中得来，往往是肤浅的"趣"。）

The only thing really hard to understand in the world is *qu*. *Qu* is like the hues of hills, the taste of water, the splendor of flowers, or the beauty of a woman. Even an eloquent person can hardly find words to put it clearly. Only those with empathy know it well… *Qu* that comes from nature is deep and mellow; if it comes from book learning, it is often shallow. (Yuan Hongdao: Preface to Chen Zhengfu's *Inspirations of the Mind*)

人道
/réndào/

Way of Man

为人之道，指人类社会必须遵循的行为规范（与"天道"相对），也是人类社会得以维持和运行的关系及法则。近代以后，西学东渐，它演变为以尊重和关爱人的生命、幸福、尊严、自由、个性发展等为原则的行为规范和权利。

The way of man refers to the code of conduct that people must observe and also the relations and norms that keep human society on the right track. The way of man stands in contrast to the way of heaven. When Western culture was introduced to China in modern times, the term gained the meaning of respect and care for people's lives, well-being, dignity, freedom, and individuality.

引例 Citations:

◎ 天道远，人道迩。(《左传·昭公十八年》)

（天之道遥远，人事之道切近。）

The way of heaven is far away; the way of man is near. (*Zuo's Commentary on The Spring and Autumn Annals*)

◎尧、舜不易日月而兴，桀、纣不易星辰而亡，天道不改而人道易也。（陆贾《新语·明诫》）

（尧、舜没有改变日月的运行而兴起，桀、纣也没有改变日月的运行而灭亡，这是因为天道没有改变而人道改变的缘故。）

The rise of Yao and Shun did not change the sun and the moon. The fall of Jie and Zhou did not change the stars. This is because the way of man does not change the way of heaven. (Lu Jia: *New Thoughts*)

人文化成

/rénwén-huàchéng/

Edify the Populace to Achieve a Harmonious Society

根据社会文明的进展程度与实际状况，用合于"人文"的基本精神和原则教化民众，引导民心向善，最终实现有差等又有调和的社会秩序。"人文"指的是诗书、礼乐、法度等精神文明的创造；"化"是教化、教导（民众）并使之改变，"成"指社会文治昌明的实现。"人文化成"的核心在于强调文治，实际上是中华"文明"理想的又一表达形式。

The term is used to describe efforts to teach people essential ideals and principles of *renwen*（人文）and guide them to embrace goodness with the aim of building a harmonious – albeit hierarchical – social order, according to the level of development of a civilization and the specifics of the society. *Renwen* refers to poetry, books, social norms, music, law, and other non-material components of civilization. *Hua*（化）means to edify the populace; *cheng*（成）refers to the establishment or prosperity of rule by civil means (as opposed to force). The concept emphasizes rule by civil means, and is another expression of the Chinese concept of "civilization."

引例 Citation：

◎观乎天文，以察时变；观乎人文，以化成天下。（《周易·彖上》）

（观察日月星辰的运行状态，可以知道四季的变换；考察诗书礼乐的发展状况，可以用来教化天下百姓，实现文治昌明。）

By observing the movement of constellations, we can learn about the change of seasons; by observing development of human culture, we can enlighten the people and build a civilized society. (*The Book of Changes*)

仁

/rén/

Ren (Benevolence)

"仁"的基本含义是爱人，进而达到人与人之间、天地万物之间一体的状态。"仁"既是道德行为的基础和依据，又是一种内在的与道德行为相应的心理意识。大体来说，"仁"有如下三重含义：其一，指恻隐之心或良心；其二，指根源于父子兄弟关系基础上的亲亲之德；其三，指天地万物一体的状态和境界。儒家将其作为最高的道德准则，并将"仁"理解为有差等的爱，即爱人以孝父母敬兄长为先，进而关爱其他家族成员，最终扩大为对天下之人的博爱。

The basic meaning of the term is love for others. Its extended meaning refers to the state of harmony among people, and the unity of all things under heaven. *Ren* (仁) constitutes the foundation and basis for moral behavior. It is also a consciousness that corresponds to the norms of moral behavior. Roughly put, *ren* has the following three implications: 1) compassion or conscience; 2) virtue of respect built upon the relationship between fathers and sons and among brothers; and 3) the unity of all things under heaven. Confucianism holds *ren* as the highest moral principle. *Ren* is taken as love in the order of first showing filial piety to one's parents and elder brothers, and then extending love and care to other members of the family, and eventually to everyone else under heaven.

引例 Citations：

◎克己复礼为仁。(《论语·颜渊》)

（克制自己的言行以符合礼的要求就是仁。）

To restrain yourself and practice propriety is benevolence. (*The Analects*)

◎仁者，爱之理，心之德也。（朱熹《论语集注》卷一）
（仁，是爱的道理，心的德性。）

Ren is the principle of love and the moral nature of human mind. (Zhu Xi: *The Analects Variorum*)

仁民爱物
/rénmín-àiwù/

Have Love for the People, and Cherish All Things

仁爱百姓，爱惜万物。这里的"物"泛指一切禽兽草木，而"爱"意思是取之有时、用之有节。它是孟子（前372？—前289）提出的一种思想。孟子认为，人类对待自己亲人的态度是亲爱，对待百姓的态度是仁爱，对待动植物的态度是爱惜，这是自然形成的情感差异。爱虽然有亲疏差等，但君子能以"亲亲"为原点，推己及人，广被万物，即由爱亲人进而仁爱百姓，进而爱惜万物。它是一种源于家族本位而又超越家族本位，甚至超越人类本位、遍及万事万物的博大的爱，是达成人自身、人与人、人与自然关系和谐完满的基本原理。张载（1020—1077）的"民胞物与"思想与此不无渊源。

The term means to have love for the people, and cherish all things in the world. Here *wu* (物) includes plants and animals, while *ai* (爱) implies using them in a measured and appropriate way. This was first proposed by Mencius (372?-289 BC) who differentiated natural emotions as: a love for close family, a broad compassion for other people, and a sense of cherishing for plants and animals. The love could be close or distant, but a person of virtue always begins with love of close relatives, which then extends to other people and eventually to all things in the world.

Though this feeling starts within the family, it should extend beyond it, even beyond the human race to include plants and animals, to become a broad love. The goal is to achieve harmony within oneself, with others and with nature. Zhang Zai's (1020-1077) concept that "all people are my brothers and sisters, and all things are my companions" is very similar.

引例 Citations：

◎ 孟子曰："君子之于物也，爱之而弗仁；于民也，仁之而弗亲。亲亲而仁民，仁民而爱物。"（《孟子·尽心上》）

（孟子说："君子对于万物，爱惜却说不上仁爱；对于百姓，仁爱却说不上亲爱。君子亲爱亲人，因而仁爱百姓；仁爱百姓，因而爱惜万物。"）

Mencius said, "Men of virtue cherish all things but this is not benevolent love, have compassion for others but this is not love of family. Men of virtue love and care for their loved ones, they are therefore kind to other people. When they are kind to people, they treasure everything on earth." (*Mencius*)

◎ 凡人之生，皆得天地之理以成性，得天地之气以成形，我与民物，其大本乃同出一源。若但知私己而不知仁民爱物，是于大本一源之道已悖而失之矣。（曾国藩《日课四条，同治十年金陵节署中日记》）

（大凡人出生时，都禀受了天地的"理"而成就本性，都得到了天地的"气"而成就形象。我与万民、万物在根本上是同出一源的。假如我只知自私自利而不知仁民爱物，那么就和我与万民万物同根同源这个道理相背离而失去自我了。）

At birth, all humans in accordance with nature's laws are bestowed with natural tendencies, and derive their forms from vital force *qi*. I come from the same origins as all people and the myriad things on earth. If I care only about my selfish interests and ignore love for all people and things, then I turn my back on our common origins, and lose my sense of self. (Zeng Guofan: On the Four Aspects of Daily Self-improvement, Diary Written at the Residence of Jinling)

仁者爱人
/rénzhě-àirén/

A Benevolent Person Loves Others.

  仁者对他人充满仁爱之心。"仁者"即有仁德的人，是有大智大勇、德行完满、关爱他人、有人格魅力和感召力的人。"仁"在孔子（前551—前479）那里是最高的道德范畴和境界，以"爱人"为基本规定，意思是"仁"从孝父母、敬兄长开始，进而关爱家族其他成员，进而扩大至全天下的人。孟子（前372？—前289）将其提炼为思想命题，并应用于治国理政，提出君子由亲爱亲人而仁爱百姓，由仁爱百姓而爱惜万物。在儒家看来，人虽然有差等，但仁爱却是普遍的。它是构建和谐、友善社会的基础和目标。

The benevolent person has a loving heart. *Renzhe* (仁者) refers to benevolent and virtuous people or people with loving hearts, who have tremendous courage, wisdom, perfect moral character, charm, and charisma, and who love and care about others. Confucianism holds *ren* (仁) as the highest moral value. The basic meaning of *ren* is loving others, and to love others, one should first show filial piety to one's parents and respect one's elder brothers, and then extend love and care to other family members, and eventually to everyone else in the world. Mencius (372?-289 BC) synthesized and upgraded this notion into a theory to be applied to the governance of a country. He proposed that a person of virtue should love and care about first his loved ones, then other people, and finally everything on earth. Confucianism believed that love could be extended to people in a certain order, but that benevolence has general value, which is both the foundation and the goal of building a harmonious and good-will society.

引例 Citations：

◎仁者爱人，有礼者敬人。爱人者，人恒爱之；敬人者，人恒敬之。(《孟子·离娄下》)

(仁者爱别人，有礼节的人尊敬别人。爱别人的人，别人总也爱他；尊敬别人的人，别人总也尊敬他。)

Benevolent people care for others, and courteous people show respect for others.

Those who care about others can always be cared about by others; those who show respect for others will always be respected by others. (*Mencius*)

◎亲亲而仁民，仁民而爱物。(《孟子·尽心上》)

(君子亲爱亲人，因而仁爱百姓；仁爱百姓，因而爱惜万物。)

Men of virtue love and care for their loved ones, they are therefore kind to other people. When they are kind to people, they treasure everything on earth. (*Mencius*)

仁者无敌

/rénzhě-wúdí/

The Benevolent Person Is Invincible.

具有仁德的人是无敌于天下的。"仁者"指具有"仁德"的君主或施行仁政的国家。"仁德"在政治层面表现为"仁政"，以仁爱作为施政的依据和出发点，善待民众，慎用刑罚，减轻赋税，最大限度地惠及百姓。如此才能赢得民众的拥护，上下一心，众志成城，无敌于天下。其基本原理是：国家强盛的深厚源泉在于赢得民心，只有善待百姓，才能获取这一源泉。

The one who is benevolent is invincible. The benevolent refers to a ruler who has the virtue of benevolence or to a state with benevolent rule. In terms of political affairs, benevolence manifests itself as benevolent governance based on love and care for the people, use of penalties with restraint, lighter taxes, and benefiting the people to the greatest extent possible. In this way, the ruler will gain the support of the people and achieve unshakeable unity of will among his subjects and himself, so that the state will be invincible. The underlying principle is that a state's source of strength lies in winning the hearts and minds of its people; if only the people are cared for, will the state be able to draw strength from this source.

引例 Citation：

◎孟子对曰："地方百里而可以王（wàng）。王如施仁政于民，省刑罚，薄税敛，深耕易耨（nòu）；壮者以暇日修其孝悌忠信，入以事其父兄，出以事其长上，可使制梃（tǐng）以挞（tà）秦楚之坚甲利兵矣。……故曰：'仁者无敌。'"（《孟子·梁惠王上》）

（孟子回答说："有方圆百里的土地就可以使天下归顺。大王如果对老百姓施行仁政，慎用刑罚，减少赋税，深耕细作，及时除草；使年壮男子能有空余时间修养自己孝顺父母、敬爱兄长、为人尽心、待人诚信的品德，在家能侍奉父母兄长，出门能侍奉尊长上级，这样即使他们拿着加工的木棒也能抗击装备精良的秦、楚军队了。……所以说：'具有仁德的人是无敌于天下的。'"）

Mencius replied, "With a territory of a hundred square *li*, it is possible for one to rule as a true king. If Your Majesty govern with benevolence, refrain from imposing harsh punishment, and lighten taxes and imposts on the people, they will plow deeply and weed thoroughly. The able-bodied will, on their days off, care for their parents, and they will show fraternal love, loyalty and good faith. At home, they will serve their fathers and brothers, and away from home, their elders and superiors. So they are able to defeat the Qin and Chu troops even with wooden sticks… That is why I believe that the benevolent person is invincible." (*Mencius*)

任人唯贤

/rènrén-wéixián/

Appoint People Only on Their Merits

　　只任用德才兼备或出众的人担任官职或赋予其某种职权,即用人只以德才为标准,而不论其与自己亲疏远近。"唯"，只。"贤"，指德才兼备或出众的人，是古人所推崇的一种理想人格。只有德才兼备或出众的人才能切实践行、维护各种社会规范，引领社会发展。选拔、任用德才兼备或出众的人，让他们在国家治理中充分发挥作用，这是实现良好治理状态的重要条件或根本保障。它是中国古人所推崇和秉持的共通的用人原则，迄今仍被作为选拔、培养、使用和管理干部的基本准则。

Appoint a person to office or position based solely on merit or outstanding ability. In other words, the criteria for giving authority to a person do not involve any kind of personal relationship. *Wei* (唯) means "solely," and *xian* (贤) means a combination of ability and moral rectitude, an ideal much sought after by the ancients. Those with these qualities are able to observe and uphold social norms and be leaders of social progress. To appoint such wise and capable people to positions of power is the basis and guarantee of good governance. Such qualities, much revered in ancient times, continue to be the basic standards for selecting, training, managing and appointing public officials today.

引例 Citations：

◎任官惟贤材，左右惟其人。(《尚书·咸有一德》)

(任命官员只任用德才兼备的人，身边大臣也应是忠良之人。)

Only those who are both capable and upright should be appointed to official positions. High officials around the ruler should be such loyal and moral people. (*The Book of History*)

◎建官惟贤，位事惟能。(《尚书·武成》)

(建立官职只任用有德才的人，安排吏事只选用有能力的人。)

Official positions should only be filled by the moral and the upright. Official affairs should only be dealt with by those who are capable. (*The Book of History*)

◎古者以天下为公，唯贤是与。(《三国志·魏书·三少帝纪》)

(在古时候，人们把天下看成是天下人共有之物，只推举德才兼备的人来治理。)

In ancient times, it was believed that everything in the country belonged to all the people, so only the upright and capable should govern. (*The History of the Three Kingdoms*)

日 新
/rìxīn/

Constant Renewal

天天更新。努力使自身不断更新，使民众、社会、国家不断更新，持续进步、完善，始终呈现新的气象。它是贯穿在"修齐治平"各层面的一种自强不息、不断革新进取的精神。

This term refers to an ongoing process of self-renewal, which also brings new life to the people, society, and the nation. This process features continuous progress and improvement. It represents a tenacious and innovative spirit that permeates all levels of "self-cultivation, family regulation, state governance, bringing peace to all under heaven."

引例 Citation：

◎ 汤之盘铭曰："苟日新，日日新，又日新。"《康诰》曰："作新民。"《诗》曰："周虽旧邦，其命惟新。"是故君子无所不用其极。（《礼记·大学》）

（[商朝的开国君主]汤的浴盆上铸刻的铭文说："如果能够一天更新自己，就应天天保持更新，更新了还要再更新。"《尚书·康诰》上说："激励民众弃旧图新，去恶向善。"《诗经》上说："周虽然是古老的国家，却禀受了新的天命。"所以君子无时无处不尽心尽力革新自己。）

"If we can improve ourselves in one day, we should do so every day, and keep building on improvement," reads the inscription on the bathtub of Tang, founder of the Shang Dynasty. "People should be encouraged to discard the old and embrace the new, give up evil ideas, and live up to high moral standards," says *The Book of History*. "Though it was an ancient state, Zhou saw its future lying in continuously renewing itself," comments *The Book of Songs*. Therefore, men of virtue should strive to excel themselves in all aspects and at all times. (*The Book of Rites*)

镕裁

/róngcái/

Refining and Deleting

对文学作品的基本内容与词句进行提炼与剪裁，使之达到更高的水准与境界。属于文学写作的基本范畴。最早由南朝刘勰（465？—520？或532？）《文心雕龙》提出。主要指作者在写作过程中，根据所要表达的内容以及文体特点，对于创作构思中的众多素材加以提炼，同时对文辞去粗存精、删繁就简，以求得最佳表现效果。这一术语既强调文学写作的精益求精，同时也彰显了文学创作是内容与形式不断完善的过程。明清时期的戏剧创作理论也颇受其影响。

This term refers to improving a literary work by refining its basic content and making the presentation concise. Refining and deleting is a basic process in literary writing. The term was first mentioned by Liu Xie (465?-520? or 532?) of the Southern Dynasties in his *The Literary Mind and the Carving of Dragons*. It means that in producing a literary work, the author should select the right elements from all the material he has, delete unnecessary parts and keep the essence, and write in a concise way to best present what he has in mind and to best suit the styles of writing. It shows that literary creation is a process of constantly striving for perfection in terms of both content and form. This idea had a great impact on the theory of theatrical writing in the Ming and Qing dynasties.

引例 Citations：

◎ 规范本体谓之镕，剪截浮词谓之裁。裁则芜秽不生，镕则纲领昭畅。（刘勰《文心雕龙·镕裁》）

（"镕"是规范文章的基本内容和结构，"裁"是删去多余的词句。经过剪裁，文章就没有多余杂乱的词句；经过提炼，文章就会纲目清楚、层次分明。）

Refining means to shape the basic content and structure of a literary work, while deleting means to cut off redundant words or sentences. Once done, the essay will be well structured, with a clear-cut theme. (Liu Xie: *The Literary Mind and the Carving of Dragons*)

◎ [谢]艾繁而不可删，[王]济略而不可益。若二子者，可谓练镕裁而晓繁略矣。（刘勰《文心雕龙·镕裁》）

（谢艾的文章用词虽然堆砌，但都是必不可少的，不能删减；王济的语言虽然简略，但能够充分表达意思，不能增加。像这两位，可以说是精通镕裁的方法，明了繁简得当的道理了。）

Xie Ai's essays are ornate in expression yet free of unnecessary sentences or words, with nothing to be deleted. Wang Ji's writing is concise in style; it sufficiently expresses an idea without the need for using more words. Men of letters like them surely command the art of refining and deleting by using a proper amount of words and expressions. (Liu Xie: *The Literary Mind and the Carving of Dragons*)

三才

/sāncái/

Three Elements

"三才"指天、地、人。《易传》在解释《易》的卦象时提出了"三才"之说。在由"—"（阳爻）、"--"（阴爻）六画所组成的一卦中，处于下位的初爻（一爻）、二爻象征地，中间的三爻、四爻象征生活在天地之间的人，上位的五爻、六爻象征天。六画统一于一卦之中，也即象征着天、地、人是一个整体。三者遵循着共通的法则，但在各自的领域中法则的具体表现有所不同。

The three elements refer to heaven, earth, and man. When explaining the trigrams, *Commentary on The Book of Changes* proposes the idea of the "three elements." In a trigram which consists of six undivided and divided lines, the first and second lines at the bottom represent earth, the third and fourth lines in the center represent man who lives between earth and heaven, and the fifth and sixth lines at the upper part represent heaven. Collectively, the six lines united in one diagram signify the whole of heaven, earth, and man. The three elements share the same rules but have different manifestations of rules in their each field.

引例 Citations：

◎是以立天之道曰阴与阳，立地之道曰柔与刚，立人之道曰仁与义。兼三才而两之，故《易》六画而成卦。(《周易·说卦》)

（所以确立天的法则为阴与阳，确立地的法则为柔与刚，确立人世的法则为仁与义。兼有象征天地人的卦画而两画一组，因此《周易》是六画构成一卦。）

So the law of heaven is governed by yin and yang; the law of earth is governed by softness and hardness; and the law of man is governed by benevolence and righteousness. Each trigram, described in *The Book of Changes*, consists of six lines with each two being a unit representing heaven, earth and man. (*The Book of Changes*)

◎《易》一物而三才备：阴阳气也，而谓之天；刚柔质也，而谓之地；仁义德也，而谓之人。（张载《横渠易说》卷三）

（《周易》一卦而具备三才：具备阴阳之气的而称之为天，具备刚柔质性的而称之为地，具备仁义品德的而称之为人。）

Each trigram in *The Book of Changes* consists of three elements: the *qi* of yin and yang representing heaven, the quality of softness and hardness representing earth, and the virtue of benevolence and righteousness representing man. (Zhang Zai: *Zhang Zai's Explanation of The Book of Changes*)

三思而行

/sānsī'érxíng/

Think Carefully Before Taking Action

　　指经过多次思考以后再去施行（"三"原指三次，但在古书中又常表示"多"）。是一种过于谨慎的处事态度。适度的思考是正当言行的前提，但如果思虑过于谨慎，则容易心生顾虑、犹豫，使对私利的关切影响对道义的遵守。《论语》记述春秋鲁大夫季文子"三思而后行",孔子（前551—前479）认为,季文子思考两次即可,不必三思。后人在使用"三思而行"一词时,或淡化其过度谨慎之义,仅用以劝诫谨慎行事,强调在言语行事之前应反复周详地思考,从而做出符合日用伦常之道的选择。

The term refers to taking action after having reflected several times (The number three is often used in ancient literature to mean several or many times). This is a kind of attitude handling things too cautiously. An appropriate measure of reflection is a prerequisite for proper speech and action, but if one becomes too cautious, then hesitation and doubt easily arise in the mind, affecting the observance of morality in the face of personal gain. *The Analects* records that Ji Wenzi, a senior official of the State of Lu in the Spring and Autumn Period, "acted having reflected thrice." Confucius (551 - 479 BC) thought that it would suffice if Ji reflected twice and that there was no need to reflect three times. When people later used the expression "thinking thrice before acting," they weakened the meaning of being too cautious, and just used it to urge caution when acting. They stressed that one should carefully reflect before speaking or acting so as to be in conformity with accepted moral standards.

引例 Citation：

◎季文子三思而后行。子闻之,曰:"再,斯可矣。"(《论语·公冶长》)

(季文子三思之后才去行事。孔子听闻后说:"思考两次就可以了。")

Ji Wenzi acted after having reflected thrice. When Confucius heard it, he remarked, "Twice is sufficient." (*The Analects*)

三省吾身

/sānxǐng-wúshēn/

Reflect on Oneself Several Times a Day

多次反省自身。"三省吾身"是儒家所主张的一种道德修养方法。儒家认为，德行的确立取决于自身的追求与努力。因此应时时反省自己的言行与内心，并以此作为修养道德的基本方法。曾子（前505—前436）特别提出，每日应从尽己为人、诚信待人、温习课业等方面多次反省自身是否存在不足，有则改之，无则加勉。

Reflecting often on what one does – this is a way of self-cultivation of virtue advocated by Confucianism. This school of thought holds that as moral integrity is established with one's efforts of self-cultivation, one needs to constantly examine his words and deeds as well as what he has in mind as a fundamental way of improving himself. Zengzi (505 - 436 BC), in particular, stresses that one should everyday reflect many times on whether he has performed duties for others, treated others with good faith and whether he has reviewed what he learned to see if there is any room for improvement.

引例 Citation：

◎ 曾子曰："吾日三省吾身：为人谋而不忠乎？与朋友交而不信乎？传不习乎？"（《论语·学而》）

（曾子说："我每天多次反省自己：为他人谋划是否未尽心竭力？与朋友交往是否不守信诺？传授的学问是否没有温习？"）

Zengzi said: "Each day I reflect on myself several times: Have I tried all my best to help someone when offering advice to him? Have I kept my word to my friends? Have I reviewed what I learned?" (*The Analects*)

三玄

/sānxuán/

Three Metaphysical Classics

《老子》《庄子》《周易》三部著作的合称。汉代五经之学盛行，魏晋时期思想大变，《老子》《庄子》《周易》为学者所关注。经由何晏（？—249）、王弼（226—249）、向秀（227？—272）、郭象（？—312）等人的注解，这些经典被赋予了新的意义。"三玄"既是魏晋名士清谈的中心内容，也是玄学家借以发挥自己哲学思想的基本素材。"三玄"之学集中探讨了个体生命与外在世界之间的矛盾，也充分展现了儒家和道家思想之间的冲突与互补。

The term refers to three metaphysical works: *Laozi, Zhuangzi,* and *The Book of Changes*. During the Han Dynasty, the study of the Five Classics was the prevailing trend; but during the Wei and Jin dynasties, the way of thinking changed considerably. Scholars turned their attention to *Laozi, Zhuangzi,* and *The Book of Changes*. The annotations by such people as He Yan (?-249), Wang Bi (226-249), Xiang Xiu (227?-272), and Guo Xiang (?-312) gave these classics new meanings. The Three Metaphysical Classics were the focus of discourse among leading scholars of the Wei and Jin dynasties, and they were regarded by scholars of metaphysic learning as a source of inspiration when they expressed their philosophical thinking. The study of the Three Metaphysical Classics focused on probing the contradiction between individual life and the outside world. It also fully demonstrated conflict and complementarity between the thinking of Confucian and Daoist scholars.

引例 Citation：

◎洎（jì）于梁世，兹风复阐，《庄》《老》《周易》，总谓"三玄"。（颜之推《颜氏家训·勉学》）

（到了梁代，这一风气再次获得阐扬，《庄子》《老子》《周易》三部著作，总称为"三玄"。）

In the Liang Dynasty, there was a renewed interest in the study of *Zhuangzi, Laozi,* and *The Book of Changes*, which were collectively referred to as the Three Metaphysical Classics. (Yan Zhitui: *Admonitions for the Yan Clan*)

山水诗

/shānshuǐshī/

Landscape Poetry

　　一种以描写山水名胜为主要题材的诗歌流派。主要摹写自然山川的秀美壮丽并借以抒发闲情逸致，特点是写景状物逼真细致，语言表达富丽清新。东晋时期，南渡的士大夫在自然山水中寻求精神抚慰和解脱，激发了山水诗创作的灵感。其开创者是晋末宋初的大诗人谢灵运（385—433），他把自然美景引入诗歌创作，将诗歌从枯燥乏味的玄理中解放出来，后经谢朓（tiǎo，464—499）、何逊（？—518？）、阴铿等人的创作实践而逐步成为诗歌史上的一个重要诗派。到唐代特别是盛唐时期，山水诗的创作更是蔚为大观，涌现出王维（701？—761）、孟浩然（689—740）等著名山水诗人，中唐时期的刘长卿（？—789？）、韦应物（737？—791）、柳宗元（773—819）等人的创作也有特色。山水诗开启了新的诗歌风貌，标志着一种新的审美观念的产生。

Landscape poetry, as the name suggests, describes the beauty and charm of natural scenery, and landscape poets express their emotions through extolling the enchanting scenery. Landscape poetry is characterized by vivid description of sights with rich and refreshing language. During the Eastern Jin Dynasty, scholars who had fled war-torn homes in the north sought solace and escape in nature in the south, and this found expression in poetic description of mountain and river scenes. Xie Lingyun (385-433), a great poet of the late Eastern Jin and early Song Dynasty of the Southern Dynasties, created this poetic style. He introduced the depiction of natural beauty into poetry writing, freeing poetry from bland and insipid moral preaching. Further developed by Xie Tiao (464-499), He Xun (?-518?), Yin Keng, and others, landscape poetry became an important literary school. It gained prominence in the Tang Dynasty, especially in the prime of Tang, during which such landscape poets like Wang Wei (701?-761) and Meng Haoran (689-740) distinguished themselves. Mid-Tang poets including Liu Changqing (?-789?), Wei Yingwu (737?-791), and Liu Zongyuan (773-819) also became famous for writing landscape poems. This gave rise to a new form of expression in poetry and a new trend of aesthetic appreciation.

引例 Citation：

◎宋初文咏，体有因革。庄老告退，而山水方滋；俪采百字之偶，争价一句之奇，情必极貌以写物，辞必穷力而追新，此近世之所竞也。（刘勰《文心雕龙·明诗》）

（[南朝]宋初期的诗文，风格上有继承有变革，表现老庄思想的玄言诗退出诗坛，而山水诗正在崛起；文人用数百字的骈偶堆砌辞藻，为了某一句的新奇而攀比争胜，描绘外物务求穷形极胜，遣词造句必定竭力追求新异，这就是近代人们所竞相追逐的目标。）

The literature and poetry of the early Song Dynasty of the Southern Dynasties saw some changing trend: metaphysical poetry implicating Laozi and Zhuangzi's thoughts declined and landscape poetry gained in popularity. Poets sometimes used a few hundred words of parallel prose just to describe a scene, or competed with each other in writing an unusual line. In describing scenes, they tried to depict every detail; in composing a literary work, they racked their brains to achieve what is unusual. This has become the current trend in literary writing. (Liu Xie: *The Literary Mind and the Carving of Dragons*)

上兵伐谋

/shàngbīng-fámóu/

The Best Strategy in Warfare is to Foil the Enemy's Strategy.

　　用兵的上策是挫败敌方的计谋。是古代军事家孙武提出的一条军事原则。在孙武看来，军事斗争是在不同层面展开的。不同层面的斗争都可以对战争胜败产生重要的影响。其中，武力攻伐对于双方都会造成极大的伤害，因此是不得已的选择。善于用兵之人应在武力斗争发动之前，运用谋略破除敌人的进攻威胁，或为己方的武力攻伐扫清障碍，以最小的代价实现战略目标。

Foiling the enemy's strategy is an important principle proposed by Sunzi the ancient military strategist. In his view, war was waged at different levels, all of which have a significant impact on the outcome. Armed attacks will do great damage to both sides, so they should be avoided if at all possible. Those who are good at leading armies should be able to use stratagems to eliminate the threat of enemy attack in advance or clear the obstacles to their own armed forces to achieve their strategic goals at minimal cost.

引例 Citation：

◎ 故上兵伐谋，其次伐交，其次伐兵，其下攻城。攻城之法，为不得已。(《孙子·谋攻》)

(所以用兵的上策是挫败敌方的计谋，其次是破坏敌方的外交，再次是攻打敌方的军队，最下策是进攻敌方的城邑。攻城是不得已采取的办法。)

The preferred way is to foil the enemy's plans, the next best to use diplomacy, failing that to attack the enemy's forces, and the least desirable is to assault the enemy's cities. Assaulting cities is a last resort when all else has failed. (*The Art of War*)

上帝

/shàngdì/

Supreme Ruler / Ruler of Heaven

主要含义有二：其一，上古传说中指主宰宇宙万事万物的最高天神。也叫"天帝"。商周时期，巫是联通人与上帝的媒介，巫通过卜筮向上帝请示，传达上帝的旨意。其二，指帝国或王朝的最高统治者，即帝王、君主，包括远古或死去的帝王、君主，犹言"天子"。基督教传入中国后，基督教教士又借用"上帝"一词作为对其所崇奉之神God的译称。

The term has two meanings. One is the supreme ruler of the universe, also known as the Ruler of Heaven. During the Shang and Zhou dynasties, wizards were the intermediaries between humans and the supreme ruler. They asked for his orders by means of divination and conveyed them to humans. The other meaning is the supreme ruler of an empire or dynasty, that is, the emperor or monarch, including those of remote antiquity and those who had died; each was referred to as Son of Heaven. After Christianity was introduced to China, missionaries used this term as a translation of the word "God."

引例 Citations:

◎先王以作乐崇德，殷荐之上帝，以配祖考。(《周易·象上》)
(先代的君王因此制作音乐，赞美功德，以盛大的典礼奉献给上帝，并让祖先的神灵配祭。)

Former kings thus created music to extol virtue, conducted grand ceremonies to honor the Ruler of Heaven, and worshipped ancestral tablets. (*The Book of Changes*)

◎皇矣上帝，临下有赫。监观四方，求民之莫。(《诗经·大雅·皇矣》)
(伟大的上帝呀，俯察人间好分明。洞察天下四方地，努力寻求民安定。)

August is the Ruler of Heaven, beholding the mortal world in majesty. He surveys and watches the four quarters, bringing peace and stability to the people. (*The Book of Songs*)

上善若水

/shàngshàn-ruòshuǐ/

Great Virtue Is Like Water.

最完美的善就像水的品性一样，滋润万物却不与万物相争。出自《老子》。老子以水的这种柔弱之性比喻至善的执政者应有的品德。执政者面对百姓，应如水之于万物，辅助、成就百姓的自然而不与百姓相争。后多指为人处世时能像水一样滋润万物，尽己所能帮助他人却从不争名逐利，或者具有坚忍负重、谦卑居下的品格。

The greatest virtue is just like water, nurturing all things without competing with them. This term was first used by Laozi to advocate the belief that a virtuous ruler should govern with gentle and accommodating qualities as demonstrated by water. He should assist and provide for people just like what water does, instead of competing with them for resources. Later, this term came to mean that people should nourish all things as water does and try their best to help people without seeking fame or profit. It also refers to human virtues such as endurance for the sake of achieving a noble goal and modesty.

引例 Citation：

◎上善若水。水善利万物而不争，处众人之所恶（wù），故几于道。(《老子·八章》)

（至善之人具有如水一般的品德。水善于滋润万物而不与万物相争，处于众人所厌恶的卑下之处，因此水几近于道。）

Great virtue is like water. Water nourishes all things gently and does not compete with anything, content to be in a low place not sought by people. Water is therefore closest to Dao. (*Laozi*)

舍生取义

/shěshēng-qǔyì/

Give One's Life to Uphold Righteousness

舍弃生命以保全道义。出自《孟子》。孟子（前372？—前289）认为，"义"是人之所以为人的本质特征之一，舍"义"而不足以为人。生命固然可贵，但生存却并不是人之所以为人的目的或意义。因此，当保全生命与坚守道义发生冲突的时候，人不应背义苟活，而应牺牲生命以捍卫道义。

This belief is advocated by Mencius (372?-289 BC). He holds that upholding righteousness is an essential attribute of a dignified man, and without it one would lose his moral standing. Life is precious, but survival should not be the only thing that is important in life. When one faces a choice between saving life and upholding righteousness, he should give life to uphold righteousness.

引例 Citation:

◎生亦我所欲也，义亦我所欲也，二者不可得兼，舍生而取义者也。(《孟子·告子上》)

（生命是我所渴望的，义也是我所渴望的，二者不能同时获得的时候，舍弃生命以保全道义。）

Both life and righteousness are important to me. However, if I cannot have both, I will give my life so as to uphold righteousness. (*Mencius*)

社 稷
/shèjì/

Gods of the Earth and the Five Grains / State / State Power

　　古代帝王、诸侯所祭祀的土地神和五谷神。"社"是土地神，"稷"是五谷神。土地神和五谷神是以农为本的华夏族最重要的原始崇拜物。古代君主为了祈求国事太平、五谷丰登，每年都要祭祀土地神和五谷神，"社稷"因此成为国家与政权的象征。

She (社) is the God of the Earth, and *ji* (稷 millet), represents the God of the Five Grains. Chinese kings and vassals of ancient times offered sacrifices to these gods. As the Han people depended on farming, these gods were the most important primitive objects of worship. The ancient rulers offered sacrifices to the gods of the Earth and the Five Grains every year to pray for peace and good harvests in the country. As a result, *sheji* became a symbol of the nation and state power.

引例 Citation:

◎王者所以有社稷何？为天下求福报功。人非土不立，非谷不食。

土地广博，不可遍敬也；五谷众多，不可一一而祭也。故封土立社示有土尊；稷，五谷之长，故封稷而祭之也。(《白虎通义·社稷》)
（天子为何设立土地神与五谷神呢？是为了天下百姓祈求神的赐福、报答神的功德。没有土地，人就不能生存；没有五谷，人就没有食物。土地广大，不可能全都礼敬；五谷众多，不可能全都祭祀。所以封土为坛立土地神以表示土地的尊贵；稷[谷子]是五谷中最重要的粮食，所以立稷为五谷神而予以祭祀。）

Why do the Sons of Heaven worship the gods of the Earth and the Five Grains? They do so to seek blessings for all under heaven and to requite the gods' blessings. Without earth, people have nowhere to live; without grain, people have nothing to eat. The earth is too vast to be worshipped everywhere; the variety of grains is too large to be worshipped one by one. Therefore, earth altars to the God of the Earth have been set up to honor the earth; and as millet is the chief one of the five grains, it has become the God of the Five Grains and sacrifices have been instituted. (*Debates of the White Tiger Hall*)

神与物游

/shényǔwùyóu/

Interaction Between the Mind and the Subject Matter

　　文艺创作中人的精神与外物交融、自由驰骋的构思活动。在这一构思活动中，一方面人的精神感觉和想象投射到客观事物上，使客观事物具有了审美色彩；另一方面，虚无缥缈的精神感觉和想象也借助客观事物得以表达和呈现。"神"与"物"的自由融合，超越了时间与空间的限制，形成艺术形象，然后经过语言的表现，产生了美妙的文艺作品。这一术语源自《庄子》的"乘物以游心"，后经南朝刘勰（465？—520？或532？）《文心雕龙》的系统阐发，成为对"神思"这一术语的概括性论述，突出艺术构思过程中心灵与物象交融、自由想象的特点，既说明了艺术创作中的构思活动，也高度概括了文艺创作中的审美心理与创作自由的特点。

This term refers to the creative process through which a writer interacts with subject matter and gives free rein to his imagination. During the process, he projects onto real objects his mental sensations and imaginings, and endows them with an aesthetic tone. Conversely, his imaginary sensations and imaginings are given concrete expression by real objects. The free interaction between mind and subject matter, transcending the limitations of space and time, creates a superb artistic work depicted in language. The term originated in the words of "taking advantage of the circumstances to let your mind wander freely" in *Zhuangzi*. Later, this idea was systematically developed by Liu Xie (465?-520? or 532?) in *The Literary Mind and the Carving of Dragons* during the Southern Dynasties to describe imaginative contemplation. The term stresses the importance of interaction between the mind and the poetic subject matter as well as free imagination in the process of artistic creation. It demonstrates the process of thinking in artistic creation and succinctly summarizes the underlying features of aesthetic appreciation and freedom in artistic creation.

引例 Citations：

◎ 其始也，皆收视反听，耽思傍讯。精骛八极，心游万仞。其致也，情曈昽（tónglóng）而弥鲜，物昭晰而互进。（陆机《文赋》）
（在开始写文章时，必须停止一切视听活动，凝聚心神，广为求索，精神奔驰于八方极远之地，心灵飞翔至万仞极高之境。到极致时，情感由朦胧而渐趋明朗，物象也随之清晰而在眼前交替呈现。）

When starting to write an essay, one should keep away sounds and sights and keep his mind focused so as to allow the imagination to search freely in the universe. When his mind reaches the farthest end, all confusion will dissipate, and images will clearly emerge in his mind one after another. (Lu Ji: *The Art of Writing*)

◎ 故思理为妙，神与物游。神居胸臆，而志气统其关键；物沿耳目，而辞令管其枢机。（刘勰《文心雕龙·神思》）
（所以写作构思的奇妙之处，可以使思绪和想象与外在事物自由地连接交融。思绪和想象蕴藏于内心，由人的情志、气质主宰；外物通过听觉、视觉来认识，而将其表达出来却是由言辞负责的。）

What is marvelous about composing a poem is that it makes it possible for the mind and the imagination to interact freely with external objects. The feelings and imaginings that well up from within are determined by a writer's aspirations and temperament. We recognize external objects through hearing and vision, but these objects are expressed through the use of language. (Liu Xie: *The Literary Mind and the Carving of Dragons*)

神韵

/shényùn/

Elegant Subtlety

指文学艺术作品中清远淡雅的意蕴和韵味。原本是对人物的风度神情的评价，魏晋时人认为人格之美在于内在精神气韵，不同于汉代人推重外形。后来这一概念进入书画理论，指作品内在的精神韵味。明代人从书画理论引入诗歌理论，使神韵成为对诗歌风格的要求，清代王士禛（1634—1711）是"神韵说"的发扬光大者，他特意编选了《唐诗神韵集》，借编选理想的诗歌阐发自己的审美趣味，又在诗歌理论著作中大力倡导，构建起独具特色的诗歌艺术审美体系，从而使"神韵说"得以完善定型，最终成为清代诗学的一大流派。

This term refers to the subtle elegance of literary and artistic works. It was originally used to depict a person's mien and manner. During the Wei and Jin dynasties, the propriety inherent in a person was valued, whereas during the previous Han Dynasty, a person's external appearance was stressed. Later on, this concept was incorporated into the theory of calligraphy and painting to refer to the elegant subtlety of a work. In the Ming Dynasty, the concept was extended to the theory of poetry, and elegant subtlety became a requirement for composing poetry. Later, Wang Shizhen (1634-1711) of the Qing Dynasty further developed the theory of elegant subtlety. In compiling *The Elegant Subtlety of the Tang Poetry*, he elaborated on his aesthetic views. In his writings on poetry theory, Wang Shizhen championed these views and created his own unique poetical aesthetics, enriching the theory of elegant subtlety, and making it a major school of the Qing-dynasty poetics.

引例 Citations：

◎诗之佳，拂拂如风，洋洋如水，一往神韵，行乎其间。（陆时雍《诗镜·总论》）

（好诗如同拂面的清风，如同流过的浩大河水，仿佛有种神韵行进在诗的字里行间。）

Just as gentle breeze touching one's face and the river flowing past, a good poem has elegant subtlety permeating its lines. (Lu Shiyong: *A Comprehensive Digest of Good Ancient Poems*)

◎予尝观唐末五代诗人之作，卑下龇（wéi）琐，不复自振，非惟无开元、元和作者豪放之格，至神韵兴象之妙以视陈隋之季，盖百不及一焉。（王士禛《〈梅氏诗略〉序》）

（我曾经读唐末五代时的诗人作品，格调卑下猥琐，气势不振，非但没有开元、元和年间诗作的豪放风格，在神韵、兴象的绝妙方面，甚至连陈、隋衰微时期的诗作的百分之一都比不上。）

I have read the works by poets of the late Tang Dynasty and the Five Dynasties and found their poetry mean-spirited, trivial, and depressed. They were far less bold and daring than those poems written between the Kaiyuan and Yuanhe periods of the Tang Dynasty. Worse still, they did not have the slightest traces of the elegant subtlety and inspiring imagery that were evident in the poetry written in the State of Chen during the Northern Dynasties and in the Sui Dynasty when poetry was already in decline. (Wang Shizhen: Foreword to *Poetry by the Mei Family*)

慎独

/shèndú/

Shendu (Ethical Self-cultivation)

儒家提出的一种道德修养方法。"慎独"有两种不同含义：其一，将"独"理解为闲居独处。人们在独处时，没有他人的监督，最容易放纵行事。"慎独"即要求在独处时谨慎对待自己的行为，自觉遵守道德、礼法的要求。其二，将"独"理解为内心的真实状态。人们可以在言行上表现出符合道德、礼法的要求，但心中却没有对道德、礼法的认同与追求。"慎独"则要求在心上做工夫，使内心与道德、礼法所要求的言行相符。

A kind of ethical self-cultivation advanced by the Confucian school of thought, the term has two different meanings. First, *du*（独）is understood as at leisure and alone. When people are alone, without someone else's supervision, they easily act in an undisciplined and immoral way. *Shendu*（慎独）requires being careful with one's conduct when being alone, consciously following morality and the requirements of etiquette. Second, *du* is understood as an inner true state. People may in their words and actions manifest what is in accord with morality and the requirements of etiquette, but in their heart they do not accept or pursue any morality or etiquette. *Shendu* requires that one makes efforts in one's heart, so that one's inner world is in agreement with the words and actions required by morality and etiquette.

引例 Citations：

◎ 是故君子戒慎乎其所不睹，恐惧乎其所不闻。莫见（xiàn）乎隐，莫显乎微，故君子慎其独也。(《礼记·中庸》)

（因此君子在没有人看见时也是谨慎的，在没有人听到时也是有所恐惧的。没有比隐蔽的地方更容易表现的了，没有比隐微的地方更容易显明的了，因此君子应"慎独"。）

A man of virtue is cautious when he is not being watched by others and apprehensive when what he says is not being heard. There is nothing more visible than in what is secret, and nothing more obvious than in what is vague and minute. Therefore, a man of virtue is watchful when he is at leisure and alone. (*The Book of Rites*)

◎ 此谓诚于中，形于外，故君子必慎其独也。(《礼记·大学》)

（这是说实存于内心的东西，会表现在外，因此君子必须"慎独"。）

This means what one truly believes in his heart and mind will find expression in the open. That is why a man of virtue must be cautious when he is at leisure and alone. (*The Book of Rites*)

生生
/shēngshēng/

Perpetual Growth and Change

　　生生不息的变化。出自《周易·系辞上》。《周易》所言"生生"包含两层含义：其一，就万物的存在而言，"生生"指天地万物处于永恒的生成、变化之中，阴阳的交互作用构成了"生生"的内在动力。"生生"是天地万物的根本属性，也是道德之善行的来源。其二，就占筮而言，"生生"指奇画与偶画相交错，卦爻之象处于不断变化之中。

The term stands for perpetual change. According to *The Book of Changes*, *shengsheng* (生生) can be understood at two levels. First, in regard to the existence of all things, it is the interaction of yin and yang that drives the process of the endless cycle of birth, rebirth, and change of heaven, earth, and all things. This process is a fundamental attribute of the universe, and the source of ethical behavior. Second, as a term in divination, it refers to the alternation of yin and yang lines and the fact that all elements in the symbol system of *The Book of Changes* are in a perpetual state of change.

引例 Citations:

◎生生之谓易。(《周易·系辞上》)

(生生不息，称之为"易"。)

One generation gives life to another generation in perpetual change. (*The Book of Changes*)

◎生生之谓易，是天之所以为道也。天只是以生为道，继此生理者，即是善也。(《二程遗书》卷二上)

(生生不息的变化，就是天道的内容。天只是以生生不息为原则，秉承此生生不息之理的，就是善。)

Continued growth and perpetual change is essence of the way of heaven. Heaven follows this principle, and kindness is guided by this principle. (*Writings of the Cheng Brothers*)

声一无听，物一无文

/shēng yī wú tīng, wù yī wú wén/

A Single Note Does Not Compose a Melodious Tune, Nor Does a Single Color Make a Beautiful Pattern.

　　单一声响不构成动听的旋律，单一颜色不构成美丽的花纹。其本质强调文学艺术的美在于多样性的统一与和谐，只有在多样性的统一与和谐中才能创造美。这一命题后来构成中国古代文艺理论的重要原则，推动文艺的繁荣与发展。

This statement suggests that the beauty of literature and art lies in the unity and harmony of diverse elements. It became an important principle in ancient Chinese theories on literature and art, and facilitated the development of literature and art.

引例 Citations：

◎声一无听，物一无文，味一无果，物一不讲。(《国语·郑语》)
(单一声响不能构成动听的旋律，单一颜色不能构成美丽的花纹，单一味道不能成为美食，单一事物无法进行比较。)

A single note does not compose a melodious tune; a single color does not form a beautiful pattern; a single flavor does not make a delicious meal; and a single thing has nothing to compare with. (*Discourses on Governance of the States*)

◎五色杂而成黼黻（fǔfú），五音比而成韶夏，五情发而为辞章，神理之数也。(刘勰《文心雕龙·情采》)
(五色交错而成灿烂的锦绣，五音排列而组织成悦耳的乐章，五情抒发而成动人的辞章，这是自然的道理。)

When silk threads of various colors are woven together, a beautiful piece of embroidery is created. When the five musical notes are properly arranged, a beautiful melody is composed. When the five emotions are forcefully expressed, a beautiful piece of writing is created. This is all too natural and obvious. (Liu Xie: *The Literary Mind and the Carving of Dragons*)

盛唐之音

/shèngtángzhīyīn/

Poetry of the Prime Tang Dynasty

指唐玄宗开元（713—741）、天宝（742—756）年间的诗歌创作与艺术成就。与初唐、中唐、晚唐时期的诗歌相对应。这一时期是"安史之乱"前唐帝国的黄金时代，当时，社会稳定、政治清明、经济繁荣，南北文化融合，中外交通发达，这一切为"盛唐之音"营造了很好的社会氛围和文化基础。在唐诗初、盛、中、晚四个阶段中，盛唐最短，但艺术成就最为辉煌，被后人誉为"盛唐气象"。这一时期，不但出现了诗仙李白（701—762）、诗圣杜甫（712—770），而且还出现了张说（yuè，667—731）、张若虚、张九龄（673或678—740）、孟浩然（689—740）、王维（701？—761）、高适（700？—765）、岑参（shēn，715—770）、王昌龄（？—756？）、王之涣（688—742）、崔颢（？—754）、李颀（？—753？）、王翰等一大批卓有成就的诗人。他们赞美山川，向往功业，抒发个人情志，记述社会现实，诗风豪迈浑厚，意境宏阔高远，语言清新天然，富有生命活力与进取精神，创造了中国古典诗歌的最高成就。就诗派而论，这一时期则有山水田园诗派、边塞诗派等。

This term refers to the poetic creation and achievements during the Kaiyuan (713 - 742) and Tianbao (742 - 756) reign periods of Emperor Xuanzong of the Tang Dynasty, as compared with poetic writing in the early Tang, mid-Tang, and late Tang periods. This period, marked by good governance, prosperity, and stability, was a golden era for the great Tang empire before it was disrupted by the An Lushan and Shi Siming Rebellion. There was cultural infusion between the north and south, and travels to and from the outside world were frequent. All this made it possible for artistic creation to blossom. Of all the four periods of poetic creation, i.e., the early Tang, the prime Tang, the mid-Tang, and the late Tang, the prime Tang was the shortest, but its artistic attainment was most remarkable. This period produced legendary poet Li Bai (701 - 762) and poetic genius Du Fu (712 - 770) as well as a galaxy of outstanding poets such as Zhang Yue (667 - 731), Zhang Ruoxu, Zhang Jiuling (673 or 678 - 740), Meng Haoran (689 - 740), Wang Wei (701?- 761), Gao Shi (700?- 765), Cen Shen (715 - 770), Wang Changling (?-756?), Wang

Zhihuan (688-742), Cui Hao (?-754), Li Qi (?-753?), and Wang Han. These poets extolled natural scenery, expressed noble aspirations, and depicted real life. Their writing style was both vigorous and unrestrained. They were broad in vision and were adept at using fresh, natural language, and their poems were full of power, vigor and an enterprising spirit. Their poems represented the highest attainment in classical Chinese poetry. This period also saw the thriving of the natural landscape school and the frontier school in poetry writing.

引例 Citations:

◎ 盛唐诸公之诗，如颜鲁公书，既笔力雄壮，又气象浑厚。（严羽《答出继叔临安吴景仙书》）

（盛唐诸多诗人的诗作，好比颜真卿的书法作品一样，笔力既雄壮感人，气象又质朴厚重。）

Works of many poets during the prime of the Tang Dynasty struck readers with their touching, powerful expression and simple yet dignified style, just like the calligraphy of Yan Zhenqing. (Yan Yu: *Letter in Reply to Uncle Wu Jingxian in Lin'an*)

◎ 盛唐气象浑成，神韵轩举。（胡应麟《诗薮·内编五》）

（盛唐时期的诗歌气象浑然一体、天然生成，其精神气韵也就自然昂扬飞举。）

Poetry in the prime of the Tang Dynasty is noted for being expressive, smooth and natural, creating a soaring and uplifting spirit. (Hu Yinglin: *An In-depth Exploration of Poetry*)

师出有名

/shīchū-yǒumíng/

Fighting a War with a Moral Justification

兴兵开战要有正当的名义或理由。泛指做事有正当的理由。它包含两层意思：其一，师直为壮，谓出兵理由正当，则士气旺盛，战斗力强，否则难以服众；其二，无故不得兴兵，防止因贪、怒而穷兵黩武。其核心在于强调战争的正义性。这是文明精神的体现。

To wage a war, one must have a legitimate cause, just as we ought to have such a reason in doing all things. The term has two meanings. The first is that moral justification is a source of strength when waging a war. With moral justification, the troops will have high morale and strength in fighting. Without it, it would be difficult to command the troops. The second meaning is that war must not be waged without a just cause. Greed or anger should not be allowed to lead to militarism and aggression. The underlying notion of this concept is that war can only be fought with a just cause, which represents the spirit of civilization.

引例 Citations:

◎师必有名。(《礼记·檀弓下》)
(出兵必须有正当理由。)

A military campaign must have a moral justification. (*The Book of Rites*)

◎顺德者昌，逆德者亡。兵出无名，事故不成。(《汉书·高帝纪上》)
(顺应道德就会昌盛，违背道德就会灭亡。出兵没有正当名义，事情所以不会成功。)

Those who have virtue thrive; those who go against virtue perish. If a war is waged without moral justification, it will not succeed. (*The History of the Han Dynasty*)

◎庶几义声昭彰，理直气壮，师出有名，大功可就矣。(朱鼎《玉镜台记·闻鸡起舞》)
(希望正义的声音广为传扬，理由正大而气势雄壮，出兵有正当的名义，这样才可建成大功业。)

I hope the voice of justice will be heard everywhere. Be bold and confident when fighting a just war. When a military campaign has a moral justification, great victory can be achieved. (Zhu Ding: *A Tale of a Jade Dressing Table*)

师法之化

/shīfǎzhīhuà/

Enlightenment Through Education

教师和法度的教化。"师法之化"是由荀子（前313？—前238）提出的。荀子认为，人天生具有对外物的欲求，这是人的本性。如果放纵人的这种本性，就会导致人与人之间的纷争，社会将陷入混乱。因此，需要通过后天的教化，在恰当安顿人的欲望的同时，确立起对道德、礼法的认同与遵守。而教化的基本方式就是通过教师的传授和法度的规范，实现对人的欲望与言行的引导。

Enlightenment through education was a notion first put forward by Xunzi (313?-238 BC). He believed that people by nature desire external things. However, If unrestrained, this natural desire will lead to conflicts between people and plunge society into chaos. Therefore, they need to be enlightened through education to both meet their desires and make them understand and observe ethics and etiquette. The basic form of enlightenment is guiding their desires, words and deeds through teaching.

引例 Citation：

◎ 然则从人之性，顺人之情，必出于争夺，合于犯分（fèn）乱理而归于暴。故必将有师法之化、礼义之道，然后出于辞让，合于文理，而归于治。(《荀子·性恶》)

（那么放纵人的本性，顺从人的欲望，必然会发生争夺，出现违反名分扰乱秩序的行为而导致暴乱。因此必须要有教师和法度的教化以及礼义的引导，然后才会实现相互辞让，言行合乎文明秩序，从而实现社会的安定。）

If people's natural impulses are allowed to surge without check, conflicts are certain to break. This will lead to violation of social norms and disruption of social order, resulting in social unrest. Therefore, it is necessary to have teachers and models to give guidance to people and enlighten them through teaching of etiquette and ethical principles. When this is done, courtesy and deference will develop, people will observe social order in their words and deeds, and peace and stability will prevail. (*Xunzi*)

诗史
/shīshǐ/

Historical Poetry

指诗歌的内容能够真实反映某一历史时期广阔的社会现实和重大的历史事件而具有"史"的价值。《诗经》有些诗篇反映当时历史，孔子（前551—前479）据此提出《诗经》"可以观"，即包含了对《诗经》以诗征史的肯定，汉代学者很看重诗歌承载历史的功能。后来的诗论家大都强调优秀诗歌须将审美与反映现实结合起来，从而彰显诗歌的审美与认识、教育功能的统一。唐代诗人杜甫（712—770）的诗歌被称作"诗史"，就是因为他的诗能够反映"安史之乱"时的真实社会，体现出深刻的忧国忧民之情。

This term refers to poetry that reflects social realities and major events of a historical period, thus possessing historical value. Some of the poems in *The Book of Songs* were about the realities of its time, which prompted Confucius (551-479 BC) to exclaim that "*The Book of Songs* enables one to understand society." This means that he viewed *The Book of Songs* as using poetry to reflect history. Han-dynasty scholars stressed the importance of poetry as a means of recording history. Subsequently, Chinese scholars of poetry believed that poetry should reflect reality through aesthetic means so as to provide aesthetic enjoyment, understanding as well as education. The poems of Tang poet Du Fu (712-770) are called "historical poetry" because they reflected what the country went through during the An Lushan-Shi Siming Rebellion and the author's acute sense of sadness about the misery the country and its people suffered in times of national crisis.

引例 Citations：

◎杜逢禄山之难，流离陇蜀，毕陈于诗，推见至隐，殆无遗事，故当时号为"诗史"。（孟棨（qǐ）《本事诗·高逸》）

（杜甫遭逢安禄山叛乱引发的灾难，先后漂泊甘肃、四川一带，所经历的一切，全都写在诗中，后人由此推知当时的很多隐约细节，几乎没有什么遗漏，所以当时人称他的诗为"诗史"。）

Du Fu fled to the provinces of Gansu and Sichuan to escape turbulences caused by the An Lushan-Shi Siming Rebellion and wrote about his experiences in poems. As his poems gave vivid and detailed accounts about events of the time, they became known as "historical poetry." (Meng Qi: *The Story of Poetry*)

◎昔人评杜诗为"诗史"，盖其以咏歌之辞，寓纪载之实，而抑扬褒贬之意，粲然于其中，虽谓之"史"可也。（文天祥《集杜诗自序》）

（过去的人评价杜甫诗为"诗史"，大概是因为他能够以诗歌形式记载真实的事件，同时批评讥刺与表扬赞美的意旨显然蕴含其中，所以称他的诗为"史"完全合适。）

People regarded the poems of Du Fu as historical poetry mostly because they described what really happened in his age, and they contained criticisms or praises of historical events. So his poems were aptly called "historical poetry." (Wen Tianxiang: Preface to *Poems Composed by Rearranging Du Fu's Verses*)

诗言志

/shī yán zhì/

Poetry Expresses Aspirations.

诗歌表达作者内心的志向。"志"指诗歌作品中所表达的作者的内心志向、思想，兼及情感因素。"诗言志"最先见于儒家经典《尚书·舜典》，是中国诗论的"开山纲领"（朱自清语），经过历代诗论家的演绎，其蕴涵不断得以丰富，并由此确立了中国文论关于文学特征的基本观念。

A poem expresses aspirations in one's heart. *Zhi* (志) here means the author's aspirations, emotions, and thoughts. The concept of "poetry expressing aspirations," first seen in the Confucian classic *The Book of History*, was hailed by Zhu Ziqing as the "manifesto" of Chinese poetry. Enriched by poetry critics through the generations, it was later established as a basic concept in Chinese literary criticism.

引例 Citations：

◎ 诗言志，歌永言。(《尚书·舜典》)

（诗是表达内心志向的，歌是用语言来吟唱的。）

Poems express aspirations deep in one's heart, whereas songs are verses for chanting. (*The Book of History*)

◎ 诗者，志之所之也，在心为志，发言为诗。(《毛诗序》)

（诗是内心情感意志的表达，藏在心里就是情感意志，用语言把它表达出来就是诗歌。）

Poetry is an expression of a person's feelings and aspirations. When hidden in his heart, it is just his feelings and aspirations. When put forth through the medium of words, it becomes what is known as poetry. (Introductions to *Mao's Version of The Book of Songs*)

诗缘情

/shī yuán qíng/

Poetry Springs from Emotions.

诗歌缘于诗人内心的情感。西晋陆机（261—303）《文赋》提出，诗人情动于心，而后才有诗歌创作。"诗缘情"说与"诗言志"说互为补充，强调文学的抒情性与审美特征，表现出魏晋时代文学观念的变迁。因此，"诗缘情"也成为中国古代关于诗歌与文学本质看法的另一代表观点。

Poems originate from the poet's heart-felt feelings. Lu Ji (261-303) of the Western Jin Dynasty said in "The Art of Writing" that a poet must have a surge of feeling deep in his heart before he could create a poem. This view, complementing the concept of "poetry expressing aspirations," stresses the lyrical and aesthetic nature of literary works and echoes the evolution of literary tastes during the Wei and Jin dynasties. "Poetry springing from emotions" represents another viewpoint on the nature of poetry and literature in ancient China.

引例 Citations:

◎ 诗缘情而绮靡。(陆机《文赋》)

(诗歌源于情感因而形式华丽好看。)

Poetry, springing from emotions, reads beautifully in its form of expression. (Lu Ji: The Art of Writing)

◎ 人禀七情，应物斯感，感物吟志，莫非自然。(刘勰《文心雕龙·明诗》)

(人具有喜、怒、哀、惧、爱、恶、欲等七种情感，受到外物的刺激而心有所感，心有所感而吟咏情志，所有的诗歌都出于自然情感。)

People have the seven emotions of joy, anger, sadness, fear, love, loathing and desire. He expresses his feelings and aspirations in a poetical way when he is stimulated by the external world and his heart is touched. All poems come from natural emotions. (Liu Xie: *The Literary Mind and the Carving of Dragons*)

诗中有画，画中有诗
/shī zhōng yǒu huà, huà zhōng yǒu shī/

Painting in Poetry, Poetry in Painting

诗中有画意，画中有诗情。指诗歌与绘画作品所呈现出的审美意境融合相通的美学效果。语出苏轼（1037—1101）《书摩诘〈蓝田烟雨图〉》。绘画是造型艺术，通过众多物象构成画面给人以审美感受；诗歌是语言艺术，通过文字营造意境给人以审美感受。前者是"无声有形"的艺术，后者是"有声无形"的艺术。这一术语旨在提倡"诗歌"与"绘画"的相互渗透与融合，进而创造出天然清新、具有"诗情画意"的审美境界。苏轼这一思想对后世文学与绘画艺术的发展有着深远的影响。

This expression highlights the connection between poetry and painting in their ability to create aesthetic imagery. This idea was first put forward by Su Shi (1037-1101) in his "Notes to Wang Wei's Painting 'Mist and Rain over Lantian.'" Painting creates an aesthetic effect through images presented. Poetry, on the other hand, is a language art, which creates an aesthetic effect through the use of words. The former is an art that has shape but no sound, while the latter is an art that has sound but no shape. The term means that good poetry and painting should be fused so that a spontaneous and novel aesthetic realm can be created by a "picturesque poem" or a "poetic picture." This idea of Su Shi's had a far-reaching influence on the subsequent development of literature and painting in China.

引例 Citations:
◎味摩诘之诗，诗中有画；观摩诘之画，画中有诗。(苏轼《东坡题跋·书摩诘〈蓝田烟雨图〉》)
(品味王维的诗，诗中有画的意境；观看王维的画，画中有诗的情感。)
When reading Wang Wei's poems, one can conjure up a picturesque image. When viewing Wang Wei's paintings, one can experience a poetic sentiment. (Su Shi: *A Collection of Su Dongpo's Prefaces and Postscripts*)

◎诗中画，性情中来者也，则画不是可拟张拟李而后作诗；画中诗，乃境趣时生者也，则诗不是便生吞生剥而后成画。真识相触，如镜写影，初何容心？今人不免唐突诗画矣。(石涛《大涤子题画诗跋》卷一)
(所谓诗中有画，源自诗人的本真性情，故而诗中的画不是随便描摹哪个姓张姓李的人的画便能写出诗来；所谓画中有诗，乃是由当时特定的意境、情趣生发出来的，故而画中的诗不是生搬硬套某一首诗便能画成画。内心的识见与自然碰撞相融，如同镜子显现物象那么逼真，起初哪里是有意于此，今天的人 [不懂得这一点] 所以免不了要胡乱冒犯诗画了。)
Painting in poetry is a natural creation deriving from a poet's true aspiration; such poems cannot be composed by imitating others' paintings. Poetry in painting is inspired by a specific scene or sentiment at a given time, so it is not possible to artificially insert a poem into a painting. The way that a mind interacts with nature is as direct and unaffected as a life-like image reflected in a mirror. The effect is not deliberately intended at first. Nowadays, people do not understand this point. No wonder poetry and painting have become abused. (Shi Tao: *Dadizi's Comments on His Own Poems Inscribed on Paintings*)

时 中
/shízhōng/

Follow the Golden Mean

　　随时而符合中庸之道。"时中"一说出自《礼记·中庸》。儒家以"中庸"作为行事的最高准则，强调处事应无过、无不及。但无过、无不及的标准，并不是固定不变的教条，而是随时变化的。人们需要在每一个具体的生活处境中，思考道德、礼法的要求，时时、处处践行"中庸"的准则，也即"时中"的要求。

This term, which originated from *The Doctrine of the Mean* (a section of *The Book of Rites*), means that one should at all times follow the principle of the mean. Confucian scholars regarded the mean as the supreme principle guiding people's behavior. They stressed that when handling things one should not act excessively or insufficiently. However, the criteria for determining what were appropriate or not did not remain unchanged. When taking a specific action, one should always bear in mind the need to follow ethical standards and rites, namely, the principle of the mean.

引例 Citation：

◎仲尼曰："君子中庸，小人反中庸。君子之中庸也，君子而时中；小人之中庸也，小人而无忌惮也。"(《礼记·中庸》)

(孔子说："君子遵行中庸，小人违背中庸。君子遵行中庸，随时而符合中庸之道；小人违背中庸，行事而无所忌惮。")

Confucius said, "A man of virtue follows the mean and a petty man goes against it. A man of virtue seeks to be in keeping with the mean at all times, whereas a petty man goes against it and acts unscrupulously." (*The Book of Rites*)

实事求是

/shíshì-qiúshì/

Seek Truth from Facts

　　根据事物实际情况，正确地对待和处理问题。本指古人治学时注重事实，以求得出正确的见解或结论。后多指依据实际情况进行思考或表达，如实、正确地对待和处理问题。它既是一种关于思维或认识的方法论原则，也是一种做人的基本态度或伦理操守。其基本理念是求真、务实或诚实。

This term means handling things correctly according to realities of the situation. The term was originally used to describe the rigorous attitude of ancient Chinese scholars who paid great attention to acquiring solid facts in order to arrive at the correct understanding or conclusion. Later, it has come to mean expressing ideas or handling matters according to reality. It is a methodological principle on cognition and a fundamental principle underpinning behaviors and ethics. Basically, it calls for behaving in a practical, realistic, and honest way.

引例 Citation：

◎河间献王德……修学好古，实事求是。(《汉书·景十三王传·河间献王德》)

（河间献王刘德……喜欢学习和古代事物，在充分掌握事实的基础上求得正确的见解。）

Liu De, Prince Xian of Hejian… loved to study history and always sought the right understanding based on thorough grasp of evidence. (*The History of the Han Dynasty*)

史
/shǐ/

History

　　在甲骨文与金文中,"史"的字形是手执笔或简簿,其义指记载史事的官吏。东汉许慎(58？—147)《说文解字》说:"史,记事者也。从又(手)持中。中,正也。""史"与"事"同源,记"事"的人叫"史",人所记叫"事"。后来史官所记述的史事或史实以及按一定原则编集整理的关于史事或史实的各种记载及评述也称作"史",即今之"历史"。按许慎说法,"史"字"从又持中",所谓"持中"就是坚持客观公正、无所偏袒的原则。中国有重史的传统,在很长时期内,史官甚至有不受当政者干涉的特殊地位。一方面,史家可以通过秉笔直书对当政者形成一定程度的制约,使其谨言慎行;另一方面,又可以通过总结、评述历史人物与历史事件汲取经验教训,为当政者提供借鉴。这一传统构成了中国人的人文精神和理性精神的重要特征。

In ancient inscriptions on tortoise shells and ox scapula, together with inscriptions on ancient bronze objects, the pictographic Chinese character *shi* (史) represents a hand holding a writing brush or a hand holding a bamboo slip, referring to a court official in charge of keeping historical records. *Explanation of Script and Elucidation of Characters* by Xu Shen (58?-147) in the Eastern Han Dynasty goes: "*Shi* is the person who keeps records of events. A hand in the middle implies maintaining justice." Same in sound, two differently-written Chinese characters *shi* (史 history) and *shi* (事 events) are from the same origin, and those who keep notes of what happens are called *shi* (史 record keeper) and what they write down is *shi* (事 records). Later, what the officials in charge of keeping records of historical incidents or events or collections of these incidents or events as well as comments about them are also called *shi* (史), which literally means history. According to Xu Shen, the original pictograph representing the Chinese character *shi* looks like a hand kept in the middle, which means keeping records of historical incidents or events objectively without lending favor to any side of an issue. Great emphasis was once placed on keeping records of history, and during certain periods, even the sovereign rulers were not allowed to interfere with the work of officials in charge of keeping records of historical incidents or events. On the one hand, by keeping records of historical incidents or events, such officials posed a deterrent to rulers, who had to be careful about what they said and what they did. On the other hand, by keeping records of or commenting on historical figures or events, lessons could be summed up or examples be set up, which rulers could draw on and learn from. This tradition constitutes an important aspect of Chinese people's humanistic and rationalistic spirit.

引例 Citations:

◎ 此人皆意有所郁结，不得通其道也，故述往事、思来者。(《史记·太史公自序》)

（这些人都是感情郁结，不能实现志向，所以记述往事，希望将来的人能够了解。）

They were depressed over what had prevented them from fulfilling their aspirations, so they wrote down what had happened in the hope that future generations would understand them. (*Records of the Historian*)

◎ 千古兴亡之理，得自简编；百王善恶之由，闻于经史。其间祸淫福善，莫不如影随形，焕若丹青，明如日月。(赵普《上太宗请班师》)

（自古以来国家兴亡的道理，从书中都能找得到；数百个帝王行善作恶的缘由，从经史记述中也都听说过。史籍中所记述的淫乱招致祸殃、行善得到福报的事情，都像影子跟随形体一样密不可分，像图画一样鲜明，像日月一样光亮。）

Reasons for the rise and fall of all states since antiquity can all be found in books; reasons why hundreds of emperors did good or evil deeds can also be read in classics and history books. The examples recorded of how licentiousness invited disasters and good deeds brought about fortune are omnipresent like our own shadows, and they are as obvious as the sun and moon and as evident as a painting. (Zhao Pu: *Memorial Urging Emperor Taizong to Withdraw Troops*)

世外桃源

/shìwài-táoyuán/

Land of Peach Blossoms / Land of Idyllic Beauty

晋陶渊明（365或372或376—427）在《桃花源记》中所描述的一个安乐而美好的地方。那里景色优美，与世隔绝，远离战乱，没有政治压迫，人们过着平等、自由、安宁、祥和、快乐而美好的生活。后喻指为人向往的美好世界或理想社会，也指脱离世俗、安乐自在的隐居之所。

In his essay "The Peach Blossom Spring," Tao Yuanming (365 or 372 or 376-427) of the Jin Dynasty describes an idyllic place of natural beauty, cut off from the outside world and far from the ravages of war, free from political oppression, where people live in equality, freedom, harmony, peace, and happiness. Later, the expression came to mean an imagined ideal society or place; also a refuge, away from material temptations where one could live in seclusion and tranquility.

引例 Citation：

◎土地平旷，屋舍俨然，有良田美池桑竹之属。阡陌交通，鸡犬相闻。其中往来种作，男女衣着，悉如外人。黄发垂髫（tiáo），并怡然自乐。（陶渊明《桃花源记》）

（眼前是平坦宽广的土地，房舍整整齐齐。有肥沃的田地、美丽的池沼和桑树竹林之类的景色。田间小路四通八达，鸡鸣狗叫都能听到。人们在田野里往来耕种劳作，男女的穿戴跟外人完全一样。老人和小孩个个都安适愉快，自得其乐。）

Before the eyes, the land lies wide and flat, dotted with neatly-built houses. There are fertile fields, picturesque ponds, and clumps of bamboo and mulberry trees. The paths in the fields branch in all directions, chickens cluck and dogs bark. People work in the fields, dressed in exactly the same manner as people outside. White-haired elders and tufted children alike seem happy and content. (Tao Yuanming: The Peach Blossom Spring)

书道

/shūdào/

The Way of Calligraphy

指通过书法创作追求身心合一进而体悟宇宙与生命真谛的艺术境界。受孔子（前551—前479）"志于道，据于德，依于仁，游于艺"的思想影响，尤其是庄子（前369？—前286）"技进乎道"的美学精神导引，书家对书法有更高的艺术追求，希望超越书法的形式与技艺，达到"道"的境界。因唐代书家重视书写的笔法、技法，故改称"书法"。"书法"是"书道"的初级阶段，属于技法的、有形的、形而下的范畴；"书道"是"书法"的最高阶段，属于普遍的、抽象的、形而上的范畴。"书道"这一术语后来传至日本，被赋予了更多修身、养性、悟道等方面的内容，这些又影响了中国近现代书法艺术的发展。

This term refers to an artistic state wherein a calligraphic artist pursues a unity between body and soul through calligraphic creation, so that he may embrace the truths about the universe and life. It was influenced by Confucius (551-479 BC) who said: "[Cultivated people] should follow Dao, adhere to virtues, embrace benevolence, and are well versed in various arts and skills." It was influenced even more by Zhuangzi's (369?-286 BC) aesthetic view, "If we can achieve perfection in a particular area of skill, we come close to the great Way itself." The calligrapher aims higher than the mere art of calligraphy, aspiring to attain the great Way by transcending calligraphy as a mere skill or form of art. By the Tang Dynasty, because calligraphers put more emphasis on the different forms and skills of calligraphy, they started to use a new term "calligraphic technique." Calligraphic technique represented an initial stage of calligraphy – a tangible, superficial and somewhat "lower" level. The calligraphic Way, on the other hand, was an advanced stage of calligraphic technique, paying attention to universal, abstract and therefore much "higher" aspects of calligraphy. This latter concept spread to Japan and took on the broader implications of self-cultivation and enlightenment later on. It, in turn, influenced the development of modern Chinese calligraphic art.

引例 Citations：

◎唐中叶以后，书道下衰之际，故弗多得云。（黄伯思《东观余论·跋叚（xiá）柯古靖居寺碑后》）

（唐代中期之后，书道开始走向衰落，故而上乘书作不可多得。）

After the mid-Tang Dynasty, the way of calligraphy started to decline, and excellent works of calligraphy became scarcely available. (Huang Bosi: *A Chief of Imperial Archives' Other Works Appended to a Collection of Essays*)

◎隶书生于篆书，而实是篆之不肖子，何也？篆书一画、一直、一钩、一点，皆有义理，所谓指事、象形、谐声、会意、转注、假借是也，故谓之"六书"。隶既变圆为方，改弦易辙，全违父法，是六书之道由隶而绝。（钱泳《履园丛话·书学》）

（隶书由篆书生发出来，实际上是篆书的不肖之子，为什么这么说呢？篆书的一画、一直、一钩、一点，都蕴藏着义理规律，即通常所说的指事、象形、谐声、会意、转注、假借，故而称之为"六书"。隶书将篆书圆润的书写形态变为方正，全然改变篆书的结构规律，违背了篆书的造字方法，所以六书所蕴含的造字规律由隶书而开始断绝了。）

Clerical script was derived from seal script. It was an "unfilial son" of seal script. Why? In seal script, the execution of each horizontal or vertical line, hook or dot is governed by certain reasons and laws. They are ideographic, pictographic, ideophonetic, associative compound, or with transferred meaning and borrowed meaning, hence the term "six ways of constituting characters." The clerical script, by changing seal script from smooth roundness to angular abruptness, transforms the structural pattern altogether and violates the methodology of forming seal script. Thus, the reasons and laws implicit in the six ways of forming characters became lost as clerical script came to prevail. (Qian Yong: *Collected Writings on the Study of Calligraphy at Lüyuan*)

书契

/shūqì/

Documents on Bamboo or Wooden Slips

主要有两种含义：一指书写于简牍上的文字；二指纸张发明以前用竹木制作的券契或文书凭证，竹木正面用文字记录事项，竹木的一侧刻有一定数量的齿，通常会有两份，由当事双方各执其一，便于将来复验。两汉以后，简牍书写逐渐退出历史舞台，但作为券契或文书凭证用的竹木书契仍有使用。

This term has two meanings. One refers to script in general inscribed on bamboo or wooden slips. The other refers to documentary proofs, particularly proof of property ownership inscribed on bamboo or wooden slips before paper was invented. Various activities and matters were recorded on the front side. A number of tooth-like marks were carved on one side. There are usually two copies of the document, each held by one of the two parties concerned for future re-verification. After the Western and Eastern Han dynasties, script inscribed on bamboo or wooden slips gradually fell into disuse, whereas documents of proof carved on the same medium continued to be used.

引例 Citations：

◎上古结绳而治，后世圣人易之以书契。(《周易·系辞下》)

（上古时期的人通过结绳的方法来记录事情，后世的圣人用文字记录取代了这一做法。）

In Chinese high antiquity people tied knots to keep records. The sages of later generations, on the other hand, used writing for the same purpose. (*The Book of Changes*)

◎书者文字，契者刻木而书其侧，故曰"书契"也。一云：以书契约其事也。(陆德明《经典释文·尚书音义上》)

（"书"指的是文字，"契"是在竹木的一侧刻上与事项有关的标识，所以称之为"书契"。另一种说法是："书契"是就有关事项进行约定的文书凭证。）

The character *shu* refers to written characters, whereas *qi* means the marks made on one side of bamboo or wooden slips to record matters and activities. Another interpretation is that *shuqi* refers to documents that guarantee the validity of a pledge or proof. (Lu Deming: *An Interpretation of Confucian and Other Classics*)

书者，散也

/shū zhě, sǎn yě/

Calligraphy Expresses Inner Conditions.

写好书法，先要抒放情性、摒除一切杂念。是东汉著名书法家蔡邕（133—192）在《笔论》中提出的书法观念。它论述了书法艺术抒发主体情怀的创作心态，强调书家在创作时应先抒放情性、排除一切牵累与功利之心，并将其视为决定书法作品成功与否的关键要素。

To become a good calligrapher, one must first set one's mind at ease and dismiss all distracting thoughts. This is an argument raised by Cai Yong (133 - 192), a famous Eastern Han calligrapher, in his treatise "On Calligraphic Script." He says that the art of calligraphy discloses the calligrapher's personal feeling, stressing the need to unleash one's true self and to eliminate all of life's burdens and practical considerations. This view takes such actions as being crucial to the success of a calligraphic work.

引例 Citations：

◎书者，散也。欲书先散怀抱，任情恣性，然后书之，若迫于事，虽中山兔豪不能佳也。（蔡邕《笔论》，见陈思《书苑菁华》卷一）

（从事书法活动，先要抒放情性、排除一切杂念。动笔之前，必须舒展心胸，任凭性情恣意挥洒，然后再展毫书写，如果是被迫应事，即使是用中山产的兔毫佳笔，也写不出优美的书法作品来。）

To engage in the practice of calligraphy, one should first unleash his pent-up feelings and eliminate all distracting thoughts. Before setting brush to paper, he is advised to open his heart and give free rein to his fantasy. Only then can he expect to carry out his actual task. If he is reluctant to do it, even if he uses a rabbit-hair brush from Zhongshan, he will still fail to produce a fine work of calligraphy. (Cai Yong: On Calligraphic Script)

◎ 夫欲攻书之时，当收视反听，绝虑凝神，心正气和，则契于玄妙。心神不正，字则攲（qī）斜；志气不和，书必颠覆。（李世民《笔法诀》，见陈思《书苑菁华》卷十九）

（想要书写之时，首先应当对外界之事不看不听，杜绝思虑，凝聚心神，心思纯正，气息平和，才能写出玄妙的作品。如果心神不端正，那么所写的字就会歪斜；气息不平和，所写作品就会失败。）

When doing calligraphy, he should stay totally free from what is going on outside, let go of all worries and anxiety, concentrate his energy, purify his mind, and breathe with perfect ease. Only thus would he be able to produce a real piece of work of art. If his mind is in a jumble, his written characters will be crooked; if his breath is uneven, his work will turn out a failure. (Li Shimin: The Craft of Calligraphy)

率性
/shuàixìng/

Acting in Accordance with Human Nature

　　遵循、发挥人的道德本性。率：遵循。出自《礼记·中庸》。《中庸》认为，人具有道德的本性，道德本性是源自于天的。人应遵循、发挥这一天赋的德性，将其实现为外在的言行。符合天赋德性的言行即构成人伦生活中的道德。后世儒者将人的道德本性视为天理在人性中的体现，因此"率性"也被看作是对天理的依循。

The notion of acting in accordance with human nature first appears in *The Doctrine of the Mean*, a section of *The Book of Rites*. According to this text, all humans possess an innate virtuous quality that originates from heaven. People should follow and give full play to this heavenly bestowed virtue and realize it in their words and deeds. Behavior in keeping with this inherent nature constitutes a person's virtuous quality. Later scholars regarded this virtuous nature as the heavenly law manifested in human nature. Acting in accordance with human nature was therefore seen as following the heavenly law.

引例 Citation:

◎ 天命之谓性，率性之谓道，修道之谓教。(《礼记·中庸》)

(天所命令赐予人的本性称为性，依循道德本性而行事称为道，对道德的修养称为教。)

What heaven has bestowed upon people is called human nature. Acting in accordance with this moral nature is called the Way (Dao); cultivation of this moral nature is called education. (*The Book of Rites*)

水墨画
/shuǐmòhuà/

Ink Wash Painting

指中国画中纯用水墨、不用色彩的一种绘画形式。也称国画、中国画。以水、墨、毛笔和宣纸作为主要材料，通过调配清水的多少，引为浓墨、淡墨、干墨、湿墨、焦墨等，画出浓淡层次不同的作品。一般的水墨画，只有水与墨，黑色与白色。进阶的水墨画，也有工笔花鸟画，色彩艳丽，又称彩墨画。中国水墨画讲究远处抽象、近处写实，渲染色彩、营构意境，崇尚"气韵生动"。

This refers to a style of painting in which ink shades are manipulated through dilution, and color use is minimal. It is also known as traditional Chinese or typically Chinese painting. The materials used include ink and water, a painting brush, and rice paper. Through adjusting the proportion of water to ink, the final image varies between light and dark, wet and dry, and thick and thin ink, thus producing varying degrees of color intensity. An ink wash painting normally consists of only ink and water, or of black and white. A more refined ink wash painting, on the other hand, may also feature an elaborate style of painting with flowers and birds in splendid hues, also known as "colored ink wash painting." On the whole, Chinese ink wash painting is impressionistic when depicting distant objects, but realistic about nearby ones. Through the skillful manipulation of color contrasts and the production of artistic ambience, the painter brings forth the value of a painting's "spiritual liveliness."

引例 Citations:

◎ 夫画道之中，水墨最为上。肇自然之性，成造化之功。或咫尺之图，写千里之景。东西南北，宛尔目前；春夏秋冬，生于笔下。（旧题王维《画学秘诀》）

（在绘画技法之中，水墨画法是最上层的一种。它发端于水墨的自然质性，却成就了天地造化的神奇。数尺长的画幅，能绘制出长达几千里的景色。它将天下四方的景色，都呈现在观者眼前；四季的物象，都通过画笔表现出来。）

Ink wash is the cream of all painting techniques. Making use of the natural properties of ink and water, it creates a miraculous view of heaven and earth. About several *chi* (3 *chi* ≈ 1 meter) of a painting would suffice to demonstrate a several-thousand-*li*-long landscape. It captures the scenic beauty of all quarters of the world, showing seasonal changes through the execution of a painting brush. (Wang Wei: *Key to Good Paintings*)

◎ 余曾见破墨山水，笔迹劲爽。（张彦远《历代名画记》卷十）

（我曾见[王维]用破墨之法创作的山水画，它的线条很是劲健、爽朗。）

I saw some landscape paintings produced by Wang Wei rendered with the use of an "alternating technique," namely alternating light ink with thick ink or vice versa, or alternating wet ink with dry ink. They struck me as vigorous and bold. (Zhang Yanyuan: *Famous Paintings Through History*)

顺天应人
/shùntiān-yìngrén/

Follow the Mandate of Heaven and Comply with the Wishes of the People

顺应上天的旨意和民众的意愿。"天"即"天命",指上天旨意。古人认为,有德行的人秉承上天意志而确立政权,成为君主,故称为"天命"。"人"指人心、民意。它与西方"君权神授"思想相似,但它还强调人心、民意,体现了人本思想。在古代它常被用于称扬新朝代的建立和社会重大变革的实施,以表明其正当性、合法性。

The ancient Chinese believed that virtuous men followed the will of heaven in establishing a political regime and becoming its sovereigns; hence their success came from the mandate of heaven. This thought is similar to the Western notion of the divine right of kings; but it also emphasizes the wishes and will of the people, or people-centered thinking. In ancient China, this phrase was often used in praise of the founding of a new dynasty, and the implementation of major social reforms to justify its legitimacy.

引例 Citation：

◎ 天地革而四时成。汤武革命,顺乎天而应乎人。(《周易·彖下》)
（天地有阴阳的变化而形成一年四季。商汤、周武王变革天命 [推翻旧政权,建立新政权],是顺应了上天的旨意和人民的意愿。）

Changes of yin and yang in heaven and earth give rise to the four seasons. Following the mandate of heaven and complying with the wishes of the people, King Tang and King Wu overthrew old regimes and established the Shang and Zhou dynasties respectively. (*The Book of Changes*)

思

/sī/

Reflecting / Thinking

　　心所具有的思考与辨别的能力。儒家认为"思"是人心所独有的重要功能。心能"思",因此可以不像耳目之官一样被外物牵引或遮蔽。人只有通过心之"思",才能发现内在于心的道德品性的根基,并由此通达于"天道",从而确立人之所以为人的本质。如果缺少"思"的工夫,人将丧失其主体性与独立性。

The term means the ability to reflect and evaluate. Confucian scholars considered this a unique quality of the human mind. By reflecting, a person will keep himself from being led astray or getting confused by what he sees or hears. Through reflecting, a person will discover the foundation of morality. This leads to understanding the way of heaven, and eventually, the essence of being human. Without reflecting, humans will lose their individual consciousness and independence.

引例 Citations:

◎学而不思则罔,思而不学则殆。(《论语·为政》)

(只"学"而不"思",则会迷茫昏乱;只"思"而不"学",则会疑惑危殆。)

Learning without reflecting leads to confusion; reflecting without learning leads to danger. (*The Analects*)

◎耳目之官不思,而蔽于物,物交物,则引之而已矣。心之官则思。思则得之,不思则不得也。此天之所与我者,先立乎其大者,则其小者不能夺也。(《孟子·告子上》)

(耳目等器官不能思考,因而被外物的表象遮蔽。耳目与外物相接触,就会被其引向歧途。"心"这一器官能够思考,思考便能有所得,不思考便无所得。这是天赋予我的,先确立心作为大者的官能,如此则不会被耳目之官的欲望遮蔽。)

The sensory organs like ears and eyes cannot think. Therefore, they tend to be misled by the appearance of external objects, and they tend to be led astray when coming into contact with such objects. The heart, however, is an organ capable of thinking. Thinking creates insight, while lack of it will lead one to a dead end. So thinking is the gift Heaven bestows on us. One should first establish the primary function of the heart, thus not be misled by eyes and ears. (*Mencius*)

斯文
/sīwén/

Be Cultured and Refined

即"文"或"人文",包括礼乐教化、典章制度等,也即诗书、礼乐、法度等精神文明的创造以及与之相关的既有差等又有调和的社会秩序。"斯",此,这个。后"斯文"连用,也用于指读书人或文人;又衍生出文雅之意,形容一种教养或风度。

Literally, the term means "this culture." It encompasses the cultural and ethical progress created by rites, music, education, codes, and systems as well as a social order which is hierarchical but harmonious. Later, this term came to refer to the literati and extended to mean being cultured and refined.

引例 Citation:

◎天之将丧斯文也,后死者不得与于斯文也。(《论语·子罕》)

(上天如果要消灭周代的礼乐制度,那我也不可能掌握它了。)

If Heaven wished that this culture should perish, then I could do nothing about it. (*The Analects*)

四端

/sìduān/

Four Initiators

　　仁、义、礼、智四德的端始、萌芽。孟子（前372？—前289）认为仁、义、礼、智根于心。恻隐之心是仁之端，羞恶之心是义之端，辞让之心是礼之端，是非之心是智之端。"四端"是每一个人天生所具有的，是人之所以为人的本质特征。人只要充分扩充、发挥自己内心所固有的善端，就能够成就仁、义、礼、智四德，从而成为君子乃至圣人。

The four initiators are buds of four virtues: ren (仁), yi (义), li (礼), and zhi (智), or roughly benevolence, righteousness, propriety, and wisdom, which Mencius (372?-289 BC) believed were all rooted in man's mind. Commiseration is the initiator of benevolence. Shame is the initiator of righteousness. Deference is the initiator of propriety and a sense of right and wrong is the initiator of wisdom. The four initiators are naturally possessed by man. They are fundamental features defining a human being. Man should fully cultivate and develop his inherent kindness, then he can accomplish the four virtues, and consequently become a man of virtue or even a sage.

引例 Citation：

◎凡有四端于我者，知皆扩而充之矣，若火之始然，泉之始达。苟能充之，足以保四海；苟不充之，不足以事父母。（《孟子·公孙丑上》）

（凡是具有"四端"的人，知道把它们扩充起来，就好像火刚开始燃烧，泉水刚开始涌出。如果能够扩充"四端"，就足以安定天下；如果不能扩充"四端"，都不足以奉养父母。）

All who have the four initiators in them should know how to cultivate them, so that these initiators will grow, just like a fire that has started burning, or a spring that has started gushing out. If people can cultivate and expand the four initiators, they can bring stability to the world. Otherwise, they can hardly provide for their parents. (*Mencius*)

四海

/sìhǎi/

Four Seas

全国各地或世界各地。古人认为中国的疆域四面环海，各依方位称"东海""南海""西海"和"北海"，合称"四海"。它蕴含着远古中国人关于中国和世界的地理图景："九州"居"天下"之中，"天下"由"九州"及其周边"四海"组成，中国是"海内"，外国则是"海外"。在古人那里，"四海"大多统指天下，并不确指某个海域，有时用来指陆地四周的海，有时又指"四海"所环绕的陆地。

Four Seas refer to the territory of China or the entire world. The ancient Chinese believed that China was a land surrounded by Four Seas – the East, West, North, and South seas. The term suggests what the ancient Chinese conceived to be the map of China and the world: Nine *zhou* (regions) were located at the center of *tianxia* (all under heaven). *Tianxia* consisted of nine *zhou* and its surrounding Four Seas. China was within the Four Seas, while foreign lands were outside the Four Seas. In ancient China, Four Seas referred to all under heaven in most cases, and did not denote a specific body of water. Therefore, the term was used sometimes to mean the seas surrounding the land, and sometimes to specify the land surrounded by the Four Seas.

引例 Citation：

◎君子敬而无失，与人恭而有礼，四海之内皆兄弟也。(《论语·颜渊》)

（君子做事认真而不出差错，待人谦恭而合于礼，那么天下所有的人都是他的兄弟。）

A man of virtue always does things conscientiously without making any mistakes and treats people respectfully and appropriately. Then all within the Four Seas will be his brothers. (*The Analects*)

四海之内皆兄弟

/sìhǎi zhī nèi jiē xiōngdì/

All the People Within the Four Seas Are Brothers.

全天下的人都亲如兄弟。也说"四海皆兄弟"。"四海"即东海、西海、南海、北海。古人认为天圆地方，中国居陆地中间，陆地四周由四海环绕。"四海之内"指当时已知的人类生活空间，犹言"天下"，意指全国或全世界。它昭示了中国人兼济天下的博大胸怀、仁爱友善的人文精神。

This saying means that all the people in the world are as close as brothers. The Four Seas are the East, West, South, and North seas. The ancient Chinese believed that heaven was round and the earth was square, with China in the middle of the earth, which was surrounded on all four sides by the Four Seas. "Within the Four Seas" refers to the world inhabited by humans, which was also called "all under heaven," referring to the whole country or the whole world. This saying shows the inclusive and broad mind of the Chinese and their compassion, love and friendship towards other human beings.

引例 Citation：

◎君子敬而无失，与人恭而有礼，四海之内皆兄弟也。(《论语·颜渊》)

（君子做事认真而不出差错，待人谦恭而合于礼，那么天下所有的人都是他的兄弟。）

A man of virtue always does things conscientiously without making any mistakes and treats people respectfully and appropriately. Then all within the Four Seas will be his brothers. (*The Analects*)

四书

/sìshū/

Four Books

《论语》《孟子》《大学》《中庸》等四部儒家经典的合称。《大学》《中庸》原是《礼记》中的两篇，在唐代以前，并没有引起人们的特别重视。随着唐宋以来儒学的复兴，《大学》《中庸》经过唐代韩愈（768—824）、李翱（772—836）的表彰，宋代程颢（1032—1085）、程颐（1033—1107）兄弟和朱熹（1130—1200）的推崇，被赋予了新的意义，其地位逐渐提升，与《论语》《孟子》并列，合称"四书"。朱熹所著《四书章句集注》确立了"四书"的经典地位。"四书"成为了宋明理学家创建、阐发自身思想的重要素材，对后世儒学的发展产生了深远影响。

This term refers collectively to the four Confucian classics: *The Analects*, *Mencius*, *The Great Learning*, and *The Doctrine of the Mean*. *The Great Learning* and *The Doctrine of the Mean* originally were two sections of *The Book of Rites*, but before the Tang Dynasty they did not attract much attention. Following the revival of Confucianism which began in the Tang and Song dynasties, through the advocacy of Han Yu (768-824) and Li Ao (772-836) of the Tang Dynasty, Cheng Hao (1032-1085), Cheng Yi (1033-1107) and Zhu Xi (1130-1200) of the Song Dynasty, *The Great Learning* and *The Doctrine of the Mean* were given new meaning. Their standing was gradually elevated, and they were regarded just as important as *The Analects* and *Mencius*. The four were then collectively known as the Four Books. *Commentaries on the Four Books*, written by Zhu Xi, established the dominant position of the Four Books, which formed the foundation for the Neo-Confucian scholars of the Song and Ming dynasties. The Four Books became the source from which the Neo-Confucian scholars drew inspiration to further their learning, and thus exerted a profound influence on the development of Confucianism.

引例 Citation：

◎ 如《大学》《中庸》《语》《孟》四书，道理粲然。（《朱子语类》卷十四）

（如《大学》《中庸》《论语》《孟子》四部经典，其中的道理明白易懂。）

The principles in the Four Books, i.e., *The Great Learning*, *The Doctrine of the Mean*, *The Analects*, and *Mencius*, are illuminating and easy to follow. (*Categorized Conversations of Master Zhu Xi*)

四象
/sìxiàng/

Four Images

"八卦"生成过程中由"两仪"分化出的四种物象或特性。《周易·系辞上》言:"《易》有太极,是生两仪,两仪生四象,四象生八卦。""两仪"继续分化形成相互区别而又相互关联的四种物象或特性,就是"四象"。对于"四象"的具体内容,古人有着不同的理解:其一,从万物生成的角度来看,"四象"或指春、夏、秋、冬四时,或指金、木、水、火四种基本元素。其二,从占筮的角度来理解,"四象"或指揲(shé)分蓍草时每组被分出的四根蓍草,或指画卦时所确定的太阴、太阳、少阴、少阳等四种爻象。

This term means the four images, or features of the four images, which are engendered through the division of the two modes in the process of the formation of the eight trigrams. As explained in *The Book of Changes*, "Changes involve *taiji* (太极 the supreme ultimate), which produces two modes. The two modes generate the four images, and the four images generate the eight trigrams." The four images are distinct from one another while also mutually related. There was no agreement among ancient scholars with regard to what the four images represent. From the point of view of the coming into being of all things, the four images might stand for the four seasons: spring, summer, autumn, and winter; or four basic elements: metal, wood, water, and fire. Alternatively, as a term in divination, the four images could refer to the four stalks in each group when the divination stalks are divided in a fortune-telling exercise, or to four line images for divination: greater yin, greater yang, lesser yin, and lesser yang.

引例 Citations：

◎ 大衍之数五十，其用四十有九。分而为二以象两，挂一以象三，揲之以四以象四时。(《周易·系辞上》)

(用来广泛推演变化的数是五十，使用的有四十九根蓍草。将这些蓍草分为两份，以象征"两仪"。从其中一份抽出一根蓍草，以象征天、地、人"三才"。其余蓍草则每四根为一组进行划分，以象征"四时"。)

The total number of divination stalks is fifty; those that are used are forty-nine. These are divided into two groups representing the pair of modes. One stalk is taken from one group to represent the three elements of heaven, earth, and man, and the rest are counted out in fours to represent the four seasons. (*The Book of Changes*)

◎ "两仪生四象"者，谓金木水火，禀天地而有，故云"两仪生四象"。(《周易·系辞上》孔颖达正义)

(所谓"两仪生四象"，是指金木水火四种基本元素，禀受于天地而存有，所以说"两仪生四象"。)

The four images generated by the two modes refer to metal, wood, water, and fire. They come into existence thanks to heaven and earth, and therefore it is said that the two modes generate the four images. (Kong Yingda: *Correct Meaning of The Book of Changes*)

岁寒三友
/suìhán-sānyǒu/

Three Friends of Winter / Steadfast, Loyal Friends

严寒时节的三位友人，具体指松、竹、梅三种植物。在中国传统文化中，有些植物因其自然属性而被赋予某种人文蕴涵。松、竹四季常青，历冬不凋；梅花凌霜傲雪，美丽绽放。三者都不怕严寒，在严寒中展现自身的生命力和自然美，宛如在严寒中相伴生长的好友，故被世人合称为"岁寒三友"。它常被用来喻指忠贞不渝的友谊，寄托对于孤傲高洁人格的崇尚和向往。

"Three friends of winter" refer to the pine, bamboo and plum. In traditional culture, certain human characteristics are attributed to plants and animals based on their natural qualities. The pine and bamboo remain green all year round even in the coldest season, and the plum blooms in early spring when snow and frost are still frequent. These three plants are cold-resistant and retain their beauty even in harsh weather, just like good friends keep each other's company during an icy winter. This term is often used to refer to loyal and steadfast friendship, and also represent the fine qualities of high-mindedness and detachment.

引例 Citations:

◎岁寒，然后知松柏之后凋也。(《论语·子罕》)
(每年到了天气最寒冷的时节，才知道松树与柏树是最后凋谢的。)
Only when the year turns deadly cold do we see that pines and cypresses are the last to wither. (*The Analects*)

◎到深秋之后，百花皆谢，惟有松竹梅花，岁寒三友。(无名氏《渔樵闲话》第四折)
(到了深秋之后，各种花都凋谢了，只有松、竹、梅花依然生机盎然，是岁寒三友。)
By late autumn, all the other flowers have withered. Only the pine, bamboo and plum remain vibrant, thus described as three steadfast friends in the cold. (*Casual Talk Between a Fisherman and a Woodcutter*)

太虚
/tàixū/

***Taixu* (Great Void)**

虚空的境地或事物虚空的状态。张载（1020—1077）对"太虚"的含义进行了深入的阐发。他认为，天地万物都是由"气"构成的。而

"太虚"是"气"的一种无形而虚静的状态。这一状态是"气"的本然状态。"太虚"凝聚而为"气","气"消散而复归于"太虚"。"太虚"只是无法被人感知,并不是绝对的空虚无有。"太虚"的属性通过"气"而赋予天地万物。

Taixu (太虚) refers to a state of void in both space and things. Zhang Zai (1020-1077), a thinker in the Song Dynasty, elaborated on the meaning of *taixu*, or great void. He believed that all things in heaven and on earth were made up of *qi* (气), and that *taixu* was its natural state, which was formless and motionless. When *taixu* coalesced, it turned into *qi*; when *qi* dissipated, it became *taixu*. Though *taixu* could not be felt by humans, it was not absolute emptiness and nothingness. *Taixu* gave life to all things in heaven and on earth by means of *qi*.

引例 Citations:

◎ 是以不过乎昆仑,不游乎太虚。(《庄子·知北游》)

(因此不能越过昆仑之山,不能巡游于太虚之中。)

And so, they will not be able to go beyond Mount Kunlun, nor can they wander in the great void. (*Zhuangzi*)

◎ 太虚无形,气之本体,其聚其散,变化之客形尔。(张载《正蒙·太和》)

(太虚是无形的,是气的本来状态,气或聚或散,不过是太虚变化的暂时形态罢了。)

Taixu, or the great void, is formless; it is the original state of *qi*. Whether *qi* coalesces or dissipates, it is just a temporary form of *taixu*. (Zhang Zai: *Enlightenment Through Confucian Teachings*)

体

/tǐ/

Ti

"体"作为文艺学、美学范畴，主要含义有三：其一，指文学艺术的某一门类、流派、体式、作品区别于其他文学艺术门类、流派、体式、作品的整体特征。它是包含了文学艺术的体式、内容、语言、风格等诸要素在内所呈现出的总体形态与艺术特征。其二，指文学艺术作品的风格，不包括体式、形式等方面的内容。其三，指文学作品的基本样式，即文体或文学体制。历代文论家对文体的分类不尽相同，比如南朝梁昭明太子萧统（501—531）《文选》将文体分为38种。中国古代文学的文体丰富多样，各有自己的基本样式与写作要求，而风格即是作者的艺术个性在作品中的显现，有时也表现为一个时代、一个流派的文学特征。这一术语经常与人名、朝代名等结合，如骚体、陶体、建安体等，用来指称与作品风格相关的艺术特征并广泛运用于文艺批评与鉴赏中。

Ti (体) has three different meanings in the study of literature, art, and aesthetics. First, it refers to features that distinguish one particular category, form, or literary school from others. These features represent the overall form and artistic characteristics, including the structure, content, language, style, and other essential elements. Second, it refers only to literary and artistic style, not their form or shape. Third, it refers to the basic literary and artistic form, i.e., the writing style and literary genre. Scholars of literary theory in different historical periods did not use the same standards to classify literary styles. For example, Xiao Tong (501-531, Crown Prince Zhaoming of the Liang Dynasty during the Southern Dynasties) classified literary and artistic works into 38 styles or categories in his *Selections of Refined Literature*. There is a wide range of writing styles and literary genres in classical Chinese literature, each with its own style and writing requirements. The style of a literary work reflects the author's individual artistic temperament, and, sometimes, also the literary and artistic trend in a particular era. This term is often used together with the name of a person or a dynasty to describe literary and artistic features peculiar to a school of literature. Examples are the Sao Style (represented by the famous poem, "*Lisao*", written by renowned poet Qu Yuan), Tao Style (represented by poet Tao Yuanming), and Jian'an Style (named after the period of Jian'an during the Han Dynasty). The term is widely used in literary criticism and appreciation.

引例 Citations:

◎ 夫人善于自见，而文非一体，鲜能备善，是以各以所长，相轻所短。(曹丕《典论·论文》)

(人总是善于看到自己的优点，然而文章不止一种文体，很少有人擅长所有文体，因此各人总是以自己所擅长的文体写作而轻视别人所不擅长的文体。)

People are always quick to see their own strengths. However, given the rich variety of literary styles, few people are accomplished in all of them. Therefore, people always write in the styles they are good at while taking lightly other people's works written in styles they happen to be weak in. (Cao Pi: On Literary Classics)

◎ 自汉至魏，四百余年，辞人才子，文体三变。(《宋书·谢灵运传论》)

(自汉至魏，四百多年，写诗文的才子[众多]，而诗文的体制风格，也经历了三次大的变化。)

For more than 400 years from the Han Dynasty to the Wei Dynasty, numerous talented poets came to the fore, and the styles of poetry and essay writing went through three major transformations. (*The History of Song of the Southern Dynasties*)

体用

/tǐyòng/

Ti and Yong

"体用"有三种不同含义：其一，形体、实体为"体"，形体、实体的功能、作用为"用"。其二，事物的本体为"体"，本体的显现、运用为"用"。其三，行事、行为的根本原则为"体"，根本原则的具体施用为"用"。在"体用"对待的关系中,"体"是基础,"用"是依赖于"体"的。

Ti (体) and *yong* (用) can be understood in three different ways: 1) a physical thing and its functions or roles; 2) the ontological existence of a thing and its expression and application; and 3) the fundamental code of conduct, and its observance. In any *ti–yong* relationship, *ti* provides the basis on which *yong* depends.

引例 Citations：

◎ 天者定体之名，乾者体用之称。(《周易·乾》孔颖达正义)

("天"是确定实体的名称，"乾"是表现实体之功用的名称。)

Tian (天) means heaven in the physical sense, while *qian* (乾) means its functions and significance. (Kong Yingda: *Correct Meaning of The Book of Changes*)

◎ 至微者理也，至著者象也。体用一源，显微无间。(程颐《程氏易传·序》)

(最隐微的是理，最显著的是象。作为本体的理和作为现象的象出自同一来源，显著与隐微之间没有差别。)

What is most subtle is *li* (理), while what is most conspicuous is *xiang* (象). *Li* as the ontological existence and *xiang* as its manifestation are of the same origin; there is no difference between them. (Cheng Yi: *Cheng Yi's Commentary on The Book of Changes*)

天

/tiān/

Tian (Heaven)

"天"是中国古代思想中具有神圣性和终极意义的一个概念。主要有三种不同的含义：其一，指自然意义上的天空或人世之外的整个自然界，其运行呈现出一定的规律和秩序。其二，指主宰万物的具有人格意志的神灵。其三，指万事万物所遵循的普遍法则，同时也是人的心性、道德以及社会和政治秩序的依据。

Tian（天）is a sacred and fundamental concept in ancient Chinese philosophy. It has three different meanings. The first is the physical sky or the entirety of nature (not including human society), the operations of which manifest certain laws and order. The second refers to a spiritual being, which possesses an anthropomorphic will and governs everything in the universe. The third denotes the universal law, which is observed by all things and beings, and which is also the basis of human nature, morality, and social and political orders.

引例 Citations：

◎ 天行有常，不为尧存，不为桀亡。(《荀子·天论》)
（天的运行有其常道，不因为尧在位而存在，不因为桀在位而消失。）

Nature's ways are constant. They did not exist because Yao was on the throne or disappear because Jie was the ruler. (*Xunzi*)

◎ 上天孚佑下民。(《尚书·汤诰》)
（上天信任并保佑百姓。）

Heaven trusts and blesses the people. (*The Book of History*)

◎ 天者，理也。(《二程遗书》卷十一)
（天就是宇宙的普遍法则。）

Heaven is the overarching law of the universe. (*Writings of the Cheng Brothers*)

天经地义

/tiānjīng-dìyì/

Natural Rules and Orderliness

天地的规则与秩序。据《左传》的记载，郑国子产（？—前522）提出了"天经地义"之说，以解释礼的本质及依据。在子产看来，天地的运行遵循着恒常的规则，并呈现出稳定的秩序，具有最高的合理性。人应效法于天地，符合"天经地义"的言行与秩序即是合理的、正当的。礼对人的言行及人伦秩序的规定，正是"天经地义"的体现。"天经地义"一词后来被广泛地用以描述各种事物的正当性及不容置疑的道理。

Literally, this term means the rules and orderliness of heaven and earth. According to *Zuo's Commentary on The Spring and Autumn Annals*, Zichan (?-522 BC) of the State of Zheng proposed the concept to explain the essence and justification of rites. Zichan believed that the movements of heaven and earth followed eternal rules that created a consistent and rational order. Man too should imitate this in word and deed in an orderly, rational, and proper way. The constraints that rites place on human behavior, and the resulting social ethics and harmony are all manifestations of these laws of nature. The expression later came to mean anything that is proper, or any reasoning that is justified.

引例 Citation：

◎夫礼，天之经也，地之义也，民之行也。(《左传·昭公二十五年》)

(礼是天地运行的法则，民众行为的规范。)

Rites represent the rules governing the movement of heaven and earth as well as the code of conduct for the people. (*Zuo's Commentary on The Spring and Autumn Annals*)

天命

/tiānmìng/

Mandate of Heaven

天的命令与赐予。"天命"主要包含三种不同含义：其一，指天对于人事的命令。命令的内容最初集中于王权的更替，即上天授命有德者征讨并取代失德之君，享有至高无上的权力和福禄。其二，指命运，具有不可抗拒之义，标志着人力的限度。其三，指天赋予人的禀性。《中庸》称"天命之谓性"。宋儒发挥这一思想，以"天命之性"指称人禀受于天的纯善的本性。

The term means order and bestowment from Heaven. "Mandate of heaven" mainly contains three different meanings. The first is the order of heaven over human affairs. Such order first of all focuses on a change of the supreme ruler's authority. Heaven empowers the virtuous to attack and replace a ruler who has lost his virtue, and thus enjoy the highest and unsurpassed power and benefits. Secondly, mandate of heaven means fate, which is irresistible and imposes limit on human power. Thirdly, the term indicates the natural disposition bestowed by heaven upon human being. According to *The Doctrine of the Mean*, "Mandate of heaven endows one with his nature." Song-dynasty Confucian scholars developed this idea, proposing that human nature was the "nature of mandate of heaven," that is, the inherent pure and good nature one receives from heaven.

引例 Citations：

◎ 天命靡常。(《诗经·大雅·文王》)

（上天的命令没有恒常不变的。）

Heaven-bestowed supreme power is not eternal. (*The Book of Songs*)

◎ 莫之为而为者天也，莫之致而至者命也。(《孟子·万章上》)

（没有人能做到却做到了，这是天意；没有人求它来它却来到了，这是命运。）

That which no man can do but is accomplished is the mandate of heaven. That which no man asks but comes is from fate. (*Mencius*)

天命靡常

/tiānmìng-mǐcháng/

Heaven-bestowed Supreme Power Is Not Eternal.

  上天的命令没有恒常不变的。出自《诗经·大雅·文王》。古人相信，上天的命令决定着人世中至高无上的王权的归属。但天命所赐予的王权并不是恒常不变的，殷周的更迭就是由于天命发生了改易。而天命的改易遵循着固定的法则，君主有德则授命，失德则剥夺天命。因此，"天命靡常"的观念警醒着统治者，时刻修养自身的德行以保有天命。

This term first appears in *The Book of Songs*. It means that there is no one who can forever remain a recipient of the bestowed supreme power by the Ruler of Heaven. The ancients believed that the heavenly order determined to whom the supreme royal power belonged. However, the choice of the recipient of such a conferment was not forever. Replacement of the Shang Dynasty by the Zhou Dynasty was brought about by the change of the recipient of Heaven's bestowal of the mandate to rule. However, the change of the recipients of the mandate followed a fixed principle: such bestowal could fall only on a ruler who was virtuous. Once he had lost virtue, the mandate to rule would be withdrawn from him. Therefore, the concept of the change of the recipient of Heaven's mandate served as a warning to the ruler, who must constantly cultivate his virtue in order to keep his rule.

引例 Citation：

◎ 侯服于周，天命靡常。殷士肤敏，祼（guàn）将于京。厥作祼将，常服黼（fǔ）冔（xǔ）。王之荩（jìn）臣，无念尔祖。(《诗经·大雅·文王》)

（于是殷人臣服于周，上天的命令没有恒常不变的。归顺的殷人优美而敏捷，到京师行祼礼助祭，他们穿旧黼衣、戴旧冠。今周王任用臣下，不应该感念祖先的德行吗？）

Thus the officials of the Yin became the subjects of the Zhou. This follows the rule that there is no one who can forever remain the recipient of Heaven's mandate to rule. The Yin officials, healthy and agile, wearing costumes embroidered with black-and-white designs and traditional caps, came to the capital to assist in the ritual ceremonies. Shouldn't they, now appointed by the Zhou as officials, be grateful for the virtue of their ancestors? (*The Book of Songs*)

天人合一

/tiānrén-héyī/

Heaven and Man Are United as One.

一种认为天地人相通的世界观和思维方式。这种世界观旨在强调天地和人之间的整体性和内在联系，突出了天对于人或人事的根源性意义，表现了人在与天的联系中寻求生命、秩序与价值基础的努力。"天人合一"在历史上有不同的表现方式，如天人同类、同气或者同理等。如孟子（前372？—前289）认为通过心的反思可以知性、知天，强调心、性和天之间的统一。宋儒寻求天理、人性和人心之间的相通。老子则主张"人法地，地法天，天法道"。根据对天和人理解的不同，"天人合一"也会具有不同的意义。

The term represents a world outlook and a way of thinking which hold that heaven and earth and man are interconnected. This world outlook emphasizes the integration and inherent relationship between heaven, earth, and man. It highlights the fundamental significance of nature to man or human affairs, and describes the endeavor made by man to pursue life, order, and values through interaction with nature. The term has different ways of expression in history, such as heaven and man being of the same category, sharing the same vital energy, or sharing the same principles. Mencius (372?-289 BC), for one, believed that through mental reflection one could gain understanding of human nature and heaven, emphasizing the unity of mind, human nature, and heaven. Confucian scholars of the Song Dynasty sought to connect the principles of heaven, human nature, and the human mind. Laozi maintained that "man's law is earthly, earth's law is natural, and heaven's law is Dao." Depending on a different understanding of heaven and man, the term may have different meanings.

引例 Citations：

◎以类合之，天人一也。（董仲舒《春秋繁露・阴阳义》）

（以事类相合来看，天与人是一体的。）

In terms of integration of categories, heaven and man are one. (Dong Zhongshu: *Luxuriant Gems of The Spring and Autumn Annals*)

◎ 儒者则因明致诚，因诚致明，故天人合一，致学而可以成圣，得天而未始遗人。（张载《正蒙·乾称》）

（儒者则由明察人伦而通达天理之诚，由通达天理之诚而洞明世事，因此天与人相合为一，通过学习而可以成为圣人，把握天理而不曾遗失对人伦的洞察。）

A Confucian scholar is sincere because of his understanding, and he achieves understanding because of his sincerity. That is why heaven and man are united as one. One can become a sage through studies, and master heaven's law without losing understanding of man's law. (Zhang Zai: *Enlightenment Through Confucian Teachings*)

天人之分

/tiānrénzhīfēn/

Distinction Between Man and Heaven

一种认为天与人相分别的世界观和思维方式。此说最初由荀子（前313？—前238）所提出，他反对将人世的道德、秩序的来源或依据寄托于天。荀子认为，天与人各有其职分，不应混淆。天地日月的运行、寒暑水旱的出现，都属于天职的领域，有其常道，与人事无关，也非人力所及。而人的道德、人世的治乱则属于人职的范围，人应对道德的养成及社会的治理负责。只有明确了"天人之分"，人才能在天所赋予和确立的基础之上发挥人的能力而不是僭越到人无法用力的领域。

This term refers to a world outlook and a way of thinking which hold that heaven and man are different. This explanation was first put forward by Xunzi (313?-238 BC), who did not believe that human morality and the order of human society emanated from heaven. He argued that heaven and man each had a different role and that they should not be mixed. Temporal changes of heaven and earth as well as the occurrence of seasonal changes in temperature and rainfall all belonged to the domain of heaven. They had their normal path, unrelated to human affairs, and were beyond the reach of human power. On the other hand, man's morality and order in the world belonged to the realm of man. People should be responsible for moral development and social order. Only by making a clear distinction between heaven and man could one develop his abilities on the basis established by heaven, without overstepping into a domain where man was unable to exert his power.

引例 Citation：

◎ 天行有常，不为尧存，不为桀亡。……强本而节用，则天不能贫；养备而动时，则天不能病；修道而不贰，则天不能祸。……故明于天人之分，则可谓至人矣。(《荀子·天论》)

(天的运行有其常道，不因为尧在位而存在，不因为桀在位而消失。……加强农事而节省用度，则天不能使之贫乏；供养充足而活动适时，则天不能使之疾病；循行正道而坚定不移，则天不能加以灾祸。……因此能够明晓天与人的区分，就可以称之为最高明的人了。)

Nature's ways are constant. They did not exist because Yao was on the throne or disappear because Jie was the ruler... When you work diligently in agriculture and are frugal in expenditures, nature cannot impoverish you. When you are well provided for with what you need and work at the proper time, nature cannot make you sick. When you firmly follow the right path, nature cannot bring you disaster... Therefore, he who understands the distinction between nature and man may be called the wisest man. (*Xunzi*)

天时地利人和

/tiānshí dìlì rénhé/

Opportune Time, Geographic Advantage, and Unity of the People

"天时"本指作战时的有利气候，泛指时间上的各种有利条件，包括天气、时机、机遇等；"地利"本指作战时的有利地形，泛指空间上的各种有利条件，包括地形、地势、区位等；"人和"本指得到人们拥护，上下同心，团结一致，泛指人的优势。古人认为，它们是事关成败的三种最重要的因素；而且"天时不如地利，地利不如人和"，其中起决定作用的是"人和"。它反映了中国人考虑问题的三个基本向度——时间（时机）、空间（环境）和人，体现"以人为本"的基本理念。

"Opportune time," which originally referred to the favorable weather at the time of war, now generally refers to various temporal advantages, including weather, timing, opportunity, and so on. "Geographic advantage," which originally referred to advantageous positions in battle, now refers to generally various favorable spacial conditions, including terrain, position, location, and such. "Unity of the people," which originally referred to popular support, unity of all ranks, and societal solidarity, now refers in general to advantages in personnel. Ancient Chinese believed that these three were the most important factors for success. Among them, "unity of the people" is decisive because "opportune time is not as valuable as geographic advantage, and geographic advantage is not as valuable as unity of the people." The saying reflects the three fundamental dimensions of a problem the Chinese people take into consideration: time (opportunity), space (environment), and people. It reflects the basic notion of putting people at the center of everything.

引例 Citations：

◎ 天时、地利、人和，三者不得，虽胜有殃。(《孙膑兵法·月战》)
（有利的气候条件、有利的地理条件、人的齐心协力，这三者如不齐备，即便打了胜仗，自己也会蒙受损失。）

Favorable weather conditions, geographic advantages, and the unity of the people all must be in place. If not, victory will be costly. (*Sun Bin's Art of War*)

◎ 天时不如地利，地利不如人和。(《孟子·公孙丑下》)
（有利的气候条件不如有利的地理条件，有利的地理条件不如人的齐心协力。）

Favorable weather conditions are not as valuable as favorable geographic conditions, and favorable geographic conditions are not as valuable as the unity of the people. (*Mencius*)

天下
/tiānxià/

Tianxia (All Under Heaven)

  古多指天子统治范围内的全部土地及统治权。古人认为，大夫的统治范围是"家"，诸侯的统治范围是"国"，天子的统治范围是"天下"。"天下"字面义是"普天之下"，实质指天子统治或名义之下的"家国"统合体所覆盖的全部疆域，并包括天下所有的人及国家的统治权。后演变指全民族或全世界。

This term referred mainly to all the land under the name of the Son of Heaven and the right to rule on such land. The ancient Chinese held that the rule of senior officials was over their enfeoffed land, and that of dukes and princes was over feudal states. The rule of the Son of Heaven was over all the land. Literally, *tianxia* (天下) means "all under heaven." It actually refers to all the territory embracing the enfeoffed land and feudal states under the rule or in the name of the Son of Heaven, as well as all the subjects and the right to rule. The term has later evolved to refer to the whole nation or the whole world.

引例 Citations：

◎ 溥天之下，莫非王土；率土之滨，莫非王臣。(《诗经·小雅·北山》)

（普天之下，无一不是天子的土地；四海之内，无一不是天子的臣民。）

All land under heaven falls within the domain of the Son of Heaven; all those on this land are his subjects. (*The Book of Songs*)

◎ 大道之行也，天下为（wéi）公。选贤与能，讲信修睦。(《礼记·礼运》)

（大道实行的时代，天下为天下人所共有。品德高尚、才能突出的人被选拔出来管理社会，人与人之间讲求诚实与和睦。）

When the Great Way prevails, the world belongs to all the people. People of virtue and competence are chosen to govern the country; honesty is valued and people live in harmony. (*The Book of Rites*)

◎ 天下兴亡，匹夫有责。（梁启超《痛定罪言》三）

（天下的兴盛与衰亡，[关乎到每个人，因此]每个人都有责任。）

The rise and fall of a nation is the concern of every individual. (Liang Qichao: Painful Reflections on Current Affairs Despite Possible Incrimination)

天下为公
/tiānxià-wéigōng/

The World Belongs to All.

　　天下是公众的，天下为天下人所共有。"天下"，本义是"普天之下"，喻指君位、国家政权或整个国家，后泛指整个世界。"公"，大家、公众，狭义指贤人、德才兼备的人，广义指全体国民或天下所有的人。"天下为公"主要有两层意思：其一，君位非一人一姓所私有，而为有才德的人所共有，即所谓传贤不传子。其二，国家非一人一姓所私有，而为公众所共有。其中包含着反对君位世袭、主张推举有才德之人掌权的"尚贤"和"民本"思想。古人相信，"天下为公"是实现"大同"社会、人民生活幸福的政治前提和保障。至近代，"天下为公"又演变成为推翻专制、实现民主的标志性关键词，后来成为一种美好的社会政治理想。

The world is a public realm and therefore belongs to all the people. *Tianxia* (天下), which literally means everything under heaven, used to refer to the monarch, state power, or the nation; later it extended to mean the whole world. In the narrow sense, *gong* (公) refers to figures with both integrity and competence, while in the broad sense it refers to all the people of a country, or everyone in the world. This term has two meanings. The first is that the position of a ruler is not the private property of just one person or his family, but rather belongs to all people of virtue and ability. Hence, the throne should be passed on to people according to their merit rather than through bloodline. The second meaning is that a country does not belong to a single individual or family, but belongs to the public. This is a people-centered vision, which opposes hereditary rule and believes that people with virtue and competence should be selected to exercise power. Ancient Chinese held this to be the foundation and guarantee for people to enjoy a happy life and realize universal harmony. In modern times, it evolved into a key concept calling for overthrowing autocracy and realizing democracy and later into a longing for an ideal society.

引例 Citation:

◎大道之行也，天下为公。选贤与能，讲信修睦。(《礼记·礼运》)
（大道实行的时代，天下为天下人所共有。品德高尚、才能突出的人被选拔出来管理社会，人与人之间讲求诚实与和睦。）

When the Great Way prevails, the world belongs to all the people. People of virtue and competence are chosen to govern the country; honesty is valued and people live in harmony. (*The Book of Rites*)

天子

/tiānzǐ/

Son of Heaven

"天"之子，指帝王、君主，即帝国或王朝的最高统治者。古人认为，帝王、君主秉上天旨意统治天下，其权力乃天所授，故称帝王、君主为天子。这个名称肯定了帝王、君主的权力来自上天所赐的正当性和神圣性，同时也对之构成一定的约束。这和西方的"君权神授"的观念相似，但有根本不同：中国的"天"不同于西方的"神"，而且蕴含着"天人感应"的思想，即"天"的旨意与人心、民意相贯通。

The Son of Heaven refers to the emperor or monarch, the supreme ruler of an empire or dynasty. People in ancient times believed that a monarch ruled the world by Heaven's decree and with its mandate, hence he was called the Son of Heaven. This term asserted that a ruler's authority was legitimate and sacred, as it was bestowed by Heaven, but to some extent, it also restricted the exercise of this power. This has some commonality to the Western concept of the divine right of kings by the grace of God, but there are fundamental differences. *Tian* (天), the Chinese word for Heaven, is not the same as the Western term "God." Rather, the Chinese term also implies the idea of interaction between Heaven and man, which means that the decree of Heaven also embodies popular will and popular support.

引例 Citations:

◎明明天子，令闻不已。(《诗经·大雅·江汉》)

(勤勤勉勉的周天子，美好的声誉流传不息。)

So diligent is the Son of Heaven! His fame will forever be remembered. (*The Book of Songs*)

◎德侔天地者称皇帝，天祐而子之，号称天子。(董仲舒《春秋繁露·三代改制质文》)

(道德可与天地齐等的人做皇帝，上天保佑他，以他为子，所以号称"天子"。)

A man whose virtue is equal to that of heaven and earth can be an emperor. Heaven blesses him and takes him as his son, so he is called the Son of Heaven. (Dong Zhongshu: *Luxuriant Gems of The Spring and Autumn Annals*)

田园诗

/tiányuánshī/

Idyllic Poetry

一种以描写田园景色和田园生活为主要题材的诗歌流派。由东晋诗人陶渊明（365或372或376—427）开创。陶渊明的诗大部分取材于田园生活，语言质朴，画面平淡，但清新自然，意境深远，韵味醇厚。田园诗为中国古典诗歌开辟了一个新的境界，影响了六朝之后的诗歌发展。

A genre created by Tao Yuanming (365 or 372 or 376-427) of the Eastern Jin Dynasty, idyllic poetry depicts rural life and scenery. Taking country life as his favored theme, Tao Yuanming used plain language to portray rural scenes. His poems were unpretentious, refreshing, and natural, thus creating a far-reaching aesthetic conception and a lasting charm. Idyllic poetry represented a new stage in classical Chinese poetry and shaped poetic development in the Six Dynasties period and beyond.

引例 Citation:

◎以康乐之奥博，多溺于山水；以渊明之高古，偏放于田园。(白居易《与元九书》)

(谢灵运的诗深奥博大，但是多耽溺于山水；陶渊明的诗超拔古朴，却又多放情于田园。)

Xie Lingyun's poems are profound in implication, but focused excessively on mountain and water scenes, while Tao Yuanming's poems are graceful and simple, depicting mainly rural scenes. (Bai Juyi: Letter to Yuan Zhen)

同归殊途

/tóngguī-shūtú/

Arrive at the Same Destination via Different Routes / Rely on a Common Ontological Entity

虽然有着相同的目标，但所走的道路不同。语出《周易·系辞下》，大致包含两方面的含义：其一，指不同学派、不同人对于社会秩序、价值的理解虽然不同，主张的社会治理方法也有差异，但他们的目标是一致的，都是谋求社会的安定、繁荣。其二，指万事万物虽然呈现出不同的样态，但他们都归附或依赖于一个共同的本体。

This term means to reach the same goal through different routes. Coming from *The Book of Changes*, the term has two meanings. First, different schools of thought and different people have different understandings of social order and values, and the ways of governance they advocate also vary, but their goals are the same – stability and prosperity of society. Second, though things under heaven manifest themselves in different ways, they all belong or rely on a common ontological entity.

引例 Citations:

◎天下同归而殊途，一致而百虑。(《周易·系辞下》)
（天下之人有着相同的目标，但所走的道路不同；有着相同的道理，但有上百种不同的想法。）

All people under heaven have the same goal, though they take different routes; they cherish the same principles, but they hold different views. (*The Book of Changes*)

◎子曰"天下同归而殊途，一致而百虑"，一本万殊之谓也。（王夫之《周易外传》卷六）
（孔子说"天下同归而殊途，一致而百虑"，是说天下万物依赖于一个共同的本体［本体表现在不同的事物之中］。）

Confucius said, "Under heaven, people have the same goal but they go by different routes." This means that all things under heaven rely on the same ontological entity. (Wang Fuzhi: *Explanatory Notes to The Book of Changes*)

推己及人

/tuījǐ-jírén/

Put Oneself in Another's Place

以自己的心思推测别人的心思。亦即儒家所说的"恕道"，是实现仁民爱物的重要原则和方法。它首先承认人类在精神上的根本一致，进而以此为原点，弘扬宽和、仁爱精神，设身处地为他人着想，以自身的所思所欲去理解别人：自己不希望的，不要强加给别人；自己所希望的，也要帮助别人实现。

This term means to infer others' thoughts with one's own. It is exactly what Confucianism advocates as tolerance toward others, which is an important principle or method of caring for the people and cherishing all things. In the first place, such thinking believes that people basically share a common spirit. On this basis, tolerance and benevolence need to be advanced. One should show consideration for others by putting oneself in their place, and understand others by walking in their shoes. We should never do unto others what we would not want others to do unto ourselves, and whatever we would wish for ourselves, we should also help others to achieve.

引例 Citations:

◎他人有心，予忖度之。(《诗经·小雅·巧言》)

(别人有什么心思，我能揣测得到。)

We can guess how others feel by putting ourselves in their place. (*The Book of Songs*)

◎强恕而行，求仁莫近焉。(《孟子·尽心上》)

(努力按照将心比心的恕道去做，没有比这更接近仁的了。)

Nothing comes closer to benevolence than trying to empathize with others by standing in their shoes. (*Mencius*)

◎忠恕违道不远，施诸己而不愿，亦勿施于人。(《礼记·中庸》)

(忠和恕离大道不远，如果施加在自己身上而自己不愿意接受，那么也不要强加给别人。)

Loyalty and forgiveness is very close to the principle of integrity, which means we should never impose upon others what we are not willing to accept ourselves. (*The Book of Rites*)

婉约派
/wǎnyuēpài/

The *Wanyue* School / The Graceful and Restrained School

宋词两大流派之一。内容多写儿女之情、离别之绪，其特点是"专主情致"，表情达意讲究含蓄柔婉、隐约细腻，音律婉转谐和，语言圆润清丽。婉约词出现较早，名家辈出，唐五代有温庭筠（？—866）、李煜（937—978），宋初有柳永（987？—1053？）、晏殊（991—1055）、欧阳修（1007—1072）、晏几道（1038—1110），之后又有秦观（1049—1100）、贺铸（1052—1125）、周邦彦（1056—1121）、李清照（1084—1151？），南宋则有姜夔（1155？—1209）、吴文英（1212？—1272？）、张炎（1248—1314后）等一大批词人。在一千多年的词学发展中，婉约词风支配词坛，无论是数量还是质量，婉约派都占据主流和正统地位。需要说明的是，婉约派词人也抒写感时伤世之情，只是多将家国之恨、身世之感寓于抒情咏物，别有寄托，故不能一概以柔媚视之。

As one of the two *ci* (词) lyric schools of the Song Dynasty, the graceful and restrained school mainly dealt with romantic love or parting sorrow. It featured sentimental and nuanced expression of one's feelings, graceful and melodious metric patterning, and mellow and subtle use of language. *Ci* lyrics of this school emerged early, and many poets were famed for writing this style of *ci*, especially Wen Tingyun (?-866) and Li Yu (937-978) of the Five Dynasties period, Liu Yong (987?-1053?), Yan Shu (991-1055), Ouyang Xiu (1007-1072), Yan Jidao (1038-1110), Qin Guan (1049-1100), He Zhu (1052-1125), Zhou Bangyan (1056-1121), and Li Qingzhao (1084-1151?) of the Northern Song Dynasty, as well as Jiang Kui (1155?-1209), Wu Wenying (1212?-1272?), and Zhang Yan (1248-1314?) of the Southern Song Dynasty. The graceful and restrained school occupied a dominant position in terms of both quantity and quality in over one thousand years of poetry's development. It should be mentioned that poets of this school also cared deeply about the fate of the nation, but they tended to express their concerns in a personal and sentimental way, often through depicting scenery. Therefore, their poems should not be regarded as lacking of vigor and energy.

引例 Citations：

◎ 至论其词，则有婉约者，有豪放者。婉约者欲其辞情蕴藉（jiè），豪放者欲其气象恢弘，盖虽各因其质，而词贵感人，要当以婉约为正。（徐师曾《文体明辨序说·诗余》）

（至于说到词，则有婉约风格的，有豪放风格的。婉约词其词句和情感追求含蓄而有意蕴，豪放词则追求气魄和境界宏大壮阔。这虽然是词作者的气质不同所致，但是词讲究以情动人，大体还是应该以婉约为正宗。）

Some *ci* lyrics are graceful and restrained, and some are bold and exuberant. The former are written in a nuanced way, whereas the latter are powerful and unrestrained. This difference is due to different temperament of poets. But *ci* lyrics are about expressing one's nuanced feelings, so the graceful and restrained school is representative of *ci* lyrics. (Xu Shizeng: *A Collection of Introductory Remarks on Various Styles*)

◎ 易安为婉约主，幼安为豪放主，此论非明代诸公所及。（沈曾（zēng）植《菌阁琐谈》）

（李清照是婉约词第一人，辛弃疾是豪放词第一人，这一见解明代诸位评论家并未提及。）

Li Qingzhao was the best *ci* poetess of the graceful and restrained school, whereas Xin Qiji was the best of the bold and unrestrained school. This view, important as it is, was not mentioned by literary critics of the Ming Dynasty. (Shen Zengzhi: *Random Notes on Ci Lyrics from Junge Studio*)

王者富民

/wángzhě-fùmín/

A Ruler Should Enrich People.

　　想要推行王道的君主会使百姓富足。"王者"本指想要推行王道、统一天下的君主，泛指成就伟大事业的领导者。其中隐含的道理是：伟大的事业必须有民众的广泛拥护才能成功，为此，有作为的领导者必须把广大民众利益放在首位，而不能着眼于一部分人的利益，更不能着眼于个人利益。这和"民惟邦本""藏富于民"的思想息息相通。

A great ruler who conducts benevolent governance will enrich his people and unify the country. The implication of this term is that a great cause can succeed only when it is supported by the people. Therefore, a visionary leader must give top priority to the interests of all the people, not just the interests of some people, still less those of some individuals. This term echoes the thinking of "people being the foundation of the state" and "keeping wealth with the people."

引例 Citation：

◎ 故王者富民，霸者富士，仅存之国富大夫，亡国富筐箧、实府库。筐箧已富，府库已实，而百姓贫……则倾覆灭亡可立而待也。（《荀子·王制》）

（所以想要推行王道的君主会使民众富足，想要称霸诸侯的君主会使士兵富足，勉强能存活的国家会使大夫富足，而亡国的君主只是富了自己的箱子、塞满自己的仓库。自己的箱子已装满了，仓库已塞满了，而老百姓却贫困了……那么，这样的政权离倾覆灭亡的日子也就不远了。）

So a ruler who conducts benevolent governance will enrich his people. But a ruler who wants to control all dukes and princes can only enrich his army. A state that only enriches its ministers can barely survive; a state that only keeps the ruler's coffer and his storehouses full is doomed. Inevitably, the people in such a state will be plunged into poverty... It will not be long before such a state collapses. (*Xunzi*)

韦编三绝
/wéibiān-sānjué/

Leather Thongs Binding Wooden Strips Break Three Times.

　　编联竹简或木简的熟皮条断了好多次。中国古人在竹片或木片上书写、记事，然后在这些竹片或木片（称为"简"）上钻孔，用熟皮条

("韦")按顺序编联成册("韦编")。据《史记·孔子世家》记载,孔子(前551—前479)晚年喜欢《周易》,百读不厌,以致编联《周易》简册的皮条多次断裂。后以此形容勤奋读书,好学不倦。

In ancient China, people recorded events by writing on bamboo or wooden strips. They used boiled leather thongs threaded through little holes made on those strips to bind them together into a book according to a certain order. According to the *Records of the Historian*, Confucius (551 - 479 BC) avidly read *The Book of Changes* in his old age. He used the book so often that the leather thongs binding the wooden strips broke three times. Later on, this term is used to describe a person who reads diligently.

引例 Citation:

◎ 孔子晚而喜《易》…… 韦编三绝。(《史记·孔子世家》)

(孔子晚年喜欢《周易》…… 编联《周易》简册的皮条多次断裂。)

In his old age Confucius loved to study *The Book of Changes*… He used this book so much that the leather thongs binding the wooden strips wore out three times. (*Records of the Historian*)

为政以德
/wéizhèng-yǐdé/

Governance Based on Virtue

以道德原则执掌国政、治理国家。孔子(前551—前479)在西周统治者一向秉承的"明德慎罚"的基础上提出了为后世儒家所遵循的"德政"理念。"德政"与"威刑"相对。"为政以德"并非不要刑法,而是突出强调道德对政治的决定作用,将道德教化视为治国的根本原则与方法。

Governance of a state should be guided by virtue. Confucius (551 - 479 BC) expounded this philosophy – which his followers in later eras promoted – on the basis of the approach advocated by the rulers in the Western Zhou Dynasty that prized high moral values and the virtue of being cautious in meting out punishment. Governance based on virtue stands in contrast to rule by use of harsh punishment as a deterrent. It does not, however, exclude the use of punishment, but rather highlights the decisive role of virtue in governance, and regards moral edification both as the fundamental principle and the essential means for achieving good governance.

引例 Citation：

◎ 为政以德，譬如北辰居其所，而众星共（gǒng）之。(《论语·为政》)

（以道德教化来治理政事，就像北极星位于天空一定的方位，而众星都环绕着它运行。）

Governance based on virtue is like the North Star taking its place in the sky, while all the other stars revolve around it. (*The Analects*)

为己之学

/wèijǐzhīxué/

Learning for Self-improvement

以自我修养为目的的学问。儒家将"学"作为一种成就道德生命的方式。学者通过对经典和礼法的学习以及对圣贤的效法，不断培养自身的德性，以成就理想的人格。因此，"学"是一个自我修养的过程，是"为己"的。"学"并不是为了向他人展示自己的学问或德行，以获取外在的利益。

The term refers to learning for the purpose of self-cultivation. Confucian scholars view learning as a means of improving our moral life. By studying the classics and rules of etiquette, and by learning from the sages, we may constantly improve our morality in order to develop an ideal character. Therefore, learning is a process for self-cultivation and is practiced for our own good. The pursuit of learning is not to make a show of our knowledge or virtuous conduct in return for benefit.

引例 Citations：

◎子曰："古之学者为己，今之学者为人。"（《论语·宪问》）
（孔子说："古时的学者是为了自身的道德修养而学习，现在的学者是为了向他人展示学问。"）

Confucius said: "People in ancient times learned to cultivate their own moral character. People today learn to impress others." (*The Analects*)

◎大抵为己之学，于他人无一毫干预。圣贤千言万语，只是使人反其固有而复其性耳。（《朱子语类》卷八）
（一般而言，为己之学不受他人的任何影响。圣人、贤人所说的千言万语，归根结底是令人回归其固有的本性。）

Generally speaking, learning for self-improvement has nothing to do with others. Everything the sages said, in the final analysis, was meant to help people restore their original inherent nature. (*Categorized Conversations of Master Zhu Xi*)

温故知新

/wēngù-zhīxīn/

Review the Old and Learn the New

温习旧有的知识并获得新的理解与体会。有时也指回顾历史，对当代有新的指导意义。"温"，温习；"故"，指旧的、已知的知识；"新"，指新的、未知的知识。前人对"温故知新"的理解主要有两种：其一，将"温故"与"知新"理解为并列的两方面，认为在"温故"的同时就逐步获得新知，"知新"在"温故"的过程中得以实现。其二，将"温故"理解为"知新"的前提与基础，认为没有"温故"，就不可能"知新"；"新"是"故"的进一步发展，并且摒弃了其中陈腐的旧见。"温故知新"

在今天已经超出一般学习方法的意义，也是个体、企业、组织甚至一个国家自我成长的基本机理。其中包含新与旧、古与今、已知与未知、继承与创新的辩证思想。

This term means to review what has been learned and to gain new understanding and new insights. It also means to obtain guidance in the present moment by recalling the past. *Wen* (温) means to review; *gu* (故) means knowledge that has been acquired in the past; *xin* (新) means new and unexplored knowledge. Our predecessors had two main approaches to interpreting this term. According to one approach, reviewing the knowledge acquired in the past and understanding new knowledge should be understood as two actions taking place at the same time. In other words, one gains new knowledge in the course of reviewing the old. According to the other, reviewing the knowledge acquired in the past should be viewed as the basis and precondition for understanding new knowledge. Without reviewing, one would not be able to understand new knowledge. Furthermore, the new knowledge is a development of the old on the basis of rejecting stale and outdated ideas of the past. Today, what this term offers is more than a simple methodology for studying, but rather a fundamental mechanism for the development of an individual, an enterprise, an organization, or even a country. The term expresses a dialectical logic between the old and new, past and present, known and unknown, and inheritance and innovation.

引例 Citation：

◎温故而知新，可以为师矣。(《论语·为政》)

(温习旧有的知识，并获得新的理解与体会，这样就可以成为他人的老师了。)

Reviewing what you have acquired and learning anew, this way you can be a teacher for others. (*The Analects*)

温柔敦厚
/wēnróu-dūnhòu/

Mild, Gentle, Sincere, and Broad-minded

指儒家经典《诗经》所具有的温和宽厚的精神及教化作用。秦汉时期的儒学认为，《诗经》虽然有讽刺、劝谏的内容，但是重在疏导，不直言斥责，大多数诗篇情理中和，在潜移默化中使读者受到感化，养成敦实忠厚的德性，从而达到以诗教化的目的。温柔敦厚的诗教观是儒家中庸之道的体现，以中正、平和为审美标准，这也成为对于文艺创作风格的要求，体现为以含蓄为美、以教化为重。

This term refers to the mild and broad-minded manner with which the Confucian classic, The Book of Songs, edifies people. Confucian scholars during the Qin and Han dynasties believed that although some poems of The Book of Songs were satirical and remonstrative in tone, it still focused on persuading people instead of just reproving them. Most of the poems in the book were moderate in tone and meant to encourage the reader to learn to be moderate and honest. Encouraging people to be mild and gentle, sincere and broad-minded is a manifestation of Confucian doctrine of the mean, and being fair and gentle is an aesthetic value, which is also a standard for literary and artistic style that stresses the need for being gentle in persuasion and for edification.

引例 Citations：

◎入其国，其教可知也。其为人也，温柔敦厚，《诗》教也。(《礼记·经解》)

(进入一个国家，能看出国民的教养。民众的为人如果温柔敦厚，那就是《诗经》的教化之功。)

When you enter a state, you can find out whether its people are proper in behavior. If they show themselves to be mild and gentle, sincere and broad-minded, they must have learned it from The Book of Songs. (The Book of Rites)

◎温柔敦厚，诗教之本也。有温柔敦厚之性情，乃能有温柔敦厚之诗。(朱庭珍《筱(xiǎo)园诗话》卷三)

(温柔敦厚，是诗歌教化的根本。只有具备温柔敦厚的性情，才能写出温柔敦厚的诗歌。)

Teaching people to be mild and gentle, sincere and broad-minded is the basic purpose of poetry education. One can write poetry with such characteristics only if one is endowed with such good qualities. (Zhu Tingzhen: *Xiaoyuan's Comments on Poetry*)

文明

/wénmíng/

Wenming **(Civilization)**

指社会文治教化彰明昌盛的状态。"文"指"人文"，指礼乐教化以及与此相关的有差等又有调和的社会秩序；"明"即光明、昌明、通达之义。中华民族崇文而不尚武，自古便将文治教化的彰明昌盛作为自己的最高理想和追求，并以此作为评判异国他域政治是否清明的重要标准。

This term refers to a thriving, prosperous, and perceptibly refined society in which people behave in a cultured fashion. *Wen* (文) refers to the arts and humanities, including social norms, music education, moral cultivation, and a social order that is hierarchical yet harmonious. *Ming* (明) means bright, prosperous, and highly civilized. The Chinese nation has always preferred *wen* to *wu* (武 force). This is the loftiest ideal pursued by the Chinese nation since ancient times. It was also the criterion by which to judge whether the governance of a nation was well conducted.

引例 Citation：

◎文明之世，销锋铸耜（sì）。（焦赣（gòng）《易林·节之颐》）
(文明时代，销毁兵器而铸造农具。)

In a civilized society weapons are destroyed to make farming tools. (Jiao Gong: *Annotations on The Book of Changes*)

文气

/wénqì/

Wenqi

  作品中所表现出的作者的精神气质与个性特点。是作家的内在精神气质与作品外在的行文气势相融合的产物。"气"原指构成天地万物始初的基本元素，用在文论中，既指作家的精神气质，也指这种精神气质在作品中的具体表现。人禀天地之气而形成不同的个性气质，表现在文学创作中，便形成不同的文气，呈现出独特的风格特点及气势强弱、节奏顿挫等。

Wenqi（文气）is the personality an author demonstrates in his works, and is a fusion of his innate temperament and the vitality seen in his works. Originally, *qi*（气）referred to the basic element in the initial birth and formation of all things, as well as heaven and earth. In literary criticism, it refers to an author's distinctive individuality and its manifestation in his writings. Humans are believed to develop different characters and traits endowed by the *qi* of heaven and earth. Reflected in literary creation, such different characters and traits naturally find expression in distinctive styles and varying degrees of vigor as well as rhythm and cadence.

引例 Citations：

◎文以气为主，气之清浊有体，不可力强而致。(曹丕《典论·论文》)

（文章由作家的"气"为主导，气有清气、浊气两种形态 [决定人的气质优劣与材质高下]，不是强行可以获得的。）

Literary writing is governed by *qi*. Either clear or murky, *qi* determines the temperament of a writer, refined or vulgar, and his talent, high or low. *Qi* cannot be acquired. (Cao Pi: *On Literary Classics*)

◎气盛则言之短长与声之高下者皆宜。(韩愈《答李翊（yì）书》)

（文章的气势很强，那么句子长短搭配和音调的抑扬顿挫自然都会恰当。）

If a piece of writing has a vigorous style, the length of the sentences will be well-balanced and the choice of tone and cadence will be appropriate. (Han Yu: *A Letter of Response to Li Yi*)

文学
/wénxué/

Literature / Scholars / Education Officials

原义为博通前代文献,"文"指文献,"学"是关于文献的学问。后泛指文章、文献以及关于文章、文献的各种知识与学问。主要含义有三:其一,先秦两汉时期,指关于古代文献特别是诗书礼乐、典章制度等人文方面的知识与学问。魏晋南北朝以后,"文学"一词大体与今天的文学概念接近,但包含人文学术的内容。近代以来,西方的文学观念传入中国,"文学"一词逐步演变指用语言创造审美形象的一门艺术,但传统意义上的"文学"范畴仍为章太炎(1869—1936)等少数学者沿用。这一术语的最初含义决定中国现当代主流的文学观念仍坚持从大文化的意义上看待文学现象,强调文学的审美价值与人文学术的内在联系,而与西方的"文学"术语强调文学之独立审美价值有所区别。其二,泛指古代各类文章及文献。其三,指以著书立说、教学等方式传播学问的文人与掌管文教的官员。

Originally, the term meant to command a good knowledge of documents from pervious dynasties. *Wen* (文) referred to documents, and *xue* (学) referred to the study of these documents. Later, the term referred to articles and documents in general as well as the knowledge about those documentations. The term had three main meanings. Firstly, from the pre-Qin period to the end of the Eastern Han Dynasty, it meant knowledge of ancient literature, especially that of humanities including poetry, history, rites and music, as well as works of laws and regulations. Starting from the Wei and Jin dynasties, the term basically became equivalent to today's concept of literature, but it also referred to academic writings on humanities. With the introduction of the Western concept of literature in recent history, the term gradually evolved to mean a pursuit that uses language to create aesthetic images. However, a few scholars, such as Zhang Taiyan (1869-1936), stuck to its traditional definition. The original meaning of the term determined the mainstream view on literature in contemporary China, which focuses on examining a literary phenomenon in the broader cultural context and emphasizing the intrinsic relationship between the aesthetic values of literature and liberal arts. This is somewhat different from the Western notion of literature which highlights the independent nature of literary appreciation. Secondly, the term refers broadly to various kinds of articles and documents in ancient times. Thirdly, it refers to scholars who promote learning through writing and teaching, as well as officials in charge of culture and education.

引例 Citations：

◎文学：子游、子夏。(《论语·先进》)

([弟子中]博学与熟悉古代文献的，是子游和子夏。)

Among the disciples of Confucius, Ziyou and Zixia have a good knowledge of ancient literature. (*The Analects*)

◎于是汉兴，萧何次律令，韩信申军法，张苍为章程，叔孙通定礼仪，则文学彬彬稍进，《诗》《书》往往间(jiàn)出矣。(《史记·太史公自序》)

(这时汉朝兴起，萧何编订法令，韩信申明军法，张苍订立历数和度量衡标准，叔孙通确定礼仪，而后文章与学问出众的人才逐渐进入朝廷，失传的《诗经》《尚书》等典籍也不断被发现。)

At that time, the Han Dynasty was on the rise, with Xiao He codifying laws, Han Xin promulgating military rules, Zhang Cang formulating the calendar and measurements, and Shusun Tong establishing ceremonial rites. Soon, literary talent who excelled in writing and learning took up positions in the imperial court. Lost classics such as *The Book of Songs* and *The Book of History* were rediscovered one after another. (*Records of the Historian*)

◎大抵儒学本《礼》，荀子是也；史学本《书》与《春秋》，马迁是也；玄学本《易》，庄子是也；文学本《诗》，屈原是也。(刘熙载《艺概·文概》)

(大致来说，儒学以《礼》为依据，荀子即是这样；史学以《尚书》和《春秋》为典范，司马迁即是这样；玄学以《周易》为根基，庄子即是这样；文学以《诗经》为本源，屈原即是这样。)

Generally speaking, Confucian studies are based on *The Book of Rites*, as exemplified by Xunzi. Historiography is modeled on *The Book of History* and *The Spring and Autumn Annals*, as exemplified by Sima Qian. Metaphysical studies are based on *The Book of Changes*, as exemplified by Zhuangzi. Literature has its root in *The Book of Songs*, as exemplified by Qu Yuan. (Liu Xizai: *Overview of Literary Theories*)

文以载道
/wényǐzàidào/

Literature Is the Vehicle of Ideas.

儒家关于文学与道关系的论述。"文"指的是文学创作及作品;"道"指的是作品中的思想内容,但古代文学家与理学家将"道"主要理解为儒家所倡导的思想和道德。中唐时期古文运动的领袖韩愈(768—824)等人提出"文以明道"的观点,认为文章主旨应合乎并发挥圣人的经典。宋代理学家周敦颐(1017—1073)进一步发展为"文以载道",提出文学像"车","道"即是车上运载的货物,文学不过是用以传播儒家之"道"的手段和工具。这一命题的价值在于强调文学的社会功用,强调文学作品应该言之有物、有正确的思想内容。但它轻视文学自身的审美特性,故后来受到重视文学自身价值的思想家与文学家的反对。

This term is a Confucian statement about the relationship between literature and ideas. *Wen* (文) refers to literary creations and works, while *dao* (道) refers to the ideas conveyed by literary works. Writers and philosophers in ancient China explicated these ideas as Confucian thought and ethics. Han Yu (768-824), leader of the mid-Tang-dynasty Classical Prose Movement advocating the prose style of the Qin and Han dynasties, and some others proposed that the purpose of writings should be in line with the classics of the ancient sages as well as promote them. Zhou Dunyi (1017-1073), a Neo-Confucian philosopher of the Song Dynasty, expounded the principle of literature serving as a vehicle of ideas. He concluded that literature was like a vehicle while ideas were like goods loaded on it, and that literature was nothing but a means and a vehicle to convey Confucian ideas. This theory was valuable because it stressed the social role of literature and emphasized that writers should know what they were writing about to ensure that their works conveyed correct ideas. However, it underestimated the aesthetic value of literature and later met opposition from thinkers and writers who emphasized the value of literature per se.

引例 Citation:

◎文所以载道也。轮辕饰而人弗庸,徒饰也,况虚车乎?文辞,艺也;道德,实也。(周敦颐《通书·文辞》)

（文章是用来承载思想和道德的。车轮与车辕过度装饰而没人使用，白白装饰了，更何况那些派不上用场的车呢？文辞，只是一种技艺，而道德才是文章的实质。）

Writings are meant to convey ideas and ethics. When vehicles are not used, even if the wheels and shafts are excessively decorated, it is simply a waste. Fine language is only a means for writing, whereas ethics are the essence of writings. (Zhou Dunyi: *The Gist of Confucian Thought*)

文章

/wénzhāng/

Literary Writing

　　泛指一切著述，包括今天意义上的文章和著作。先秦时这一术语包含在文学之内，两汉时"文章"一词与"文学"对举，指一切用文字写下来的文辞、篇章、史书、论著，六朝时"文章"与"文学"并列，开始指后世所说的审美范畴的"文学"，但仍作为统括一切文体的范畴使用。"章"意为一曲音乐演奏完毕，或一首完整的音乐，故此术语强调作品意义和结构的完整，注重文章写作手法与技巧；"文"和"章"都有花纹、色彩错杂的意思，"文章"相当于美的形式，故此术语隐含了审美观念。早期"文章"的概念与"文学"概念有一定联系又有所区别。"文章"偏重于辞章美文，说明了人们对于文章审美价值的逐渐重视。

The term refers to all kinds of writings, including what we call essays and books today. In the Pre-Qin period, this term was subsumed under literature. During the Han Dynasty, the term referred to writings other than *wenxue* (文学 documents of previous dynasties) to specifically mean essays, articles, history books, and treatises. In the Six Dynasties, the term, together with *wenxue*, began to assume the meaning of what later generations meant by literature, that is, writings for aesthetic appreciation which encompass every type of literary works. *Zhang* (章) also implies a movement of music played to its finish, or a single piece of music.

Therefore, the term focuses on both meaning and structure as well as writing skills and techniques. Both Chinese characters in the term have the meaning of interwoven patterns and colors. Together, they signify a beautiful form, giving the term an aesthetic connotation. The earlier concept of the term is related to but different from that of wenxue, with the former focusing more on elegant diction and style, indicating increasing attention to the aesthetic value of literary works.

引例 Citations：

◎文章者，盖情性之风标，神明之律吕也。蕴思含毫，游心内运，放言落纸，气韵天成。(《南齐书·文学传论》)

（所谓文章，乃是人的感情性格变化的风向标、内在精神的一种量器。下笔之前蓄积文思，内心思绪自由驰骋，等到形诸纸墨时，文章的气韵自然天成。）

Literary writings reflect one's moods and disposition, or give expression to one's inner world. Before writing, one should gather his thoughts and free his mind so as to transcend the limitations of time and space. Thus, once he starts writing, his work will achieve its flavor naturally. (*The History of Qi of the Southern Dynasties*)

◎圣贤书辞，总称"文章"，非采而何？(刘勰《文心雕龙·情采》)

（古代圣贤的著作文辞，都叫做"文章"，这不是因为它们都具有文采吗？）

Writings by sages in ancient times are all called "literary writings." Isn't this because they all have literary elegance? (Liu Xie: *The Literary Mind and the Carving of Dragons*)

闻知
/wénzhī/

Knowledge from Hearsay

听闻而得的知识。"闻知"是墨家提出的一种知识类别，同时也标志着一种认知方式。墨家认为，知识的获取有三种方式，即"亲知""闻知""说知"。"闻知"指通过他人的告知或传授而认知事物，是一种间接的认知方式。

Knowledge from hearsay is a type of knowledge and a way of acquiring it proposed by the Mohist School. In their opinion, knowledge is gained in three ways: by personal experience, by hearsay, and by explanation. To learn by hearsay means being told or taught by others, and is an indirect way of gaining knowledge.

引例 Citations：

◎知，闻、说、亲。(《墨子·经上》)
（知，分为闻知、说知、亲知。）
Knowing comes from hearsay, explanation, or personal experience. (*Mozi*)

◎传受之，闻也。(《墨子·经说上》)
（他人传授而知，就是"闻知"。）
Receiving something that is being told is knowing by hearsay. (*Mozi*)

卧游
/wòyóu/

Enjoy Sceneries Without Physically Travelling

以观赏山水画代替游历山水，借以体味山水之乐。南朝画家宗炳（375—443）晚年因病无法游历名山大川，于是将游玩过的山水绘成画作挂在墙上，以卧游的方式权当山水之游。这一术语体现了古代文人乐（yào）山乐水的传统，还肯定了艺术对于人生的特殊意义，推动了绘画艺术的发展。

Artists often admire natural scenery beholding landscape paintings rather than traveling to actual spots. When the Southern Dynasty painter Zong Bing (375-443), due to illness in old age, could no longer tour great mountains and rivers, he painted the landscapes he had once seen and then hung the works on the wall, thus fulfilling his dream of seeing those beautiful sights again. This term illustrates the tradition of loving mountains and rivers among ancient literati, affirms the significance of art to life, and promotes the art of painting.

引例 Citations:

◎（宗炳）有疾还江陵。叹曰："老疾俱至，名山恐难遍睹，唯当澄怀观道，卧以游之。"凡所游履，皆图之于室。(《宋书·宗炳传》)
（[宗炳]生病之后回到江陵。感叹说："我老了，又病了，恐怕难以遍游名山，只有放空心灵，向内省察而领悟真谛，在屋里躺着观看山水画而权当亲身游历。"于是将自己游玩过的地方都画出来挂在室内墙上。）

Zong Bing returned to Jiangling to convalesce. With a sigh he said, "I'm old and sick, so touring famous mountains and rivers is now quite beyond me. What I should do is to unleash my soul and look inwardly to seek truth. I can look at landscape paintings even when lying in bed, as if I were actually there." Thus he hung on the wall all the paintings he had done of the places he had been to. (*The History of Song of the Southern Dynasties*)

◎一畦杞菊为供具，满壁江山入卧游。(倪瓒《顾仲贽过访闻徐生病差（chài）》)
（以一畦枸杞和菊花为酒食，满壁的山水画都可躺着观赏。）

With a plot of wolfberries and chrysanthemums to go with my wine, I rove the landscapes covering the walls while reclining in my bed. (Ni Zan: *Gu Zhongzhi Visits to Find Mr. Xu Fully Recovered*)

无为
/wúwéi/

Non-action

"为"的一种状态。道家以"有为"与"无为"相对。所谓"有为"，一般是指统治者把自己的意志强加给他人或世界，不尊重或不顺应万物的本性。"无为"的意义与之相反，包含三个要点：其一，权力通过自我节制的方式遏制自己的干涉欲望。其二，顺应万物或百姓的本性。其三，发挥万物或者百姓的自主性。"无为"并不是不作为，而是更智慧的作为方式，通过无为来达到无不为的结果。

Wuwei (non-action) refers to a state of action. Daoism contrasts "action" to "non-action." "Action" generally means that the rulers impose their will on others or the world without showing any respect for or following the intrinsic nature of things. "Non-action" is the opposite of "action," and has three main points: 1) through self-control containing the desire to interfere; 2) following the nature of all things and the people; and 3) bringing into play the initiative of all things and people. "Non-action" does not mean not doing anything, but is a wiser way of doing things. Non-action leads to the result of getting everything done.

引例 Citations:

◎ 是以圣人处无为之事，行不言之教。(《老子·二章》)

（因此圣人以无为的方式处理世事，以不言的方式教导百姓。）

Therefore, sages deal with the world's affairs by way of non-action, and teach people without uttering a word. (*Laozi*)

◎ 道常无为而无不为。(《老子·三十七章》)

（道总是对万物不加干涉而成就万物。）

Dao always makes all things possible through non-interference with them. (*Laozi*)

无为而治

/wúwéi'érzhì/

Rule Through Non-action

不过度作为而把国家治理得很好。"治"指国家治理达到良好状态；"无为"不是不作为，而是不妄为。在道家那里，其要义在于顺其自然，即治国者充分尊重治理对象（民众）自身的禀性、状态和趋向，不过分干预民众的生活，使之遵循人自身固有的本性、意愿和逻辑，自我发展，自我实现，以无为而达到无不为，其哲学基础是"道法自然"。在儒家那里，其要义在于以德化民，即治国者不以政令、刑法等强加于人，而是从自身做起，以自身的道德和功业使民众受到影响和感化，使民众"不令而行"，实现天下大治，犹言"人文化成"。儒、道两家的共通点在于：治国者不妄加作为，不过度干预，充分尊重民众或社会的主体性。

Zhi (治) here means a state of good governance; *wuwei* (无为 non-action) does not mean doing nothing, but instead not acting in an over-assertive manner, in other words, not imposing one's will. In Daoist thinking, this expression means the ruler must respect the natural conditions of those governed (the people); he must not interfere unduly in their lives but allow them to follow their own desires and ways to fulfill themselves. Through "non-action" everything will be actually achieved. The focus is "Dao operates naturally." In Confucian thinking, "non-action" means the ruler governs by influencing and motivating his subjects through his moral example and achievements, not through decrees, or coercive punishments, so that they act without being ordered, and social harmony is achieved. The focus here is something similar to "teaching people essential ideals and principles and guiding them to embrace goodness so as to build a harmonious social order." Both the Confucian and Daoist schools of thought advocate governance through respect for the intrinsic nature of people and society, not through too much interference or imposition.

引例 Citations：

◎ 道常无为而无不为。侯王若能守之，万物将自化。(《老子·三十七章》)

（道总是对万物不加干涉而成就万物。君主如果能够持守住它，万事万物就会自我生长。）

Dao always makes all things possible through non-interference with them. If the ruler can strictly follow this, then all things and creatures will grow of their own accord. (*Laozi*)

◎ 子曰："无为而治者，其舜也与(yú)！夫何为哉？恭己正南面而已矣。"(《论语·卫灵公》)

（孔子说："能够无所作为而天下治理得很好的人，大概只有舜吧？他作了些什么呢？只是庄严端正地坐在天子之位上罢了。"）

Confucius said, "Who was the best at ruling through non-action? Probably Shun. And what did he do? Just sat solemnly upright on his imperial throne." (*The Analects*)

无欲则刚

/wúyù-zégāng/

People with No Covetous Desires Stand Upright.

人没有非分的贪欲，就能做到刚正凛然。"欲"指各种私欲、贪欲；"刚"即刚正公道、正直有力。"无欲"并不是绝对禁止人们有"欲"，而是提倡克制自己的私欲、贪欲。"无欲则刚"讲的是立身处事尤其是执政做官的基本道理：一个人面对来自各方的种种诱惑，应该大公无私、端正品行、淡泊守志，不要有非分的贪图，这样就能一身正气，无所畏惧，就像高高的峭壁一样，挺立于天地之间，坚不可摧。

People with no covetous desires stand upright and maintain integrity. *Yu*（欲）refers to all sorts of selfish and covetous desires. *Gang*（刚）means fairness, justice, integrity, and forcefulness. *Wuyu*（无欲）does not mean that people should not have any desires, but rather, people should not harbor any selfish or covetous desires. The term tells us a basic principle for people to follow in conducting themselves, and especially for officials in handling office affairs, that is, no temptations should ever sway anyone. One must always conduct oneself properly without seeking to gratify personal interests; one must always seek compliance without seeking fame or wealth; and one must never harbor any greed. This is the way for one to stand upright, firm, and fearless. Like towering cliffs, one may stand tall and indestructible.

引例 Citations：

◎子曰："吾未见刚者。"或对曰："申枨（chéng）。"子曰："枨也欲，焉得刚？"（《论语·公冶长》）

（孔子说："我没见过刚正的人。"有人回应说："申枨就是。"孔子说："申枨欲望太多，哪里能够刚正呢？"）

Confucius said, "I have never seen any person of rectitude." Someone responded, "Shen Cheng is such a person." Confucius said, "Shen Cheng has too many desires. How can he be of rectitude?" (*The Analects*)

◎ 海纳百川，有容乃大；壁立千仞，无欲则刚。（林则徐对联）

（大海广阔接纳无数江河，人有度量才能[像大海那样]有大成就；千仞崖壁巍然屹立，人没有贪欲就能[像山崖那样]刚正凛然。）

The vast ocean accepts hundreds of rivers emptying into it; people with a broad mind can achieve greatness. Thousands of cliffs stand tall and lofty; people with no covetous desires stand firm and upright. (A couplet composed by Lin Zexu)

吴越同舟

/Wú-Yuè-tóngzhōu/

People of Wu and Yue Are in the Same Boat.

　　吴、越两国人同乘一条船。比喻双方虽有旧怨，但面临共同的危难困境，也会团结一致，相互救助。春秋时代，吴、越是相互仇视的邻国，但当两国人同船渡江，遭遇风浪时，他们却相互救援，如同一个人的左右手一样。它包含的思想是：敌友不是绝对的，也不是永恒的，在一定的境遇下可以化敌为友。

In the Spring and Autumn Period, Wu and Yue were neighboring states which were hostile to each other. Wu and Yue people being in the same boat is a metaphor for overcoming old grievances to face common danger. When people from these two states were crossing a river in the same boat and encountered a storm, they had to work together to save themselves; in that sense, they were just like the left and right hands of the same person. The story implies that there is no absolute and perpetual enmity or friendship. Under certain circumstances, an enemy can be turned into a friend.

引例 Citation：

◎吴越之人，同舟济江，中流遇风波，其相救如左右手者，所患同也。（《孔丛子·论势》）

（吴、越两国的人同乘一条船渡江，中途遭遇风浪，他们之所以像一个人的左右手一样相互救援，是因为他们遇到共同的危难。）

People of the states of Wu and Yue were crossing a river in the same boat when they encountered strong winds and waves midstream. To save themselves from a common peril, they worked together like the left and right hands of the same person. (*Collected Works of the Confucian Family*)

五经

/wǔjīng/

Five Classics

《诗》《书》《礼》《易》《春秋》等五部儒家经典的合称。先秦时期有"六经"之说，指《诗》《书》《礼》《乐》《易》《春秋》，因《乐》已亡佚（一说无文字），故汉代多称"五经"。从汉武帝（前156—前87）立"五经博士"起，"五经"之学成为中国学术、文化和思想的根本。从内容上来说，"五经"各有所偏重，如《诗》言志、《书》言事等，因其不同而互补，故构成一个整体。历代儒者通过对文本的不断解释，为这些经典赋予了丰富的意义。"五经"之学包括了中国传统文化对于世界秩序与价值的根本理解，是"道"的集中体现。

The term refers to the five Confucian classics: *The Book of Songs, The Book of History, The Book of Rites, The Book of Changes,* and *The Spring and Autumn Annals*. In the pre-Qin period, the term "Six Classics" was used, referring to *The Book of Songs, The Book of History, The Book of Rites, The Book of Music, The Book of Changes,* and *The Spring and Autumn Annals. The Book of Music,* did not exist in written form, hence people often used the term "Five Classics" during the Han Dynasty. After Emperor Wu of the Han Dynasty (156-87 BC) established the title of "Academician of the Five Classics," study of these works became the foundation of Chinese learning, culture, and thought. In terms of content, the Five Classics each has its own focus; for instance, *The Book of Songs* deals with aspirations, and *The Book of History* chronicles events. Different in focus but complementing each other, they form an integral collection of classics. Throughout history, Confucian scholars added significant meaning to these classics with their interpretations of the original texts. The Five Classics comprise traditional Chinese culture's fundamental understanding of world order and values, epitomizing the concept of Dao.

引例 Citation：

◎ "五经"何谓？谓《易》《尚书》《诗》《礼》《春秋》也。(《白虎通义·五经》)

("五经"是什么？是《易》《尚书》《诗》《礼》《春秋》等五部典籍。)

Which are the Five Classics? They are: *The Book of Songs*, *The Book of History*, *The Book of Rites*, *The Book of Changes*, and *The Spring and Autumn Annals*. (*Debates of the White Tiger Hall*)

五行相生

/wǔxíng-xiāngshēng/

The Five Elements, Each in Turn Producing the Next

五行循环生成。"五行"本指五种基本事物，即木、火、土、金、水。世间万物都由这五种事物构成，或具有这五种事物的属性。"五行相生"之说描述了这五种事物之间所具有的循环生成关系。木生火，火生土，土生金，金生水，水生木。同时，具有这五种属性的事物之间也遵循这样的生成关系。

This refers to the concept of the five basic elements, each in turn giving rise to the next. The five basic elements are: wood, fire, earth, metal, and water. All things in the world are composed of these five elements or possess their properties.

According to this concept, wood produces fire; fire produces earth; earth produces metal; metal produces water; and water produces wood. Similarly, things with the properties of these five elements also have similar relations between themselves.

引例 Citation：

◎五行者，五官也，比相生而间（jiàn）相胜也，故为治，逆之则乱，顺之则治。（董仲舒《春秋繁露·五行相生》）

（五行，如同五个官职，相邻的事物依次生成而相互间隔的事物依次克胜。因此治理国家人事，悖逆了五行次序就会混乱，顺应了五行次序则会安定。）

The five elements are comparable to five official positions. Adjacent things emerge in a certain sequence. If things do not emerge in order, each will check the next. This principle also applies to the governance of a state and all social affairs. Chaos grows if the order of the five elements is disrupted; peace prevails if the five elements are in good order. (Dong Zhongshu: *Luxuriant Gems of The Spring and Autumn Annals*)

五音

/wǔyīn/

The Five Notes

　　五声音阶，即宫、商、角、徵、羽等五个音高递增的音符，大致对应于今天简谱中的1、2、3、5、6。在角后、徵前加变徵，在羽后加变宫，即为七声音阶。音阶细分意味着旋律多变，不过基于五声音阶的古典音乐尽管变化相对较少，亦自有一种单纯、质朴、静穆、悠扬的美。因为古代雅乐、民歌多用五声音阶，所以常用"五音"泛指音乐。

The term refers to the five musical notes that rise in pitch, from *gong* (宫), *shang* (商), *jue* (角), *zhi* (徵), to *yu* (羽), which correspond roughly to the notes of 1, 2, 3, 5, and 6 in today's numbered musical notation. When a *zhi* minus is placed before *zhi* and a *gong* plus after *yu*, this pentatonic scale becomes heptatonic. Such division of the musical notes gives rise to a variety of tunes. Although Chinese classical music based on a five-note scale does not vary that much, it retains the beauty of a simple, quiet, and lyrical style. As ancient refined music and folksongs were mostly based on a five-note scale, this term often referred to music in general.

引例 Citations：

◎ 高渐 (jiān) 离击筑，荆轲和 (hè) 而歌，为变徵之声，士皆垂泪涕泣。(《战国策·燕策三》)

(高渐离敲着筑，荆轲和着节拍唱歌，发出变徵的音调，送行的人都流着眼泪低声哭泣。)

Gao Jianli struck the *zhu* instrument. Jing Ke sang to the beat, uttering a *zhi*-minus note. Those who saw him off broke out in tears. (*Strategies of the Warring States*)

◎ 五色令人目盲；五音令人耳聋；五味令人口爽；驰骋畋 (tián) 猎，令人心发狂；难得之货，令人行妨。是以圣人为腹不为目，故去彼取此。(《老子·十二章》)

(缤纷的色彩，使人眼花缭乱；嘈杂的音调，使人听觉失灵；丰盛的食物，使人舌不知味；纵情狩猎，使人心情放荡发狂；稀有的物品，使人行为不轨。因此，圣人但求吃饱肚子而不追逐声色之娱，所以摒弃物欲的诱惑而保持安定知足的生活方式。)

A riot of color makes one dizzy; discordant melody damages one's hearing; plenty of food numbs one's taste bud; hunting to excess causes one to lose control over oneself; and a valuable object tempts one into stealing it. Therefore, a sage, once having eaten enough, will not seek sensual pleasures. Rather, he will abandon the desire for material comfort and be content with living a simple life. (*Laozi*)

◎ 五色杂而成黼黻 (fǔfú)，五音比而成韶夏，五情发而为辞章，神理之数也。(刘勰《文心雕龙·情采》)

(五色交错而成灿烂的锦绣，五音排列而组织成悦耳的乐章，五情抒发而成动人的辞章，这是自然的道理。)

When silk threads of various colors are woven together, a beautiful piece of embroidery is created. When the five musical notes are properly arranged, a beautiful melody is composed. When the five emotions are forcefully expressed, a beautiful piece of writing is created. This is all too natural and obvious. (Liu Xie: *The Literary Mind and the Carving of Dragons*)

物化

/wùhuà/

Transformation of Things

  事物彼我界限的打破及相互转化，是事物的一种存在状态。"物化"一说出自《庄子·齐物论》。庄子（前369？—前286）通过"庄周梦蝶"的寓言来说明"物化"的意义。庄子认为，自身与他者、梦与醒以及一切事物之间的界限与区别都可以被破除，从而实现物与物之间的转化与流通。如果执著于彼我的区别，就不能体认"物化"，如在梦中一般；但如果执著于"物化"，同样会跌入梦中。

This is a form of the existence of things when the boundary between things is broken and one thing transforms into another. The term "transformation of things" comes from *Zhuangzi*, in which the author Zhuangzi (369?-286 BC) illustrated the concept in the fable Zhuangzi Dreamed of Becoming a Butterfly. He believed that the boundary and difference between oneself and others, between in a dream and being awake, and between all things can be broken. Consequently, one may achieve the transformation between one thing and another. However, if one holds onto the difference between oneself and the others, one cannot achieve the transformation of things, as if in a dream. If one is bent on transforming things, one may still fall into a dream.

引例 Citation：

◎昔者庄周梦为胡蝶，栩栩然胡蝶也，自喻适志与（yú）! 不知周也。俄然觉，则蘧（qú）蘧然周也。不知周之梦为胡蝶与？胡蝶之梦为周与？周与胡蝶，则必有分矣。此之谓物化。(《庄子·齐物论》)

（从前庄周梦见自己变成了蝴蝶，翩翩飞舞的一只蝴蝶，遨游各处悠游自在，不知道自己是庄周。忽然醒过来，自己分明是庄周。不知道是庄周做梦化为蝴蝶呢，还是蝴蝶做梦变化为庄周呢？庄周与蝴蝶必定是有所分别的。这就叫做"物化"。）

Once I, Zhuangzi, dreamed that I became a flying butterfly, happy with myself and doing as I pleased. I forgot that I was Zhuangzi. Suddenly I woke up and I was

Zhuangzi again. I did not know whether Zhuangzi had been dreaming that he was a butterfly, or whether a butterfly had been dreaming that it was Zhuangzi. There must be a difference between the two, which is what I call the "transformation of things." (*Zhuangzi*)

徙木立信

/xǐmù-lìxìn/

Establish One's Credibility by Rewarding People for Moving a Log

通过让人搬动大木头（兑现赏金）来树立威信。据《史记》记载，商鞅（前390？—前338）变法之前，为了取信于民，命人在都城集市南门立一根三丈长的大木头，宣布无论是谁，只要把木头搬到集市北门，就会得到丰厚的赏金。有人壮着胆子作了，商鞅立刻赏了重金。人们由此确信商鞅说到做到，因而新法颁布后得以畅行无阻。其中最重要的是"立信"——取信于民：若要国家政令畅通无阻，首先必须取信，令出必行，这样才能得到百姓的支持和拥戴。

According to *Records of the Historian*, in order to gain the people's trust before initiating his political reforms, Shang Yang (390?- 338 BC) announced that, regardless of whoever it might be, if anyone was able to move a huge log 3 *zhang* long (approx. 7 meters) from the southern gateway to the northern gateway of the market in the capital city, he would be amply rewarded. A person was bold enough to attempt this task and succeeded; hence he was immediately rewarded with a generous sum of money. After that, the people were convinced that Shang Yang was one who kept his word, and hence, he was able to issue his new decrees unimpeded. The important thing here is "the establishment of credibility" – winning the people's trust. In order to pass a country's decrees unimpeded, one must first gain trust, which is imperative for issuing a decree. Only in this way can the support and allegiance of the common people be gained.

引例 Citation：

◎令既具，未布，恐民之不信，已乃立三丈之木于国都市南门，募民有能徙置北门者予十金。民怪之，莫敢徙。复曰"能徙者予五十金"。有一人徙之，辄予五十金，以明不欺。卒下令。(《史记·商君列传》)

（法令已经完备，还没有公布，（商鞅）恐怕百姓不相信，于是在国都集市南门立了一根三丈长的大木头，向百姓招募，如果有人将木头从集市南门搬到北门，就赏给他十镒（yì，古人以一镒为一金，一镒相当于二十两或二十四两）黄铜（金钱）。百姓对此感到奇怪，没有人敢去搬木头。（商鞅）又宣布："谁能搬过去，就赏给他五十镒黄铜（金钱）。"有一个人将大木头搬到了集市北门，商鞅立即赏给他五十镒黄铜，以表明没有欺骗他。于是商鞅最终颁布了变法的命令。）

After the decrees for reform being drawn but before being issued, Shang Yang, fearing that the people wouldn't take the decrees seriously, he had a 3-*zhang*-long (approx. 7 meters) log erected in front of the southern gateway of the market place in the capital city. He declared that whoever could move the log from the southern gateway to the northern gateway would be given a reward of 10 *yi* (equivalent of 200 taels of copper). People found it very strange and nobody came forward to move the log. Shang then said, "Whoever can move the log will be awarded 50 *yi* (equivalent of 1,000 taels of copper)." One man came up and moved the log to the market's northern gateway. Shang kept his words and immediately gave him the promised amount of reward. Thus Shang was able to issue the decrees of reform thereafter. (*Records of the Historian*)

相反相成

/xiāngfǎn-xiāngchéng/

Being both Opposite and Complementary

处于对立关系中的两个事物之间既相互排斥又相互成就、相互转化。一切事物都处于与他者的对立之中。对立双方具有相反的性质或意义，因而彼此间是相互排斥的，如有与无、长与短、高与下、善与恶、美与丑等。但同时，事物的性质或意义又是借由与之对立的事物而获得确立的，对立双方在一定条件下还可以相互转化。这一观念在先秦时期即已出现，在班固（32—92）《汉书·艺文志》中始被概括为"相反相成"。

This term refers to two things that are mutually opposite to but complementing each other and that they mutually transform between them. Everything is an antithesis to something else. Both antithetic sides are opposite to each other. Therefore there is mutual exclusion between them, such as *you* and *wu*, long and short, high and low, good and bad, and beautiful and ugly. On the other hand, the nature or the identity of a thing is established due to something antithetic to it. The two opposing sides can transform into each other under certain conditions. This concept emerged in the pre-Qin period. In *The History of the Han Dynasty* written by Ban Gu（32-92）, the idea was first defined as "two things being both opposite and complementary."

引例 Citations：
◎ 天下皆知美之为美，斯恶已；皆知善之为善，斯不善已。故有无相生，难易相成，长短相形，高下相倾，音声相和，前后相随。（《老子·二章》）
（天下都知道美之所以为美，丑恶的观念也就产生了；都知道善之所以为善，不善的观念也就产生了。因此有和无相互生成，难和易相互成就，长和短相互形成，高和下相互包含，音和声相互调和，前和后相互随顺。）

People all know that ugliness exists as an antithesis of beauty and that evil exists as an antithesis of goodness. Likewise, *you* and *wu* produce each other; what is difficult and what is easy complement each other; long and short exist in contrast, so do high and low; tone and sound are in harmony with each other, and front and back exist because of each other. (*Laozi*)

◎仁之与义，敬之与和，相反而皆相成也。（《汉书·艺文志》）
（仁与义、敬与和，既相互排斥又相互成就。）

The relationship between benevolence and righteousness and between respect and harmony is one of mutual opposition and complementation. (*The History of the Han Dynasty*)

逍遥

/xiāoyáo/

Carefree

  人的心灵的一种自由、无待的状态。最初由庄子（前369？—前286）提出并以之名篇。庄子认为，人的心灵可以超越于形体无法逃避、无可奈何的境遇之上，消除对于物的依赖，进而达到心灵的自由、无碍。西晋郭象（？—312）重新解释了"逍遥"之义，认为有待之物能够安于各自的性分（fèn）即达到了"逍遥"。

The term refers to a state of mind totally free from all constraints. It was first proposed by Zhuangzi (369?-286 BC) in one of his most well-known essays. According to him, people's minds can go beyond predicament in a way that their bodies cannot, so mentally they can be independent of material concerns and free of all worries. Guo Xiang (?-312) of the Western Jin Dynasty had a new definition of the term: By acting in accordance with its own nature, everything can be free of troubles and worries.

引例 Citations：

◎芒然彷徨乎尘垢之外，逍遥乎无为之业。（《庄子·大宗师》）

（安闲无待地神游于尘世之外，逍遥自在于自然无为的境地。）

People should seek carefree enjoyment beyond the constraints of the human world. (*Zhuangzi*)

◎夫小大虽殊，而放于自得之场，则物任其性，事称其能，各当其分（fèn），逍遥一也。（郭象《庄子注》卷一）

（事物虽然有大小的不同，但若安放于自得的范围内，则每一事物都按照其本性发展，功用与其本性相合，担当各自的职分，则它们所达到的逍遥是一样的。）

Things, big and small, are different from each other. But when they are placed where they should be, each of them will develop as its nature dictates, shoulder their proper responsibilities, and ultimately achieve the same degree of freedom. (Guo Xiang: *Annotations on Zhuangzi*)

小人

/xiǎorén/

Petty Man

"小人"最初用以表明人的社会身份与地位，通常指被统治者或地位低下之人。后世又以人的德行高下来界定"小人"，德行卑下者被称作"小人"（与"君子"相对）。"小人"只关注和追逐个人的权力或利益，为了获取私利不惜违背道义，缺乏对"道"的理解与尊重。

The term was originally used to indicate a person's social status, usually referring to the rulers' subjects or those low in social ranking. Later generations also used the term to indicate one's moral standard in a disapproving way. Those of base character were called petty men as opposed to men of virtue. A petty man only pursues his personal interests or profits, even by violating morality and righteousness; and such people have no understanding of or regard for Dao.

引例 Citations：

◎君子喻于义，小人喻于利。(《论语·里仁》)
（君子知晓并遵循义，小人知晓并追逐利。）

A man of virtue understands and observes what is morally right; while a petty man only has his eyes on and goes after what brings him personal gains. (*The Analects*)

◎苟安务得，所以为小人。（朱熹《论语集注》卷二）
（苟且偷安务求得利，因此是小人。）

They are petty men because they only seek ease and comfort of the moment and pursue personal gains. (Zhu Xi: *The Analects Variorum*)

小说

/xiǎoshuō/

Fiction

　　以人物形象刻画为中心，通过完整的故事情节和环境描写来反映社会生活的一种文学体式。人物、情节、环境是小说的三要素。按照篇幅及容量，小说可分为长篇、中篇、短篇。中国古典小说，按照所表现的内容，可分为神怪小说、历史演义小说、英雄传奇小说、世情小说等几大类；按照体制可分为笔记体、传奇体、话本体、章回体等；按照语言形式，可分为文言小说和白话小说。中国古典小说经过了不同的发展阶段，有着鲜明的时代特点：先秦两汉时期的神话传说、史传文学，以及诸子散文中的寓言故事等，是中国古代小说的源头；魏晋南北朝时期出现的文人笔记小说，是中国古代小说的雏形；唐代传奇标志着古典小说的正式形成；宋、元出现的话本小说，为小说的成熟奠定了坚实的基础；明清小说标志着中国古典小说发展的高峰，出现了《三国演义》《水浒传》《西游记》《红楼梦》等古典名著。"五四"新文化运动之后，现代白话小说创作大量涌现，传播着现代的科学与民主精神。

Fiction is a literary genre primarily concerned with depicting characters to tell a complete story about social life within a setting. Fiction has three main elements, namely, characters, a plot, and a setting. Depending on the length, fiction can be divided into novels, novellas, and short stories. In terms of content, traditional Chinese fiction can be divided into the following broad categories: fantasy stories of gods and spirits, historical fiction, heroic legendary tales, and stories about human relations and social mores. In terms of genre, traditional Chinese fiction is divided into literary sketches, legendary tales, story-tellers' prompt-books, and chapter-based novels. In terms of language, there is fiction in the classical language and vernacular fiction. Traditional Chinese fiction has evolved through different stages, with distinctive features for each period. The myths, legends and historical biographies of the pre-Qin and Han dynasties, and the fables in the works of the earlier Chinese thinkers were the sources of traditional Chinese fiction. The literary sketches by men of letters in the Wei, Jin, Northern and Southern dynasties were embryonic forms of traditional fiction. The legendary tales of the Tang Dynasty marked the eventual emergence of Chinese fiction. The story-tellers' prompt-books in the Song and Yuan dynasties laid the foundation that allowed traditional fiction to reach maturity. The novels of the Ming and Qing dynasties marked the peak in the development of pre-modern fiction. That period is famous for producing great Chinese classical novels, namely, *Romance of the Three Kingdoms*, *Journey to the West*, *Outlaws of the Marsh* and *Dream of the Red Chamber*. During and after the New Culture Movement and the May 4th Movement around 1919, a large amount of modern vernacular fiction appeared, bringing forth a message of science and democracy of the modern age.

引例 Citations：

◎若其小说家合丛残小语，近取譬论，以作短书，治身理家，有可观之辞。(《昭明文选》卷三十一李善注引桓谭《新论》)
(像那些小说家将零散的论述整合起来,用身边发生的事情打比方进行述说劝诫,所写文章都不长,其中论述个人修身和治理家庭的内容,有不少可看的地方。)

Those writers of stories put together scattered statements. Drawing on what happens around them, they make up parables, writing short pieces. The parts about how to improve one's character and keep good family life are worth reading. (Huan Tan: *New Treatise*, as cited in *Selections of Refined Literature Compiled by Prince Zhaoming*, Vol. 31 Li Shan's Note)

◎小说，正史之余也。(笑花主人《〈今古奇观〉序》)
(小说，是正史之外的一种文学形式。)

Fiction is a literary supplement to formal historical accounts. (Xiaohuazhuren: Foreword to *Strange Tales New and Old*)

孝
/xiào/

Filial Piety

　　子女对父母的顺从与敬爱。就言行而论，"孝"包含以下三点要求：其一，要谨慎保护受之于父母的身体，以免伤病，令父母担忧。其二，不能违背父母的教导、要求，即便不能认同，也应顺从遵循。其三，应以高尚的德行，成就自己的声誉与功业，以彰显父母的教导。"孝"植根于子女内心对父母的亲爱与尊敬。儒家认为，"孝"是个人德行养成的基础，并将其作为维系和强化父子关系乃至君臣关系的根本。

Filial piety is obedience to, and respect and love for your parents. To observe this, you must do the following. First, attentively keep your body, born by parents, safe from injury and illness so as to relieve them of their worries. Second, do not go against your parents' teachings, guidance and requests; obey them even if you do not agree with them. Third, gain fame and become accomplished through moral integrity, so as to highlight their teachings and guidance. Filial piety is rooted in children's love and respect for their parents. Confucians believe that filial piety is the foundation of a person's moral integrity and the basis for maintaining and strengthening the parent-child relationship, and even the sovereign-subject relationship.

引例 Citations：

◎子游问孝。子曰："今之孝者，是谓能养。至于犬马，皆能有养。不敬，何以别乎？"（《论语·为政》）

（子游请教什么是孝。孔子说："今日所谓的孝，是能奉养父母。对于犬、马，都能够饲养。如果不能尊敬父母，那么如何将奉养父母与饲养犬马相区别呢？"）

Ziyou asked Confucius about filial piety and Confucius replied, "Filial piety nowadays means taking care of your parents. But even dogs and horses can be taken care of; without respect, what is the difference between taking care of your parents and taking care of dogs and horses?" (*The Analects*)

◎夫孝，始于事亲，中于事君，终于立身。（《孝经·开宗明义》）

（孝，初始于服侍父母，发展为侍奉君主，归终于处事、为人之道。）

Filial piety starts with serving parents; it proceeds to serving the sovereign; it is completed by working and behaving within the rules of conduct. (*Classic of Filial Piety*)

心

/xīn/

Heart / Mind

"心"是人之情感、认识和价值的基础，生命的主宰。与耳、目、鼻、口等被动地感知外物不同，"心"具有思考的能力，可以辨别和整理感官所获得的材料，进行知识和道德判断。孟子（前372？—前289）认为"心"包含恻隐、辞让、羞恶、是非等四端，道德实践的核心就是保存并扩充人固有的善心。道家则认为虚静是心的根本状态，如静止之水，由此可以把握天地万物的本原。

The heart, a vital organ of life, underpins one's emotions, awareness, and value judgments. Different from the ears, eyes, nose, and mouth, which sense the outer world in a passive way, the heart is capable of thinking and performing intellectual and moral evaluations on the basis of analyzing and sorting out what these organs have sensed. Mencius (372?-289 BC) believed that the heart consists of four aspects: compassion, deference, sense of shame or detestation, and conscience. Preserving and expanding one's good heart is the central aim in practicing moral teachings. According to Daoism, a serene and uncluttered heart is the highest state for a human being, much like a peaceful pool of still water. Such calmness is the way in which the heart can capture the essence of all things in the world.

引例 Citations：

◎耳目之官不思，而蔽于物。物交物，则引之而已矣。心之官则思，思则得之，不思则不得也。（《孟子·告子上》）

（耳目等器官不能思考，因而被外物的表象遮蔽。耳目与外物相接触，就会被其引向歧途。"心"这一器官能够思考，思考便能有所得，不思考便无所得。）

The sensory organs like ears and eyes cannot think. Therefore, they tend to be misled by the appearance of external objects, and they tend to be led astray when coming into contact with such objects. The heart, however, is an organ capable of thinking. Thinking creates insight, while lack of it will lead one to a dead end. (*Mencius*)

◎心者，一身之主宰。(《朱子语类》卷五）

（心是人身体的主宰。）

Heart is the dominant organ of one's body. (*Categorized Conversations of Master Zhu Xi*)

心斋

/xīnzhāi/

Pure State of the Mind

心灵进入完全虚静的状态。出自《庄子·人间世》。书中借由孔子（前551—前479）之口向颜回（前521—前481）讲解"心斋"之义。庄子（前369？—前286）认为，耳和心在感知外物时，有彼我、是非之别。而气则虚无恬淡，处于万物之中而不与之分别、冲突。因此应使心变得如气一般虚无，与外物相接触，却不与之分别、对立。心游离于事物之外，摆脱事物的限制与影响，这便是"心斋"。

The term refers to a state of mind that is completely empty and void. It originates from the book *Zhuangzi*, in which the meaning of the term was explained by Confucius (551-479 BC) to Yan Hui (521-481 BC). Zhuangzi (369?-286 BC) believed that one's ears and heart distinguish between oneself and others and between right and wrong, while *qi* (气 vital force), shapeless and empty, exists in everything and does not come into conflict with anything. Therefore, one's mind should be empty like *qi* when coming into contact with external things so that one will not be different or clash with them. When one's mind roams beyond physical things, freeing itself from the constraints and influence of other things, it maintains a state known as the "pure state of mind."

引例 Citation：

◎ 回曰："敢问心斋。"仲尼曰："若一志，无听之以耳而听之以心，无听之以心而听之以气。听止于耳，心止于符。气也者，虚而待物者也。唯道集虚，虚者心斋也。"（《庄子·人间世》）

（颜回说："请问什么是'心斋'？"孔子说："你心志专一，不用耳去听而用心去体悟，不用心去体悟而用气去感应。耳的作用止于聆听外物，心的作用止于应合事物。气乃是虚无而能容纳外物的。道只能集于虚无之气中，虚静的心灵就是'心斋'。"）

Yan Hui said, "Could I ask what the 'pure state of the mind' means?" Confucius answered, "You should get totally focused. You need not listen with your ears but listen with your mind; you need not even listen with your mind but listen with *qi*. Listening stops at the ears, and the mind reaches only what fits it. *Qi* is empty and accommodates all external things. Dao gathers and presents itself in an unoccupied and peaceful mind; being unoccupied means the pure state of the mind." (*Zhuangzi*)

心知

/xīnzhī/

Mind Cognition

　　基于心的一种认识活动。由于人们对心及其与外物关系的理解不同，因此对"心知"的认识也有所差异。有人强调，人需要通过心的作用认识日用伦常之道，并使之成为某种内在的诉求。"心知"是人实现道德行为与伦理生活的必要条件。而人心时常处于被遮蔽或不确定的状态，只有通过对心的培养与引导，才能发挥其应有的作用。但也有人认为，"心知"会使人焦灼于变动、繁复的外物，从而造成生命的不安。因此需要排除"心知"，使心进入虚静的状态，不受外物的干扰。

The term means cognitive activities of the mind. As there are different views on the relationship between the mind and the external world, people's understanding of the mind's cognitive process also varies. Some people emphasize the role of the mind in shaping ethical standards in daily life and making them a source of inner strength. Cognition of the mind is a prerequisite for moral cultivation and ethical living. As the mind is often in a blocked or unstable state, it needs to be nurtured with proper guidance before it can play its due role. However, others argue that the mind's cognitive activities make one concerned about the evolving complexity of the external world and feel anxious about life. It is therefore necessary to get rid of the mind's cognitive activities so as to leave the mind in a state of tranquility free from outside interference.

引例 Citation：

◎ 人何以知道？曰：心。心何以知？曰：虚壹而静。(《荀子·解蔽》)

（人如何能够知晓道？回答：用心。心如何能够知晓？回答：做到"虚壹而静"。）

How can people learn to know Dao? The answer is to use one's heart and mind. How can the heart and mind know? The answer is to achieve open-mindedness, concentration, and tranquility. (*Xunzi*)

信言不美，美言不信

/xìn yán bù měi, měi yán bù xìn/

Trustworthy Words May Not Be Fine-sounding; Fine-sounding Words May Not Be Trustworthy.

可信的话并不漂亮，漂亮的话多不可信。老子鉴于当时社会风气与文风的浮华不实，倡导返朴归真与自然平淡的生活方式和文学风格。魏晋时代，文人崇尚自然素朴，反对虚浮华丽的创作风气，出现了像陶渊明（365或372或376—427）这样伟大的诗人，文艺创作也倡导真实自然的思想与风格。自此之后，中国古代文艺以素朴自然为最高的审美境界。

To address the extravagance in social mores and in the style of writing of his time, Laozi advocated simple and natural lifestyles and literary presentations. During the Wei and Jin dynasties, men of letters valued natural and simple literary styles and were opposed to extravagant and superficial styles. This line of thought led to the emergence of great poets like Tao Yuanming (365 or 372 or 376 - 427), and shaped literary writings to reflect direct thoughts and natural expressions. Subsequently, ancient Chinese literature and art took simplicity and naturalness as the highest aesthetic standards.

引例 Citations：

◎信言不美，美言不信。善者不辩，辩者不善。（《老子·八十一章》）

（可信的话并不漂亮，漂亮的话多不可信。善良的人往往不能能言善辩，能言善辩的人往往不善良。）

Trustworthy words may not be fine-sounding; fine-sounding words may not be trustworthy. A kind-hearted person may not be an eloquent speaker; a glib person is often not kind. (*Laozi*)

◎老子疾伪，故称"美言不信"，而五千精妙，则非弃美矣。（刘勰《文心雕龙·情采》）

（老子憎恶虚伪矫饰，所以他认为"漂亮的话多不可信"。但他自己写的《道德经》五千言，思想深刻而文笔优美，可见他并没有摒弃文章之美。）

Laozi detested pretense, so he said, "Flowery rhetoric words may not be trustworthy." However, the 5,000-word *Dao De Jing* (another name of *Laozi*) he wrote is not only profound in ideas but reads beautifully. That means he was not opposed to writings using fine words. (Liu Xie: *The Literary Mind and the Carving of Dragons*)

兴利除害

/xīnglì-chúhài/

Promote the Beneficial; Eliminate the Harmful

兴办对民众有利的事情，消除对民众有害的事情。作为执政者，应将百姓利益放在首位，多做利于天下百姓的事，除去为害百姓的事。中国古人，无论儒家、墨家、法家，都认为这是治国理政者的基本职责，也是治国理政者获得民众拥护的根本前提，因而也是权力正当性的依据所在。今之所谓"执政为民"，与此不无渊源。

Promote what is beneficial to the people; eliminate what is not. Those in power should place the interests of the public at the forefront of their concerns, focusing on what is beneficial and eliminating what is harmful. In ancient China, Confucians, Mohists, and Legalists all held that this was the fundamental duty of a ruler, and determined whether or not there was public support and hence political legitimacy for his rule. Today "govern for the people" has its roots in this concept.

引例 Citations:

◎先王者善为民除害兴利，故天下之民归之。所谓兴利者，利农事也；所谓除害者，禁害农事也。（《管子·治国》）

（远古的贤明君王善于为人民除害兴利，所以天下人民都归附他。所谓兴利，就是有利于农业生产；所谓除害，就是禁止有害于农业生产的事情。）

Wise ancient rulers promoted what was beneficial for the people and eliminated what was harmful, thus winning their allegiance. Beneficial means what is good for farming, harmful what is not. (*Guanzi*)

◎仁人之事者，必务求兴天下之利，除天下之害。（《墨子·兼爱下》）

（仁人的事业，应当努力追求兴办对天下人都有利的事情，去除天下人共同的祸害。）

Benevolent rule means doing what is in the best interests of all people and eliminating common ills. (*Mozi*)

◎汤武者，修其道，行其义，兴天下同利，除天下同害，天下归之。(《荀子·王霸》)

(商王汤、周武王都遵循这个原则，奉行这个道理，兴办对天下人都有利的事情，去除天下人共同的祸害，因此天下人都归顺了他们。)

King Tang of Shang and King Wu of Zhou both followed this principle: promote what benefits all and eliminate what harms all. For this reason, their peoples gave them allegiance. (*Xunzi*)

行己有耻

/xíngjǐ-yǒuchǐ/

Conduct Oneself with a Sense of Shame

对自己的言行保持羞耻之心。出自《论语》。在孔子（前551—前479）看来，一个人的德行的养成不只是言语、行为符合外在的规范，更要在内心对于自身的不足或违礼背德之行感到羞耻，进而能够在羞耻心的刺激下，按照德礼的要求改正、完善自己的言行。羞耻心的确立是儒家教化的重要目标。

The term is from *The Analects*. From the point of view of Confucius (551 - 479 BC), the cultivation of moral conduct is not only words and deeds in accordance with social norms, but more importantly one should have a sense of shame about personal inadequacies and violations of moral conduct. Moreover, stimulated by a sense of shame, one can correct and perfect self-conduct in accordance with moral and social norms. The establishment of a sense of shame is an important goal of Confucian teaching.

引例 Citations：

◎子贡问曰："何如斯可谓之士矣？"子曰："行己有耻，使于四方，不辱君命，可谓士矣。"(《论语·子路》)

(子贡请教："如何做才可以称为士？"孔子说："对自己的言行保持羞耻之心，出使四方诸侯，不辱没君主赋予的使命，就可以称为士了。")

Zigong asked, "What qualifies a person to be called a *shi* (roughly referring to those at the social stratum between the aristocracy and the common people)?" Confucius said, "He who conducts himself with a sense of shame, and does not disgrace the tasks entrusted by his sovereign when dispatched elsewhere, may be called a *shi*." (*The Analects*)

◎ 子曰:"道(dǎo)之以政,齐之以刑,民免而无耻。道之以德,齐之以礼,有耻且格。"(《论语·为政》)

(孔子说:"用政令加以引导,用刑罚加以规范,民众能免于罪过,但没有羞耻之心。用道德加以引导,用礼义加以规范,民众不但有羞耻之心,而且能够自觉合于规范。")

Confucius said, "If people are guided by governmental decree and made to behave themselves through punishments, they will avoid punishment, but will have no sense of shame. If they are guided by morality and behave themselves in accordance with social norms, they will have a sense of shame and will follow rules." (*The Analects*)

行书
/xíngshū/

Running Script

介于草书和楷书之间的一种书法艺术形态。它保留了隶书的基本结构,以自然连笔、书写流畅便捷、容易辨识为主要特征。一般认为行书起源于东汉刘德升,盛行于魏晋。行书有"行进"和"行云流水"的意思,它没有固定的形态和写法,不属于一种独立的字体,适合于任何书写工具,不同人的书写各有特色。东晋王羲之(303—361,一作307—365,又作321—379)的《兰亭集序》、颜真卿(708—784)的《祭侄季明文稿》、苏轼(1037—1101)的《寒食诗帖》是三大行书法帖典范,风格鲜明,具有极高的审美价值。

Running script is a calligraphic form between cursive script and regular script. A Chinese character written in the style of running script retains the basic structure of characters written in official script. Running script features smoothly-linked strokes, and the characters written in this style are easy to recognize. Generally, people believe that running script was created by Liu Desheng of the Eastern Han Dynasty and became popular in the Wei and Jin eras. This writing style reminds one of drifting clouds and flowing water. It has no fixed arrangement for the radicals of a character and can be executed with any writing tools. The same characters written in this style by different people are different in appearance. The best-known masterpieces in this style are Wang Xizhi's (303 - 361, or 307 - 365, 321 - 379) "Preface to the Collection of Poems Composed at the Orchid Pavilion," Yan Zhenqing's (708 - 784) "Draft Elegy to Nephew Jiming," and Su Shi's (1037 - 1101) "The Cold Food Observance." They are distinctive in style and have great aesthetic value.

引例 Citations：

◎行书者，后汉颖川刘德升所作也。即正书之小伪（é），务从简易，相间流行，故谓之"行书"。（张怀瓘（guàn）《书断》卷上）

（行书，是后汉颖川郡的刘德升创造的书写方法。也就是对楷书稍加改变，致力于简单方便，书写时时不时像流水一样行进，所以叫做"行书"。）

Running script was a writing form created by Liu Desheng from Yingchuan in the Eastern Han Dynasty. It is a variation of regular script, easy and convenient to write. Since writing the script sometimes resembles running water, hence the name running script. (Zhang Huaiguan: *Commentary on Calligraphy*)

◎所谓"行"者，即真书之少纵略，后简易相间而行，如云行水流，秾纤间出。非真非草，离方遁圆，乃楷隶之捷也。（宋曹《书法约言·论行书》）

（所谓行书，就是在楷书基础上稍稍自由简略一些，其后简省笔画，不时出现连笔而行，如行云流水一样，笔道粗细相间。它既不是楷书也不是草书，字形既不方也不圆，是楷书和隶书基础上的一种快捷书体。）

Running script is a freer and more concise form of regular script. Later on, strokes of some characters were sometimes linked to make writing easy and simple, looking like drifting clouds and running water. The thickness of strokes of characters keeps changing, sometimes thick, and sometimes thin. It is neither regular script nor cursive script. The form of each character is neither square nor round. It is a quickly-written calligraphic form based on regular script and official script. (Song Cao: *Comments on Different Styles of Script*)

行先知后
/xíngxiān-zhīhòu/

First Action, Then Knowledge

对"知""行"关系的一种认识。王夫之（1619—1692）等人在"知""行"关系问题上提出了"行先知后"的主张。王夫之承认对人伦日用之道的体认与践行是相互关联的，但就先后而言，只有先"行"才能获得"知"。"行"是"知"的来源，对"知"起着决定性的作用。能"行"必然对所行之事有所"知"，但能"知"却未必能"行"。

The term represents one interpretation of the relationship between "knowledge" and "action." Regarding the relationship between "knowledge" and "action," Wang Fuzhi (1619-1692) and others argued that "action precedes knowledge." Wang acknowledged that an understanding of the principles underlying human relations in everyday life is interrelated with the application of these principles, but in terms of sequence, only through "action" can one obtain "knowledge." "Action" is the source of "knowledge" and has a decisive impact on "knowledge." If one can "act," one inevitably "knows" about one's actions, but the ability to "know" does not necessarily translate into the ability to "act."

引例 Citation：

◎行焉而后知其艰，非力行焉者不能知也。(王夫之《四书训义·论语九》)

(践行之后才知道其中的艰难，若没有努力践行就不能知晓。)

Only after acting can one know the difficulties involved; without efforts to act one cannot know. (Wang Fuzhi: *Explicating the Lessons of the Four Books*)

形而上
/xíng'érshàng/

What Is Above Form / The Metaphysical

　　无形或未成形质，一般以此指称有形事物的依据。出自《周易·系辞上》（与"形而下"相对而言）。"形"指形体，"形而上"是指在形体出现之前，也即无形者。此无形者被称为"道"。

The term means what is formless or has no formal substance yet. It generally indicates the basis of physical things. The term "what is above form" comes from *The Book of Changes* and is used as the opposite of "what is under form." "Form" indicates physical shape. "What is above form" refers to the state before a physical shape emerges, namely, formlessness. That which is formless is called "Dao."

引例 Citation：

◎形而上者谓之道，形而下者谓之器。(《周易·系辞上》)
（未成形质者称为"道"，已成形质者称为"器"。）

What is above form is called Dao, and what is under form is called "an object." (*The Book of Changes*)

形而下
/xíng'érxià/

What Is Under Form / The Physical

　　有形或已成形质，一般指实际存在的具体事物。出自《周易·系辞上》（与"形而上"相对而言）。"形"指形体，"形而下"指在形体出现之后，也即有形者。此有形者被称为"器"。"形而下"的存在以"形而上"为依据。

The term means what has a form or what has a formal substance. It generally indicates existing and concrete things. The term "what is under form" comes from *The Book of Changes*. It is used as the opposite of "what is above form." "Form" indicates physical shape. "What is under form" refers to the state after a physical shape has emerged, namely, physical existence. That which has a form is called "an object." What is under form takes what is above form as the basis of its existence.

引例 Citation:

◎形而上者谓之道，形而下者谓之器。(《周易·系辞上》)
（未成形质者称为"道"，已成形质者称为"器"。）

What is above form is called Dao, and what is under form is called "an object." (*The Book of Changes*)

形具神生

/xíngjù-shénshēng/

Physical Form Gives Birth to Spirit.

人的形体具备以后精神活动随之产生。"形"指人的形体，"神"指包括情感、意识在内的各种精神活动。荀子（前313？—前238）提出，人的形体和精神，与万物一样，都是在天道的运行中自然生成的。人的形体先于精神而生成，形体的具备构成了精神产生的条件。人的精神依存于形体之中。

When a person's physical form has fully developed, he will develop spiritual activity accordingly. Here "form" refers to the physical form of a human being, and "spiritual" refers to various mental activities, including emotions and consciousness. Xunzi (313?-238 BC) pointed out that a person's physical form and spirit, just like everything else, develop naturally in the course of the movement of the way of heaven. Spirit is born in the wake of physical formation of a human being. Full physical form is a prerequisite to the birth of spirit. A person's spirit exists within his physical form.

引例 Citation:

◎ 天职既立，天功既成，形具而神生。好恶、喜怒、哀乐藏焉，夫是之谓天情。（《荀子·天论》）

（天的职能已经确立，天的功效已经实现，人的形体具备了，人的精神活动也随之产生。好恶、喜怒、哀乐等情感蕴藏在形体之中，这就叫做天然的情感。）

When the functions of nature have been established and brought into play, one's physical form emerges and one's spirit is born. Love and hate, delight and anger as well as sadness and joy all develop within one's physical form; and they are called natural emotions. (*Xunzi*)

兴
/xìng/

Evocation

主要指由外物触发内心情感而产生的审美感受和心理状态。作为美学范畴的"兴"接受了"兴观群怨"之"兴（譬喻）"与"赋比兴"之"兴（六义之一）"的双重影响而兼有两者的含义。从欣赏的角度来看，孔子（前551—前479）所提出的"兴观群怨"之"兴"，注重读诗而引发的心理感受和教育功能，并非纯粹的文学理论；从创作的角度来看，"兴"是《诗经》"六义"（风、雅、颂、赋、比、兴）之一，一般说来，前三者为《诗经》的内容与体裁分类，后三者为《诗经》的创作手法。"兴"的基本特征为：由相类似的事物引发开来，运用想象与联想，达成譬喻，由此及彼，将所要表达的意义蕴含在形象中，使诗歌的韵味更加含蓄、深邃。"兴"将诗歌的发端与联想完整地融为一体，使人在鉴赏中回味无穷，是中国古代诗歌创作的特有手法。"兴"起初与"比"结合紧密，魏晋南北朝时它的蕴含和审美特征逐渐获得独立的发展，成为与"比兴"分立的诗学范畴，"兴"更注重外物对内心的感发触动。

This term refers to the state of mind in which external things evoke one's inner feelings, thus creating aesthetic appreciation. As an aesthetic term, evocation means both stimulation and association. In artistic appreciation, Confucius (551-479 BC) used evocation to refer to the psychological effect and educational function of reading poetry, and it was not meant to be a literary term only. In artistic creation, evocation means association, which is among the six poetic forms, namely, ballad, narrative, analogy, association, court hymns, and eulogy, as described in *The Book of Songs*. The first three refer to the content and subtypes of classic Chinese poetry, whereas the latter three elements are creative means employed by *The Book of Songs*. Evocation is defined by the use of similar or relevant things to create a metaphor which, by virtue of imagination and association, conveys a message through imagery and highlights the nuances of poetry. Evocation arouses one's imagination through reading a poem, making such experience an enjoyable one. It is a rhetorical means frequently used in classical Chinese poetry. At first, evocation was closely linked to analogy. Its implication and aesthetic properties started to grow independently in the Wei, Jin and Southern and Northern Dynasties period, and finally became a poetic term different from analogy and association. Evocation focuses on the impact of external things on one's emotions.

引例 Citations：

◎兴于诗，立于礼，成于乐（yuè）。(《论语·泰伯》)
（以诗感发意志，以礼规范行为，以乐成就人格。）

One uses poetry to evoke volition, rituals and etiquette to regulate behavior and music to shape one's character. (*The Analects*)

◎兴者，起也。取譬引类，起发己心。《诗》文诸举草木鸟兽以见意者，皆兴辞也。(《毛诗序》孔颖达正义引郑众语)
（兴，就是起意。借相类似的事物取譬喻，引发自己的情感、心志。《诗经》文本中列举草木鸟兽以表现作者情感、心志的情况，都是"兴"一类的词句。）

Evocation means using certain things in the outer world to arouse one's emotions and aspirations. *The Book of Songs*, for example, cites trees, grass, birds and beasts to evoke such feelings. (Zheng Zhong, as quoted in Kong Yingda: Correct Meaning of "Introductions to *Mao's Version of The Book of Songs*")

◎《诗》有六义，其四为兴。兴者，因事发端（duān），托物喻意，随时成咏。（王闿运《诗法一首示黄生》）

(《诗经》有六义，第四为兴。兴，就是依凭事物而感发，借事物寄托自己的意旨，随时吟诵成诗。)

The Book of Songs contains six genres: ballads, narratives, analogies, associations, court hymns, and eulogies. The fourth one, namely "association," means that the poet makes use of things from the outer world to voice his feelings and volition, thus creating a poem. (Wang Kaiyun: A Poem Written to Show Mr. Huang How to Write Poetry)

兴观群怨
/xìng-guān-qún-yuàn/

Stimulation, Contemplation, Communication, and Criticism

孔子（前551—前479）所提出的《诗经》的四种主要功能，实际也是对文学基本功能与价值的高度概括。"兴"是指通过作品的欣赏引发联想，激发欣赏者对于社会人生的思考与志趣提升；"观"是通过作品认识自然与社会人生的各种状况，透视政治得失；"群"是围绕作品与别人展开讨论，交流思想感情；"怨"是表达对社会时政的不满，宣泄内心的情感。这四种功能有着内在的联系，涉及文学的审美功能、认识功能与教育功能。后世学者对此不断有新的阐发。

According to Confucius (551-479 BC), *The Book of Songs* served these four purposes, which summarize the basic functions and values of literature. "Stimulation" means that the appreciation of literary works arouses imagination, stimulates reflection on society and life, and inspires aspirations and interests. "Contemplation" means that reading leads to understanding nature, society, life, and politics. "Communication" means that reading encourages discussion with others, and exchange of thoughts and feelings. "Criticism" means learning how to critically express oneself about state affairs and voice inner feelings. These four functions are closely associated and involve the aesthetic, cognitive, and educational functions of literature. Later scholars have continued to make original contributions to the study of these themes.

引例 Citations：

◎《诗》可以兴，可以观，可以群，可以怨；迩之事父，远之事君；多识于鸟、兽、草、木之名。(《论语·阳货》)

(《诗经》可以感发志向，引发思考，认识世界，可以交流思想感情，表达不满情绪。在家可以用它来侍奉父母，出外可以用它来侍奉国君，还可以从中学到鸟兽草木等众多事物的知识。)

The Book of Songs stimulates the mind, inspires contemplation, enables one to understand society, exchange feelings and thoughts with others, and express resentment. The book guides one on how to support and wait on one's parents at home and how to serve one's sovereign in public life. One can also learn about birds, beasts, and plants from the book. (*The Analects*)

◎于所兴而可观，其兴也深；于所观而可兴，其观也审；以其群者而怨，怨愈不忘；以其怨者而群，群乃益挚。(王夫之《姜斋诗话》卷一)

(经过作者感兴后的作品又具备认识价值，那么这种感兴一定深刻；经过认识又能够激发情感的，那么这种认识一定真实明察；因为聚在一起而产生某种怨恨，那么这种怨恨更加使人难忘；因为某种怨恨而聚成群体，这样的群体一定会更加紧密。)

If works created on the basis of the author's understanding have the value of cognition, his understanding must have been profound. If his feelings are based on recognition, his observation must have been sharp. If certain resentment arises from discussions among a group of people, it must be unforgettable. If a group of people have come together because they share certain resentment, they must be closely knit. (Wang Fuzhi: *Desultory Remarks on Poetry from Ginger Studio*)

兴寄
/xìngjì/

Xingji (Association and Inner Sustenance)

运用比兴、寄托等艺术手法，使诗歌情感蕴藉、内涵深厚、寄托感慨。由初唐时代的陈子昂（659—700）首次提出。"兴"是由外物触发而兴发情感，"寄"是寄托某种寓意。兴寄最初是指诗人的感兴要有寓意，达到托物言志的目的；后来引申为诗歌要有赞美或讽刺的寓意。兴寄这一术语继承了先秦时代感物起兴的诗歌传统，强调诗歌的感兴之中要有深沉的寄托，是比兴理论的重要发展，对于盛唐诗歌摆脱齐梁时代诗歌追求华彩而摒弃寄托的创作态度、推动唐诗健康发展有很大作用。

The term means the use of analogy, association, and inner sustenance in writing a poem to give implicit expression to one's sentiments, thus enabling the poem to convey a subtle message. The term was first used by the Tang-dynasty poet Chen Zi'ang (659-700). *Xing* (兴) means the development of inner feelings invoked by external objects, and *ji* (寄) means finding sustenance in them. Later it was extended to mean that poetry should be written to convey a message of praise or satire. The term carried on the pre-Qin poetical tradition of creating inspiration by writing about a subject and stressed that while depicting sentiments in poetry, the poet should find sustenance in it. The term represented an important development of the theory of analogy and association. It played a major role in ensuring that poets in the prime of the Tang Dynasty broke away from the poetic style of the Qi and Liang of the Southern Dynasties, which pursued ornate language instead of inner sustenance, thus enabling Tang poetry to develop in a healthy way.

引例 Citations：

◎仆尝暇时观齐梁间诗，彩丽竞繁而兴寄都绝。每以永叹，思古人常恐逶迤颓靡、风雅不作，以耿耿也。（陈子昂《修竹篇（并序）》）
（我曾经在闲暇时读齐梁时期的诗歌，这些诗辞藻堆砌、竞相华丽，但是兴寄的味道一点儿都没有。我常为此长叹，推想古人经常担心诗风渐至颓废华靡，《诗经》的风雅传统不再振兴，心中定会耿耿不平。）

When I read the poems of the Qi and Liang of the Southern Dynasties in my leisure time, I found them full of ornate rhetoric heaped together without sustenance. I often feel resigned as I can well imagine that the ancients were always concerned about poetry becoming decadent and the tradition of objectively reflecting reality as shown in *The Book of Songs* getting lost. (Chen Zi'ang: "The Bamboo" with a Preface)

◎仆尝病兴寄之作堙（yīn）郁于世，辞有枝叶，荡而成风，益用慨然。（柳宗元《答贡士沈起书》）

（我曾经担忧那些有兴寄特色的作品被埋没掉，文章追求浮华枝叶，恣纵成为风尚，这个时候更需要作品有感慨和意味。）

I was concerned that the works based on association and inner sustenance would get lost and that writings with only elaborate rhetoric would prevail. We really need works that have substance. (Liu Zongyuan: Letter to Scholar Shen Qi)

兴趣

/xìngqù/

Xingqu (Charm)

"兴"中所蕴含的趣或者是"兴"发时心物交会所产生的趣（情趣、意趣等）。是诗歌中所蕴含的、读者通过欣赏而获得的特定的审美趣味。南宋诗论家严羽（？—1264）在《沧浪诗话》中倡导诗歌的感染力，反对直接说理，主张让读者在品读和感悟中得到愉悦和满足。这一术语后来成为评价诗歌的重要标准，明清诗学也受到积极影响。

The term refers to charm inherent in an inspiration, or charm created when the object or scene depicted in a poem is appreciated. It is a type of aesthetic enjoyment contained in a poem which is gained through the reader's act of appreciation. In *Canglang's Criticism on Poetry*, Yan Yu (?-1264), a poetry critic of the Southern Song Dynasty, voiced his love for poetry's emotional charm and argued against direct expression of an idea in poetry. He stressed the need to enable readers to gain insight and satisfaction in a natural way through personal reflection and contemplation. This term later became an important criterion for evaluating poetry, exerting a strong influence on the poetry theories of the Ming and Qing dynasties.

引例 Citations：

◎诗者，吟咏情性也。盛唐诸人惟在兴趣，羚羊挂角，无迹可求。（严羽《沧浪诗话·诗辨》）

（诗歌吟咏的是本性真情。盛唐诗人的诗作特别着意兴趣，如同羚羊晚上将角挂在树上睡觉，没有任何痕迹可寻。）

One should write poetry only to express one's true sentiments and personality. In their poems, Tang-dynasty poets made particular efforts to inspire meaning, charm, and emotion. Their style is like an antelope hooking its horns onto a tree when sleeping at night, so that its trace cannot be found. (Yan Yu: *Canglang's Criticism on Poetry*)

◎古诗多在兴趣，微辞隐义，有足感人。而宋人多好以诗议论。夫以诗议论，即奚不为文而为诗哉？（屠隆《文论》）

（古代诗作多注重审美情趣的传达，用词含蓄而寓意隐微，足以感染读者。而宋代诗人大多借诗歌来论事说理。用诗歌论事说理，那为何不写成文章而非要写成诗呢？）

Classical poems mostly focused on inspiring meaning, charm, and emotion through hints with subtle wording and implied meanings, and that is why they moved readers. Poets during the Song Dynasty, however, tended to use poetry to comment on public affairs or make arguments. If that was what they wanted to achieve, why didn't they write essays instead of poems? (Tu Long: *On Essay Writing*)

性分

/xìngfèn/

Natural Attribute

　　万物的本性所规定的内容与限度。郭象（？—312）提出，每个人或每一事物都有各自的本性，且本性有着具体的内容与限度，如事物的大小、形状，人的年寿、智愚等。人和事物的本性是天生所具、不得不然的，因此也是不能改变的。万物都应该安于自身的"性分"。人和事物如果能够按照本性的要求，在"性分"的范围内活动行事，就是自由、逍遥的。

This term refers to the features and limitations determined by the intrinsic nature of all things. Guo Xiang (?-312), a scholar in the Western Jin Dynasty, pointed out that each person or object has his or its own intrinsic natural attributes, such as size and shape of an object, or the life expectancy and intelligence or lack of it of a person. The natural attributes of a person or an object are inborn and therefore unchangeable. All things should remain content with their natural attributes. If people and objects follow their own nature and act within the scope of their natural attributes, they can enjoy unhindered freedom of movement.

引例 Citation：

◎天性所受，各有本分，不可逃，亦不可加。（郭象《庄子注》卷二）

（人和事物所禀受的天性，各有各的内容与限度，不能够逃避，也不能够改变。）

People and objects each have their own natural attributes and limitations, which they cannot ignore or alter. (Guo Xiang: *Annotations on Zhuangzi*)

性灵
/xìnglíng/

Xingling (Inner Self)

　　本指相对于客观外物的人的心灵世界，包括性情、才智两个方面。南北朝时期，"性灵"成为文学创作与文学批评术语，主要指与社会伦理、政治教化与传统创作观念相对的个体的精神才智与性情气质，强调文艺应该发自并表现人的性灵。明清时期，随着个性伸张与思想解放，袁宏道（1568—1610）、袁枚（1716—1798）等著名文士用"性灵"倡导文学应该直抒胸臆，表现内心真实的思想情感、兴趣见解，强调创作中的精神个性和艺术个性，反对宋明理学、传统创作观念以及复古思潮对于人性与文学的束缚，并因此成为文学创作上的一个重要流派。

The term refers to an individual's inner mind vis-à-vis the outside world, which consists of two aspects, namely, temperament and talent. During the Southern and Northern Dynasties, *xingling* (inner self) became widely used in literary writing and criticism. It refers to the combination of a writer's temperament and talent, other than his social ethics, political beliefs, and literary traditions; and it stresses that literature is inspired by traits of individuality and should give expression to them. During the Ming and Qing dynasties, along with the trend of giving free rein to individuality and shaking off intellectual straitjacket, renowned scholars such as Yuan Hongdao (1568-1610) and Yuan Mei (1716-1798) advocated giving full expression to one's inner self, namely, one's thoughts, sentiment, emotion and views. They underscored the role of intellectual and artistic individuality in literary creation as opposed to the rigid School of Principle of the earlier Song and Ming dynasties, literary dogma and blind belief in classicism which constrained people from expressing human nature and inhabited literary creativity. The Xingling School thus became an important school in literary creation.

引例 Citations:

◎惟人参（sān）之，性灵所钟，是谓三才。为五行之秀，实天地之心。心生而言立，言立而文明，自然之道也。（刘勰《文心雕龙·原道》）

（只有人身上钟聚了性情才智，可以与天地并称为"三才"。人是天地万物中最杰出的种类，实际是天地的核心与灵魂。心灵活动产生语言，语言表达出来就形成文章，这是自然规律。）

Temperament and talent are found only in man, constituting his inner self. One of the three elements of existence along with heaven and earth, man stands out among all species and is the essence and soul of the world. In the natural course of events, the need to express man's inner self leads to the emergence of language, which in turn gives rise to literary creation. (Liu Xie: *The Literary Mind and the Carving of Dragons*)

◎ 大都独抒性灵，不拘格套，非从自己胸臆流出，不肯下笔。(袁宏道《叙小修诗》)

（[他的诗]大都抒发自己真实独特的性情，不拘泥于任何格式套路。只要不是出自本心，绝不肯下笔。）

Most of his poems express his inner self, without being constrained by any particular regulations or formulas. He would not commit to paper anything not flowing naturally from his inner world. (Yuan Hongdao: *Preface to Xiaoxiu's Poetry*)

◎ 自三百篇至今日，凡诗之传者，都是性灵，不关堆垛。(袁枚《随园诗话》卷五)

（从《诗经》到今日，凡是能够广泛流传的诗歌，都是因为表达了自己的性灵，与堆砌辞藻和典故没有关系。）

Ever since *The Book of Songs* was written, all those poems which have remained popular were created to give full expression to the authors' inner self, instead of being loaded with clichés and classical references. (Yuan Mei: *Suiyuan Remarks on Poetry*)

性三品

/xìngsānpǐn/

Human Nature Has Three Levels.

人性分为三个等级。"性三品"说是古代的一种人性论观点。该说认为，人的本性是不同的，分为上、中、下三个等级。上品之人性善，下品之人性恶。中间之人，本性或无善无恶，或善恶相混。有些人认为，人天生所具有的人性等级，尤其是上下二品，是不可改易的。也有人主张，后天的教化可以改变人性，甚至超越固有的品级。

Human nature may be categorized as having three levels. This is a view of human nature held by ancient Chinese people. According to this theory, different people have different inherent natures, which can be divided into upper, middle, and lower levels. People of the upper level have a good nature. People of the lower level have an evil nature. The nature of those in the middle level is either devoid of the distinction between good and evil, or is a mixture of good and evil. Some believe that human nature is inborn, particularly in those of the upper and lower levels, and is unchangeable. Others think that education can change human nature, allowing people to advance to the next level.

引例 Citations：

◎余固以孟轲言人性善者，中人以上者也；孙卿言人性恶者，中人以下者也；扬雄言人性善恶混者，中人也。（王充《论衡·本性》）
（我认为孟子所言人性善，是指中等以上的人；荀子所言人性恶，是指中等以下的人；扬雄所言人性善恶混杂，是指中等的人。）

Mencius said that people were good by nature. I believe the people he referred to are those above the middle level. Xunzi said that people were evil by nature. I believe the people he referred to are those below the middle level. Yang Xiong said that the nature of people was mixed with good and evil. I believe the people he referred to are those in the middle level. (Wang Chong: *A Comparative Study of Different Schools of Learning*)

◎性之品有上中下三。上焉者，善焉而已矣；中焉者，可导而上下也；下焉者，恶焉而已矣。（韩愈《原性》）

（人性的品类有上中下三等。上等之人，性本就善罢了；中等之人，可以引导而性善或性恶；下等之人，性本就恶罢了。）

Human nature can be divided into three levels, namely: upper, middle, and lower levels. The nature of people in the upper level is innately good. The nature of people in the middle level can be guided towards good or evil. The nature of people in the lower level is innately evil. (Han Yu: An Inquiry into Intrinsic Nature)

修齐治平

/xiū-qí-zhì-píng/

Self-cultivation, Family Regulation, State Governance, Bringing Peace to All Under Heaven

"修身""齐家""治国""平天下"的缩写。以个人自身修养为基础逐步向外扩展，先治理好家庭，进而治理好邦国，更进而安抚和治理天下百姓。这是中国古代儒家伦理哲学和政治抱负的一个重要命题，体现了儒家由个人而家而国而天下层层递进的道德政治观。在逐步向外扩展的过程中，个人的德行和修养与不同层面的政治抱负息息相关。

Self-cultivation is the starting point of several steps moving outward. The next step is managing family affairs, followed by governing the state. The final step is moving to provide peace and sound governance to all under heaven. This process is a fundamental theme in Confucian moral philosophy and discourse on politics. It is a gradually expanding process beginning with the individual and emanating outward into serving and benefiting an ever-larger whole. In such a process an individual's virtue and self-improvement are inseparable from his political aspirations.

引例 Citation：

◎古之欲明明德于天下者，先治其国。欲治其国者，先齐其家。欲齐其家者，先修其身。(《礼记·大学》)

（过去想要在全天下彰明光明德性的人，先要治理好自己的邦国。想要治理好自己的邦国，先要治理好自己的家［周朝时为封地］。想要治理好自己的家，先要做好自身的修养。）

The ancients, who wished to promote illustrious virtue under heaven, first had to rule their own states well. Wishing to govern their states well, they first had to manage their fiefdoms well. Wishing to manage their fiefdoms well, they first had to cultivate themselves. (*The Book of Rites*)

虚
/xū/

Xu (Void)

"虚"指世界或者心灵的一种状态。大体有两种不同的含义：其一，指世界的本原，万物皆由虚无中来。但古人对"虚"的这一含义又有不同理解：或认为"虚"就是空虚无有；或认为"虚"指"气"的存在状态，因为"气"的存在隐微无形，故以"虚"称之，但并非完全空无。其二，指虚静的或没有成见的内心状态。

Xu refers to a state of the cosmos or a state of mind. Basically, it has two different meanings. The first refers to the origin of the universe, indicating that everything originates from *xu*. Different ancient thinkers have different interpretations of this notion: Some take *xu* as being devoid of anything; others believe it is the state of existence of *qi* (气). Because *qi* is invisible and formless, it is said to be empty, but not a vacuum totally devoid of anything. The second meaning of *xu* refers to a state of mind that is peaceful, not preoccupied or simply free of any preconceptions.

引例 Citations：

◎ 太虚无形，气之本体。（张载《正蒙・太和》）

（太虚是无形的，是气的本来状态。）

Taixu, or the great void, is formless; it is the original state of *qi*. (Zhang Zai: *Enlightenment Through Confucian Teachings*)

◎ 唯道集虚，虚者心斋也。(《庄子·人间世》)

（道只能集于虚无之气中，虚静的心灵就是"心斋"。）

Dao gathers and presents itself in an unoccupied and peaceful mind; being unoccupied means the pure state of the mind. (*Zhuangzi*)

虚静
/xūjìng/

Void and Peace

　　排除一切欲望与理性思维的干扰，达到心灵的纯净与安宁。由道家老庄最先提出，荀子（前313？—前238）也用它说明专心致志所达到的一种精神状态。由于这种心境与文艺审美中无物无我、无知无欲的心理特性相通，因此，古代思想家与文艺批评家也用"虚静"来说明文艺活动中的审美心理。这一术语强调文艺创作中的心灵自由，认为它是达到审美最高境界的重要前提。

Void and peace mean that all distractions, such as desires and rational thoughts, should be dispelled to attain peace and purity of the soul. The idea of void and peace was first proposed by Laozi and Zhuangzi (369?- 286 BC), the founders of Daoism, and then used by Xunzi (313?- 238 BC) to refer to a state of mental concentration. Such a state of mind is similar to the psychological conditions in appreciation of works of literature and art, which are characterized by being totally free from the awareness of oneself and the outside world, and free from any urge and desire. Therefore, thinkers and literary critics of earlier times used this term to explain the state of mind in literary and artistic creation and appreciation. It stressed the need for spiritual freedom in artistic creation, suggesting that this is an important precondition for reaching the highest level of aesthetic appreciation.

引例 Citations:

◎ 致虚极，守静笃。(《老子·十六章》)

（达到虚空境界，没有任何杂念；坚守安宁心境，不受外物干扰。）

When one attains the state of void and peace, his mind becomes peaceful and free of any distractions. He can withstand the temptations of the outside world. (*Laozi*)

◎ 是以陶钧文思，贵在虚静，疏瀹（yuè）五藏（zàng），澡雪精神。（刘勰《文心雕龙·神思》）

（因此构思文章，最重要的是虚静，不受外物干扰，身体舒泰如同五脏贯通了一样，精神洁净如同洗洁过一样。）

In conceiving an essay, one should strive for a mental state of quiet emptiness and not let oneself be bothered by external interferences, and be relaxed and at ease just like all his internal organs are put in perfect comfort and his spirits refreshed by a thorough wash. (Liu Xie: *The Literary Mind and the Carving of Dragons*)

虚壹而静

/xūyī'érjìng/

Open-mindedness, Concentration, and Tranquility

荀子（前313？—前238）所提出的一种用以把握日用伦常之道的心灵状态。荀子认为，需要通过心的作用才能知"道"。但人心时常处于被遮蔽的状态，只有进入"虚壹而静"的状态才能发挥应有的作用。"虚"是不使已收藏在心中的知识妨碍将要接受的东西。"壹"是使同时兼得的知识类目分明，彼此无碍。"静"是不以虚妄而混乱的知识妨碍正常的心灵活动。

This refers to a state of mind Xunzi (313?-238 BC) proposed as a way to master the Dao of general morality. He believed that one gets to know Dao through the action of one's heart and mind. But since the human heart and mind are often closed, they can only function normally when one is open-minded, concentrated, and consequently tranquil. *Xu* (虚), or open-mindedness, prevents prior knowledge from hindering the acquisition of new knowledge. *Yi* (壹), or concentration, allows one to assimilate knowledge of different categories while keeping them from interfering with each other. *Jing* (静), or tranquility, is to keep the false and confusing knowledge from obstructing one's normal process of contemplation.

引例 Citation：

◎人何以知道？曰：心。心何以知？曰：虚壹而静。(《荀子·解蔽》)

（人如何能够知晓道？回答：用心。心如何能够知晓？回答：做到"虚壹而静"。）

How can people learn to know Dao? The answer is to use one's heart and mind. How can the heart and mind know? The answer is to achieve open-mindedness, concentration, and tranquility. (*Xunzi*)

玄览
/xuánlǎn/

Xuanlan (Pure-minded Contemplation)

原指在深远虚净的心境下览知万物，是老子提出的认识"道"的一种方法。老子认为，只有摒弃一切杂念与成见，保持内心明澈如镜，才能静观万物，从而认识"道"，体会其精要。后世文艺评论家因为"玄览"所主张的心境与文艺创作及鉴赏所要求的审美心境相契合，遂用为文艺思想的重要术语，以说明文艺创作与鉴赏时应具有的超越一切欲望与功利的特殊心境。

This term was first used by Laozi as a way to understand Dao. He believed that one cannot understand Dao by calmly observing everything unless one abandons all distracting thoughts and biases, and keeps one's mind as clear as a mirror. Later literary critics believed that the state of mind as required for *xuanlan* has similarities with the state of mind required for literary writing and appreciation, thus they made it an important term to mean one's state of mind must transcend all desires and personal gains in literary writing and appreciation.

引例 Citations：

◎涤除玄览，能无疵乎？（《老子·十章》）

（涤除一切杂念，在深远虚静的心境下观照一切，就没有瑕疵了吗？）

Is it for sure that there will be no flaws when one cleanses away all distracting thoughts and watches the world with a clear, peaceful mind? (*Laozi*)

◎伫中区以玄览，颐情志于典坟。（陆机《文赋》）

（久立于天地间以深远虚静的心境观照一切，在典籍的阅读中颐养性情、培养志向。）

Standing between heaven and earth and watching the world with a clear, peaceful mind, the writer enriches and improves himself through reading great works of the past. (Lu Ji: The Art of Writing)

玄言诗

/xuányánshī/

Metaphysical Poetry

一种以阐发老庄、佛教和《周易》哲理为主要内容的诗歌流派，起于西晋末年而盛行于东晋，其主要特点是以玄理入诗，代表诗人有孙绰（314—371）、许询（314—361）、庾亮（289—340）、桓温（312—373）等。魏晋时期社会动荡，士大夫专心老庄与佛学，贵玄理，尚清谈，以此全身远祸。到西晋后期，玄谈之风逐步影响到诗歌创作，形成玄言诗，后玄言诗与山水诗相融合。

This term refers to a poetic style that chiefly explicated Laozi, Zhuangzi (369?-286 BC), Buddhism, and *The Book of Changes*. Metaphysical poetry emerged at the end of the Western Jin Dynasty and flourished during the subsequent Eastern Jin Dynasty. Represented by Sun Chuo (314-371), Xu Xun (314-361), Yu Liang (289-340), and Huan Wen (312-373), this genre featured the expounding of abstruse and metaphysical thinking in poetry. During the turbulent years of the

Wei and Jin dynasties, scholars stayed away from politics and focused on the study of Laozi, Zhuangzi, and Buddhism to explore abstruse and philosophical ideas unrelated to current social developments. By the end of the Western Jin Dynasty, this rarefied discourse found its way into writing, creating the metaphysical style of poetry, which later merged with landscape poetry.

引例 Citation：

◎ 自中朝贵玄，江左称盛，因谈余气，流成文体，是以世极迍邅（zhūnzhān），而辞意夷泰。诗必柱下之旨归，赋乃漆园之义疏。（刘勰《文心雕龙·时序》）

（自从西晋崇尚玄学，到东晋风气更盛，因袭清谈风气，逐渐形成新的文风。因此，虽然时势极其艰难，而文章的辞意却显得平和宽缓。诗歌必定以老庄为宗旨，辞赋也成了老庄的注解。）

In the Western Jin Dynasty, discourse of metaphysics was hot, which became even more popular during the Eastern Jin Dynasty, giving rise to a new literary style. Consequently, despite the tumultuous times, writers composed literary works characterized by detachment and aloofness. Poetry invariably illustrated the ideas of Laozi and Zhuangzi, and prose-poetry became commentaries on these two thinkers. (Liu Xie: *The Literary Mind and the Carving of Dragons*)

悬梁刺股

/xuánliáng-cìgǔ/

Tie One's Hair on the House Beam and Jab One's Side with an Awl to Keep Oneself from Falling Asleep while Studying

"头悬梁，锥刺股"的略语。字面意思是把头发拴在屋梁上，用锥子扎大腿。来源于古人刻苦读书的故事。东汉的孙敬经常关起门，独自一人从早到晚不停读书。疲倦和劳累时就将头发拴在屋梁上，只要一低头，头发就被拉住，人马上清醒，再接着读。战国时代的苏秦（？—前

284），每当困乏欲睡的时候，就用锥子扎自己的大腿，以保持头脑清醒，继续苦读。后人常以这两个故事鼓励年轻人发愤读书，努力学习。今天，这种有损身体健康的极端方式已不再提倡，但其刻苦求知的精神仍广为称颂。

The term literally means to tie one's hair on the house beam and jab one's side with an awl. The idiom comes from the ancient story about how assiduously people studied. Sun Jing of the Eastern Han Dynasty would incessantly read books from dawn to dusk alone. When he felt tired or fatigued, he would tie his hair to the beam of the house, so that the moment he began to nod off, his head would be jerked back and this would immediately rouse him, and he could continue reading. During the Warring States Period, Su Qin (?-284 BC) would use an awl to jab at his own thigh whenever he felt sleepy, to make sure he stayed awake and lucid enough to be able to continue reading. Later, people started to tell these stories in order to encourage young people to study hard. Today, this kind of extreme measures which are physically harmful are no longer encouraged. However, this kind of assiduous spirit in the pursuit of knowledge is still highly lauded.

引例 Citation：

◎头悬梁，锥刺股。彼不教，自勤苦。(《三字经》)

(孙敬读书时把头发拴在屋梁上[以免打瞌睡]；苏秦读书，[每到困倦时就]用锥子扎大腿。他们不用别人督促，而是自觉地勤奋苦读。)

Sun Jing tied his hair to a roof beam to prevent himself from falling asleep while reading; Su Qin jabbed at his own thigh with an awl to keep himself from dozing off while studying. They both studied hard on their own initiative without other's supervision. (*Three-character Classic*)

学

/xué/

Learn

学习，儒家认为它是成就道德生命的一种修养和教化方式。一般意义上的"学"主要指对知识的理解和掌握，而儒家所言之"学"则更多指向道德品性的养成。个人通过后天对经典和礼法的学习以及对圣贤的效法，不断培养、完善自身的德性，以成就理想的人格。道家则反对"学"，如老子主张"绝学无忧"，认为"学"会带来内心不必要的忧虑，乃至破坏人的自然状态。

To Confucianism, learning is the way to cultivate oneself to achieve moral integrity. The usual meaning of the term is to acquire knowledge and understanding, but for Confucianism it focuses more on the cultivation of moral and ethical qualities to achieve personal growth. Through learning classics and rites, and following the practices of sages, a person is able to cultivate and improve his moral standards and thus become a person of ideal qualities. Daoists, on the other hand, are against learning, and Laozi said that "fine-sounding arguments" only cause unnecessary worries, and can disrupt a person's natural state of mind.

引例 Citations：

◎学而时习之，不亦说（yuè）乎？(《论语·学而》)

（学习并按一定的时间熟习所学的内容，不也是愉快的吗？）

Isn't it a pleasure to learn and apply from time to time what one has learned? (*The Analects*)

◎君子博学而日参（cān）省乎己，则知明而行无过矣。(《荀子·劝学》)

（君子广泛学习并且每天坚持自我参验、反省，就可以做到智慧明达而行为不会有错了。）

Men of virtue, who study extensively and reflect on themselves every day, become wise and intelligent and are free from making mistakes. (*Xunzi*)

血气
/xuèqì/

Vitality / Vital Force

　　反映着人与动物的身体需求与生命状态的气。"血气"是人天生所具有的，反映着血肉之躯对于外在物质的需求。"血气"的状态在人的各个生命阶段中是不同的，其盛衰反映着生命力的强弱。年轻时"血气"并不稳定，及至壮年则"血气"强盛，年老则"血气"衰弱。此外，不同人的"血气"强弱程度也有所差异。有的人"血气"刚强，有的则较为柔和。"血气"可以通过礼乐教化而加以改变。同时，"血气"也构成人的道德情感发生的基础。

The term refers to vitality which is needed for the human or animal body to sustain its life and which reflects the state of life. It is something one is born with, representing the body's needs of material things. A person exhibits different levels of vitality at different stages of life, reflecting changes in the strength of life. Vitality is unstable in youth; it reaches its peak in the prime of life, and in old age it wanes. Furthermore, different people have different levels of vitality, some overflowing with vigor, while others are subdued. People's vitality can be changed by means of rites, music and through education; it is the basis for shaping a person's moral and emotional trait.

引例 Citations：

◎孔子曰："君子有三戒：少之时，血气未定，戒之在色；及其壮也，血气方刚，戒之在斗；及其老也，血气既衰，戒之在得。"（《论语·季氏》）

（孔子说："君子有三件事应该警惕戒备：年轻的时候，血气不稳定，要戒备迷恋美色；等到壮年，血气旺盛，要戒备好勇斗狠；到了老年，血气已经衰弱，要戒备贪得无厌。"）

Confucius said, "One should guard against three things in life. In his youth his vital force is unstable and he should guard against lust. As his vital force strengthens in the prime of life, he should guard against aggressive behavior. In his old age his vital force weakens, and he should guard against greed." (*The Analects*)

◎凡生乎天地之间者，有血气之属必有知，有知之属莫不爱其类。（《荀子·礼论》）

（凡是生于天地之间的人和物，只要有血气的就必然会有知觉，有知觉的没有不亲爱其同类的。）

All things born between heaven and earth with vital force have consciousness; and with consciousness they all love their own kind. (*Xunzi*)

循名责实

/xúnmíng-zéshí/

Hold Actualities According to Its Name

依据名而衡量其所指之实。"循名责实"是古人治理国家的重要手段。在现实的人伦关系中，每一个特定的角色或身份都有其名，名也即规定了这一角色或身份应该具有的性质或职责。对使用或拥有某一名分的人，需要依据其名分考核、要求其实际的言行与名所规定的性质或职责相符。

An actual object should be assessed according to the name referring to it. Holding actualities according to its name was an important means for ancient Chinese to govern the state. In actual human relations concerning ethics and morality, every specific role or status had its name, which determined the character or responsibilities of that status. People with certain status had to be assessed on the basis of their status, and it was required that their actual words and actions corresponded to the character and responsibilities determined by the name of their status.

引例 Citations：

◎术者，因任而授官，循名而责实，操杀生之柄，课群臣之能者也。（《韩非子·定法》）

(所谓术，是根据个人的能力而授予官职，依照官职名分而要求其履行相应的职责，掌握生杀大权，考量群臣中能力出众的人。)

The way of governance is to bestow office according to responsibilities, who was required to carry out duties as was required by the name (i.e. the office), to exercise power over life and death, and examine and weigh officials with outstanding capabilities. (*Hanfeizi*)

◎ 循名责实，实之极也；按实定名，名之极也。(《邓析子·转辞》)
(依据名而衡量其所指之实，是要求实的标准；依据实在的内容去确定事物的名号，是要求名的标准。)

To assess the actual thing or substance according to its name means to demand an actual standard. To determine the name of a thing or substance according to actualities is the standard for naming the name. (*Dengxizi*)

雅 俗

/yǎsú/

Highbrow and Lowbrow

指文艺作品品味的雅正与通俗、高尚与低俗。是文艺批评中评论作品品味高下的一对范畴。"雅"指作品的品味高雅正统，符合主流的意识形态；"俗"多指流行于大众与民间的世俗审美标准。从文艺创作上说，高雅文艺优美精良，但人工雕琢的痕迹较重；而通俗文艺源自民间，自然清新，质朴粗放。唐以后，不少文人从通俗文艺中汲取养分，通俗文艺逐渐增多，丰富了社会文艺生活，推动了文艺形态的丰富和发展。

Highbrow and lowbrow, a dichotomy in literary criticism, refer to two kinds of literary and artistic works, namely, the refined versus the popular, and the lofty versus the vulgar. Highbrow describes works that are elegant and reflect what conforms with mainstream ideology, whereas lowbrow-art forms tend to meet popular aesthetic standard. From the perspective of art creation, highbrow art may be exquisite, but often appears affected, whereas lowbrow art, which has a folk origin, is natural, refreshing, unaffected, and unconstrained. From the Tang Dynasty onward, it became a trend for men of letters to borrow the best from popular art, thus further spurring the growth of lowbrow art, enriching cultural life and leading to more diversified artistic expressions.

引例 Citations：

◎ 子曰："恶紫之夺朱也，恶郑声之乱雅乐也，恶利口之覆邦家者。"(《论语·阳货》)

(孔子说："我厌恶用紫色取代红色，厌恶用郑国的音乐扰乱雅正的音乐，憎恶伶牙俐齿而使国家倾覆的人。")

Confucius said, "I detest replacing red with purple and interfering refined classical music with the music of the State of Zheng. I loathe those who overthrow the state with their glib tongues." (*The Analects*)

◎ 是以绘事图色，文辞尽情，色糅而犬马殊形，情交而雅俗异势。(刘勰《文心雕龙·定势》)

(因此绘画要讲究色彩，写文章要尽力表现思想感情。调配不同的色彩，所画出的狗和马形状才有区别；思想感情有了交错融合，文章的雅俗才显出不同的体势。)

The art of painting requires masterful use of colors, while the art of writing entails effective expression of thoughts and emotions. One needs to blend different colors in order to depict the different shapes of dogs and horses. Only writings that integrate thoughts and emotions demonstrate their highbrow or lowbrow qualities. (Liu Xie: *The Literary Mind and the Carving of Dragons*)

言不尽意

/yánbùjìnyì/

Words Cannot Fully Express Thought.

言语不能完全表达对世界的根本认识。语出《周易·系辞上》，指语言在表意上有所不足，因而设立卦象来表达圣人之意。荀粲（209？—238）、王弼（226—249）等魏晋玄学家进一步阐发了这一思想。他们对语言与思想关系的认识，是由其对世界本体或本原的理解所决定的。他们认为，世界的本体或本原是超越于有形事物之上的"无"。"无"没有具体的形态或属性，也就无法被命名和言说。因此，言语对思想的表达被认为是有局限的。

Words cannot fully express the fundamental understanding of the world. According to *The Book of Changes*, words are inadequate for expressing what one means and that was why the hexagram images were made to convey the ideas of the sages. Xun Can (209?-238), Wang Bi (226-249), and other metaphysicians of the Wei and Jin dynasties further elucidated this concept. Their understanding of the relationship between language and thinking was determined by their understanding of the ontological existence or original source of the world. They believed that the world's ontological existence or original source was *wu* (无), which was beyond anything tangible. *Wu* had no specific form or attribute, and it was therefore impossible to name or describe it. Thus, language was found to have its limitations in expressing thought.

引例 Citations：

◎书不尽言，言不尽意。(《周易·系辞上》)

（书面文字不能完全表达作者的语言及全部意义，语言也不能完全表达作者心中所想及全部认识。）

Written characters cannot fully express what the author wants to say, nor can words fully express his thought and knowledge. (*The Book of Changes*)

◎斯则象外之意，《系》表之言，固蕴而不出矣。(《三国志·魏书·荀彧传附子恽》裴松之注引)

（［这是］卦象之外的思想、《系辞》之外的言辞，本来就是蕴藏其中而无法用言辞文字能够表达的。）

The notions beyond the images and the words beyond "The Great Treatise" are deeply stored in them, and so they cannot be expressed. (As Cited in Pei Songzhi: *Annotations on The History of the Three Kingdoms*)

炎黄
/Yán-Huáng/

The Fiery Emperor and the Yellow Emperor / Emperor Yan and Emperor Huang

炎帝和黄帝。是历史传说中上古的两个帝王，亦即两个部落首领。炎帝姓姜，号"神农氏"；黄帝姓公孙，号"轩辕氏"。他们居住在中原，与东方部落和南方部落逐渐融合，不断繁衍，形成华夏族主体（汉朝以后称为汉族，唐朝以后又称唐人），因而他们被尊为华夏民族的祖先。他们的部落尤其是黄帝部落，文明程度最高，上古的许多重要的文化、技术发明都是由他们两个部落创造的，因而他们又被视为华夏文明的始祖。近代以后，他们又成为整个中华民族和中华文明的一种象征。至今散居世界各地的华裔也大多认同自己是"炎黄子孙"或"黄帝子孙"。"炎黄"实际上已成为中华民族共同的文化符号。

Emperor Yan (the Fiery Emperor) and Emperor Huang (the Yellow Emperor), legendary Chinese rulers in pre-dynastic times, were actually tribal leaders. Emperor Yan, whose family name was Jiang, was known as Shennongshi while Emperor Huang, whose family name was Gongsun, was known as Xuanyuanshi. They originally lived in central China where their tribes gradually merged with those in eastern and southern China. People in these tribes proliferated and made up the main body of the Chinese nation (who were referred to as the Han people after the Han Dynasty and Tang people after the Tang Dynasty). Hence, they have been revered as the ancestors of the Chinese nation. Their tribes, and the tribe headed by the Yellow Emperor in particular, achieved the highest level of civilization. Many important cultural advancements and technical innovations in ancient China were believed to be created by these two tribes. They have therefore been seen as the forefathers of the Chinese civilization. In modern times, they have been considered as symbols of the Chinese nation and Chinese culture. Today, Chinese descendants residing in different parts of the world proudly regard themselves as "descendants of the Fiery Emperor and the Yellow Emperor" or simply "descendants of the Yellow Emperor." In this regard, "Yan and Huang" have become cultural symbols of the Chinese nation.

引例 Citations：

◎周室既坏，至春秋末，诸侯耗尽，而炎黄唐虞之苗裔尚犹颇有存者。(《汉书·魏豹、田儋（dān）、韩王信传赞》)

（周天子的统治秩序已经崩溃，至春秋末期，诸侯国消灭殆尽，但炎黄尧舜的后代仍大有人在。）

With the collapse of the ruling order of the emperors of the Zhou Dynasty, by the end of the Spring and Autumn Period, various vassal states had been defeated, but numerous descendants of Emperors Yan, Huang, Yao, and Shun remained. (*The History of the Han Dynasty*)

◎我们大家都是许身革命的黄帝子孙。(国民政府《告抗战全体将士书》)

We, descendants of the Fiery Emperor and the Yellow Emperor, have devoted ourselves to the revolution. ("To All Officers and Soldiers Fighting the War Against Japanese Aggression" issued by the then national government of China)

养民
/yǎngmín/

Nurture the People

养育人民，包括满足人民的生活需要和对人民进行教育。《尚书·大禹谟》将其作为"善政"（良好政治）的目的；为了实现这一目的，治国者必须治理、协调好"六府三事"。"六府"是指金、木、水、火、土、谷，即人民生活所需的各种物质资料；"三事"是指"正德"（端正人民品德）、"利用"（使物质资料为百姓所用）、"厚生"（使人民生活充裕）。这是一种以民为本、物质文明和精神文明兼顾并举的治国理念。

This term means to provide the people with necessities of life and educate them. According to *The Book of History*, this is what constitutes good governance. To reach this goal, the ruler must manage well the "six necessities and three matters," the six necessities being metal, wood, water, fire, land, and grain, and the three matters being fostering virtue, proper use of resources, and ensuring people's livelihood. This concept of governance, which focuses on promoting both economic and ethical progress, is people-centered.

引例 Citations：

◎ 德惟善政，政在养民。水、火、金、木、土、谷，惟修；正德、利用、厚生，惟和。九功惟叙；九叙惟歌。（《尚书·大禹谟》）

（帝王的德行要体现为良好的施政，施政要以养育民众为目的。水、火、金、木、土、谷六种生活资料一定要准备充足；端正德行，物尽其用，使民众富裕，这三项工作要兼顾协调。这九个方面的事情都要安排有序，九件事做好了，就会得到歌颂了。）

The king's virtue is reflected in good governance, which means to nurture the people. The people's need for water, fire, metal, wood, land, and grain must be well satisfied; and fostering virtue, proper use of resources, and ensuring people's well-being should be pursued in a coordinated way. When these nine things are accomplished in an orderly way, the king will win people's respect. (*The Book of History*)

◎ 夫贫生于富，弱生于强，乱生于治，危生于安。是故明王之养

民也，忧之劳之，教之诲之，慎微防萌，以断其邪。（王符《潜夫论·浮侈》）

（贫困由富足中产生，衰弱由强盛中产生，动乱由太平中产生，危险由平安中产生。所以贤明的君主养育人民，经常担忧他们的疾苦，慰劳他们的艰辛，加强对他们的教诲，小心谨慎地防患于未然，断绝一切邪恶产生的源头。）

Poverty stems from wealth, weakness from strength, turmoil from stability, and danger from security. Therefore, as he nurtures the people, a wise ruler cares about their sufferings, thanks them for their work, and teaches and instructs them so as to eradicate the seeds of evil no matter how tiny they might be. (Wang Fu: *Views of a Hermit*)

养气
/yǎngqì/

Cultivate *Qi*

　　涵养道德精神、调养身心健康以达到良好的心态，从而创作出优秀的文艺作品。这一术语具有多重蕴涵：其一，先秦孟子（前372？—前289）强调君子应善于培养道德精神的"浩然之气"。其二，东汉王充（27—97？）在《论衡》中有《养气篇》，专门从养生角度提倡"养气"。其三，南朝刘勰（465？—520？或532？）《文心雕龙·养气》，汲取上述思想，主张在从事文艺创作的初始阶段，要保持良好的身体状态和从容自由的心态，不应过度消耗精神。后来"养气"成为文艺心理学的重要术语。

This term suggests cultivating one's moral spirit and improving one's physical and mental well-being to achieve the best state of mind in order to write excellent works. "Cultivating *qi* (气)" has three implications: 1) in the pre-Qin period Mencius (372?-289 BC) emphasized that the virtuous and the capable should foster a "noble spirit" conducive to moral cultivation; 2) *A Comparative Study* of Different Schools of Learning by Wang Chong (27-97?) of the Eastern Han Dynasty has a chapter entitled "Treatise on Cultivating *Qi*," which emphasizes *qi* cultivation primarily in regards to maintaining good health; 3) Liu Xie (465?-520? or 532?) of the Southern Dynasties, in *The Literary Mind and the Carving of Dragons*, drew upon the foregoing ideas and suggested maintaining good physical condition and a free, composed mental state in the initial phase of literary creation, while opposing excessive mental exertion. "Cultivating *qi*" subsequently became an important term in the lexicon of literary psychology.

引例 Citations：

◎我知言，我善养吾浩然之气。(《孟子·公孙丑上》)

（我能够察知各种言辞的真意，善于培养自己的刚强正直之气。）

I can perceive the true meaning of various statements, and I am good at self-cultivating righteousness. (*Mencius*)

◎是以吐纳文艺，务在节宣，清和其心，调畅其气；烦而即舍，勿使壅滞。(刘勰《文心雕龙·养气》)

（因此从事写作必须学会节制和疏导，让内心纯净平和，将气调理顺畅，内心烦乱时就应停止，不要让思路滞涩。）

Hence, when engaging in writing one must learn how to constrain and regulate oneself, keep one's mind pure and peaceful, and modulate one's mental vitality and activities. One should stop writing when upset so as not to disrupt one's train of thinking. (Liu Xie: *The Literary Mind and the Carving of Dragons*)

叶落归根

/yèluò-guīgēn/

Leaves Fall Returning to the Roots.

树叶凋落，回到树根周围。比喻事物总有一定的归宿，多指久居异乡的人终究会返回故里。和"安土重迁"一样，它包含着中国人自古普遍具有的一种思乡观念和情感。虽不免消极或保守，但也体现了人们热爱故土、思念亲人的纯良品格和家国情怀，是文化认同的原点之一。

Leaves wither and fall on the ground by the tree roots. This metaphor implies that all creatures have an old home to return to even after a long sojourn in distant parts. It expresses nostalgia for one's native place that has been common among Chinese people since ancient times. Although such feelings are inevitably conservative, they embody people's good and honest love for their native soil and next of kin, and their feelings for the nation. It is a mainspring of their identification with their culture.

引例 Citation：

◎云闲忘出岫，叶落喜归根。（陆游《寓叹》）
（白云悠闲已忘了从群山升起，树叶飘落都喜欢回归树根。）
Clouds float leisurely, forgetting to rise from the peaks, / leaves fall happily seeking the roots. (Lu You: A Sigh at Home)

一

/yī/

The One

"一"有三种不同含义：其一，指万物的本体或本原，即"道"的别称，或称"太一"。其二，指天地未分之时的混沌状态。"一"分化形成天地，天地万物都产生于这样一个混沌的统一体。其三，指事物的统一性，与"多""两"相对，意在强调有差异或对立的事物之间的统一性。

The term has three meanings. First, it indicates the original essence of all things. It is another name for *dao* (way). It is also referred to as *taiyi* (the supreme one). Second, it refers to the state of chaos before the separation of heaven and earth. The one was divided and transformed into heaven and earth. All things in heaven and on earth were produced from this Chaotic entity. Third, it indicates the unity of things, as opposed to "many" or "two." The idea is to emphasize the unity among things which are different or opposite.

引例 Citations：

◎一者，万物之所从始也。（董仲舒《举贤良对策》）
（"一"是万物产生的端始。）

The one is the origin of everything. (Dong Zhongshu: *Replies to the Emperor's Questions After Being Recommended*)

◎两不立则一不可见，一不可见则两之用息。（张载《正蒙·太和》）
（没有相反两方的对立则统一体不可得见，统一体不可得见则相反两方的对立也就消失了。）

Unity cannot be seen without the contradiction between two opposite sides, while the two opposite sides cannot exist without unity. (Zhang Zai: *Enlightenment Through Confucian Teachings*)

一物两体

/yīwù-liǎngtǐ/

One Thing in Two Fundamental States

作为统一体的"气"之中包含着对立的两个方面。张载（1020—1077）认为，天地万物都是由"气"构成的。"气"是完整的统一体，也即"一物"。同时，"气"又有虚实、动静、聚散、清浊等对立的状态，即是"两体"。没有对立面的相互作用，则没有统一体的存在；没有统一体的存在，则对立的相互作用也会消失。统一体之中的对立，是"气"及其所构成的事物产生变化的根源。

Qi (气), or vital force, consists of two opposing aspects. According to the Song-dynasty philosopher Zhang Zai (1020 - 1077), everything in the world consists of *qi*. On the one hand, *qi* is a whole and one thing; on the other, it consists of pairs of contradictory states, such as the real and the unreal, motion and stillness, concentration and diffusion, and clarity and opacity. Without interaction between the opposite states, the whole cannot exist. Likewise, without the whole, there can be no interaction between the opposite states. Contradictions within the whole constitute the source of changes of *qi* and all things made of *qi*.

引例 Citation:

◎一物两体，气也。一故神，两故化，此天之所以参（sān）也。（张载《正蒙·参两》）

（统一的事物之中包含着对立的两个方面，这就是"气"的状态。作为统一体，因此有神妙的运动。两个对立面相互作用，因此有无穷的变化。这也就是天所具有的"三"的意义。）

One thing with two states, that is *qi*, or vital force. As one whole thing, *qi* has miraculous movements, caused by interaction between the two opposites; and such movements create endless changes. This is why heaven has three aspects (the whole and the two states). (Zhang Zai: *Enlightenment Through Confucian Teachings*)

一言兴邦
/yīyán-xīngbāng/

A Single Remark Makes a Country Prosper.

一句话而使国家兴盛。治国理政是一项复杂的工作，不可能通过简单地依循一句话所表述的某个具体要求，就实现国家的兴盛。但如果执政者能够充分意识到治理天下的困难，并因此在为政中谨言慎行，始终不懈怠，那么凭借为政者的这种观念，则可能实现国家的兴盛。这种观念的作用即接近于"一言兴邦"。

A single remark can help a country thrive. As governance is a highly complex undertaking, it is impossible to make a country prosperous simply by following an idea expressed in a single remark. However, if a ruler thoroughly understands how difficult it is to run a country and exercises governance with prudence and dedication, it is quite possible for him to make his country prosper. In this sense, the effect of such concept, which can almost be likened as a single remark, will make a country flourish.

引例 Citation：

◎ 定公问："一言而可以兴邦，有诸？"孔子对曰："言不可以若是其几（jī）也。人之言曰：'为君难，为臣不易。'如知为君之难也，不几乎一言而兴邦乎？"（《论语·子路》）

（鲁定公问："一句话就可以使国家兴盛，有这回事吗？"孔子回答说："不可以对一句话有这样的期待。人们说：'做君主难，做大臣也不容易。'如果君主懂得做君主的艰难，不也就近乎一句话而使国家兴盛了吗？"）

Duke Ding of the State of Lu asked: "Is there a single remark that can make a country thrive?" Confucius replied: "No single remark can be expected to perform such a deed. There is a saying: 'It is not easy to be a ruler, nor is it easy to be a court official.' However, a ruler who truly understands how hard it is to govern a country will have a vision, which is almost like a single remark, and that will make his country prosper." (*The Analects*)

一以贯之

/yīyǐguànzhī/

Observe a Fundamental Principle Throughout One's Pursuit

用一个根本性的原则贯通学问、行事的始终。贯：贯通，统摄。按照儒家的要求，立身处事需要掌握多方面的知识和技能，遵守各种道德与礼法的规范。而孔子（前551—前479）强调，这些看似繁复的知识、技能与规范，贯穿着一个根本性的原则。孔子引导学生去认识、把握这一原则，并以此统摄学问、行事中的各种具体要求。后世学者对这一根本性的原则究竟为何有不同的解释，曾子（前505—前436）认为就是"忠恕"之道。

One needs to observe a fundamental principle in the entire process of academic and other pursuits. According to Confucianism, to establish oneself, one should gain a good command of knowledge and skills in a wide range of areas and abide by moral principles and norms. Confucius (551 - 479 BC) himself stressed that there is a fundamental principle running through all such knowledge and skills as well as moral standards. He taught his disciples how to master this fundamental principle so as to meet the requirements for doing things with knowledge and skills acquired. Scholars of later generations have different interpretations about what this fundamental principle is. Zengzi (505 - 436 BC) believed that it is loyalty and forbearance.

引例 Citations：

◎子曰："参（shēn）乎！吾道一以贯之。"曾子曰："唯。"子出，门人问曰："何谓也？"曾子曰："夫子之道，忠恕而已矣。"（《论语·里仁》）

（孔子说："曾参呀！我的学说贯穿着一个根本性的原则。"曾子说："是。"孔子出去后，其他弟子问曾子："是什么意思呢？"曾子说："老师的学说，只是忠和恕罢了。"）

Confucius said: "Zeng Shen, there is one thing that runs through my doctrine." Zengzi said: "Yes." When Confucius went out, other disciples asked him: "What did he mean?" Zengzi said: "Confucius' doctrine is simply this: loyalty and forbearance." (*The Analects*)

◎子曰："赐也，汝以予为多学而识之者与（yú）？"对曰："然。非与？"曰："非也，予一以贯之。"（《论语·卫灵公》）

（孔子说："端木赐，你以为我是个学了很多而又能够记得住的人吗？"子贡回答说："对啊，难道不是吗？"孔子说："不是的，我用一个根本性的原则来贯穿它们。"）

Confucius said: "Duanmu Ci (styled Zigong), you think I have learned a lot and am able to remember them all, do you?" Zigong replied: "Yes. Don't you think so too?" Confucius said: "No, what I have done is to master a fundamental principle that runs through them all." (*The Analects*)

移风易俗
/yífēng-yìsú/

Change Social Practices and Customs

转移风气，改变习俗。"移风易俗"是"乐"的重要功能。风俗是社会群体长期以来形成的共同的行为习惯，可能会包含某些违礼的成分。群体习惯的改变十分困难，不能单纯依赖强制的规范，而是需要发挥"乐"对于人心的深刻影响。通过"乐"的教化，引导人心进入恰当的状态，进而逐渐改变社会的风气和习俗，使之自觉符合礼的要求。

This is one of the important functions of music. Social practices are common forms of behavior formed within communities over time, and they can also include aspects that do not conform to rites. Changing such widespread habits is extremely difficult and cannot be accomplished by mandatory regulations alone. This is where music comes into play by affecting and stirring people's emotions so that they gradually change their ways and willingly conform to the requirements of rites.

引例 Citation：

◎乐者，圣人之所乐（lè）也，而可以善民心，其感人深，其移风易俗，故先王导之以礼乐而民和睦。（《荀子·乐论》）

（"乐"是圣人所喜好的，可以使百姓之心向善，对人有极强的感染力，能移风易俗，因此先王用礼乐引导民众，使他们和睦相处。）

Music was appreciated by the sages; it improves people's behavior, stirs and moves them, so they change social practices and customs. Thus the sage kings guided their subjects with music and rites, so that the subjects treated each other with friendship and good will. (*Xunzi*)

以无为本
/yǐ wú wéi běn/

***Wu* Is the Origin.**

将"无"作为世界的本体或本原。老子曾提出"有生于无"。魏晋时期的何晏(?—249)、王弼(226—249)等人进一步发挥这一思想,主张天地万物都"以无为本"。他们认为,任何具体的事物都不能作为另外一个具体事物的本体或本原,更不能成为整个世界的本体或本原。天地万物的发生与存在都依赖于一个更根本的、超越于有形事物之上的"无"。只有无形无名的本体才能使众多的具体事物发挥各自的功用。

Wu (无) is regarded as the original source or ontological existence of the world in classical Chinese thinking. Laozi claimed that "*you* (有) is born out of *wu*." This concept was further developed by He Yan (?-249), Wang Bi (226-249), and other thinkers of the Wei and Jin dynasties, who maintained that heaven, earth, and all things in the world originate from *wu*. No specific being, they argued, can be the original source or ontological existence of another being, much less of the world. The formation and existence of everything depend on *wu*, which is the fundamental source that transcends all tangible beings. Only an intangible and unidentifiable ontological existence gives countless specific beings their functions.

引例 Citation:

◎ 天下之物,皆以有为生。有之所始,以无为本。将欲全有,必反于无也。(王弼《老子注》)

(天下的事物都以有形的状态存在着,有形之物的发生,以"无"作为其本体。想要保全有形之物,必须返归于"无"。)

All things under heaven exist by means of *you*. The formation and existence of *you* originate from *wu*. To maintain *you* we must return to *wu*. (Wang Bi: *Annotations on Laozi*)

以形媚道

/yǐxíng-mèidào/

Natural Shapes Adapting to Dao

　　山水以其外在形貌与"道"亲近、契合。南朝画家宗炳（375—443）在《画山水序》中发挥孔子（前551—前479）"仁者乐（yào）山，智者乐水"的思想，认为山水不仅向人类竞相展示了大自然的造化之功，也向人类婉转展示了宇宙天地的变化规律，因而为有德行的人所喜爱。这一术语表现出六朝人的山水审美观念。

Mountains and rivers accord with Dao by way of their shapes. Zong Bing (375 - 443), a painter of Song of the Southern Dynasties, in his "On the Creation of Landscape Paintings" expanded on a saying by Confucius (551 - 479 BC) – "A virtuous man loves mountains and a wise man loves water." Zong held that mountains and rivers not only displayed their natural splendor to humanity, but also demonstrated the natural law of changes. Therefore, they were loved by men of virtue. This term shows the aesthetic view of people in the period of the Six Dynasties.

引例 Citations：

◎知者乐水，仁者乐山；知者动，仁者静；知者乐，仁者寿。(《论语·雍也》)

（有智慧的人喜爱水，有德行的人喜爱山；有智慧的人好动，有德行的人好静。有智慧的人快乐，有德行的人长寿。）

Confucius said, "A wise man loves water, a virtuous man loves mountains. A wise man is active; a virtuous man stays peaceful in mind. A wise man is happy; a virtuous man enjoys longevity." (*The Analects*)

◎夫圣人以神法道，而贤者通；山水以形媚道，而仁者乐（yào）。不亦几（jī）乎？（宗炳《画山水序》）

（圣人精神上效法道，而德才杰出的人可以通达于道；山水以其自然形质婉转契合道，使仁者对之喜爱。这难道不是很微妙吗？）

Sages follow Dao with their spirit. Men of virtue and talent may comprehend and practice Dao. Mountains and rivers conform to Dao through their natural shapes. That is why they are loved by benevolent people. Isn't this subtle and profound? (Zong Bing: On the Creation of Landscape Paintings)

以义制事
/yǐyì-zhìshì/

Handle Matters According to Morality and Justice

　　按照道义做事，即遵循道义、正义的原则处理政治、军事等重大事务。在中国古代政治话语中，没有权力可以任性一说；相反，要求权力的产生必须有正当性依据，权力的行使也必须遵循道义，这一点历来为古人所注重。道义、正义高于权力、规制权力，这是中国古人所推崇的政治生态。

To act based on morality and justice, that is, to manage major political and military matters according to the principles of morality and justice. In ancient Chinese political discourse, it was never right to suggest that power could be exercised arbitrarily. On the contrary, it was expected that there should be a legitimate basis for the creation of power, and that power would be exercised according to moral precepts. The ancient Chinese always attached great importance to this point. Morality and justice overrode and regulated power – such was the political ecology they highly esteemed.

引例 Citation：

◎ 王懋（mào）昭大德，建中于民，以义制事，以礼制心，垂裕后昆。（《尚书·仲虺（huǐ）之诰》）

（大王要努力显扬崇高的德行，在人民中间树立中正之道，按照道义裁断国家事务，按照礼制管理人心，使丰厚的功业能传给后人。）

The ruler must work hard to promote high moral standards and advocate the correct path among the people; he should handle affairs of state according to moral precepts and guide people's thinking to accord with the rules of etiquette, so as to leave a rich legacy to those who come after him. (*The Book of History*)

以直报怨
/yǐzhí-bàoyuàn/

Repay a Grudge with Rectitude

以正直之道对待怨恨的人。"以直报怨"是孔子（前551—前479）提出的一种报答仇怨的原则。对待怨恨的人，孔子认为"以怨报怨""以德报怨"这两种处理方式都不正确。孔子主张，不可因一时的愤恨情绪而肆意施加报复，也不可隐匿仇怨报答以恩惠友善，而应该分辨造成仇怨之事的是非曲直，以正直的原则做出回应。

Treat a person you hold a grudge against with upright behavior. "Repaying a grudge with rectitude" was a principle proposed by Confucius (551-479 BC) for dealing with grudges. He felt that both "repaying a grudge with a grudge" and "repaying a grudge with kindness" were incorrect. Confucius argued that one should not deliberately seek vengeance out of momentary anger, nor should one conceal resentment over a grudge and repay it with kindness. Rather, one should analyze the rights and wrongs of the episode which created the grudge, and respond according to the principles of rectitude.

引例 Citation：

◎ 或曰："以德报怨，何如？"子曰："何以报德？以直报怨，以德报德。"（《论语·宪问》）

（有人说："以恩惠友善来报答怨恨之人，怎么样呢？"孔子说："用什么来报答有恩德之人呢？应以正直之道回应怨恨之人，以恩惠友善回应有恩德之人。"）

Someone asked, "How about repaying a grudge with kindness?" Confucius said, "Then how would you repay kindness? Repay a grudge with rectitude, and repay kindness with kindness." (*The Analects*)

义

/yì/

Righteousness

"义"的基本含义是合理、恰当，引申而有两重含义：其一，指人行事的合理依据与标准。其二，指在道德意识的判断与引导下，调节言行使之符合一定的标准，以获得合理的安处。宋代学者用"理"或"天理"的概念来解释"义"，认为"义"就是"天理"所规定的合理的标准，同时要求言行符合"天理"。

The basic meaning of *yi* (义) is "reasonable" and "proper." It has two extended meanings. One is the proper basis and standard for people's actions. The other is to adjust one's words or deeds to meet certain standards, under the guidance of moral judgments. Scholars in the Song Dynasty used *li* (理) or "principles of heaven" to interpret *yi*, and considered *yi* to be the reasonable standard defined by the "principles of heaven," and hoped that people's words and deeds would fall in line with the "principles of heaven."

引例 Citations：

◎君子喻于义。(《论语·里仁》)

（君子知晓并遵循义。）

A man of virtue understands and does what is morally right. (*The Analects*)

◎义者，心之制，事之宜也。(朱熹《孟子集注》卷一)

（义就是约束自己的内心，使事情合宜。）

Righteousness means exercising self-restraint in order to do everything properly. (Zhu Xi: *Mencius Variorum*)

义法

/yìfǎ/

Yi Fa (Guidelines for Writing Good Prose)

　　清代方苞（1668—1749）提出的关于文章写作的方法，包括文章的思想内容及形式结构、剪裁取舍等方面的规范要求。源于《春秋》《史记》等史传文章的结撰方法，"义法"是将这些经典的写作方法推广为文章写作的典范。"义"指文章的意蕴和事理，重在"言有物"，即文章的思想内容要充实、有意义；"法"指文章的组织结构和写作技法，重在"言有序"，即语言得当、有条理次序。"义"为根本，"法"随"义"而变化，根据"义"的表达需要而选择灵活多样的写作技法，在叙事之中寓褒贬论断。义法论是清代桐城派古文理论的起点和基础。

Yi fa refers to the guidelines and criteria for prose writing advocated by Fang Bao (1668-1749) of the Qing Dynasty, which concerns content, structure, and editing. He held up the structural composition of the historical texts *The Spring and Autumn Annals* and *Records of the Historian* as examples of fine prose, and popularized them. Yi (义) refers to content and meaningfulness, with an emphasis on substance and logic; fa (法) refers to structure and writing techniques, with an emphasis on appropriate language and sequence. Yi is primary and fa adjusts accordingly to express the content in a flexible and varied way, so as to ensure that the author's opinion is clearly stated and the argument is powerful. The concept of yi fa is the cornerstone for the prose-writing theory of the Tongcheng School of the Qing Dynasty.

引例 Citations：

◎孔子明王道，干（gān）七十余君，莫能用，故西观周室，论史记旧闻，兴于鲁而次于《春秋》。上记隐，下至哀之获麟，约其辞文，去其烦重（chóng），以制义法。(《史记·十二诸侯年表》)

（孔子懂得以仁政治理天下，他用王道学说拜谒了七十多个君主，但都不被采用。因此，他西行去观览周王室的典藏，详列、评论历史记载及过去的传闻，按鲁国历史顺序编成《春秋》。上起鲁隐公元年，下至鲁哀公捕获麒麟之年，简省《春秋》的文辞，删除其中繁琐重复的记载，以此制定了史书编撰的义理和规范。）

Confucius understood the need to rule with benevolence, and took this message to over seventy different rulers, but no one heeded him. So he went westward to the Court of Zhou to consult its archives. There he carefully went through the documents and compiled the historical accounts and ancient stories of the State of Lu into *The Spring and Autumn Annals* in chronological order. He started from the first year of the reign of Duke Yin of Lu, and finished with the year in which Duke Ai of Lu caught a *qilin*, a legendary animal. He condensed the texts, eliminated repetitions and redundancies, and thus laid out the guidelines for writing historical annals. (*Records of the Historian*)

◎《春秋》之制义法，自太史公发之，而后之深于文者亦具焉。义即《易》之所谓"言有物"也，法即《易》之所谓"言有序"也。义以为经而法纬之，然后为成体之文。（方苞《又书〈货殖传〉后》）
(《春秋》所制定的义理和规范，自从司马迁加以阐发以来，后代擅长写文章的人也都具备了"义法"。"义"就是《周易》所说的"文章或言论得有内容"，"法"就是《周易》所说的"文章或言论得有条理和次序"。以内容为经，以条理和次序为纬，然后就能写出体式完整的文章。）

The example set by *The Spring and Autumn Annals* was later commented on by Sima Qian, and since then, all who wrote good prose have followed these guidelines. *Yi* is described in *The Book of Changes* as "texts and speech should be meaningful," and *fa*, "texts and speeches should be logical and orderly." These are like woof and web, and only then can a good text be written. (Fang Bao: On Rereading "Profit from Trade" in *Records of the Historian*)

艺术
/yìshù/

Art

原指儒家六艺及各种方术，后引申指艺术创作与审美活动。儒家的"六艺"指礼、乐、射、御、书、数等六种用以培养君子人格的教育内容，包括后世意义上的艺术；有时也指《诗》《书》《礼》《乐》《易》《春秋》六部经书。庄子（前369？—前286）则强调技与艺相通，是一种体悟道的融身心为一体的创作活动。儒家、道家与佛教关于艺术的思想，是中国艺术的内在精神与方法。中国艺术追求艺术与人生的统一、感知与体验的结合、技艺与人格的融会等，以意境为旨归。近代西方艺术学传入中国后，艺术成为人类主观精神与物态化作品相结合的技艺与创作，成为专门的学科，涵盖各类艺术。现在的艺术概念是传统艺术内涵与现代西方艺术学的有机融合。

Originally, the term referred to six forms of classical arts and various crafts, but it later extended to include artistic creation and aesthetic appreciation. The six forms of arts as defined by Confucianism are rituals, music, archery, charioteering, writing and mathematics. These constituted the basic requirements for cultivating a man of virtue. These six arts also included what later generations deemed as arts. Sometimes, the term also meant the six classics, namely, *The Book of Songs*, *The Book of History*, *The Book of Rites*, *The Book of Music*, *The Book of Changes*, and *The Spring and Autumn Annals*. Zhuangzi (369?- 286 BC), on his part, emphasized the connection between crafts and arts, regarding them as physical and mental creative activities that help one gain insight into Dao. The various ideas about arts put forward by Confucian, Daoist, and Buddhist scholars defined the nature and method of Chinese arts, which seek unity between artwork and real life, fusion of senses and experiences, and integration of techniques and personality, with achieving artistic conception as the ultimate aim. Since the introduction of Western art theories in modern China, arts have become an independent discipline covering all types of arts created with skill and innovation. The concept of arts today incorporate both traditional Chinese and contemporary Western notions of arts.

引例 Citations：

◎子曰："志于道，据于德，依于仁，游于艺。"（《论语·述而》）

（孔子说："有志于行道，执守于美德，依从于仁义，游学于礼、乐、射、御、书、数六艺之间。"）

Confucius said, "One should follow Dao, adhere to virtues, embrace benevolence, and pursue freely the six arts of rituals, music, archery, charioteering, writing, and mathematics." (*The Analects*)

◎ "蓺（yì）"谓书、数、射、御，"术"谓医、方、卜、筮。（《后汉

书·伏湛传》李贤注）

（"艺"指的是六书、算术、射击、驾驶车马等基本技能，"术"指的是医术、方技、卜卦、占筮等专门之学。）

Arts refer to such basic skills as writing, mathematics, archery, and charioteering. Crafts refer to such professions as medicine, fortune-telling, divination, and necromancy. (*The History of the Later Han Dynasty*)

◎ 艺术之兴，由来尚矣。先王以是决犹豫，定吉凶，审存亡，省祸福。(《晋书·艺术传序》)

（方术的兴起，有着久远的历史。古时的帝王通过方术来决断犹疑，判定吉凶，审度存亡，省察祸福。）

Fortune-telling has a long history. In ancient times, kings used fortune-telling to make decisions, weigh consequences, foresee fate, and judge outcomes. (*The History of the Jin Dynasty*)

意境
/yìjìng/

Aesthetic Conception

指文艺作品所描绘的景象与所表现的思想情感高度融合而形成的审美境界。"境"本指疆界、边界，汉末魏晋时期佛教传入中国，认为现实世界皆为空幻，唯有心灵感知才是真实的存在，"境"被认为是人的心灵感知所能达到的界域。作为文艺术语，"境"有多重含义。"意境"由唐代著名诗人王昌龄（？—756？）提出，侧重指文艺作品中主观感知到的物象与精神蕴涵相统一所达到的审美高度，其特点是"取意造境""思与境偕"。相对于"意象"，"意境"更突出文艺作品的精神蕴涵与美感的高级形态，它拓展了作品情与景、虚与实、心与物等概念的应用，提升了文艺作品及审美活动的层次。后经过历代丰富发展，"意境"

成为评价文艺作品水准的重要概念，是历代经典作品层累的结果，也是优秀文艺作品必须具备的重要特征。"意境"这一术语也是外来思想文化与中华本土思想融合的典范。

The term refers to a state where the scene described in a literary or artistic work reflects the sense and sensibility intended. *Jing* (境) originally meant perimeter or boundary. With the introduction of Buddhism into China during the late Han, Wei and Jin dynasties, the idea gained popularity that the physical world was but an illusion, and that only the mind was real in existence. So *jing* came to be seen as a realm that could be attained by having sensibilities of the mind. As a literary and artistic term, *jing* has several meanings. The term *yijing* (意境) was originally put forward by renowned Tang poet Wang Changling (?-756?). It describes an intense aesthetic experience in which one's perception of an object reaches a realm of perfect union with the implication denoted by the object. Aesthetic appreciation in the mind is characterized by "projecting meaning into a scene" and "blending sentiment with scenery." In contrast with the term *yixiang* (意象 image), *yijing* fully reveals the implication and the heightened aesthetic sense that an artistic work is intended to deliver. The concept is extended to include other notions such as sentiment and scene, actual and implied meanings, or mind and object. It also raises literary and artistic works to a new realm of aesthetic appreciation. After evolving through several dynasties, this concept developed into an important criterion to judge the quality of a literary or artistic work, representing an accomplishment drawing on classical writings through ages. It has also become a hallmark for all outstanding literary and artistic works. The term also represents a perfect union between foreign thoughts and culture and those typically Chinese.

引例 Citations：

◎ 诗有三境：一曰物境，二曰情境，三曰意境。物境一：欲为山水诗，则张泉石云峰之境，极丽绝秀者，神之于心，处身于境，视境于心，莹然掌中，然后用思，了然境象，故得形似。情境二：娱乐愁怨，皆张于意而处于身，然后驰思，深得其情。意境三：亦张之于意而思之于心，则得其真矣。（王昌龄《诗格·诗有三境》）

（诗歌有三种境：一是物境，二是情境，三是意境。第一，物境：想作山水诗，就要尽所能扩大你对泉石、高耸入云的山峰的观察，将其中极秀丽的景色及神韵印之于心，置身其间，再于内心审视所得到的物境，直至如同在手掌上观察一样真切，然后进行构思，对所要描绘的具体物象了然于心，所以能得形似。第二，情境：欢乐、悲愁、哀怨等情绪，都要尽量扩大你对它们的认识，切身感受，然后构思，就能将这些情感深刻地表现出来。第三，意境：也同样需要扩大你对它的认识，在内心反复思索，然后就能得到意境的本真。）

A poem accomplishes aesthetic conception in three ways. The first is through objects, the second is through sentiments, and the third is through an imagined scene. 1) Through objects: If you want to write poems about landscape, you need to observe intensely springs and creeks, rocks and towering peaks, imprint their extraordinary beauty and charm on your memory, put yourself in the scene created in your mind, and view in your mind's eye the image you obtain until you can see it as vividly as if it were right on your palm. By then, you can start to think about writing the poem. A deep appreciation of the scene and its objects is instrumental in achieving a true poetic image. 2) Through sentiments: Sentiments such as happiness, pleasure, sorrow, and anger should be allowed to develop in your mind. You should experience them personally to fully grasp the nature of these emotions. This will enable you to express them in a profound way. 3) Through an imagined scene: This requires you to reach aesthetic appreciation by reflecting it in your mind time and again. Then you can capture the genuine nature of an idea. (Wang Changling: *Rules of Poetry*)

◎作诗之妙，全在意境融彻，出音声之外，乃得真味。（朱承爵《存余堂诗话》）
（作诗的妙处，全在于意境的浑融相通，超出声音之上，才能品味诗歌的本真韵味。）

A beautifully composed poem is one in which the blending of image and concept is such that it transcends that of sound and music. Only then can one savor the real charm of poetry. (Zhu Chengjue: *Commentaries on Poetry from Cunyutang Study*)

◎盖诗之格调有尽，吾人之意境日出而不穷。（周炳曾《〈道援堂诗集〉序》）
（大概是诗的体制、声律是有限的，而我们这些诗人的意境却每天有新创，无穷无尽。）

Poems might have limited verse forms and rhythmic patterns, but we poets are capable of creating fresh ideas every day, all the time. (Zhou Bingzeng: Preface to *Collection of Poems from Daoyuantang Study*)

意象
/yìxiàng/

Yixiang (Imagery)

　　文学作品中表达作者主观情感和独特意境的典型物象。"意"指作者的思想情感;"象"是外在的具体物象,是寄寓了作者思想情感的艺术形象。在文学创作中,"意象"多指取自大自然中能够寄托情思的物象。"意象"强调文学作品的思想内容与形象之美的和谐生成,是一种成熟的文艺形态。

Imagery refers to a typical image in literary works, which embodies the author's subjective feelings and unique artistic conceptions. *Yi* (意) literally means an author's feelings and thoughts, and *xiang* (象) refers to the image of a material object in the external world, an artistic image reflecting the author's thoughts and feelings. In literary creation, imagery often refers to those images in nature with which an author's feelings and thoughts are associated. Emphasizing the harmonious relationship between beauty in both form and content, it is a mature state of literary creation.

引例 Citations:

◎窥意象而运斤。(刘勰《文心雕龙·神思》)
(探寻心中的意象而构思运笔。)

An author explores the imagery in his mind, conceives a work, and writes it down. (Liu Xie: *The Literary Mind and the Carving of Dragons*)

◎意象欲出,造化已奇。(司空图《二十四诗品·缜密》)
(诗歌的意象浑欲浮现,大自然是这般奇妙。)

What a wonderful state of nature it is when the imagery of a poem is about to emerge! (Sikong Tu: *Twenty-four Styles of Poetry*)

意兴

/yìxìng/

Inspirational Appreciation

"兴"中所蕴含的意或者"兴"发时心物交会所产生的意（意义、趣味等）。是作者通过对景物感受到某种意趣、意味等之后直接创作出富有一定含义的艺术形象。这一术语主张作者将思想情感自然而然地融入对于描写对象的感受之中，并通过艺术形象和审美情趣传达出来，从而激发读者的联想，产生更丰富的领悟。

The term refers to the meaning implicit in an inspiration, or meaning and charm generated when poetic emotion encounters an external object or scene. It is an artistic image an author creates when appreciating the beauty and charm intrinsic in an object or scene. According to this term, an author should incorporate his sentiments and thoughts into the object or scene depicted to convey them through artistic images and aesthetic appreciation. This will spark the reader's imagination and thus enable him to gain a deeper appreciation of a poem.

引例 Citations:

◎凡诗，物色兼意下为好。若有物色，无意兴，虽巧亦无处用之。（王昌龄《诗格·论文意》）

（但凡诗歌，景物描写、意义与趣味兼备最好。如果只注重景物描写，缺少意兴，描写技巧再高超也用处不大。）

A good poem instills meaning and inspiration in its description of scenery and imagery. If a poem only describes scenery and fails to inspire people, no matter how eloquent the description may be, it will have little appeal. (Wang Changling: *Rules of Poetry*)

◎南朝人尚词而病于理，本朝人尚理而病于意兴，唐人尚意兴而理在其中，汉魏之诗，词、理、意兴无迹可求。（严羽《沧浪诗话·诗评》）

（南朝诗人追求辞藻而说理不足；本朝诗人崇尚说理，作品缺乏意兴；唐代诗人注重意兴同时蕴含道理；汉魏诗歌的文辞、道理和意兴自然融合在一起而不露痕迹。）

Poets of the Southern Dynasties were good at using rhetoric but weak in logic. The poets of our Song Dynasty champion logic but are weak in creating inspirational ideas. Poets of the Tang Dynasty gave equal weight to both meaning and inspiration, with logic implicit in both. The poems of the Han and Wei dynasties blended the choice of words, logic, and the inspiration imperceptibly. (Yan Yu: *Canglang's Criticism on Poetry*)

阴阳

/yīnyáng/

Yin and Yang

　　本义指物体对于日光的向背，向日为"阳"，背日为"阴"。引申而有两重含义：其一，指天地之间性质相反的两种气。其二，指两种最基本的矛盾势力或属性，凡动的、热的、在上的、向外的、明亮的、亢进的、强壮的为"阳"，凡静的、寒的、在下的、向内的、晦暗的、减退的、虚弱的为"阴"。"阴""阳"或"阴气""阳气"的相互作用决定着万物的生成及存在状态。阴阳理论后来成为古人说明和理解宇宙万物、社会和人伦秩序的基础，如天阳地阴、君阳臣阴、夫阳妻阴等，阳贵阴贱，阳主阴从。

The primary meaning of yin and yang is the orientation of things in relation to the sun, with yang meaning the sunny side and yin the shady side. There are two extended meanings: 1) two opposite kinds of *qi* (气) in nature; and 2) two basic contrary forces or qualities that coexist, thus the active, hot, upward, outward, bright, forward, and strong are yang, while the passive, cold, downward, inward, dark, backward, and weak are yin. The interaction between yin and yang, or yin *qi* and yang *qi*, determines the formation and existence of all things. The theory of yin and yang later became the basis for ancient Chinese to explain and understand the universe and everything in it, social order, and human relations. For example, heaven is yang and earth is yin, ruler is yang and subordinates are yin, husband is yang and wife is yin, noble is yang and ignoble is yin, leading is yang and following is yin.

引例 Citations：

◎万物负阴而抱阳，冲气以为和。(《老子·四十二章》)
(万物背阴而向阳，阴阳两气互相激荡而成调和状态。)

All things stand, facing yang and against yin. The interaction between yin and yang creates a state of harmony. (*Laozi*)

◎阴阳无所独行。(董仲舒《春秋繁露·基义》)
(阴与阳不能单独发生作用。)

Yin and yang cannot work without each other. (Dong Zhongshu: *Luxuriant Gems of The Spring and Autumn Annals*)

音
/yīn/

Musical Sounds

指音乐，是由心中情感触动而发出的有节奏和韵律的声音。古人常以"音"与"声"相对：凡自然物所发声音叫做"声"，由人的内心情感触动而发出的声音叫做"音"；单一的声响叫做"声"，不同"声"的比配叫做"音"，不同的"音"组成有节奏的曲调叫做"乐"。古人认为，"音"发自人的内心，一国或一个地区的音乐往往反映该国或地区的民心民意和世风世情，由此儒家提出了文艺反映政治得失及具有社会教化功能的理论主张。

Musical sounds, or simply music, are artistically rhythmical sounds flowing forth from one's stirring emotions. Ancient Chinese often made a distinction between musical sounds and plain sounds. Sounds created by a natural environment are plain sounds, while those created when emotions well up in one's heart is music.

A single sound is called *sheng* (声), different sounds that come together are called *yin* (音); when these sounds beautifully fit together, they are called music (*yue* 乐). Ancient Chinese believed that musical sounds derive from one's inner motions, and that the music of a country or a region reflects the popular sentiments and the social mores there. Hence Confucian scholars believed that art and literature demonstrate both virtues and flaws in a country's governance and therefore play the role of moral education.

引例 Citations：

◎凡音者，生人心者也。情动于中，故形于声。声成文，谓之音。（《礼记·乐记》）

（大凡音乐都产生于人的内心。情感在心中激荡，所以表现为各种声音。声音组合成曲调，就叫做音乐。）

All music is born in people's minds. One's stirring emotion is manifested in sounds. When these sounds are arranged into tunes, they constitute musical notes. (*The Book of Rites*)

◎音，声也。生于心，有节于外，谓之音。（许慎《说文解字·音部》）

（音是声音的一种。产生于内心，有节奏地表现出来后，叫做音乐。）

Music is a particular kind of sounds. What flows forth from the heart in a rhythmical pattern is music. (Xu Shen: *Explanation of Script and Elucidation of Characters*)

隐 秀
/yǐnxiù/

Latent Sentiment and Evident Beauty

诗歌与文章既隐含丰富的思想感情，又有秀美的名言佳句。出自《文心雕龙》篇名。"隐"是隐含，指在叙事或写景中隐含超出事、景之外的意义，能引发读者的无限联想；"秀"是秀美，指一篇之中应该有能凸显这一意义的精妙词句。二者密不可分，共同构成优秀文学作品的审美特征。后来也作为诗文写作的一种修辞手法。

This term means that prose and poetry may contain latent sentiments and thoughts, as well as expressions and sentences that present an apparent sense of beauty. "Latent sentiment and evident beauty" first appeared as the title of a chapter in *The Literary Mind and the Carving of Dragons*. There, "latent sentiment" means what lies beyond events and landscapes in a narrative or a description, triggering imaginations on the part of the reader. On the other hand, "evident beauty" refers to the kind of beauty created by expressions and sentences in a piece of writing, which bring out that latent meaning. The latent and the apparent qualities are inseparable, constituting an aesthetic feature of good literary works. Later, this term developed into a rhetorical device in writing prose and poetry.

引例 Citations:

◎ 是以文之英蕤，有秀有隐。隐也者，文外之重旨者也；秀也者，篇中之独拔者也。（刘勰《文心雕龙·隐秀》）
（因此优秀的文章要兼具"秀"和"隐"。所谓"隐"，就是指文章在语言之外隐含有多重意蕴；所谓"秀"，则是有既彰显主旨又独到突出的秀美词句。）

Thus, an excellent piece of writing should have both beautiful in language and a message hidden between the lines. The former refers to beautiful sentences and expressions that accentuate the message of the writing while the latter represents the multiple significance that lies beyond the text. (Liu Xie: *The Literary Mind and the Carving of Dragons*)

◎ 情在词外曰隐，状溢目前曰秀。（张戒《岁寒堂诗话》卷上引刘勰语）
（思想感情隐含于语言背后叫做"隐"，寄寓思想感情的景象鲜活地展现在读者眼前叫做"秀"。）

Latency happens when feelings and thoughts are hidden between the lines of a literary work. Evident beauty occurs when messages of sentiment and feelings are vividly portrayed by the images the author creates. (Zhang Jie: *Notes on Poetry Written in the Pine and Cypress Studio*)

永明体

/Yǒngmíng tǐ/

The Yongming Poetic Style

　　南朝齐武帝永明年间（483—493）出现的、以讲求声韵对偶为主要特征的诗歌风格。也称"新体诗"（与汉魏以来的"古体诗"相对而言）。代表人物是谢朓（tiǎo，464—499）、沈约（441—513）和王融（467—493）。"永明体"标志着诗人已经熟练掌握声韵对偶的规律并自觉运用于诗歌创作，增加了诗歌的形式美感与艺术表现力，为近体诗的产生奠定了基础。不足的是，"永明体"过于受声韵拘束，内容有所削弱，受到当时一些诗论家的批评，在新变中也蕴藏了危机。

Poems of this style first emerged during the reign of Emperor Wu of Qi of the Southern Dynasties. That period, lasting from 483 to 493, assumed the regal title of Yongming, hence the name of this poetic style. Yongming poems featured metrical structure and parallelism. They were also known as the "new poetry," as opposed to the "old poetry" of the Han Dynasty and the Wei period. Xie Tiao (464-499), Shen Yue (441-513), and Wang Rong (467-493) were leading poets of the Yongming style. This style was marked by a poet's deft use of metrical structure and parallelism, thus enhancing the stylistic beauty and artistic expressiveness of poetry. It laid the foundation for the emergence of the "early modern" poetry, or regulated verse. However, the Yongming poetic style was weakened by an excessive emphasis on tonal patterns at the cost of content, drawing criticism of some poetry critics of the time. The style was thus burdened by this inherent risk in its quest for innovation.

引例 Citation：

◎永明末，盛为文章，吴兴沈约、陈郡谢朓、琅琊王融以气类相推毂，汝南周颙（yóng）善识声韵。约等文皆用宫商，以平上去入为四声，以此制韵，不可增减，世呼为"永明体"。（《南齐书·陆厥传》）

（永明末年，文学创作大盛，吴兴人沈约、陈郡人谢朓、琅琊人王融等以共同的志趣相互推举，汝南人周颙精通声韵。沈约等人的创作都讲求音律，以平声、上声、去声、入声为四声，以此来创制韵律，不能随意增加或减少，世人称之为"永明体"。）

Literary writing flourished towards the end of the Yongming period. Shen Yue from Wuxing, Xie Tiao from Chenjun, and Wang Rong from Langya, encouraged and praised each other out of their shared artistic aspirations. Zhou Yong from Runan was well versed in metrical patterning. The poems by Shen Yue and the others were very strict about the use of metrical schemes, namely, the level tone, the rising tone, the falling-rising tone, and the falling tone, and departure from the strict use of such metrical schemes was forbidden. This particular style of poetic creation became known as the Yongming style. (*The History of Qi of the Southern Dynasties*)

咏史诗
/yǒngshǐshī/
Poetry on History

以历史事件或历史人物等作为创作题材并借以抒写诗人情志、感悟的诗歌。史实、史识与史情紧密结合是其主要特点。咏史诗多以"述古""怀古""览古""感古""古兴""读史""咏史"等为题，也有直接以被描写的历史人物、历史事件为标题的。

Poetry on history refers to poems written to convey a poet's sentiments by reflecting on historical events or historical figures. A poem on history touched on historical events and expressed the poet's historical insight as well as his emotional attachment to history. Such poems recounted, relived, revived, interpreted, or chanted about history. Some poets used historical figures or events as titles for such poems.

引例 Citation：
◎怀古者，见古迹，思古人其事。无他，兴亡贤愚而已。（方回《瀛奎律髓》卷三）

（怀古之作，是诗人见到古迹，于是追思古人的往事。不为别的，不过是抒写对历史兴亡和古人贤愚的看法与感悟罢了。）

Poems on history are written when poets see historical sites that take their minds to the past. In these poems, poets reflect on the rise and fall of past dynasties as well as the wisdom and folly of historical figures. (Fang Hui: *The Best Regulated Poems of the Tang and Song Dynasties*)

勇
/yǒng/
Courage

"勇"的基本含义是勇敢。"勇"作为一种德行，要求在行事之时，不畏惧困难，不计较个人利害，始终坚守道义的原则，敢于制止违背道义的行为。"勇"的表现需要基于对道德、礼法的认知与遵守。如果缺少对道德、礼法的遵守，勇敢之行就会流于好勇斗狠或铤而走险，并导致社会混乱。

The basic meaning of *yong* (勇) is courage, which is a virtue. When necessary, a courageous person is expected to fearlessly stop any act that violates ethical principles without giving any consideration to his own personal interests. Acts of courage must be based upon recognition and observance of ethical and social norms. Otherwise, such acts may become ruthless, brutal and risky, and cause social chaos.

引例 Citations：

◎子曰："非其鬼而祭之，谄也。见义不为，无勇也。"（《论语·为政》）

（孔子说："不是自己应该祭祀的鬼神而去祭祀它，是谄媚。遇见合乎道义的事却没有作为，是无勇。"）

Confucius said: "One who offers sacrifices to other people's ancestors is a flatterer.

One who knows what is right but takes no action is lacking in courage." (*The Analects*)

◎子路曰："君子尚勇乎？"子曰："君子义以为上。君子有勇而无义为乱，小人有勇而无义为盗。"（《论语·阳货》）
（子路说："君子崇尚勇敢吗？"孔子说："君子以道义为最崇高的要求。君子只有勇敢而不守道义就会作乱，小人只有勇敢而不守道义就会当盗贼。"）

Zilu asked: "Should a person of virtue act with courage?" Confucius answered: "A man of virtue should observe ethical principles above everything else. One who has courage but ignores ethical principles will become a trouble maker. A petty person who has courage but ignores ethical principles will become a thief or a robber." (*The Analects*)

有德者必有言

/yǒu dé zhě bì yǒu yán/

Virtuous People Are Sure to Produce Fine Writing.

品德高尚的人一定有著述或妙文传世。儒家认为作家的人品（道德修养）与作品（文章价值）往往有内在的联系，品德高尚的人文章自然高妙，而善写文章的人却未必道德高尚，以此提出作家著述应以传播道德为使命，道德文章要相互统一。但后世儒家文士有时过于强调文章的道德作用与作家个人品德对文章的影响从而忽视了文学自身的创作特点与价值。

Virtuous people are sure to write fine works which will be passed on to later generations. According to Confucianism, the moral character of a writer determines the value of his work, virtuous people would naturally write well, but those who wrote well might not necessarily be virtuous. Therefore, authors should write to disseminate moral values; virtue and writings should be consistent.

However, later Confucian scholars sometimes overemphasized the influence that ethics and the authors' moral character had on their writings to the neglect of the characteristics and values of literary creation per se.

引例 Citations:

◎子曰："有德者必有言，有言者不必有德。"（《论语·宪问》）

（孔子说："道德高尚的人，一定有名言传世；有名言传世的人，不一定道德高尚。"）

Confucius said, "Virtuous people are sure to have good writings or words to pass on to later generations, but it is not always true the other way round." (*The Analects*)

◎丈夫处世，怀宝挺秀。辨雕万物，智周宇宙。立德何隐，含道必授。（刘勰《文心雕龙·诸子》）

（大丈夫活在世上，应该身怀才能，超群出众，雄辩的文辞可以摹写万物，周全的智慧可以穷尽宇宙奥秘。何须隐藏自己立德的志向，掌握了道就一定要广泛传授。）

A man of character should possess exceptional capability and his eloquent expressions should portray everything truthfully. His great wisdom should enable him to explain all things under heaven. He does not need to hide his aspirations to serve as a model of virtue. If he has come to a good understanding of Dao, he surely will disseminate it extensively. (Liu Xie: *The Literary Mind and the Carving of Dragons*)

有教无类

/yǒujiào-wúlèi/

Education for All Without Discrimination

任何人都可以或必须接受教化；而人接受了教化，也就没有了因贵贱、贫富等而产生的差异。（一说：在教学时对学生一视同仁，不会按地位、贫富等将学生分成差等。)"教"指礼乐教化，即"人文"；"类"即种类，指贵贱、贫富、智愚、善恶、地域、种族等差别、区分。"有教无类"所昭示的是一种超越等级、地域、种族等差别的普及教育思想，更是一种主张平等待人、反对种种歧视的"人文"精神。

Education can and must be provided for all. It eliminates the differences in social status and wealth. (Another explanation is that education should be provided to students without discrimination on the basis of social status or wealth.) Education consists of teaching of social norms, music, and moral principles. A non-discriminatory approach to education means making no distinction between students based on their social status, wealth, mental capability, moral character, geographic location, or ethnicity. Transcending differences in social status, geography, and ethnicity, education for all without discrimination is a humanistic ideal that champions equal treatment of all people and rejects all forms of discrimination.

引例 Citation：

◎圣人之道无不通，故曰"有教无类"。彼创残之余，以穷归我。我援护之，收处内地，将教以礼法，职以耕农……何患之恤？(《新唐书·突厥传上》)

(圣人的道德教化无处不相通，所以说"只要接受了统一的教化，就不会再有因地域、种族产生的差异"。他们突厥人遭受战争创伤，因处困境而归顺于大唐。我们帮助、保护他们，把他们迁入内地定居，教他们礼仪法度，使他们以耕田务农为业……有什么可忧虑的呢？)

The moral values promoted by ancient sages are universal. That is why "once the same education is provided, differences in geography and ethnicity would be smoothed out." When the Tujue people who suffered from war trauma and were in predicament submitted themselves to the Tang Dynasty, we should assist and protect them, let them settle down among us, teach them social norms and law, and help them engage in farming... What should we be worried about? (*The New Tang History*)

有容乃大
/yǒuróng-nǎidà/

A Broad Mind Achieves Greatness.

　　有包容，才能有大成就。"有容"即器量大，能包容一切；"大"指气魄、事业伟大。"有容"是一种道德修养，更是一种生存智慧。它是在承认并尊重个体及社会差异基础上调处自我与他人关系、寻求社会和谐的一种道德自觉，但又不是故意纵容或作无原则的妥协。"有容乃大"提醒人们立身行事尤其是为官理政，要心胸开阔，善于听取各种意见，宽和对待不同事物，就像大海接纳无数江河细流一样，这样才能养成伟大的品格，成就伟大的事业。其义与"厚德载物"相通。

A broad mind achieves greatness. *Yourong* (有容) means that one has the capacity to accommodate others. *Da* (大) refers to great courage and an important cause. *Yourong* is a moral standard, and more importantly, contains wisdom for survival. It is a conscious act of morality in pursuit of social harmony by managing and regulating relations between oneself and others on the basis of recognizing and respecting individual and social differences, without resorting to deliberate connivance or making unprincipled compromise. The term teaches people how to conduct themselves, particularly officials in exercising their administrative powers. That is, they should have a broad mind, open to different views and different things, like the sea accepting numerous rivers flowing into it. This is the way to cultivate great character and important achievements. Its meaning is similar to the term *houde-zaiwu* (厚德载物 have ample virtue and carry all things).

引例 Citations：

◎必有忍，其乃有济。有容，德乃大。(《尚书·君陈》)

(必须有所忍耐，才能有所成就。有包容，才能建立大功德。)

Tolerance and patience lead people to success, and broad-mindedness to merits and virtues. (*The Book of History*)

◎海纳百川，有容乃大；壁立千仞，无欲则刚。(林则徐对联)

(大海广阔接纳无数江河，人有度量才能[像大海那样]有大成就；千仞崖壁巍然屹立，人没有贪欲就能[像山崖那样]刚正凛然。)

The vast ocean accepts hundreds of rivers emptying into it; people with a broad mind can achieve greatness. Thousands of cliffs stand tall and lofty; people with no covetous desires stand firm and upright. (A couplet composed by Lin Zexu)

有无
/yǒuwú/

You and *Wu*

"有无"有三种不同含义：其一，指个体事物的不同部分，实有的部分为"有"，空虚的部分为"无"。其二，指个体事物在生成、存在、消亡过程中的不同阶段或状态，既有之后、未消亡之前的状态为"有"，未有之前与既终之后的状态为"无"。其三，有形、有名的具体事物或其总和为"有"，超越一切个体事物的无形、无名的本体或本原为"无"。就第三个意义而言，有些哲学家认为"无"是世界的本体或本原，"有"生于"无"；另一些哲学家则认为"有"才是更根本的，反对"有"生于"无"。在"有无"对待的关系中，"有"与"无"既相互区别，又相互依赖。

The term has three definitions. First, it describes two different dimensions of things: One is with form and the other without form. Second, it refers to two different stages or states of a thing during its generation, existence, and demise. *You* (有) refers to the state of a thing after it has come into being and before it dies out; *wu* (无) refers to the state of a thing before its birth and after its death. Third, *you* refers to any tangible or identifiable thing or the sum total of such things; *wu* refers to the original source or ontological existence, which is intangible and unidentifiable, and transcends all specific objects. With regard to the third definition, some philosophers consider *wu* to be the original source or ontological existence of the world, and *you* comes from *wu*; others believe that *you* is fundamentally significant, and dispute the notion that *you* owes its existence to *wu*. Despite their differences, *you* and *wu* are mutually dependent.

引例 Citations：

◎ 故有之以为利，无之以为用。(《老子·十一章》)

（所以说事物"有"的部分带给人便利，"无"的部分发挥了事物的作用。）

Therefore, the with-form part of an object provides ease and convenience, whereas the without-form part performs the functions of that object. (*Laozi*)

◎ 有之所始，以无为本。(王弼《老子注》)

（"有"之所以肇始存在，以"无"为根本。）

The formation and existence of *you* originate from *wu*. (Wang Bi: *Annotations on Laozi*)

愚公移山

/yúgōng-yíshān/

The Foolish Old Man Who Moved the Mountains

比喻有恒心和毅力，敢于知难而进。出自《列子·汤问》，是中国古代著名的寓言故事。愚公年近九十，门前正对大山，出门需绕行很远。为了不受大山阻隔，他终年率子孙凿山移石，遭智叟嘲笑而不放弃，终于感动天帝派天神移走了大山。在历史语境中，它蕴含着对于愚与智、有限与无穷、人力与自然力、人道与天道关系的思考。唐宋以降，寓言中勇于面对和挑战困难并且持之以恒的内涵被发掘，自此"愚公移山"成为迎难而上、坚持不懈的代名词。

This famous ancient Chinese fable from *Liezi* extols perseverance, determination and eagerness to surmount difficulty. Two huge mountains lay directly in front of the Foolish Old Man's house. The Foolish Old Man, who was almost ninety years old, had to take a long detour whenever he went out. To get rid of this inconvenience, he led his sons and grandsons in chipping away at the mountains year after year. They would not give up despite jeers of the Wise Old Man, and eventually moved God, who sent heavenly spirits to move the mountains away.

Originally, this fable pondered the relationship between foolishness and wisdom, the finite and the infinite, the forces of humans and the forces of nature as well as the relationship between the way of humans and the way of heaven. Since the Tang and Song dynasties, however, its underlying message about courage and perseverance in the face of challenge and adversity has gained increasing appreciation. Since then, the "Foolish Old Man Who Moved the Mountains" has become a synonym for forging ahead in the face of difficulties and persevering to the very end.

引例 Citations:

◎ 河曲智叟笑而止之，曰："甚矣，汝之不惠！以残年余力，曾（zēng）不能毁山之一毛，其如土石何？"北山愚公长息曰："汝心之固，固不可彻，曾不若孀妻弱子。虽我之死，有子存焉；子又生孙，孙又生子；子又有子，子又有孙；子子孙孙无穷匮也，而山不加增，何苦而不平？"（《列子·汤问》）

（河曲智叟嘲笑并阻止愚公说："你太不聪明了！就凭你在这世上最后的几年和剩下的这点儿力气，还不能毁掉山上的一根草木，能把这大山的土石怎么样呢？"北山愚公长叹了一口气说："你的脑子太顽固，顽固得不开窍，连寡妇、孤儿都比不上。即使我死了，还有我儿子在呀；儿子又生孙子，孙子又生儿子；儿子又有儿子，儿子又有孙子；子子孙孙永无穷尽，可是这两座山却不会再增高了，还愁什么挖不平呢？"）

The Wise Old Man of the River Bend laughed at the Foolish Old Man and tried to stop him, saying, "You're really too foolish! With the few years and little strength that you still have, you wouldn't even be able to fell a tree on the mountain. How can you possibly move all the soil and rocks?" The Foolish Old Man of the North Mountain heaved a long sigh and said, "You are so pigheaded! Even widows and orphans know better. It is true that I will die, but my sons will survive and they will have sons. Then their sons will have sons, and those sons will also have sons, and I will have endless sons and grandsons, but these two mountains will grow no higher. Why can't they be leveled?" (*Liezi*)

◎ 精卫填海、愚公移山，志之谓也。（杨亿《处州龙泉县金沙塔院记》）

（精卫填海和愚公移山，讲述的都是立志。）

The tales of the mythical bird Jingwei filling in the ocean and of the Foolish Old

Man moving the mountains are about determination. (Yang Yi: A Record of the Jinsha Temple in Longquan County, Chuzhou Prefecture)

◎各奋愚公之愿，即可移山；共怀精卫之心，不难填海。（蔡锷《劝捐军资文》）

（大家如果都立下愚公那样的志向，就可以搬走大山；人们都怀抱精卫那样的雄心，填平大海也不再困难。）

If everyone has the determination of the Foolish Old Man, we can move mountains; if we have the ambition of Jingwei, it will not be hard to fill in the ocean. (Cai E: A Call for Donations to the Army)

与民更始

/yǔmín-gēngshǐ/

Make a Fresh Start with the People

和民众一起革新政治。更始：重新开始。原指帝王即位改元或采取某些重大措施，后指执政者与民众一起变革现状，开创新局面。其中蕴含着悠远深厚的民本思想和君民一体、上下一心、共同革故鼎新的精神。

The term means to make political reform together with the people. *Gengshi* (更始) means to make a fresh start. The term used to refer to a new emperor ascending the throne, taking a new reign title or implementing a series of new policies. Later, it came to mean that the rulers worked together with the people trying to change the status quo and opening up new prospects. The term reflects a profound and far-reaching thought of putting people first, and highlights the spirit of monarchs and the people working with one heart and one mind to abolish what is old and establish in its place a new order.

引例 Citation：

◎朕嘉唐虞而乐殷周，据旧以鉴新，其赦天下，与民更始。（《汉书·武帝纪》）

（我赞美尧、舜而喜欢商、周，依据旧时做法并参照新规，下诏给所有罪犯免刑或减刑，和百姓一起开创新局面。）

I praise ancient emperors Yao and Shun; I like the Shang and Zhou dynasties. I have issued an imperial decree to either exempt criminals from punishment or commute their sentences on the basis of the old practice and new rules, so that we may open up a new era together with the people. (*The History of the Han Dynasty*)

缘起

/yuánqǐ/

Dependent Origination

梵文 pratītyasamutpāda 的意译。"缘起"就是"依缘（一定的条件）而起（发生）"。意思是一切事物、现象乃至社会的一切活动都是因缘和合体，都处于相续不断的因缘关系中，依一定条件而有生灭变化。"缘起"是佛教思想的起点，也是佛教各宗派所共有的理论基础。佛教以此解释宇宙万物、社会乃至各种精神现象变化无常、生灭变化的内在法则。

The term is a translation of the Sanskrit word *pratītyasamutpāda*. *Yuan* (缘) means conditions; *qi* (起) means origination. That is to say, all things, phenomena, and social activities arise out of the combinations of causes and conditions. They exist in the continuous relationship between causes and conditions. Thus all things originate, change, and demise depending upon certain conditions. Dependent origination is the fountainhead of Buddhist thought and forms the common theoretical basis for all Buddhist schools and sects. Buddhism uses this concept to explain everything in the universe, the constant changes of social and spiritual phenomena, and the internal laws of origination, change, and demise.

引例 Citation：

◎物从因缘故不有，缘起故不无。（僧肇《肇论·不真空论》引《中观》）

（万物依因缘的聚合而成，故不能说"有"；又依一定的缘而有生灭变化，故不能说"无"。）

All things originate out of the combinations of causes and conditions, thus they cannot be regarded as original existence; at the same time, they arise, change, and demise upon certain conditions, so they cannot be said as non-existence. (*Fundamental Verses on the Middle Way*, as cited in Seng Zhao: *Treatise of Seng Zhao*)

院本

/yuànběn/

Jin Opera / Scripts Used by Courtesans

有广狭二义：广义指流行于金代的一种戏曲形式，狭义指这种戏曲演唱用的脚本。因多在行院（hángyuàn）演出，故称院本。元代初年仍然流行，目前无独立完整的作品传世，其艺术特点可大致归纳为：篇幅较短，结构简单，多调笑语言及滑稽动作表演，主要角色是副净和副末，继承了唐代参军戏、宋代杂剧的戏谑手法。金院本直接影响了元杂剧的演出形式。

In a broad sense, the term means a style of traditional opera popular in the Jin Dynasty. In a narrow sense, it refers to the scores and librettos used in this type of drama, which was performed mainly in *hangyuan* (行院), or brothels, hence the name. This genre was very popular in the early Jin Dynasty but no separate, complete works have come down to us today. The format is as follows: short acts, simple plots, humorous language and comic gestures. The main performer *fujing* (副净) provides the humor while the supporting performer *fumo* (副末) provides comic backup. The form inherited a great deal from the Tang-dynasty two-person comic banter of *canjunxi* (参军戏), and Song-dynasty *zaju* comedy. The brothel scores had a great influence on the development of the later Yuan *zaju* or opera.

引例 Citation：

◎金有院本、杂剧、诸宫调。院本、杂剧，其实一也。国朝院本、

杂剧，始厘而二之。(陶宗仪《南村辍耕录》卷二十五)

(金代有院本、杂剧、诸宫调。院本、杂剧，实际是一回事。到了我们元朝，院本、杂剧才分为两种。)

In the Jin Dynasty, there were scores used by courtesans, *zaju* and *zhugongdiao*, a kind of song-speech drama with mixed modes of tunes. In fact the scores and *zaju* were the same thing. They were not divided into two separate genres until the Yuan Dynasty. (Tao Zongyi : *Stories by Master Nancun*)

载舟覆舟
/zàizhōu-fùzhōu/

Carry or Overturn the Boat / Make or Break

水既能载船航行，也能使船倾覆。"水"比喻百姓，"舟"比喻统治者。"载舟覆舟"所昭示的是民心向背的重要性：人民才是决定政权存亡、国家兴衰的根本力量。这与"民惟邦本""顺天应人"的政治思想是相通的。自古以来它对执政者有积极的警示作用，提醒他们尊重民情民意，执政为民，居安思危。

Water can carry a boat, but can also overturn it. Here, water is compared to the people, while the boat is compared to the ruler. The phrase, "carry or overturn the boat," reveals the importance of popular support: people are the critical force that decides the future of a regime and a country. This is consistent with such political doctrines as "people are the foundation of the state," and "follow the mandate of heaven and comply with the wishes of the people." Since ancient times, this term has served as a warning to the ruler, reminding him of the need to respect local conditions and popular will, to govern the country for the people, and to anticipate dangers in times of security.

引例 Citation：

◎君者，舟也；庶人者，水也。水则载舟，水则覆舟，此之谓也。(《荀子·王制》)

（君主是船，百姓是水。水既能载船航行，也能使船倾覆，说的就是这个道理。）

The ruler is the boat and the people are the water. Water can carry the boat but can also overturn it. This is the very truth. (*Xunzi*)

凿壁借光
/záobì-jièguāng/

Borrow Light from a Next Door Neighbor

凿穿墙壁，借邻居的烛光照明读书。西汉时期大文学家匡衡年幼家贫，他酷爱读书但家中没有蜡烛供他夜间读书，他就将墙凿开一个洞，借邻居的烛光发奋读书，终成一代学者。作为中国古代著名的励志故事，其意义超越了具体的行为，重在勤学苦读的精神。

By boring a hole in the next door neighbor's wall, he borrows light in order to read. Well-known scholar Kuang Heng in the Western Han Dynasty loved reading but his family was too poor to afford candles for him to read at night, so he chiseled a hole in the next door neighbor's wall to "borrow light" in order to read. He later became a great scholar. As an inspirational story in ancient times, its significance extends beyond the story itself. It tells how important it is to be diligent in gaining knowledge.

引例 Citation：

◎匡衡字稚圭，勤学而无烛。邻舍有烛而不逮，衡乃穿壁引其光，以书映光而读之。（葛洪《西京杂记》卷二）

（匡衡字稚圭，他勤奋好学，但家中没有蜡烛。邻家有蜡烛，但光亮照不到他家，匡衡就在墙壁上凿了洞引来邻家的光亮，借着光亮读书。）

Kuang Heng, also known as Zhigui, was very diligent in his studies but had no candles to allow him to read at night. The next door neighbor had candles but there was no way for him to use the light unless he chiseled a hole in the wall. He did so and was able to read with the ray of light from the next door neighbor. (Ge Hong: *Collection of Miscellaneous Stories in the Western Capital*)

正名
/zhèngmíng/

Rectification of Names

修正或端正事物的指称、名号，使名实相符。"名"是对事物的指称，规定着事物的属性及其与他者的关系。"实"是名所指称的事物、实体。名的规定应与其所指之实相符。但在现实中，名实往往不能相合。针对这种情况，就要求事物所用之名不能超过事物自身的属性，名所指之实也不能超出名所规定的范围。"正名"是维护名所构建的社会秩序的重要方法。各家都认同"正名"的主张，但其所修正的"名"的具体内容则有所不同。

This refers to the rectification of what things are called so that name and reality correspond. A name is what is used to refer to a thing, which determines the attributes of the thing and its relations with other things. "Reality" refers to a thing or an entity that its name refers to. The name of a thing should conform to what the thing actually is. However, very often name and reality do not match in real life. To deal with this situation, the name of a thing should not go beyond the nature of the thing; likewise, the reality referred to by the name must not go beyond the scope that the name implies. The "rectification of names" is an important way to maintain the social order constructed by the names. Various schools of thoughts have agreed on the necessity of rectifying names, but they differ in their views of the concrete meanings of the names to be rectified.

引例 Citations：

◎名不正，则言不顺；言不顺，则事不成；事不成，则礼乐不兴；礼乐不兴，则刑罚不中；刑罚不中，则民无所错手足。(《论语·子路》)

（名号不端正，则说话就不能顺畅；说话不顺畅，则做事就不能成功；做事不成功，则礼乐就不能兴盛；礼乐不兴盛，则刑罚就不能得当；刑罚不得当，则百姓就不知所措。）

If names are not rectified, one's argument will not be proper. If speech is not proper, nothing can be accomplished. If nothing is accomplished, rites and music will not flourish. If rites and music do not flourish, punishments will not be meted out properly. If punishments are not meted out properly, people will have no guidance as how to behave. (*The Analects*)

◎其正者，正其所实也；正其所实者，正其名也。(《公孙龙子·名实论》)

（所要正的，就是端正名所指称的实；端正名所指称的实，就是正名。）

Rectification is to bring forth what actuality is. To bring forth what actuality is is what it means to rectify the name. (*Gongsunlongzi*)

正心

/zhèngxīn/

Rectify One's Heart / Mind

使心归之于正以践行日用伦常之道。出自《礼记·大学》，与格物、致知、诚意、修身、齐家、治国、平天下并称"八条目"，是儒家所倡导的道德修养的一个重要环节。"正心"以"诚意"为前提。在真诚践行日用伦常之道的过程中，人心不可避免地会因愤怒、恐惧、欢乐、忧患等情感而有所偏邪。因此需要时常修正自己的心意，使之不受干扰，始终保持对实现日用伦常之道的追求。

This term means to rectify our mind so as to follow moral principles in daily life. Rectifying one's heart or mind is one of the eight notions from the philosophical text *The Great Learning* (a section of *The Book of Rites*), the other seven being "studying things," "acquiring knowledge," "being sincere in thought," "cultivating oneself," "regulating one's family well," "governing the state properly," and "bringing peace to all under heaven." These constitute important stages in the moral cultivation advocated by the Confucian school. "Rectifying one's mind" has as its preceding stage "being sincere in thought." In the course of following the moral principles earnestly in daily life, people are inevitably influenced by sentiments such as anger, fear, joy, and worries, which will, to some degree, lead a person astray. Therefore, one must always try to rectify one's mind and avoid being swayed by any interference, so as to keep to the observance of moral principles in daily life.

引例 Citations:

◎意既诚了，而其心或有所偏倚，则不得其正，故方可做那正心底工夫。(《朱子语类》卷十六)

("诚意"已经做到了，而心意或许有所偏颇，就不能做到端正，因此正可做"正心"方面的锻炼。)

When thought has been made sincere but the mind is perhaps still somewhat biased, then it is not possible for a person to stay pure and unbiased. Therefore one should make efforts to rectify one's mind. (*Categorized Conversations of Master Zhu Xi*)

◎著(zhuó)实致其良知而无一毫意、必、固、我，便是正心。(《传习录》卷中)

(切实地发挥良知而没有一丝妄测、武断、固执、自我之心，这便是"正心"。)

To rectify one's mind means to cultivate one's good conscience without the least conjecture, arbitrariness, stubbornness, or egoism. (*Records of Great Learning*)

正义

/zhèngyì/

Correct Meaning / Justice

古义主要有二：一谓正确或本来的含义，即对古代典籍的正确解释，常用于书名，如《周易正义》《毛诗正义》等；一谓公理、正理，即公认的正当的原则和道理。近代以来，学界用该词后一含义为理据，翻译西方的justice。时至今日，"正义"成为构建美好社会的核心价值之一。

In ancient days, this term had two meanings. One, it referred to correctness or orthodoxy, specifically in the interpretation of ancient classics. The term was often used as part of a book title, such as *Correct Meaning of The Book of Changes* and *Correct Meaning of Mao's Annotations on The Book of Songs*. Two, it referred to principles of justice that were universally accepted and righteous. In modern times, the second meaning has prevailed. Today, it has become one of the core values of the Chinese society.

引例 Citation：

◎ 正利而为谓之事，正义而为谓之行。(《荀子·正名》)

（符合利益就去做，这叫做事业；符合道义就去做，这叫做德行。）

Acting on consideration of your legitimate benefit is called business. Acting on consideration of justice is called virtue. (*Xunzi*)

政者正也

/zhèngzhě-zhèngyě/

Governance Means Rectitude.

"政"就是"正"的意思。"政"即政治、治理国家；"正"即坚持原则，端正品行，处事公正。"政者正也"有两层意思：一是强调为政者在施政层面应坚持原则、端正品行、处事公正；二是在道德层面强调为政者应严格要求自己，通过自身的示范作用，影响下属和民众一起循行正道、遵守社会规范。它是古代"人治""德政"思想的具体体现。

Zheng (政), or governance, refers to policy and managing the country, while zheng (正), or rectitude, refers to adherence to principle, decent behavior, and handling matters with fairness. This term has two meanings. First, it emphasizes that those who govern should adhere to principle, behave correctly, and handle matters with fairness. Second, it emphasizes that at a moral level, those who govern should be strict with themselves, that they should play an exemplary role and thus show their subordinates and the people how to follow the right path and comply with social norms. It is a concrete expression of the idea "rule by man" and "governing by virtue" in ancient times.

引例 Citations：

◎季康子问政于孔子，孔子对曰："政者，正也。子帅以正，孰敢不正？"（《论语·颜渊》）

（季康子问孔子如何治理国家。孔子回答说："政就是正的意思。您本人带头走正道，谁敢不跟着走正道呢？"）

When asked by Ji Kang about governance, Confucius replied, "Governance is all about rectitude. If you lead along the right path, who would dare not to follow you?" (*The Analects*)

◎子曰："其身正，不令而行；其不正，虽令不从。"（《论语·子路》）

（孔子说："执政者自身行为端正，即使不下命令，事情也能行得通；自身行为不端正，即使三令五申，百姓也不会听从。"）

Confucius said, "If a ruler is upright, he could have things done without giving orders; if he is not, people would not listen to him even if he gives repeated orders." (*The Analects*)

知常达变

/zhīcháng-dábiàn/

Master Both Permanence and Change

既掌握事物的基本规律，又懂得灵活应对具体情况或问题；既坚持原则，又能随机应变。"常"与"变"是中国古代哲学的一对范畴。事物的本质规定性、基本规律、一般原则等具有相对稳定性，故称"常"；具体事物及具体应对方法又有多样性，且随时而化，故称"变"。"常"相对于"变"而言，是存在于"变"之中的常道。"常"是根本，"变"是派生。因此，既要掌握事物的基本规律和一般原则，也要根据客观形势的变化灵活运用这些常道。"知常达变"反映了古人关于普遍性与特殊性、原则性和灵活性辩证统一的认识论和方法论。

This term means one should not only have a good command of the basic rules that govern things, but also know how to deal with exceptional situations or problems in a flexible manner. It suggests that one should not just adhere to principles, but also act according to circumstances. *Chang* (常 permanence) and *bian* (变 change) are two opposing concepts in ancient Chinese philosophy. The nature of things that decides what they are, and their basic rules or general principles that are relatively stable are called *chang* (permanence); but when it comes to specific situations or ways to deal with them, they are different and change in different circumstances, thus they are called *bian* (change). Relative to change, permanence is what endures within change. Permanence is fundamental while change is a deviation. Therefore, one needs not only to have a good command of the basic rules and general principles of things, but also know how to apply these rules and principles in a flexible manner according to objective circumstances. The mastery of both permanence and change reflects ancient Chinese people's perception of both generality and particularity as well as principles and flexibility. It also shows their methodology in the application of both.

引例 Citations：

◎归根曰静，静曰复命。复命曰常，知常曰明。(《老子·十六章》)

(返回事物的本原就叫做"静"，"静"就是回归事物的本来状态。回归事物的本来状态就是"常"，认识了"常"就达到了圣明。)

Returning to the basics leads to tranquility. Tranquility leads to the return of life. The return of life means permanence, and understanding permanence is to be enlightened. (*Laozi*).

◎盖事贵因时而达变，道在取法以自强。(王韬《越南通商御侮说》)
(大凡处理事情贵在根据时机做到灵活变化，最好的办法就是师法[他国的通商]以求自强。)

In dealing with matters, it is best to be able to be flexible; the best way is to learn to strive for self-improvement. (Wang Tao: *Vietnam's Resistance against Bullying by France Through Trade with Other European Countries*)

知耻而后勇
/zhī chǐ ér hòu yǒng/

Having a Feeling of Shame Gives Rise to Courage.

知道耻辱之后就有了勇气。源于"知耻近乎勇"（知道耻辱就接近勇敢了）。"知耻"就是有羞恶之心（对自己的过错感到羞耻,对他人的不善感到憎恶），孟子（前372？—前289）将其视为人之为人的基准或底线之一。"勇"即勇气、勇敢。在儒家那里，它和"知"（智慧）、"仁"（仁爱）一起构成"三达德"（三种普世的德行）。将"知耻"和"勇"联系起来，意在激励人们要勇于面对自己的不足，奋发进取，为达到完美境界而努力。它是个人、企业、组织、民族、国家等自尊、自励、自强精神的体现。

The notion that having a feeling of shame gives rise to courage comes from the saying that "to have a feeling of shame is to be near to having courage." Having a feeling of shame means to be ashamed of one's own mistakes as well as to hate the misbehavior of others. Mencius (372?-289 BC) believed this to be one of the basic things humans must do. In Confucian thought courage is one of three universal virtues along with wisdom and love for others. Linking shame and courage was meant to impel people to face their shortcomings squarely and work hard for improvement and perfection. The concept embodies the spirit of individuals, companies, organizations, ethnic groups, and the whole nation in achieving self-respect, self-motivation, and self-improvement.

引例 Citations:

◎知、仁、勇三者，天下之达德也。(《礼记·中庸》)
(智慧、仁爱、勇敢是天下共通普遍的德行。)

Wisdom, love for others, and courage, these three are the universal virtues of all under heaven. (*The Book of Rites*)

◎好学近乎知，力行近乎仁，知耻近乎勇。(《礼记·中庸》)
(喜爱学习就接近了智，尽力实行就接近了仁，知道耻辱就接近了勇。)

To love learning is to be near to wisdom, to practice with vigor is to be near to love for others, and to have a feeling of shame is to be near to courage. (*The Book of Rites*)

知行合一
/zhīxíng-héyī/

Unity of Knowledge and Action

对"知""行"关系的一种认识。王阳明（1472—1529）基于心学"心外无理"的主张，提出了"知行合一"说。他认为，对人伦日用之道的体认与践行不能割裂，二者是一体的两面。心中有所"知"必然会付诸行动，"行"是"知"的自然运用。若不"行"，便不是真正的"知"。另一方面，"行"也必然会带来深刻切实的认知。若没有"知"，仅仅是不自觉的或迫不得已的行为，便不能实现端正之"行"。

This is one interpretation of the relationship between "knowledge" and "action." Based on the concept in philosophy of the mind that "there are no *li* (理), or principles, outside the mind," Wang Yangming (1472-1529) made the argument that "there is unity of knowledge and action." He felt that it was impossible to separate an understanding of the principles underlying human relations in everyday life from the application of these principles, that these were two sides of the same thing. If there was "knowledge" in the mind, it would surely be put into practice, as "action" was the natural use of "knowledge." If it was not applied, it could not be true "knowledge." On the other hand, "action" would also bring about deeper knowledge. Without "knowledge," mere unconscious or forced behavior would not constitute proper "action."

引例 Citations:

◎外心以求理，此知行之所以二也；求理于吾心，此圣门知行合一之教。(《传习录》卷中)

(在心外寻求理，这是将知行分别为两件事的原因；在心中寻求理，这是圣门"知行合一"的教法。)

Searching for principles outside the mind is the reason why people separate knowledge from action; searching for principles within one's mind is how sages teach about the unity of knowledge and action. (*Records of Great Learning*)

◎知之真切笃实处，即是行；行之明觉精察处，即是知。知行工夫本不可离，只为后世学者分作两截用功，失却知行本体，故有合一并进之说。(《传习录》卷中)

(认知达到真切笃实的境地，便是"行"；践行达到明确的自觉和精微的省察，便是"知"。"知"与"行"的工夫原本不能割裂，只是因为后世的学者将二者作为两件事分别去用功，背离了"知""行"本来的状态，因此有知行合一并进之说。)

When knowledge is genuine and substantive, it becomes action; when actions bring about self-awareness and keen perceptions, they become knowledge. "Knowledge" and "action" were indivisible to begin with, and it was only because scholars later treated them as two separate things, contrary to their original nature, that there was a theory of their being united and developing together. (*Records of Great Learning*)

知先行后
/zhīxiān-xínghòu/

First Knowledge, Then Action

对"知""行"关系的一种认识。程颐（1033—1107）、朱熹（1130—1200）等人在"知""行"关系问题上主张"知先行后"。他们并不否认，对人伦日用之道的体认与践行是相互关联的，二者不可偏废。但若就先后而言，应以"知"为先。"知"是"行"的基础，"行"是在"知"的指导下实现的。只有先认识了人伦日用之道，才能使自己的言行符合道的要求。

The term represents one interpretation of the relationship between "knowledge" and "action." Regarding the relationship between "knowledge" and "action," scholars like Cheng Yi (1033 - 1107) and Zhu Xi (1130 - 1200) argued that "knowledge precedes action." They did not deny that an understanding of the principles underlying human relations in everyday life is interrelated with the application of these principles, nor did they feel that either of the two should be overlooked. However, in terms of sequence, they argued that "knowledge" came first, that it was the basis of "action," and that "action" took place through the guidance of "knowledge." Only by first understanding the principles underlying human relations in everyday life can we make our words and deeds follow the rules which govern human activities.

引例 Citations：

◎须是识在所行之先，譬如行路须得光照。(《二程遗书》卷三)
(必须是认识在行动之前，如同行路必须有光亮照明。)

Knowledge must be present before it can be acted upon, just as light must illuminate the path to be followed. (*Writings of the Cheng Brothers*)

◎知行常相须，如目无足不行，足无目不见。论先后，知为先；论轻重，行为重。(《朱子语类》卷九)
(知与行始终是相互依存的，如同眼睛没有足的功用不能前行，足没有眼睛的功用则不能视路。若说二者先后，知在行先；若说二者轻重，行更重要。)

Knowledge and action are interdependent, just as eyes cannot walk without the feet, and feet cannot see without the eyes. In terms of sequence, knowledge comes first; in terms of importance, action is more important. (*Categorized Conversations of Master Zhu Xi*)

知音
/zhīyīn/

Resonance and Empathy

体会和理解文艺作品的意蕴与作者的思想感情。原指音乐欣赏中的知己，后经魏晋南北朝时期文艺批评家的阐释，用来泛指文艺鉴赏中的心心相印、互相理解。"知音"作为文学批评的核心概念，涉及文艺创作与鉴赏中的个体差异与共性等诸多问题，有着丰富的精神蕴涵，与西方的读者反应批评理论、接受美学、解释学等基本思想有一致之处。

The term is about appreciating and understanding the ideas in literary and artistic works and the thoughts of their authors. The original meaning was feeling a sense of resonance with music. It was later extended by literary critics in the Wei, Jin, and Southern and Northern dynasties to mean resonance or empathy between writers / artists and their readers / viewers. As a core concept in literary criticism, it touches upon both general and particular issues in artistic creation and appreciation, involves rich intellectual implications, and meshes with the audience's response in Western criticism, receptive aesthetics, and hermeneutics.

引例 Citations：

◎是故不知声者不可与言音，不知音者不可与言乐，知乐则几于礼矣。(《礼记·乐记》)
(不懂自然声音的人无法与其谈论音律，不懂音律的人无法与其谈论音乐，通晓音乐的人也就接近懂得礼了。)

Talking about melody with someone who has no ear for natural sounds would be a waste of time, and so would discussing music with someone who knows nothing about melody. One who knows music is close to understanding social norms. (*The Book of Rites*)

◎ 知音其难哉！音实难知，知实难逢，逢其知音，千载其一乎！（刘勰《文心雕龙·知音》）

（理解音乐是多么困难啊！音乐实在难于理解，理解音乐的人很难遇到，要遇到理解音乐的人，恐怕是千年一遇呀！）

It is such a challenge to understand music! Since music is so hard to understand, it is difficult to find people who can appreciate it. It may take a thousand years to find someone who understands music! (Liu Xie: *The Literary Mind and the Carving of Dragons*)

直

/zhí/

Rectitude

"直"的基本含义是正直。具体而言，人们对"直"有两种不同的理解：其一，言行符合道德或礼法的要求，不因贪图个人的私利而行背德违法之事，即是"直"。不过由于人们对德礼的理解不同，对"直"的具体表现的认识也有所差异，甚至存在矛盾。其二，依据实情行事，不为迎合他人的期待或需求而隐瞒实情，也是"直"。

The basic meaning of "rectitude" is uprightness. More specifically, there are two interpretations of "rectitude." The first interpretation refers to words and deeds that meet the moral standards or the rules of propriety. To be "upright" is to refrain from doing anything immoral or illegal for the sake of personal gain. However, because there are different understandings of morality and propriety, there are also different views, even conflicting ones, of how "rectitude" is manifested. The second interpretation of being "upright" is acting in accordance with facts and not concealing the truth in order to meet the expectations or needs of others.

引例 Citations：

◎子曰："孰谓微生高直？或乞醯（xī）焉，乞诸其邻而与之。"(《论语·公冶长》)

（孔子言："谁说微生高正直？有人向他求取醋，他[不说自己没有，而]从邻居那里要来醋给他。"）

Confucius asked, "Who said Weisheng Gao is upright? Someone asked him for vinegar, and (without saying he did not have any) he got some from his neighbor for the man." (*The Analects*)

◎哀公问曰："何为则民服？"孔子对曰："举直错诸枉，则民服；举枉错诸直，则民不服。"(《论语·为政》)

（鲁哀公问道："怎么做才能让百姓信服呢？"孔子答道："将正直的人提拔起来放在邪曲的人之上，百姓就会信服；若是将邪曲的人提拔起来放在正直的人之上，百姓就不会信服。"）

Duke Ai of the State of Lu asked, "How can I win over the people?" Confucius replied, "If you promote upright people and put them above crooked ones, you will win over the people; if you promote crooked people and put them above upright ones, you will not win over the people." (*The Analects*)

直寻
/zhíxún/

Direct Quest

　　诗人即兴而感，直接抒写。这是南朝钟嵘（？—518？）《诗品》中针对诗歌过多使用典故的现象提出的创作主张，他汲取了道家的自然思想，通过考察前人的优秀诗篇，提炼出一种新的诗歌创作方式——"直寻"，即直接描写所感知事物，直接抒发内心情感并创造出情景契合的审美意象。明清时期诗学的"性灵说"受到其影响。

A poet should directly express his thoughts and sentiments when he is inspired. This is a concept for writing poems proposed by poetry critic Zhong Rong (?-518?) of the Southern Dynasties in his work *The Critique of Poetry* as a reaction to the excessive use of allusions and quotes from earlier works. Inspired by naturalist ideas of Daoism and by his own reading of the fine works of earlier poets, he developed a new form of poetic creation which he named "direct quest." By this, he meant directly describing matters that one senses and learns about, directly expressing one's inner feelings, and creating aesthetic images in which the sensibilities match up with current realities. The theory of inner self used in Ming- and Qing-dynasty poetics was influenced by this idea.

引例 Citations：

◎观古今胜语，多非补假，皆由直寻。（钟嵘《诗品》卷中）
（综观古今名篇佳句，大都不是借用前人诗句或使用典故，而是直接从自身体验中寻求而得。）

A comprehensive survey of the best-known works of ancient and current poets shows that most of the poets did not borrow favored lines or literary allusions from their predecessors, but directly sought inspirations from their personal experiences. (Zhong Rong: *The Critique of Poetry*)

◎我手写我口，古岂能拘牵！（黄遵宪《杂感》其二）
（我写出的都是我想说的话，怎能受古人的文字拘束牵制！）

I write what I want to say, Not to be constrained by old writing styles. (Huang Zunxian: Random Thoughts)

止戈为武
/zhǐgēwéiwǔ/

Stopping War Is a True Craft of War.

　　能制止战争、平息战乱才是真正的武功。这是春秋时代楚庄王（？—前591）根据"武"字的字形提出的著名的军事思想。"止"即止息；"戈"即武器，借指战争。将"武"释为止战，既符合以形表意的汉字文化特质，也表现了中国人以武禁暴的军事政治观及崇尚和平、反对战争的文明精神。

To be able to stop war is a true craft of war. This famous military view was first raised by King Zhuang of Chu (?- 591 BC) in the Spring and Autumn Period, on the basis of the structure of the Chinese character *wu* (武). *Wu* is composed of *zhi* (止), which means to stop; and *ge* (戈), which means dagger-axe or weapons and is used here in the metaphorical sense of warfare. To interpret *wu* as stopping war was consistent with the cultural characteristics of Chinese characters. It also expresses the Chinese people's thinking of using military means to stop violence and their love of peace and opposition to war.

引例 Citation：

◎仓颉作书，"止""戈"为"武"。圣人以武禁暴整乱，止息干戈，非以为残而兴纵之也。(《汉书·武五子传赞》)

（仓颉造字，由"止""戈"合成一个"武"字。圣人使用武力禁止残暴，平定动乱，止息战争，而不是为了残杀、毁灭[对方]而滥用武力。）

When Cang Jie created Chinese script, he put *zhi* (止 stop) and *ge* (戈 dagger-axe) together to make *wu* (武 war). To stop war, sages used military force to quell violence and turmoil. They did not abuse their military power to commit atrocities of killing and destroying their opponents. (*The History of the Han Dynasty*)

治内裁外

/zhìnèi-cáiwài/

Handling Internal Affairs Takes Precedence over External Affairs.

治理好国家的内部事务，才能处理好对外事务。"治内"是指国家内部的治理达到理想状态；"裁外"是指量度天下大势，制定对外政策，选择适当的政治、外交、军事等手段，影响国际格局。它告诉我们一条原理：国家内政是对外方略的基础。

A country's internal affairs must be handled well before its external affairs can be handled well. *Zhinei* (治内) means that domestic governance has achieved an ideal state; *caiwai* (裁外) means assessing the broad trends in the world, making external policies, and selecting appropriate political, diplomatic, and military measures to influence the international situation. This tells us a basic principle: a country's internal governance is the foundation of its external strategy.

引例 Citations:

◎内政不修，外举事不济。(《管子·大匡》)

(国内政务不去整治好，对外用兵就不会成功。)

If internal affairs are not handled properly, using military force externally will not succeed. (*Guanzi*)

◎三王不务离合而正，五霸不待从横（zònghéng）而察，治内以裁外而已矣。(《韩非子·忠孝》)

(夏、商、周三代开国君主没有致力于与谁疏远、与谁联合就能匡正天下，春秋五霸也没有搞合纵连横就能明察天下大势，他们不过是在治理好内政基础上再处理对外事务罢了。)

The founding rulers of the Xia, Shang, and Zhou dynasties did not try to impose order on the land by keeping their distance from some or becoming close to others, nor did the Five Most Powerful Kings of the Spring and Autumn Period discern the broad trends in the world by forming vertical or horizontal alliances. They managed external affairs only after they had handled their internal affairs well. (*Hanfeizi*)

治世之音

/zhìshìzhīyīn/

Music of an Age of Good Order

指太平时代的音乐。儒家认为，音乐与社会政治相互联通，音乐能反映一个国家的政治盛衰得失及社会风俗的变化。乐教能促使政治清明，社会秩序稳定；反过来，太平时代政治开明、和美，其音乐、诗歌作品一定充满祥和欢乐。"治世之音"也被用来指《诗经》中的某些美颂之作。

Confucian scholars believed that music interacts with both society and its political evolution; it also reflects the rise and decline of a state's political strength and changes of social customs. Music education fosters good governance and social stability. In an age of peace and stability with enlightened governance and harmony, its music and poetry are characterized by serenity and joyfulness. "Music of an age of good order" also refers to some eulogies in *The Book of Songs*.

引例 Citation：
◎ 凡音者，生人心者也。情动于中，故形于声。声成文，谓之音。是故治世之音安以乐，其政和。（《礼记·乐记》）
（大凡音乐都产生于人的内心。情感在心中激荡，所以表现为各种声音。声音组合成曲调，就叫做音乐。所以，太平时代的音乐祥和欢乐，这是因为政治宽和的缘故。）

All music is born in people's minds. One's stirring emotion is manifested in sounds. When these sounds are arranged into tunes, they constitute musical notes. Hence, the music in time of peace indicates serenity and happiness because of good governance. (*The Book of Rites*)

中道
/zhōngdào/
The Middle Way

中正不偏的行事法则。"中道"是相对于偏颇的行为而言的。古人认为，天地万物的存在与变化遵循着基本的法则。这一法则体现在人为行事中，即是"中道"。人的言行应符合于"中道"。儒家主张通过遵循"中道"，避免过度或不及的言行，以实现完美的道德。佛教则主张践行"中道"，以认识事物的真实形态，从而达到解脱。不同学派、教派对"中道"具体内容的理解会有所不同。

The middle way manifests the principle of impartiality. It stands in contrast to partial behavior. Ancient Chinese believed that the existence and changes of all things in the universe obey a single basic law, which is shown through human action and conduct. This is the middle way. People should comply with the middle way in both speech and action. It can be achieved, Confucian scholars hold, by avoiding all excessive as well as inadequate words and actions, thus attaining impeccable morality. Buddhists advocate practicing the middle way in order to see things in their true light and break free of human suffering. Different schools of thought and religious sects vary in their understanding of the specific content of this concept.

引例 Citations：

◎ 孟子曰："孔子'不得中行而与之，必也狂狷乎！狂者进取，狷（juàn）者有所不为也'。孔子岂不欲中道哉？不可必得，故思其次也。"（《孟子·尽心下》）

（孟子说："孔子讲'不能与遵循中道的人相交，也一定要结交狂者或狷者。狂者激昂进取，狷者不做有违道义的事。'孔子难道不想结交遵循中道的人吗？不一定能遇到，所以思求次一等的人。"）

Mencius commented: "Confucius said, 'If one cannot make friends with those who adhere to the middle way, at least be close to aspiring or uninhibited minds. The former aims high whereas the latter never violates moral laws.' Did Confucius not want to befriend people who pursue the middle way when he said this? An adherent to the middle way is not easy to find; that is probably why he settled for meeting people somewhat lower in stature." (*Mencius*)

◎ 莫求欲乐，极下贱业，为凡夫行。亦莫求自身苦行，至苦非圣行，无义相应。离此二边，则有中道，成眼成智，自在成定，趣（qù）智趣觉，趣于涅槃。（《中阿含经》卷四十三）

（不要追求感官的满足，它太过低劣，这是普通人的行为。也不要苛求自己履行苦修，极端的痛苦并非圣人所行，并不会带来想要的结果。远离了这两种极端，取得中道，才能够成就正见正知，导向寂静、觉醒和解脱。）

Do not seek for physical pleasures, for they are too low and are the behaviors of common people. Do not seek any ascetic practice for yourself either. Extreme suffering is not practiced by the saintly people. It won't bring the expected outcome. Only by keeping away from either extremes and by choosing the middle way can one accomplish concentration, thus getting on the way to wisdom, to peaceful mind, to awakening, and to nirvana. (*Middle Length Canonical Texts*)

中 国

/zhōngguó/

Zhongguo (China)

　　古代华夏族、汉民族以黄河中下游流域为中心生活和活动的区域。"中国"最初是一个地域兼文化的概念。华夏族多建国于黄河流域一带，以为居天下之中，故称"中国"（与"四方"相对）。后泛指中原地区以及在中原地区建立的政权和国家。近代以降，中国指我国的全部领土与主权。

This term refers to the areas along the middle and lower reaches of the Yellow River where ancient Huaxia (华夏) people or the Han people lived. Originally, the term Zhongguo (中国) meant both this region and its culture. The Huaxia people established their states along the Yellow River. Believing the areas were located in the center of the world, they called it Zhongguo (the Central Country, as against other areas around it). Later, the term was used to refer to the Central Plains in North China and the states founded in that area. Since modern times, Zhongguo has been used to refer to the entire territory and sovereignty of China.

引例 Citations：

◎惠此中国，以绥四方。(《诗经·大雅·民劳》)

（爱护京师百姓，安抚四方诸侯。）

Give benefit to the people in the capital, and reassure and pacify all the feudal dukes and princes in the country. (*The Book of Songs*)

◎若能以吴越之众与中国抗衡，不如早与之绝。(《三国志·蜀书·诸葛亮传》)

（如果能够以江东的兵力与中原抗衡，不如早与他们断绝交往。）

If the areas of Wu and Yue (under the control of Sun Quan) could stand up to confront the central region (under the control of Cao Cao), the former should better cut ties with the latter. (*The History of the Three Kingdoms*)

中和

/zhōnghé/

Balanced Harmony

　　人心所达到的中正、和谐的状态。人的喜、怒、哀、乐等情感的活动及其在言行上的表现符合礼的要求，不失偏颇进而达到一种和谐的状态，即是"中和"。治理者如果能够体认并达到"中和"的状态，以此治理天下，天地万物就会处于端正、恰当的位置，和谐、有序，就可以实现彼此间的共同繁荣与发展。

Balanced harmony is an ideal state of human mind. When people's emotions such as joy, anger, sorrow, and happiness are expressed in an unbiased way in keeping with the rites, a state of mind featuring balanced harmony is achieved. If a ruler can reach such a state of mind and exercise governance accordingly, everything in heaven and earth will be in its proper place, be orderly and in harmony with each other. This will deliver common prosperity and development for all.

引例 Citations：

◎喜怒哀乐之未发，谓之中；发而皆中（zhòng）节，谓之和。中也者，天下之大本也；和也者，天下之达道也。致中和，天地位焉，万物育焉。(《礼记·中庸》)

（喜怒哀乐还没有被事物感发时的状态，称作"中"；喜怒哀乐表现于言行而都能符合规范，称作"和"。"中"是天下的根本，"和"是天下最普遍的法则。治理者能够达到"中和"，天地就能处于正位，万物便可生长繁育了。）

When joy, anger, sorrow, and happiness are not yet expressed as a response to other things, they are in a state of balance. When they are expressed in words and deeds in accordance with the rites, harmony is achieved. Balance is the foundation under heaven, while harmony is the universal rule under heaven. If a ruler can achieve balanced harmony, both heaven and earth will be in their proper places, and all things will prosper and thrive. (*The Book of Rites*)

◎ 能以中和理天下者，其德大盛。能以中和养其身者，其寿极命。（董仲舒《春秋繁露·循天之道》）
（能够以"中和"治理天下的人，他的德政就会极大兴盛。能够以"中和"修养自身的人，他的寿命就会很长久。）

When one rules the world with balanced harmony, virtuous governance will flourish. When one achieves balanced harmony in self-cultivation, he will enjoy longevity. (Dong Zhongshu: *Luxuriant Gems of The Spring and Autumn Annals*)

中华
/zhōnghuá/

Zhonghua

　　"中华"是"中国"与"华夏"复合的简称。"华"同"花"，喻指文化灿烂。华夏的先民建国于黄河中下游，自认为居天下之中央，且又文化发达，所以称"中华"。随着华夏族为主体的多民族国家的不断扩张，凡所统辖之地，皆称中华。在近现代历史中，"中华"成为指称中国、中国人及中国文化的一种符号。

This term is an abbreviation of the compound word formed by Zhongguo (中国) and Huaxia (华夏). Here, *hua* (华) also means "flower" or "flowery," which was used as an analogy for a splendid culture. The ancestors of the Huaxia people established their state in the middle and lower reaches of the Yellow River, which they thought was the center (*zhong*) of the world and which had a flourishing culture (*hua*), so the state was called Zhonghua. This multi-ethnic state, with the

Huaxia people as the predominant group of its population, later began its territorial expansions, and the places where it extended to became part of Zhonghua. In modern times, Zhonghua became a term denoting China, the Chinese people, and its culture.

引例 Citation:

◎ 中华者，中国也。亲被王教，自属中国，衣冠威仪，习俗孝悌，居身礼义，故谓之中华。（王元亮《唐律释文》卷三）

（中华即中国。自身接受了王道教化，自然就属于中国了，穿衣戴帽有威仪，风俗讲究孝悌，立身处世追求礼义，所以称之为"中华"。）

Zhonghua refers to China. Under the wise rule of the sage king, all his subjects belong to China. They are dressed in a dignified manner, practice filial piety and fraternal duty, and follow moral norms in personal and social conduct. This is the country called Zhonghua. (Wang Yuanliang: *Commentary and Explanation on Well-Known Law Cases of the Tang Dynasty*)

中庸

/zhōngyōng/

Zhongyong (The Golden Mean)

孔子（前551—前479）和儒家所肯定的最高德行。"中"指言行没有过或不及的状态或标准。凡事都有某种限度，超过和达不到这个限度都是不好的。"庸"包含两个相关的含义：其一指平常，其二指恒常。"中"只有在平常日用之中才能恒常不易。"中庸"即指在人伦日用中始终遵循、符合无过无不及的标准。

Zhongyong (the golden mean) was considered to be the highest level of virtue by Confucius (551 - 479 BC) and Confucian scholars. *Zhong* (中) means moderate in one's words and deeds. Everything has its limits, and neither exceeding nor falling short of the limits is desirable. *Yong* (庸) has two meanings. One is common or ordinary and the other is unchanging. Moderation can be maintained for over a long time constantly only when one practices it in everyday life. *Zhongyong* means the standard of moderation that one should follow in dealing with others and in one's everyday conduct.

引例 Citations:

◎中庸之为德也，其至矣乎！（《论语·雍也》）
（中庸作为一种道德，是最高的准则吧！）
Zhongyong is the highest of virtues. (*The Analects*)

◎中庸者，不偏不倚、无过不及而平常之理。（朱熹《中庸章句》）
（中庸就是不偏颇，没有过或不及的平常的道理。）
Zhongyong does not bend one way or the other; it is the common principle of neither exceeding nor falling short of the line. (Zhu Xi: *Annotations on The Doctrine of the Mean*)

诸宫调
/zhūgōngdiào/

Song-speech Drama

　　一种源于北宋、流行于金元的说唱艺术。同一宫调的多首曲子，可组成一个套曲，诸宫调则是不同宫调的多个套曲的组合。其表演形式是唱完一个宫调的套曲，即换韵演唱另一个宫调的套曲。在套曲与套曲的演唱间隙，表演者通过说白来叙述情节，衔接前后。套曲之间，有时也夹有单曲小令。诸宫调对于元杂剧的成型与发展影响较大。董解（jiè）元创作的《西厢记诸宫调》是存世最完整的诸宫调作品，代表了金代戏曲的最高水平。

The term refers to a form of theatrical performance combining song and speech popular in the Jin and Yuan periods. The drama is composed of sets of songs. Each set of songs is composed of the same mode of music, or *gongdiao*. During the performance, one set of songs is followed by another set of songs. Between them, the performer adds spoken narrative to explain the story and string the plot together. Sometimes single ditties are added. The genre had a marked influence on the development of Yuan *zaju* or opera. The *zhugongdiao* version of *Romance of the Western Chamber* by Dong Jieyuan is the most intact extant *zhugongdiao* drama, and represents the best of Jin Dynasty opera.

引例 Citations：

◎长短句中，作滑稽无赖语，起于至和。嘉祐之前，犹未盛也。熙、丰、元祐间，兖州张山人以诙谐独步京师，时出一两解。泽州孔三传（chuán）者，首创诸宫调古传，士大夫皆能诵之。（王灼《碧鸡漫志》卷二）

（词作中，使用滑稽逗笑的语言，是从至和年间开始的。嘉祐之前，还不兴盛。熙宁、元丰和元祐年间，兖州张山人的诙谐表演在京城无人能比，时不时地就作一两首。泽州孔三传，首创用诸宫调演绎古代传奇故事，士大夫都能吟诵。）

The use of humorous and comic language in *ci* poems began in the Zhihe era (1054) of the Song Dynasty, but did not become widespread until the Jiayou era (1056-1063). During the Xining, Yuanfeng and Yuanyou periods (1068-1093), the comic performances of Zhang Shanren of Yanzhou were the best in the capital, and he would often make up verses of his own. It was Kong Sanchuan of Zezhou who first used *zhugongdiao* to tell the legendary tales of ancient times, and most literati could recite the lines and hum the tunes. (Wang Zhuo: *Musings from Biji Lane*)

◎说唱诸宫调，昨汴京有孔三传，编成传奇灵怪，入曲说唱；今杭城有女流熊保保，及后辈女童皆效此，说唱亦精。（吴自牧《梦梁录》卷二十"妓乐"）

（用诸宫调说唱，以前汴京有个孔三传，自编了一些传奇故事和有关神灵鬼怪的话本，配合乐曲说唱；现在杭州女艺人熊保保以及后辈女童都模仿他，她们的说唱技艺也很精湛。）

In the capital Bianjing, there was Kong Sanchuan who wrote dramas based on legendary tales and stories of gods and spirits, which he then combined with music to perform in *zhugongdiao* song-speech style. Today, Xiong Baobao, a female performer in Hangzhou, and other younger women who imitated him, also perform exquisitely. (Wu Zimu: *Notes of Past Dreams*)

转益多师
/zhuǎnyì-duōshī/

Learn from Many Masters, and Form Your Own Style

尽可能博采众长，以丰富自己的文艺创作。"转益"意为辗转自益，只要对自己创作有益的东西都应该加以学习吸收；"多师"谓广泛师法，不必专主一家。出自唐代诗人杜甫（712—770）《戏为六绝句》。它包含相互联系的两个方面：其一，尽可能广泛学习、师法古人或时贤的创作经验，博采众长，兼收并蓄。其二，在无所不师的同时既有继承也要有所批判。只有这样，才能合乎或接近《诗经》的风雅传统，形成自己的艺术风格。后来这一术语的使用范围由诗歌创作而扩展至文学艺术等各个领域。

The expression means to learn widely from others so as to enrich one's own artistic creation. *Zhuanyi* (转益) means to learn and absorb everything that can further one's creativity; *duoshi* (多师) means to learn from many teachers. This comes from "Six Playful Quatrains" by Du Fu (712-770) of the Tang Dynasty. There are two related meanings in this term: 1) learn from the experience and skills of all masters, past and present; and 2) while learning and carrying on the best, also be discerning, so as to approach or conform to the traditions of meaning and form as expressed in *The Book of Songs*, and then develop one's own poetic style. The expression later came to include not just poetry but also literature and art.

引例 Citations：

◎未及前贤更勿疑，递相祖述复先谁？别裁伪体亲风雅，转益多师是汝师。（杜甫《戏为六绝句》其六）

（浅薄之辈不及前贤这点不必怀疑，代代继承前人为何区分谁先谁后？甄别去除猥杂不纯的诗歌而直接亲近《诗经》的风雅传统，多方师法、博采众长，才是你真正有益的老师。）

Superficial men are clearly not the equal of past masters; why would one mind who was the first to pass on the tradition? Discard the poorly written and learn from *The Book of Songs*. And learning from many past masters means you've found the right teacher. (Du Fu: *Six Playful Quatrains*)

◎ 昔昌黎《进学》，马、扬上并《盘》《诰》。杜陵论文，卢、骆譬之江河。同工异曲，转益多师，明示轨躅（zhuó），无区畺畛（jiāngzhěn）。（陈墉《答吴子述书》，见缪荃孙《艺风堂杂钞》卷五）（过去韩愈写《进学解》，把司马相如、扬雄的作品与古代的《尚书》相提并论。杜甫谈论诗文创作，把卢照邻、骆宾王的创作比作江河奔流。韩愈、杜甫的论述对象虽然不同，思路却是一致的，都强调博采众长、多方师法，给后人明确指示了文学创作的法则，不应自我封闭、自我设限。）

In his work "Progress in Learning," Han Yu compared the writings of Sima Xiangru and Yang Xiong to *The Book of History*. In his commentary on poetry composition, Du Fu likened the works of Lu Zhaolin and Luo Binwang to rapidly flowing rivers. Han and Du were writing for different readers, but both believed in the value of learning from many teachers, and advised writers and poets not to close themselves off from multiple influences. (Chen Yong: Reply to Wu Zishu)

庄周梦蝶

/Zhuāng Zhōu mèng dié/

Zhuangzi Dreaming of Becoming a Butterfly

庄子（前369？—前286）梦见自己成为蝴蝶。"庄周梦蝶"一事见于《庄子·齐物论》。庄子梦见自己成为蝴蝶，醒来后才发现自己是庄周。庄子甚至无法区分是庄子梦见自己成为蝴蝶，还是蝴蝶梦见自己成为庄子。庄子借由这一梦境的感受提醒人们，自身与他者、梦与醒以及一切事物之间的界限与区别都是相对的，是可以破除的。事物处于转化与流通之中，庄子称之为"物化"。

Zhuangzi (sometimes also referred to as Zhuang Zhou, 369?-286 BC) dreamed that he had become a butterfly. The story appears in "On Seeing Things as Equal" in the classic *Zhuangzi*. Zhuangzi dreamed that he had become a butterfly, but woke up to find he was still himself. In fact he was not sure whether he had dreamed of becoming a butterfly or a butterfly had dreamed of becoming him.

Zhuangzi used this dream to remind people that there must be a relative difference between oneself and others, between dreaming and wakefulness, and between all other things. However, these boundaries were not absolute and could be broken. Things were in constant transformation and circulation, which he called the "transformation of things (*wuhua* 物化)."

引例 Citation：

◎昔者庄周梦为胡蝶，栩栩然胡蝶也，自喻适志与（yú）！不知周也。俄然觉，则蘧（qú）蘧然周也。不知周之梦为胡蝶与？胡蝶之梦为周与？周与胡蝶，则必有分矣。此之谓物化。(《庄子·齐物论》)

（从前庄周梦见自己变成了蝴蝶，翩翩飞舞的一只蝴蝶，遨游各处悠游自在，不知道自己是庄周。忽然醒过来，自己分明是庄周。不知道是庄周做梦化为蝴蝶呢，还是蝴蝶做梦变化为庄周呢？庄周与蝴蝶必定是有所分别的。这就叫做"物化"。）

Once I, Zhuangzi, dreamed that I became a flying butterfly, happy with myself and doing as I pleased. I forgot that I was Zhuangzi. Suddenly I woke up and I was Zhuangzi again. I did not know whether Zhuangzi had been dreaming that he was a butterfly, or whether a butterfly had been dreaming that it was Zhuangzi. There must be a difference between the two, which is what I call the "transformation of things." (*Zhuangzi*)

自强不息

/zìqiáng-bùxī/

Strive Continuously to Strengthen Oneself

自己努力向上，强大自己，永不懈怠停息。古人认为，天体出于自身的本性而运行，刚健有力，周而复始，一往无前永不停息。君子取法于"天"，也应发挥自己的能动性、主动性，勤勉不懈，奋发进取。这是中国人参照天体运行状态树立的执政理念和自身理想。它和"厚德载物"一起构成了中华民族精神的基本品格。

The term means that one should strive continuously to strengthen himself. Ancient Chinese believed that heavenly bodies move in accordance with their own nature in a vigorous and forever forward-going cycle. A man of virtue, who follows the law of heaven, should be fully motivated and work diligently to strengthen himself. This is the Chinese view on governance and self development, established with reference to the movement of heavenly bodies. Together with the notion that a true gentleman has ample virtue and carries all things, it constitutes the fundamental trait of the Chinese nation.

引例 Citations:

◎ 天行健，君子以自强不息。(《周易·象上》)

(天的运行刚健有力，一往无前，君子应像天一样，奋发图强，永不停息。)

Just as heaven keeps moving forward vigorously, a man of virtue should strive continuously to strengthen himself. (*The Book of Changes*)

◎ 自人君公卿至于庶人，不自强而功成者，天下未之有也。(《淮南子·修务训》)

(自帝王公卿到普通百姓，不奋发进取就能建立功业的，普天之下没有这样的事情。)

Neither monarchs, ministers, nor commoners have ever achieved great accomplishments in the world without first striving to strengthen themselves. (*Huainanzi*)

◎ 外有敌国，则其计先自强。自强者，人畏我，我不畏人。(《宋史·董槐传》)

(外有敌对的国家，那我们首先要谋求使自己强大。如果自己强大了，敌国就会畏惧我们，我们就不会畏惧他们。)

Facing hostile countries, we must first of all strive to become strong. If we have strengthened ourselves, enemy states will fear us and we will not fear them. (*The History of the Song Dynasty*)

自由
/zìyóu/

Acting Freely / Freedom

本义是由自己做主，依从自己的想法、意志、愿望行事，不受外来限制和约束。在古代中国，儒道都向往内心与生命不受拘系的自由。近代以来，它用作liberty和freedom的译词。作为专有名词，其含义主要有二：其一，指法律所规定并保护的国民享有其意志、行为不受干涉的权利，如言论、集会、宗教信仰等方面的自由。其二，哲学上指人对必然性的认识和对客观世界的改造的自由。它是建立在对自然、社会规律深刻把握的基础上，以人的全面发展为目的的自由，被认为是构建美好社会的核心价值之一。

The term means acting on one's own free will without being subject to external restrictions. In ancient China, both Confucians and Daoists longed for freedom both of the mind and in their lives. In modern times, this term has become the Chinese word for "liberty" and "freedom." As a technical term, it has two meanings. One is citizens' statutory and law-protected rights not to be interfered in their will and actions, such as freedom of speech, freedom of assembly, and freedom of religious belief. The other, philosophically, refers to freedom of people's understanding of necessity and their transformation of the objective world. Based on a profound understanding of the principles governing the nature and society and aiming to ensure individuals to achieve well-rounded development, freedom is considered one of the core values conducive to a good society.

引例 Citation：

◎外物尽已外，闲游且自由。（齐己《匡山寓居栖公》）
（一切皆为身外之物，四方游历身心自由。）

Realizing that all things are all external, I wander at leisure and freely follow my own inclinations. (Qi Ji: In Memory of a Recluse During My Residence on Mount Lu)

宗法
/zōngfǎ/

Feudal Clan System

　　中国古代以家族为中心，按血统、嫡庶来组织治理家族、国家、社会的原则和方法。宗法由父系氏族的家长制演化而来，定型于西周，与封建制等互为表里。宗法分为家国两个层面，在家的层面，宗族的嫡长子是家族的嫡系继承人，拥有家族的最高权力，其余家族成员依据亲疏、世系各自确定其在家族中的地位和权力。帝王公侯或者世家大族的宗族等级制扩展到国家的层面，对于王位继承与国家政治具有决定性的作用。宗法制数千年来对中国人的生活方式、思维方式影响深远。

This system was central to life in ancient China; it was a system of principles and measures by which a clan, a state, or society was run, based on bloodline or whether a son was born from the wife or a concubine. The feudal clan system evolved from the patriarchal chiefs system. Taking shape during the Western Zhou Dynasty, this system and the feudal system were mutually dependent and complementary. The feudal clan system had two levels: one was the familial level, where the eldest son by the wife was the first in line to inherit the family's property and thus enjoyed the greatest authority. Other members of the clan were allotted their status and authority according to their closeness of kinship, ancestry, or seniority. In the families of the emperor, kings, and other nobility, this pattern was extended to the state or national level. It had a decisive impact on the inheritance of the imperial throne and on state politics. The feudal clan system greatly influenced the Chinese way of life and thinking for several thousand years.

引例 Citation：

◎宗法者，佐国家养民教民之原本也。（冯桂芬《复宗法议》）
（所谓宗法，是帮助国家养育、教化民众的原始基础。）

The feudal clan system is a state's bedrock for fostering and educating its people. (Feng Guifen: My Argument for Restoring the Feudal Clan System)

中国历史年代简表
A Brief Chronology of Chinese History

远古时代 Prehistory		
夏 Xia Dynasty		c. 2070 - 1600 BC
商 Shang Dynasty		1600 - 1046 BC
周 Zhou Dynasty	西周 Western Zhou Dynasty	1046 - 771 BC
	东周 Eastern Zhou Dynasty 　春秋时代 Spring and Autumn Period 　战国时代 Warring States Period	770 - 256 BC 770 - 476 BC 475 - 221 BC
秦 Qin Dynasty		221 - 206 BC
汉 Han Dynasty	西汉 Western Han Dynasty	206 BC-AD 25
	东汉 Eastern Han Dynasty	25 - 220
三国 Three Kingdoms	魏 Kingdom of Wei	220 - 265
	蜀 Kingdom of Shu	221 - 263
	吴 Kingdom of Wu	222 - 280
晋 Jin Dynasty	西晋 Western Jin Dynasty	265 - 317
	东晋 Eastern Jin Dynasty 十六国 Sixteen States*	317 - 420 304 - 439

南北朝 Southern and Northern Dynasties	南朝 Southern Dynasties	宋 Song Dynasty	420 - 479
		齐 Qi Dynasty	479 - 502
		梁 Liang Dynasty	502 - 557
		陈 Chen Dynasty	557 - 589
	北朝 Northern Dynasties	北魏 Northern Wei Dynasty	386 - 534
		东魏 Eastern Wei Dynasty	534 - 550
		北齐 Northern Qi Dynasty	550 - 577
		西魏 Western Wei Dynasty	535 - 556
		北周 Northern Zhou Dynasty	557 - 581
隋 Sui Dynasty			581 - 618
唐 Tang Dynasty			618 - 907
五代十国 Five Dynasties and Ten States	后梁 Later Liang Dynasty		907 - 923
	后唐 Later Tang Dynasty		923 - 936
	后晋 Later Jin Dynasty		936 - 947
	后汉 Later Han Dynasty		947 - 950
	后周 Later Zhou Dynasty		951 - 960
	十国 Ten States**		902 - 979

宋 Song Dynasty	北宋 Northern Song Dynasty	960 - 1127
	南宋 Southern Song Dynasty	1127 - 1279
辽 Liao Dynasty		907 - 1125
西夏 Western Xia Dynasty		1038 - 1227
金 Jin Dynasty		1115 - 1234
元 Yuan Dynasty		1206 - 1368
明 Ming Dynasty		1368 - 1644
清 Qing Dynasty		1616 - 1911
中华民国 Republic of China		1912 - 1949

中华人民共和国1949年10月1日成立
People's Republic of China, founded on October 1, 1949

*"十六国"指东晋时期在我国北方等地建立的十六个地方割据政权，包括：汉（前赵）、成（成汉）、前凉、后赵（魏）、前燕、前秦、后燕、后秦、西秦、后凉、南凉、南燕、西凉、北凉、北燕、夏。

The "Sixteen States" refers to a series of local regimes established in the northern area and other regions of China during the Eastern Jin Dynasty, including Han (Former Zhao), Cheng (Cheng Han), Former Liang, Later Zhao (Wei), Former Yan, Former Qin, Later Yan, Later Qin, Western Qin, Later Liang, Southern Liang, Southern Yan, Western Liang, Northern Liang, Northern Yan, and Xia.

**"十国"指五代时期先后存在的十个地方割据政权，包括：吴、前蜀、吴越、楚、闽、南汉、荆南（南平）、后蜀、南唐、北汉。

The "Ten States" refers to the ten local regimes established during the Five Dynasties period, including Wu, Former Shu, Wuyue, Chu, Min, Southern Han, Jingnan (also Nanping), Later Shu, Southern Tang, and Northern Han.